an introduction to models in the social sciences

Charles A. Lave
University of California, Irvine

James G. March
Stanford University

HARPER & ROW, Publishers
New York   Evanston   San Francisco   London

Sponsoring Editor: Ronald K. Taylor
Project Editor: Lois Lombardo
Designer: Jared Pratt
Production Supervisor: Stefania J. Taflinska

An Introduction to Models in the Social Sciences

Library of Congress Cataloging in Publication Data

Lave, Charles A
    An introduction to models in the social sciences.

    Includes index.
    1.   Social sciences—Mathematical models.   I.   March,
James G., joint author.   II.   Title.
H61.L342   300'.1'5   74-18064
ISBN 0-06-043861-4

contents

preface

.

As we indicate in Chapter 1, this book is an introduction to thinking analytically about human behavior. We try to describe both a basic style of speculation and four specific speculative models that are useful and enjoyable in predicting, understanding, influencing, and appreciating human life. Our efforts are based on three simple presumptions:

(1) A central feature of modern thinking in the social and behavioral sciences is the use of formal models, normally in mathematical form.

(2) It is possible to exhibit the development and use of social science models in a way that is both precise enough to explicate important ideas and simple enough to require no mathematics beyond high school algebra.

(3) Much of the power, beauty, and pleasure of models comes from inventing and elaborating them, and from exploring their implications in new domains.

The book is about model building, but it is not a methodology book in the customary sense. The more technical questions of specifying and testing models are slighted in favor of exploring model building as a creative art. Toward that end, readers are encouraged to accept an active role in devising new models and finding new implications of old ones. The text provides frequent occasions on which the reader is asked to pause and think about the ideas being examined. In addition, there are a great many problems that include applications to a wide variety of situations. The mode of reading is intended to be active.

The book can serve a number of different instructional purposes: It can be used as a text or supplement in an introductory course or in courses in methodology or models; it can also be used as casual reading in bed. It requires neither previous exposure to the social and behavioral sciences nor college mathematics, but it is consistent with advanced training in those fields. We have used the materials with high school seniors, college freshmen, graduate students, and faculty colleagues. Anyone who reads the book and does a good sample of the problems should develop a reasonable basic grasp of how to engage in creative theoretical thinking in the social sciences.

Most of all, the book is testimony to the delights of the game. All authors have a fantasy that what they write will be useful to their readers, that something can be learned from the words so carefully chosen and cruelly edited. We endorse that fantasy and add a grander one: We hope that readers will come to enjoy not only the book but also the pleasures of imagination that it celebrates.

C.A.L.
J.G.M.

acknowledgments

We are indebted to an unusually long list of colleagues, students, and friends who have helped us. In a more than usual way, it is accurate to give them the credit and us the blame for what is written.

Our greatest debt is to over 2000 students at the University of California at Irvine, Hampshire College, University of Bergen, Copenhagen School of Economics, and Stanford University who have been our collaborators. The collaboration with students has been real, and we are grateful for it. To single out individual students among all of those who have helped us by their imagination and criticism is hard, but we should like to note particularly the contributions of Karen Anderson, John Johnson, Ronald Lewis, Warren Netz and the "Flaming Variables," Albert Nichols, and Anne Underwood.

Several colleagues have been especially generous in their comments on the text as it was developing. Among them, we should like to thank particularly John Conlisk, Jean Lave, R. Duncan Luce, Johan Olsen, Michael Rothschild, Barbara West, and Gail Whitacre.

We have also learned a great deal from colleagues who have taught with us or in similar courses. We should like to make special note of the ideas and encouragements we have taken from Michael Butler, Michael Cohen, James Danziger, Henry Hamburger, Gordon Lewis, and John Miller.

Preparing the final manuscript has involved a more than usual amount of tolerance and overtime typing from a number of important friends. Donna Dill, Gayle Hill, Marsha Mavis, and Lillian White deserve credit for dealing both with us and with some pressing deadlines in order to produce a plausible manuscript.

Finally, we should like to recognize a special debt to an institution. Our attempts at an introduction to models in the social sciences were sustained for several years in an exceptionally rewarding environment, the School of Social Sciences at the University of California, Irvine. We were fortunate to be there. Although many people made that experience possible, we should like to mention two of them in particular: Daniel Aldrich was a persistently supportive Chancellor; Mary Tomkinson Rezich was the heart of the School of Social Sciences. Without denying the heavy contributions of others, we should like to witness our gratitude to Dan Aldrich and Mary Rezich by dedicating this book to them—if they'll have it.

C.A.L.
J.G.M.

chapter
one

what
we
are
up
to

This book is about the social sciences. It is not, however, a grand tour of what the social sciences are. It is a first excursion into a few domains of social science imagination. It does not claim the scholarly virtues of comprehensiveness and balance. It is a brief introduction to the pleasures of thinking about human behavior.

To speak of pleasures is probably dangerous and certainly pretentious. Few people rely solely on any social science for their pleasures, and attaining a suitable level of ecstasy involves work. We regret the latter problem. It is a nuisance, but God has chosen to give the easy problems to the physicists. We do not regret the former problem. We have no intention of suggesting that poetry and sex be abandoned. Rather, we invite you, in the moments left between Byron and bed, to join us in speculating about ordinary human existence.

Speculation presumes observation. We rely on the difficult and creative drudgery required to retrieve the record of social events. The data are lost in the files of bureaucracies, diaries of servants, accounts of businesses, and memories of participants. They are discovered through the paraphernalia of research and manipulated by the technology of inference. Precise and imaginative empirical observation distinguishes fine work in anthropology, business administration, demography, economics, education, geography, history, journalism, law, linguistics, political science, psychology and sociology.

Many smart and patient people have accumulated knowledge from observations of individuals, groups, and institutions in society. Others have articulated the methodology of the social sciences. We are in debt to both traditions, but our approach is different. Our theme is more a way of thinking about observations than an inventory of them; it is more concerned with the invention of conjectures than with the formal rules for talking about them.

We propose a practical guide to speculation. We explore the arts of developing, elaborating, contemplating, testing, and revising models of human behavior. The point of view is that of a person trying to comprehend the behavior around him. The primary emphasis is on using a few simple concepts and a little imagination to understand and enjoy individual and collective human behavior.

Speculation is the soul of the social sciences. We cherish attempts to discover possible interpretations of behavior. The effort is complicated and subtle; it has a distinguished history. Aristotle, Smith, Toynbee, Marx, Malinowski, Camus, James, Weber, Dostoevsky, Freud, Durkheim, Cervantes and a host of other figures have added to our understanding of human behavior.

Despite such an impressive ancestry our ambitions are not heroic. We think that playing with ideas is fun. We think there are some interesting ideas in the social sciences. We think that an increase in the quality of speculation both in the social sciences and in everyday life would be good. We would like to contribute to an understanding of models in the social sciences and to enjoyment of their pleasure.

What is a model? How do you invent one? What are some common models in the social sciences? How do you apply them in new situations? What makes a good model? This book attempts to answer such questions by engaging the reader in the process of invention. By the end of the book we will have presented enough examples of models to make a definition superfluous. At the outset, however, we begin with an inelegant characterization: A model is a simplified picture of a part of the real world. It has some of the characteristics of the real world, but not all of them. It is a set of interrelated guesses about the world. Like all pictures, a model is simpler than the phenomena it is supposed to represent or explain.

Consider a scale model of a train. We call it a "model" train because it has some of the characteristics of a train. It is similar in appearance to a real train, has similar parts, and possibly moves in a similar manner. It does not have all of the characteristics of a real train, however. By examining a scale model of a train, we can learn something about a real train's general size and design, but we can not tell much about its horsepower, speed, capacity, or mechanical dependability.

Since a model has only some of the characteristics of reality, it is natural to have several different models of the same thing, each of which considers a different aspect. A diagram of the energy flow in the train's power plant would also be a model of the train. It would be useful for answering some questions that the scale model does not. Neither of these models, however, could tell us whether the train would be an economic success. To determine this we need a performance table (model) showing the relations among tonnage hauled, speed, and fuel consumption. There are many other possible models of a train, each representing some but not all of the train's attributes. Each could be used to say something, but not everything, about a real train.

Whether we are talking of modeling trains, societies, groups, or individuals, the modeling process is the same. We construct models in order to explain and appreciate the world. Sometimes we call our simplifications theories, paradigms, hypotheses, or simply ideas. In a more formal treatise we might make distinctions among some of the labels; but we will not do so here. We will talk simply of models as a generic term for any systematic set of conjectures about real world observations.

Speculative models are central to science, history, and literature. They are also a part of normal existence. We are constantly forming partial interpretations of the world in order to live in it. Because we do not always label our daily guesses about the world as "models," we sometimes overlook the extent to which we are all theorists of human behavior. The activity is not mysterious.

We will treat models of human behavior as a form of art, and their development as a kind of studio exercise. Like all art, model building requires a combination of discipline and playfulness. It is an art that is learnable. It has explicit techniques, and practice leads to improvement. We can identify a few of the necessary skills:

1. An ability to *abstract* from reality to a model. Problems in social science are complex and frequently personal. It is necessary, but not easy, to form abstract representations of a delicately intricate reality.
2. A facility at *derivation* within an abstract model. Models become rich through their implications. It is necessary to devise models that yield significant derivations and to develop skill at producing meaningful implications.
3. A competence at *evaluating* a model. Not all models are good ones. Some are unattractive because their derivations are inaccurate; some because their consequences are immoral; some because they are unaesthetic. It is necessary to know how to reject inadequate models.
4. A *familiarity with some common models*. The number of models in the social sciences is large; but a few are common enough to make familiarity with them essential. It is necessary to have command of a few standard models and to know how to apply them to a wide variety of situations.

It is possible to identify a set of common models in the social sciences that are relatively simple, easily modified to extend their scope, and suggestive of the varieties of formal reasoning that might be used. And though they do not immediately require more than high school mathematics, they do involve abstraction, derivation, and evaluation.

Beginning in Chapter 4, we consider four such models:

1. *Individual Choice.* The processes by which individuals choose among alternatives, make decisions, and solve problems. For example, investment behavior, gambling, voting, occupational choice, consumer behavior, the selection of mates. The basic model is a model of rational choice under risk. We examine the fundamentals of decision trees, expected value calculations, and alternative criteria for rational choice. The rational model is applied to a variety of choice situations found throughout the study of human behavior.

2. *Exchange.* Exchange as a special case of individual and collective choice. We introduce the basic ideas of indifference curves and the ways in which mutually acceptable trades are made in the market, the cold war, small groups, marriage, and politics. Some effort is made to apply the basic model (drawn largely from economics) to a variety of "noneconomic" situations.

3. *Adaptation.* Modification of behavior by individuals and collectivities in response to experience. The basic model is a probability learning model taken from psychology. The ideas are applied to learning, personality development, socialization, organizational change, attitude change, and cultural change. Special attention is given to superstitious learning and mutual adaptation.

4. *Diffusion.* The spread of behaviors, attitudes, knowledge, and information through a society. The basic models are borrowed from epidemiology and sociology and include both simple versions of contact, transmission, and contagion and more complicated models of the spread of a "disease" in a social structure. The models are applied to the spread of fads, innovations, rumors, political allegiances, emotions, and ideas.

These four varieties of models comprise the basic substantive content of the book. By the end of the book a reader who has worked through the problems and examples should be able to apply the models to any reasonably well-defined situation for which they are relevant. He should be able to make a first approach to asking theoretically interesting questions about almost any situation involving human behavior.

Models of choice, exchange, adaptation, and diffusion are not the only kinds of models we might have considered. Indeed, the variations are considerable and limited mostly by our ability to invent interesting metaphors. The social sciences include ideas about *transition*: how people change from one job to another, from one social class to another over time. The social sciences include ideas about *demography*: how entry (birth) rates, exit (death) rates, and the movement of people (migration) change the age distribution and other features of a population of a society or a part of society. The social sciences include ideas about *structure*: how attitudes, memory, social positions, classes, associations, and language are organized.

Each of these, as well as the four models with which we will deal, is an exhibit in modern social science art. Each has its admirers and its critics; each has its geniuses and its hacks. We hope that the identification of model building as a form of art is not empty, although it may be optimistic. It is intended to communicate the frustrations, aesthetic charm, and unanticipated discovery to be found in the analysis of human behavior.

The major pleasures of the social sciences stem from an elementary property of human beings: Man is capable of producing more complex behavior than he is capable of understanding. The behavior of an infant baffles a psychologist, and vice versa. As a result, models of human behavior are knowledge, ideology, and art. They are metaphors by which we seek to ensure that our understanding of behavior, the complexity of behavior, and the number of questions about behavior all increase over time. Our excitements are those of participating in this spiral.

We invite you to join the game. Participation requires effort, but it does not (in the beginning) require extensive knowledge about the literature of the social sciences. We have used these materials in formal courses and in casual reading, in graduate seminars and in freshman required courses, in professional schools and in high schools, in the United States and abroad. Prior exposure to the social sciences sometimes helps, but a willingness to play with ideas, to construct images, and to solve puzzles seems much more important.

Of greatest importance, however, is the commitment to working through a set of problems. These problems are found at the end of each subsequent chapter of the book. Each problem asks the reader to develop some model, its implications, use it as a basis for recommending social policy, or evaluate it. The problems range from simple exercises to complicated social questions requiring considerable ingenuity to answer. They require involvement, time, and thought on the part of the reader. The text provides a guide to possible ideas and some examples; but it is the problems at the end of the chapters that are intended to serve as the locus of major effort.

As you go through the rest of the book, we hope that you will experience some of the enjoyment that we do in the activity. We hope you will discover a general style of approaching the social sciences that encourages a playful exercise of disciplined thought, allows the invention of new ways for thinking about familiar things, and treats human behavior as mystery and social scientists as detectives or artists.

References

Robert Henri, *The Art Spirit* (Philadelphia: Lippincott, 1960; first published in 1923).

Leo Rosten, *The Joys of Yiddish* (New York: McGraw-Hill, 1968).

Richard S. Rudner, *Philosophy of Social Science* (Englewood Cliffs, N.J.: Prentice-Hall, 1966).

chapter two

an introduction to speculation

2.1 INTRODUCTION

The best way to learn about model building is to do it. In this chapter we invite you to speculate about human behavior. The procedure we have adopted is a familiar one. It is used by novelists in developing characters or events, by historians in interpreting history, by children in training their parents, and by astronomers in creating theories of the universe.

Despite such testimonials, our procedure is not the only procedure for examining human behavior. Intelligent people differ on how to give meaning to observable phenomena. They differ even more on a variety of special issues that we will happily ignore. If we had some unique vision of the only way to approach social science, we would be delighted to present it. If we knew of some major new solutions to the ancient complications of the search for interesting meanings, we would hurry to announce them. Our intentions are incomparably more modest. We have found one common approach to interpreting human behavior both fruitful and enjoyable. We hope you may find it similarly rewarding.

In this chapter we ask you to practice your skill at imagining speculations. In each section we start with an observation and then speculate about processes that might have produced the observed fact. The examples are all taken from the world of ordinary experience: government, college life, friendship, and population control. They even include one example drawn from the physical world simply to demonstrate that the process of speculation is fun there too.

2.2 CONTACT AND FRIENDSHIP

Suppose we were interested in the patterns of friendship among college students. Why are some people friends and not others? We might begin by asking all of the residents of single rooms along a particular dormitory corridor to give us a list of their friends. These lists of friends are our initial data, the result we wish to understand.

If we stare at the lists for a while to see what they mean, we eventually notice a pattern in them: Friends tend to live close to each other; they tend to have adjacent dormitory rooms. What does this mean? What process could have produced this pattern of friendship?

One feature of this book is that we will often ask you to stop and do some thinking. We are serious.

STOP AND THINK. Devote a moment's time to thinking of a possible process that might produce this observed result.

One *possible* process that might have led to this result is the following:

> Each spring the director of campus housing allows students to indicate their dormitory room preference for the following year; groups of friends take advantage of this and ask to have each other as roommates or to be put in adjacent rooms.

This process is a speculation about a prior world. *If* the real world had once been like our model world, then the observed facts would have been a logical consequence. That is, this speculative prior world would have produced our observed result, namely, that friends tend to have adjacent rooms. Thus we have found a model, a process, that accounts for the facts. We do not stop here, however. We next ask: What other consequences does this model have? What else does it imply? It also implies that the students in each dormitory friendship group must have known each other previously; hence they must have attended the university during the previous year; hence there will be fewer friendship clusters among freshmen.

Is this further implication of our speculative prior world correct? To test it we first examine the friendship patterns in a dormitory of juniors and seniors, and, as expected, we discover groups of friends living next to each other.

We also examine a dormitory that has only freshmen and discover that there are as many groups of friends clustered there too, which is not an expected result (according to the model). This result would not have been predicted by our model unless the freshmen knew each other prior to college. Perhaps the freshman friendship clusters consist of students who knew each other in high school and who asked for adjacent rooms. We look at information on the backgrounds of freshmen to see whether this is true; but we discover that almost all of the students come from different high schools.

So our speculative model world does not do a very good job of explaining what we have observed. Some process other than mutual selection by prior friends must be involved. We think about it some more and try to imagine another process that could have led to these results. Our new speculation (which is probably the one you yourself thought of when the question was first posed) is as follows:

> College students come from similar backgrounds. As a result, they have enough experiences, problems, and values in common that they are capable of becoming friends with each other. Pairs of college students who live near each other will have frequent opportunities for interaction and hence are likely to discover these common characteristics.

Thus students who live close to one another will become friends. This new speculation explains the presence of friendship clusters in freshmen dorms as well as in junior-senior dorms. Does it have any other implication?

STOP AGAIN. Think about it. *Hint:* **what about changes in these friendship clusters over time?**

Since the chance of contact increases over time, the friendship clusters should grow in size as the school year progresses. You would expect the average friendship cluster to be relatively small in October, bigger in December, and still bigger by May. To test this prediction, you would have to run questionnaires at two or three separate dates. If you did so and discovered that the prediction was correct, the model would seem somewhat more impressive.

In summary: We made an observation (friendship clusters around adjacent rooms); we speculated about a model world (mutual selection by preexisting friends) to explain this result; we looked at other implications of the model world (no friendship clusters in freshmen dorms) to see if they were true. Since they were not true, we created a new model, with a new process inherent in it (similarity of values and opportunity to meet cause friendship), we then examined the implications of the new model world (cluster size increases over time) and found that they were true.

So far we have formulated a model of college students discovering similarities. We would now like to make our model more general, to find some new model that includes this model as an implication. Can you think of such a more general model?

STOP AND THINK. **Remember you still want to include the predictions we made earlier and yet find a more general model that predicts new behaviors as well, perhaps beyond the campus scene.** *Hint:* **Look at the parts of the existing model that restrict its area of applicability.**

One possible approach to reformulation proceeds as follows: College students are people. Perhaps our speculation about college students is true about all people. Now our theory becomes:

> Most people have enough experiences, problems, and values in common that they are capable of being friends. Pairs of people are likely to discover these common characteristics when they live close to one another.

The model is a broad, powerful statement about the world. If it is true, does it have any nonuniversity implications? Racial integration is a potential area for its application. The model predicts more friendships between blacks and whites who live in integrated neighborhoods than would be found between blacks and whites who do not live near each other; it also predicts that opinions of blacks and whites toward each other will be more positive and favorable in integrated neighborhoods.

A group of social scientists decided to test some of these predictions.[1] They chose two housing areas—one segregated and the other integrated—to see whether there were differences in friendships and attitudes. Both areas were public housing projects; and both were carefully compared to assure that other variables that might also influence interracial attitudes would be similar in both projects.

The social scientists questioned white residents of the two housing projects about their relations with their neighbors and about their attitudes toward blacks. They found that whites living in the integrated project reported far more neighborly relations with blacks than was true of whites living in the segregated project. They also found that integration produced large changes in white attitudes toward blacks. Among those whites who had originally held unfavorable attitudes toward blacks before moving into the housing project, 92% of those in the segregated project still had unfavorable attitudes, while more than half of those in the integrated project now held favorable attitudes toward blacks. Thus the predictions of the model were confirmed.

With the extension of our speculation from college students to people and from dormitories into neighborhoods, we have not yet exhausted the possibilities for developing the model.

STOP AND THINK. **Reread the model, and then try to think of ways in which you might reformulate the ideas to make them even more general.** *Hint:* **Think about the process by which friendships are formed.**

Perhaps you thought of something like this. The reason people in neighborhoods discover each other's values is because they have contact through communication. Now our model becomes:

Most people have enough experiences, problems, and values in common that they are capable of being friends. Pairs of people are likely to discover these common characteristics when they communicate with each other.

Thus people who communicate with each other will become friends. Now we can use our model not only to predict some features of college life and some features of residential neighborhood life but also some consequences of communication through visiting, writing, telephoning, or television.

STOP AND THINK. **Speculate about the implications of the changing communication patterns in our society; for example, grandparents no longer live in the same household as their grandchildren, and children now leave home earlier and live farther away. Use the new extended model to predict the change in friendship patterns which might result from the change in communication patterns. Some of your speculations may seem false, but this is simply a**

sign that you are doing the job well and being imaginative. At this stage it is more important to be creative than to be critical. (You are on your own on this question—no answer will be given below.)

But now suppose, finally, that a friend of yours proposes the following:

> Most people have enough differences in experiences, problems, and values that they are capable of being enemies. Pairs of people are likely to discover these differences when they communicate with each other.

Thus people who communicate with each other will become enemies.

In reviewing our original dormitory data, we see that this new model predicts that the size of enemy groups will increase over the course of the school year. That is, the number of people disliked by any one person will increase over the year. It is possible, therefore, to revise the model to take account of both effects (friend production and enemy production) by changing it to something like the following:

> Most people have enough experiences, problems, and values in common that they are capable of being friends. At the same time, most people have enough experience, problems, and values that differ that they are capable of being enemies. Pairs of people discover their common and differing characteristics through communication.[2]

At this point we have a broad, provocative speculation. We cannot stop here, however, for we now have to deal with a major problem implicit in this model: What determines the initial pattern of communication? How do two people happen to begin by discussing shared characteristics rather than conflicting characteristics? To what extent do expectations about others become self-fulfilling? That is, do friends confine their communication to things they agree on, whereas enemies discuss each other's differences?

The fact that initially prejudiced whites changed their feelings toward blacks after moving into an integrated housing project is grounds for optimism. Perhaps communications about shared values are more powerful than communications about differences.

Perhaps closeness creates strong incentives to discover shared values. Or perhaps the experience of solving joint problems (for example, dirty streets, landlord problems, school issues) creates the incentive to discover shared values.

Since our current model places primary emphasis on the pattern of communication, you might wish to add some speculations of the following kinds:

1. Friends tend to communicate about common values; enemies communicate about differing values. As a result, two people who start out being friends (either through chance or positive expectations) will become better friends; two people who start out being enemies will become worse enemies.

2. Situations in which there is general social agreement about appropriate behavior and appropriate interpretations of behavior will more likely produce communication about shared values than will situations in which there is less general agreement. Thus two persons who initially meet in a well-defined, normatively regulated situation will be more likely to become friends than if they had met in normatively unregulated situations. (Could this be a possible reason why stable societies impose relatively elaborate politeness rules for first encounters among people?)

3. Strangers would rather be friends than enemies (because enemies are more "expensive.") Thus two people initially try to communicate about shared values. "Mistakes" occur when a person guesses wrong about which values are shared, or when he is forced to communicate to an audience of several different people. Thus two persons from similar cultures are more likely to become friends than two persons from different cultures. On the average, the smaller the group within which a first encounter between two persons occurs, the more likely they are to become friends. On the average, the larger the group of strangers, the more inane the conversation. This is one reason why, counter to intuition, large parties of strangers are duller than small parties of strangers, per gallon of liquid served.

STOP. If you have taken the time to exercise your imagination at each step of these examples, you should now have a sense of the basic nature of the model-building procedure that we are presenting and its pleasures. You may find it useful at this point to retrace the process and devote some time to your own speculations rather than ours.

2.3   *ROCKS, LAKES, AND RIVERS*

Not all speculation concerns human behavior. We can play the same game with observations made about the physical world. Figure 2.1, for example, shows an excavation in Southern California. Other excavations near this particular area all show the same structure: parallel layers of rocks with smaller rocks and sand between them. Why does the excavation look like this? What kind of geological process might have produced this end result? How did the rocks get there? Why are they layered the way they are?

STOP AND THINK. Try to think of some geological process that might have produced this result.

A possible process might be:

This area is actually the bed of an ancient ocean; the layers are the result of successive deposits of rock and sand washed there by the ocean; then the land was pushed up out of the ocean by some kind of geological upheaval.

This imagined process is a speculation about a prior world. *If* the real world had once been like our model world, then the observed facts would have been a logical consequence. Thus we have found a model, a process, that accounts for the facts.

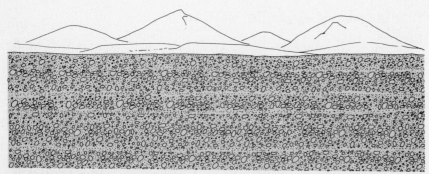

Figure 2.1: Gravel pit wall with stratified layers of rock. There are mountains in the background. Adapted from Geology Illustrated *by John S. Shelton. W. H. Freeman and Company. Copyright © 1966. Reproduced with permission.*

If our speculation about the prior world is true, are there any other facts that we should also observe?

STOP AND THINK. **Think of some other consequences that follow from the model. What are its other observable geological implications? Try to think of at least one other implication before you continue reading.**

If this were an ancient ocean bed, there should also be marine debris as well as rocks, for example, fossils of some kind. A careful examination of the excavations, however, shows no fossils or other marine debris. This causes us to doubt the ocean-bed model. A further cause of doubt is that the surface of the ground is exactly parallel to the rock layers exposed by the excavation. It is unlikely that the land would have been raised exactly straight up out of the ocean or that subsequent erosion of the surface could have worn it exactly parallel to the former floor.

So our speculation, or model, about the origin of this area is in trouble. The model correctly explains the layers of rocks, but, unfortunately, it also predicts two things that are not true. Thus it is unlikely that our model is correct. Let us try to think of some other model that might have generated the observed result.

STOP. **Can you think of an alternative?**

An alternative possible model is:

The area in the picture was formed by rocks washed down from the mountains in the background; torrential rains and flooding carried the rocks from the mountains; successive layers represent successive floods.

Could this alternative version of the prior world have created the known results? It does explain the layers of rocks; it predicts the lack of marine fossils; and it also predicts that the surface should be exactly parallel to the rock layers, since the process is presumably still going on in a slow fashion. But is there anything else that this new version of the prior world would predict? If the process we have imagined were true, would it have led to any other results?

STOP AND THINK about this for a moment.

If the model were true, we might also expect that the type of rocks in the excavation will be the same as the type of rocks found in the mountains. We might also expect that excavations closer to the mountains will show larger rocks than the ones in the drawing, since the large rocks could not have been washed so far. And, finally, we might also expect to find a very slight upslope from this area toward the mountains. All three of these predictions were confirmed by field work. The last model then appears to be a reasonable speculation.

2.3.1 A MODEL OF THE MODEL-BUILDING PROCESS

You should now have some notion of what a model is and how models are created. A model is a simplified representation of the real world. Models are created by speculating about processes that could have produced the observed facts. Models are evaluated in terms of their ability to predict correctly other new facts.

Models are simplified representations of the world because it is impossible to represent the full complexity of the world (notice that the geological model did not specify the dates of the floods, the amount of water in each, the types of rocks washed down, the names and ages of any trees that might have been uprooted, and so on) and also because minute details are unnecessary. Our simple model has only enough detail to make it applicable to other situations.

If you think back over the procedure we used to build the model, it works as follows (though usually not nearly so neatly):

Step 1
Observe some facts.

Step 2
Look at the facts *as though they were the end result of some unknown process (model).* Then *speculate about processes that might have produced such a result.*

Step 3
Then *deduce other results* (implications/consequences/predictions) *from the model.*

Step 4
Then ask yourself *whether these other implications are true and produce new models if necessary.*

First we started with some facts (the rock formations exposed by the excavation) that we wanted to explain. Next we constructed an imaginary model world (the ocean bed) that could have produced these observed facts. We then asked if there were other consequences or predictions implied by the imagined model world. We found two such predictions (presence of fossils and surface irregularity) but discovered that neither prediction was confirmed in the real world. So we rejected our initial guess about the prior world and imagined an alternative prior world (floods from the mountains). This alternative model not only accounted for all of the known facts, but from it we also predicted three new results, which were all confirmed. Thus we now feel confident that the process we imagined is what actually produced the result that we wanted to explain. Therefore, we have a good model because it explains why the rocks in the excavation look the way they do.

The explanatory procedure should now be relatively clear: It involves a constant interplay between the real world and the model world. The main difference between this explanatory procedure and the kind of thinking we usually do is that this procedure is more systematic and more creative. In ordinary thinking when we have a result to explain, we are usually content to think of some simple explanation and then stop. This is incomplete thinking; it stops before the process is fully carried out. The real fun is to continue thinking and see what other ideas the explanation can generate, to ask ourselves: *If this explanation is correct, what else would it imply?* Once you learn to do it easily, you will find genuine creative enjoyment associated with this interplay between explanation and prediction.

2.4 RESPONSIBILITY CORRUPTS

Governments frequently appoint task forces or commissions to study serious, complex issues such as crime, unemployment, education, narcotics, or student unrest. Sometimes such commissions are appointed because the sheer complexity of a problem makes concentrated, impartial study a necessity. Sometimes they are appointed for political reasons in an effort to bury a currently controversial, but probably short-lived, issue. And sometimes they are appointed to rubber stamp and legitimize a program that an administrator has already decided he wants to implement. The make-up of these commissions is usually very diverse: One often finds conservative businessmen, lawyers, professors, civil servants, and liberal labor union leaders all mixed together. In spite of the complexity of the issues being investigated, in spite of the variety of motivation for appointing the commissions, and in spite of the diversity of their memberships, there is a common pattern in the final reports of task forces or commissions. They often end up criticizing the policies of the government that appointed them; they usually make recommendations that can be characterized as moderate; and the members usually agree unanimously or nearly unanimously. That is, the diversity of opinions on the commission is usually resolved in a moderate, action-oriented direction, apparently by changing the opinions of the participants, particularly those of the more doctrinaire members.

For example, the report of President Nixon's Commission on Campus Unrest was published in 1970. Among the commission members were a police chief, a governor, a newspaper editor, an attorney, a law school dean, a retired Air Force general, a university president, a professor, and a graduate student. The commission did not issue the kind of report that might have been expected, given the probable initial biases of its members. The report expressed a good deal of criticism not only toward students but also toward the government and universities. It said:

> Most student protestors are neither violent nor extremist. . . . The roots of student activism lie in unresolved conflicts in our national life, but the many defects of the universities have also fueled campus unrest. . . . The university's own house must be placed in order. . . . Actions—and inactions—of government at all levels have contributed to campus unrest. The words of some political leaders have helped to inflame it. Law enforcement officers have too often reacted ineptly or overreacted. At times, their

response has degenerated into uncontrolled violence. . . . We recommend that the President seek to convince public officials and protestors alike that divisive and insulting rhetoric is dangerous.

In the next few pages we will show the kind of thought processes carried out by one of the authors as he tried to understand why commissions behave the way they do. Some of the steps that follow took longer to formulate than others, and some are slightly expanded to make the thinking more explicit.

STOP. **Think about the observation. Why would commissions be moderate (and critical) in their reports? See if you can form some speculations of your own.**

The reading of the newspaper story about the commission on student unrest and the observation that moderation and a tendency to criticize the government were common to such commissions was the observed *result* I wanted to explain. I asked myself *how* such a result could occur; what *process* could have led to this result? Thus my first try at an explanatory process was:

People on commissions who hold diverse opinions ultimately decide to compromise a little bit. They do so in a kind of trading process in which each gains a little and each gives up a little. Thus the final report represents a middle ground among the diverse views.

I next tried to broaden the model, to make it more general and abstract. The first step was to look at all of the verbs and nouns in the model to see if they could be made less specific. "Commission" and "final report" were broadened first, since it seems possible that the compromise process is true of all group behavior. My second try was:

People who hold diverse opinions will tend to compromise their differences and end up supporting some opinion in the middle, in order to obtain common agreement.

Notice that "commissions" was dropped altogether and that "final report" was broadened to become "opinions." This model is broader than the first try, though it is limited to opinions. Could any other verbs or nouns be broadened? It seemed possible that behavior might be changed as well. So the language was broadened to include actions as well as opinions. The third try was:

> People with conflicting goals and opinions will tend to compromise their differences in order to obtain common agreement.

The third try was substantially broader than the first, and I now had a model with applications in the whole area of human decision making. Does the model work? Are its predictions correct?

The simplest prediction is that we should observe evidence of compromise in the final reports of task forces. There was such evidence of compromise—the reports always seemed to endorse some position in the middle of the spectrum of original opinions held by the participants. But something else was also apparent. There were rarely any strong dissenting "minority reports." Nor were there many instances of commission members "repudiating" a report upon their return to private life. Perhaps most of the participants had actually *changed* their opinions rather than simply compromised them for the sake of the report. If this were true, it was not a result that would be predicted by the model. Some other process must be involved, therefore, and the model must be modified to take account of it or else be discarded in favor of a different model.

STOP AND THINK. **How would you modify the model? What sort of process might lead to an actual change in personal opinions?**

Why would the opinions of the people on the commission be changed as a result of their participation in the activities of the commission? My first try at a new model was something like this:

> It is easier to hold extreme views if you are not confronted with their consequences and if you are not exposed to alternative views. People on commissions do have the strong possibility of having their reports implemented and hence are forced to think about the actual consequences of their decisions. It is hard to cling to extreme ideas when faced with the possibility of human misery resulting from them.[3]

This seemed to be an interesting beginning, and I next tried to broaden it. The model should apply to all decision-making situations, not only to commissions, and it should apply to actions as well as opinions. A second try was:

> People in positions of responsibility tend to moderate their beliefs and actions as a result of confrontation with actual consequences and exposure to alternative ideas.

The model now suggests a reason why idealists, of either the right or the left, tend to modify their ideological purity and become more moderate once they are given real world responsibilities. What about other possible predictions from the model? It predicts the same moderating effect on successful candidates for public office, and there is at least some casual evidence of this if we look at campaign utterances and compare them with subsequent actions while in office. It also predicts that leaders of radical movements (of either left or right) will tend to disappoint their fellows if they achieve office in a larger sphere. They will probably be viewed as "sell-outs" to the establishment.

For other predictions I tried to think of examples of offices with differing amounts of responsibility and power. The model says that it is easier to maintain extremist views in relatively powerless offices. Thus the president of a local chapter of a minor political social group can easily maintain right-wing views in spite of being president. Likewise, an antibusiness member of Congress may have his views only slightly moderated by his being a congressman, for he is only one vote out of 435. But the model does say that a congressman will exercise the greatest moderation of his views in those areas in which he has committee assignments (since committees are more powerful and carry greater responsibility); and similarly the model predicts that on those occasions when Congress overrules a committee, the congressional action will be more extreme (in either direction) than the committee recommendation. Finally, the model predicts that really powerful and responsible positions such as Chief Justice of the U.S. Supreme Court or President of the United States will have the most effect upon the men or women who hold them.

STOP. **Review the argument and the derivations. Are there other speculations that might explain our original**

observation? Are the others better or worse than this set
of ideas?

2.5   THE CASE OF THE DUMB QUESTION

Suppose you are sitting in class when the person next to you asks
a really dumb question. This is your observed fact. Can you imagine
a process that might produce such an observed event? Let us
suppose that you also know that the person next to you is a football
player. Then you might begin with a simple model, particularly if
you are not a football player:

> Football players are dumb.

Using this as a base, can we generalize it into a more interesting idea? You might want to begin by broadening "football
player" to "athlete," producing the following new statement:

> Athletes are dumb.

The change has made your model more general (but not
necessarily more correct), but the model still has no sense of
process. Why might athletes appear dumb? Is appearing dumb an
inherent characteristic of people who are good at sports? Is it
due to something that happens after people take up sports in a
serious way? Or is there some other explanation?

STOP AND THINK.   Is there some possible process that
would make athletes appear dumb?

One possible model for our observations might be:

Being a good athlete requires large amounts of practice time;
being smart in class requires large amounts of study time. The
amount of free time is so limited that you cannot both study and
practice well.

This is a much more general explanation. It makes a variety of
interesting predictions. Not only does it explain why athletes appear
dumb in class, but it also predicts that any time-consuming activity

will produce the same effect. Thus people who spend large amounts of time on student government or the school paper will also appear dumb in class. Of course, this is not the only possible model. An alternative might be:

> Everyone wants to feel successful. Achieving recognition in any one area is enough to make most people content.

According to this model, athletes will not work hard to achieve recognition in academic work because they already have recognition as athletes. Thus they will appear dumb in class. It also predicts that other individuals who are successful in school in important activities (for instance, student politics, social events) will appear dumb in class.

Or you might have imagined a quite different process:

> We tend to be jealous of success in others. When we are jealous of someone, we attempt subconsciously to lower his apparent success in class by interpreting his questions as "dumb."

According to this model, athletes (who are correctly identified as athletes) will ask questions that appear simplistic to other persons (who are relatively unsuccessful in athletics). Other individuals who are successful in other nonacademic pursuits will also ask what appear to be dumb questions.

> *STOP.* Now we have three different models explaining the dumb football player, and undoubtedly you have thought of others. Which of the models is best? We will consider this question in the next chapter, but you might think a little about it now.

2.6 THE CASE OF THE SMART WOMEN

The data collected to test the various ideas of this partially true story were often casual and nonrigorous. A social scientist noticed that women having a particular religious background tended to do better academic work at his university than women having other religious backgrounds. Religion Z maintains a private educational system that many of its members attend instead of public schools. The Z schools have a certain amount of religious content, are often relatively strict, and are usually segregated by sex.

> ***STOP.*** **Why do Z women do better academic work than non-Z women? What kind of process could produce this result?**

The social scientist who made the initial observation immediately thought of two possible explanations:

Model 1. Z women are inherently smarter than non-Z women.

Model 2. There is something special about Z high schools that prepares students better for college work.

Model 1 is not a good model because it has no sense of process to it. Nonetheless, there is a possible test to check it out. We might simply give IQ tests to random samples of Z and non-Z girls in order to test the assumptions of the model. As a general rule, however, we will discourage assumption testing as a way of validating models. A little bit of imagination devoted to looking for testable predictions will generally be more profitable. In this case we suspect, from general biological knowledge, that if there were a systematic genetic-linked difference between the intelligence of Z women and that of non-Z women, there would be a similar systematic difference between Z men and non-Z men. Now we can avoid the tedious task of administering intelligence tests to everyone. Instead, we simply (and cleverly) check to see if Z men have better grade records than non-Z men. We do so and discover that there is no difference between the two groups of men. This leads us to doubt Model 1.

Model 2 asserts that there is something superior about the Z schools. But if this were true, then again we would expect Z men to be outstanding compared to non-Z men. Perhaps it is only the Z women's schools that are special, however. Casual conversation with Z men and women did not reveal any plausible differences between the Z schools that they attended. Thus Model 2 does not seem valid either, although we might want to keep it in mind. The differences between schools might be subtle. Are there any alternative models?

STOP AND THINK. What other explanations might there be for the social scientist's observation?

If you have read any modern discussions on educated women, you might have thought of the following model, which was also suggested by one of the Z women:

Model 3. Men seem to confuse masculinity and intelligence; a smart woman is threatening to them. So when a woman shows her intelligence, she gets criticized or ignored. After a while, women who want male approval learn to act dumb so as not to offend men. Since the Z schools are segregated by sex, their women graduates haven't been conditioned to be quiet in class and play dumb. With only other women around they get more chance to develop their intellectual potential.

Is this a good model? The process is certainly clear, and it does account for the original observation of disproportionately smart Z women and average Z men. Can we now make some interesting predictions? The essential variables in the model seem to be the degree of contact with men and the values of the men contacted. This in turn suggests some possible natural experiments:

1. Z women should gradually, over time, become conditioned by their new college environment. So the difference between Z women and non-Z women should be much smaller in senior classes than in freshmen classes.
2. There are many noncoeducational colleges. Graduates of women's colleges should do better in graduate school than women graduates of coeducational colleges.
3. Some women are largely indifferent to additional male approval, perhaps because they are strongly career oriented, perhaps because they are certain of their standing (either high or low) among men. Women in career-oriented programs will do better than women in liberal arts programs; women who are married will do better than women who are not; women who are distinctively unattractive to men will do better than others.

STOP. Is Model 3 a good one? Or are there other models? Perhaps professors like the way in which Z women deal with teachers. Maybe you can think of some other explanation. See what predictions you can derive from your own model.

2.7 ON BECOMING A SOCIAL SCIENTIST

Recruitment into college majors is not a random process; rather, there are systematic biases in the motivations, attitudes, and abilities of students who select certain majors. Students make choices that at least in a modest way match their expectations about a field with their own aspirations and their own views of their personal abilities. Counseling from parents, friends, and teachers guides a student into a commitment that is relatively consistent with his talents. As a result, students with greater interest and aptitude in art are disproportionately represented among art majors, and students with greater interest and aptitude in mathematics are disproportionately represented among mathematics majors. In a reasonably efficient "market" these simple mechanisms serve to attract students to interests and careers that are generally consistent with their abilities; but, as we know well from an examination of the ways in which sex biases permeates such a system, the market is far from perfect.

STOP. Think about how you might form a model of the process by which people become committed to a field of study. *Hint:* Maybe they learn to like what they are good at.

Consider the following simple model of the process:

1. There exists a set of alternative fields (for example, political science, history, mathematics).
2. There is a set of basic ability dimensions (for example, verbal fluency, problem solving, imagery). Success in the various fields depends upon the possession of some combination of these talents; the talents leading to success in the various fields overlap considerably, though they are not identical. There is also a random component (error) in success within each field.

The magnitude of the random component varies from field to field.

3. Each child is characterized by a value (score) on each basic ability dimension. Although the correlation among these values is strongly positive, it is not perfect.

4. Initially, a child has no preferences among these fields; children develop preferences on the basis of experience, tending to prefer those in which they are successful; they modify subsequent experiences (insofar as possible) to increase the time spent in fields that are preferred.

Within the model the process by which preferences are developed is simple. A child is presented with a series of opportunities to choose an academic interest; a choice is made on the basis of initial preferences; some level of success or failure is experienced, depending on the relation among the child's abilities, the abilities necessary for success in the field, and some random component; preferences among the various alternative interests are modified on the basis of success.

Such a model is hardly adequate to explain all features of the choice of major; it does, however, capture (or at least is consistent with) the major features of currently received doctrine about (1) individual abilities, (2) the relation between talent and performance in a field, and (3) individual learning of preferences.

STOP AND THINK. **What does the model leave out? Are there important factors omitted by this simplification?**

You may have noted two conspicuous factors that have been ignored by our gradual commitment model.

1. *Market Value.* A strict adaptation model ignores anticipations of future economic and social successes associated with various occupations and thus with various fields. At least some of the enthusiasm for medicine as a career stems from expectations on the part of students (and their parents) of the economic and social position that such a career confers.

2. *Social Norms.* The appropriateness of certain fields (and cer-

tain talents) for certain people is regulated by social rules as well as by adaptation to intrinsic talent. Most conspicuous among rules are the regulations related to ethnic group status and sex. Moreover, expectations with respect to the match between ethnic group or sex on the one hand and performance on the other form a major filter for the interpretation of succcess.

This description of an individual adaptation model subject to the outside press of the market and social norms is reasonable. It is also prima facie efficient and neutral; the process will tend to match up abilities and interests.

The model also predicts some other things. For example, it predicts that the speed of commitment by an individual to a field will depend on the variance of abilities in the individual (that is, those whose abilities are relatively specialized will become committed earlier than those whose ability levels are relatively equal for a wide range of fields); on the relative specialization of the field (that is, fields requiring abilities that are not required by other fields will tend to secure commitment relatively early); on the general level of ability of the individual (that is, those with relatively high ability will tend to become committed before those with relatively low ability); and on the magnitude of the random component in determining success in a field (that is, fields with a high random component will tend to secure later commitment and to attract relatively less able individuals).

According to this model, the social and behavioral sciences, for example, will tend to recruit those students with high abilities in relevant areas, although it will lose some students having high social science ability to other fields when those students also had high abilities relevant to the other fields (particularly to fields with heavy overlap in the abilities required for success). Subject to "errors" in allocation due to chance elements in rewards, time limitations on experience, variations in market values, and social norms, the process allocates students to the places in which their abilities lie.

The errors of allocation, however, are important. If we are interested in understanding some features of how one becomes a social science major, we may be particularly interested in discovering features in the process that might produce systematic errors in the choice of social science.

STOP. Review the process we have specified. Can you see any way in which the selection of a social science major might be systematically biased?

If our model is correct, development of interest in behavioral and social science is subject to several sources of error:

1. Virtually nothing of the behavioral and social sciences is taught in the first 12 years of American schools. The exceptions are small and somewhat misleading: Geography (that is, maps, place names, and the distribution of natural and human resources), civics (that is, constitutional and legal forms), and modern history comprise the normal fare (perhaps supplemented with an exposure to sex and family living). In some schools there is an effort to introduce a bit of economics, psychology, cultural anthropology, or sociology; but these efforts touch an insignificant number of students rather late in their precollegiate days. "Social studies" in the American school is frequently history with an hour's discussion of current events on Friday.

2. The skills required in the social and behavioral sciences are far from unique to those fields. If we assume that the skills required for a modern social or behavioral scientist include the skills of analysis, model building, hypothesis forming, speculation, data interpreting, and problem solving, it is clear that social science deals in widely demanded skills. In particular, it seems obvious that such skills are highly correlated with the skills involved in mathematics, natural sciences, history, and creative writing.

3. Social norms leading students toward social science tend to be antianalytical. The behavioral sciences are associated (quite appropriately) with human beings and social problems. As a result, they are associated (quite inappropriately) with a rejection of things, quantities, abstractions, and special skills. The norms tend often to be relatively "antiprofessional."

4. The social sciences appear to have a relatively high random component in their evaluation procedures. The reliability of grading appears to be less than in some other fields. As a result, students of relatively low ability do, on the average, better in social science than in other fields—even if the average preformance and average ability levels are held constant.

When we superimpose these facts on the basic model, we obtain a series of predictions about possible errors in the choice of social science as a field of interest:

1. Since the abilities appropriate to the social and behavioral sciences are similar to, or correlated with, the abilities appropriate to fields more commonly offered at the precollegiate level (for example, mathematics, natural science, history, English), many students with high potential for work in social science will have learned to prefer (and have a commitment to) another field by the time they come to college.

2. A disproportionate share of those students who say they want to be social scientists on entering college will be "residual students," students who have not as yet found a field for commitment. In effect, this means that many will be students who are not particularly good at mathematics, physics, chemistry, English, history, or biology.

3. Insofar as a student has learned to prefer social science in his precollegiate training, he will have learned to prefer social science in terms of some combination of current events, social and human problems, and institutional description, or (disproportionately) because of error in the earlier evaluation scheme.

The fundamental conclusion can be stated in a grossly simple way: If our model is correct, many social science students will be either inept at necessary skills or persuaded that those skills are irrelevant; many students with the skills necessary for social science will be strongly committed to competitive fields long before college or graduate school. This will be true in general, but it will be less true of individuals (for instance, women, blacks) who are channeled into social science by social norms than of other groups; it will be less true of fields that provide good economic prospects (for instance, economics, law) than other fields.

We have pondered the implications of such a model for the teaching of social science. As teachers, we have sometimes feared that some of our students might be expecting the wrong things from social science; that some students who would be good social scientists never took the right courses; and that some of the enthusiasm and intelligence of our students was buried beneath learned instincts for pedantry. This book, in fact, is a partial response to these concerns.

We have also pondered the implications of the model for understanding why we became social scientists. Was it really because we were not very good at anything else? We do not think so, and we have taken solace in the observation that good models of human behavior are rarely precise interpretations of individual actions.

For example, suppose one of our models generates the following prediction: Wealthy people tend to be more politically conservative than poor people. This is a good prediction about human behavior. But it does not necessarily describe an individual. Former Mayor Lindsay of New York is both wealthy and liberal. So are many other people. We do not expect such a model to predict individual human behavior; we only expect it to predict appreciably better than chance. If we questioned wealthy people about their political views and discovered that 60% were conservative, while only 20% of poor people were conservative, we would say that the model did a reasonably good job of predicting aggregate human behavior.

The prediction that wealthy individuals will tend to be politically conservative is still useful and interesting even if you know some wealthy individuals who are not. Thus if you were soliciting votes for a liberal cause, you would know that your chances of obtaining support from wealthy people would be relatively low. You might concentrate your efforts on other segments of the population and advertise in *Newsweek* rather than in the *Wall Street Journal*.

Thus although our model of how errors are made in the discovery of an interest in social science suggests that there will be more mistakes in social science than in some other fields, it does not necessarily apply to us, or to you. On the other hand, even if it does apply and we are here for all kinds of "erroneous" reasons, we have nevertheless rather grown to like it; and you might also.

2.8 THE POLITICS OF POPULATION

Human societies sometimes face a population problem. A population problem exists when it is generally agreed within the society that the natural processes of birth and death are creating economic or social difficulties and should be modified. Historically, different societies have reacted to this situation in different ways. For example, some societies have increased the average life expectancy of their citizens through improved health-care systems. Some societies have increased the death rate selectively with respect to age, sex, and social class through wars, infanticide, or inefficient health care. Some societies have decreased, or increased, the birth rate through modifying social norms with respect to homosexuality or marriage, through encouraging women to work outside the home or to stay home, through contraceptives, or through moral persuasion.

STOP. Since this kind of question is profoundly important ethically, we might wish to speculate about the process by which societies arrive at different solutions to the population problem. Under what circumstances will societies engage in infanticide, birth control, medical research, women's liberation, or war? What is the process involved?

A possible way of looking at the problem follows. Since any population is limited by some kinds of scarce resources, a society decides who will share in those resources. One aspect of that decision is the question of who will live and who will not. Any combination of policies with respect to health care, birth control, work, war, and social norms is a decision about whose life will be relatively favored in the society and whose will be relatively unfavored. In this sense every society discriminates in favor of some people and against others.

Suppose we think of society as consisting of various age groups (for example, old people, young adults, children, unborn). Various possible population control procedures clearly have different consequences for the different age groups. A society that invests money in research on cancer and heart disease, for example, discriminates in favor of middle- and old-age people. A society that practices infanticide discriminates against babies. A society that practices birth control discriminates against the unborn.

If we look at the problem this way, our task becomes that of identifying a process by which a society might come to discriminate in one way or the other.

STOP AND THINK. Can you form any hypotheses about the decision process within a society?

You might have said something like this:

Individuals and groups within a society pursue their own self-interests. It is in the interest of every individual to promote discrimination in favor of his own age group and other age groups to which he expects to belong. Each group of individuals within the society has a certain amount of power. The greater the relative power of a group, the greater the discrimination in its favor.

A moment's reflection on the power structure within societies immediately suggests two predictions:

1. All societies will tend to discriminate against the unborn. That is, faced with an overpopulation problem, they will tend to prefer birth control to increasing the death rate.
2. The broader the sharing of power within the living society (for example, the more democratic it is), the greater the discrimination against the unborn.

The first of these predictions sounds interesting and provocative, but it is not easy to evaluate. The second, however, can be examined. A social scientist who did not have this specific problem in mind has invented a measure of the democracy of a political system and has applied it to some modern political systems. His results are presented in Table 2.1 along with crude birth and death rates.

Our model says that relatively democratic countries will discriminate more against the unborn than will relatively undemocratic countries. This means that we would expect to find that relatively democratic countries had relatively low birth rates and relatively long life expectancies. Is this the case?

STOP. **Think about how you would decide whether these data support the model.**

One procedure that might have occurred to you is to plot pairs of observations as we have done in Figures 2.2 and 2.3. In Figure 2.2 each country is a point. Each country is located on the figure according to the democratic index for that country and the crude birth rate for that country.

STOP AGAIN. **What does the model predict about such a figure?**

TABLE 2.1   *Democracy, Birth Rates, and Death Rates*

COUNTRY	DEMOCRATIC INDEX	CRUDE BIRTH RATE	DEATH RATE 60–64 YR. OLD (MALES)
Great Britain	236.3	18.3	27.6
France	231.4	17.7	26.1
Finland	229.2	16.9	34.6
Sweden	225.8	15.9	18.6
Netherlands	220.9	19.9	33.1
Belgium	214.9	16.4	29.1
Japan	212.7	18.6	—
Luxembourg	210.1	16.0	24.7
Norway	209.7	17.5	16.5
New Zealand	209.4	22.8	26.3
Denmark	205.7	18.0	19.3
Israel	203.2	25.8	26.8
W. Germany	199.4	17.9	—
Italy	198.6	19.2	21.8
Canada	196.8	21.4	23.5
United States	190.9	19.4	29.2
Venezuela	188.3	—	—
Austria	186.9	17.9	—
Chile	184.6	32.8	—
Ireland	181.4	22.1	27.0
India	172.7	—	—
Switzerland	169.3	18.8	25.6
Mexico	121.9	44.2	41.8

Source: Deane E. Neubauer, "Some Conditions of Democracy," *American Political Science Review* **61** (1967) 1002–1009. Reprinted with permission.

According to our model more democratic countries will discriminate *more* against the unborn. Thus a high democratic index should lead to a low birth rate. This appears to be generally true. One quick and inelegant way of checking is to draw a vertical line through the middle (*median*) value with respect to birth rate. These are the dashed lines in Figure 2.2. These lines divide the space into four rectangular areas. If our model is correct, we should find that the points are concentrated in the upper left and lower right areas. If you check, you will find that there are fourteen points in these two areas and only four points in the other two.

In Figure 2.3 each country is again a point. Here the points are located according to the democratic index for that country and the crude death date for 60–64-year-old males in that country. We have drawn the equivalent dashed lines.

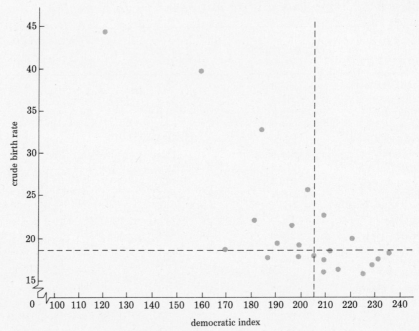

Figure 2.2: Democracy and birth rates.

STOP. **What does the model predict?**

Our model predicts that the more democratic countries will discriminate *less* against 60–64-year-olds. Thus we predict that a high democratic index will be associated with low death rate. This does not appear to be true. Our data arrange themselves so that there are exactly four points in each of three of the quadrants and five points in the fourth.

STOP. **Can you generate any other predictions that might be wrong? So far we have talked mostly about good predictions, but much of the art of model building lies in finding bad predictions.**

At least one other problematic prediction occurs to us. We have talked entirely about age groups and the relatively weak political position of the unborn. In effect, we have developed the implications of a pure political model in which the powerful discriminate against the less powerful. There are other political groups that are relatively weak. Consider blacks in the United States, who have, by almost any plausible measure, less political power on the average than whites. Thus, according to the model, you would expect that age-specific death rates would be higher and age-specific birth rates lower among blacks than among whites. In fact, the first proposition is true, but the second is not.

One possible explanation is that this is something unique to the problems of blacks in America. However, this thought can be quickly dispelled. Spanish-speaking Americans also have less political power on the average than do Anglos. Yet birth rates and death rates are both high among Spanish-speaking Americans. Such a situation appears to have been true historically for many minority groups within the United States. American society seems systematically to discriminate against living members of ethnic minority groups and against unborn children of dominant social groups.

Thus it is possible that our model is simply wrong. One of the important realities of model building is that not all predictions

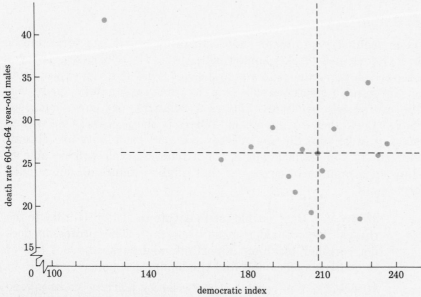

Figure 2.3: Democracy and death rates.

are correct. Indeed, as we will suggest in more detail in the next chapter, although we enjoy being right, most theoretical development comes from being wrong.

2.9 THREE RULES OF THUMB FOR MODEL BUILDING

Model building as you have done it in this chapter is not a novel activity. It is something we all do all the time. We speculate about things that happen to us or that we see happening to others. It is not mysterious, but it probably can be improved by a little attention to some elementary rules. In Chapter Three we will suggest some more detailed rules of thumb. Here we will simply note three general rules that we have been using repeatedly in making the speculations in this chapter. They are probably sensible much of the time, though they are not absolute truths.

> *Rule 1: Think "Process."   A good model is almost always a statement about a process, and many bad models fail because they have no sense of process. When you build a model, look at it for a moment and see if it has some statement of process in it.*

Example

Your chemistry professor shows up in class but has forgotten to bring along last week's homework papers. He apologizes, and you turn to the person next to you and say, "What can you expect from absent-minded professors?" This is your explanatory model for the professor's behavior. This is a common, ordinary, but poor model. Look at it for a moment. Where is the process? One way to put a process into the model is to ask *why* professors are absent-minded. If you think about it for a moment, you will be able to think of a number of processes that might produce absent-minded professors.

> *Model 1.*   Busy people try to devote their limited time to the things they consider most important. The professor does not consider teaching important, and so he did not bother to go by his office and find the homework papers.

> *Model 2.*   You become a professor by learning to be a good problem solver. Good problem solving involves almost single-

minded concentration. So the professor occasionally forgets to do one thing because he is concentrating on another.

The models are different from each other, but each involves a sense of process, or relationship. One way to be certain that your models involve a sense of process is to see if you can derive general relational statements from them, that is: The greater X is, the greater Y will be. Thus Model 1 contains the following general relational statement: The busier someone is, the more likely he is to concentrate on important things. And Model 2 contains this general relational statement: The tougher the problem and the harder someone is concentrating on it, the more likely he is to forget other things.

> *Rule 2: Develop Interesting Implications. Much of the fun in model building lies in finding interesting implications in your models. In the problems associated with this course you will repeatedly be asked to develop interesting implications from some model. Whether something is considered interesting obviously involves a judgment, but there is a good strategy for producing interesting predictions: Look for natural experiments.*

Example

An uninteresting prediction from Model 1 would be: Make the professor value his students more, and he will then become less absent-minded. Or from Model 2: Get the professor to work on easier problems, and he will become less absent-minded. These are relatively uninteresting because they ask us to run an experiment in a situation in which we probably cannot.

The way to find more interesting predictions is to think about the process involved in each model and then look for natural instances in which the key variables in the process vary. In Model 2, for example, it is not simple to vary the difficulty of the professor's problems, but you can easily find instances of similar situations and hence can predict that people (business executives, architects, football coaches) in other occupations that demand concentrated, abstract thought will occasionally forget things, too. Or you can predict that the professor will be just as absent-minded when engaged in his laboratory research as when he is engaged in teaching.

Or, for Model 1, you cannot easily make the professor value

some given class of students more, but you can search for natural occurrences of this event. For example, if you believe that he values the students in his graduate research seminar more than the students in his freshman introductory class, you would predict less absent-minded behavior with respect to the graduate students. Suppose you did make such observations and discovered that he was equally forgetful in his graduate classes; and furthermore that his freshmen lectures are well prepared, that he seems to have great quantities of careful notes, and that he often spends so much time answering questions after the freshman class that he is late for his next class. You would then be highly skeptical of the truth of Model 1.

> ***Rule 3: Look for Generality.*** *Ordinarily, the more situations a model applies to, the better it is and the greater the variety of possible implications. Finding generality involves the ordinary process of generalizing nouns and verbs.*

Example

Expand "college professors" to "busy people"; expand "forgetting homework papers" to "forgetting anything"; expand "bringing papers" to "one kind of work." Finding generality also involves asking repeatedly why the process we have postulated is true. We ask: Is there another model that, if true, would include our model as an implication? That is, we look for a more general model that predicts our model and other things as well. Model 2, for instance, can be generalized to a large family of learning models that can be formulated to predict what would happen if people learned to be good social scientists (see Section 2.7) or executives (see Chapter Six).

From such simple heuristics, a little experience, some playfulness, and a bit of luck come good models, and some bad ones. Indeed, it is the creativity with which we specify bad models that leads us to good ones.

References

Herbert A. Simon, *Models of Man* (New York: Wiley, 1957).

Arthur L. Stinchcombe, *Constructing Social Theories* (New York: Harcourt Brace Jovanovich, 1968).

Josephine Tey, *The Daughter of Time* (London: Macmillan, 1951).

Notes

[1] Martin Deutsch and Mary Evan Collins, "Interracial Housing," in William Peterson, ed., *American Social Patterns*, (Garden City, N.Y.: Doubleday, 1956).

[2] Actually, the process implicit in this model should be clarified somewhat. We are *not* saying that out of every 100 people there are 70 who are inherently like us and who could become our friends and 30 people who are inherently different from us who could become our enemies; and communication allows us to identify the two different groups. Rather, the model says that almost anyone is capable of becoming either a friend or enemy, depending on whether you communicate about your similarities or your differences.

[3] Note an alternative theory: People on commissions want to have their reports implemented. They believe (from experience?) that extreme reports rarely are implemented.

Problems

A Note for Instructors. The problems in this book are designed to stimulate thought. For many of the problems, especially those in Chapters 2 and 3, there are no unique correct answers; rather, there are only thoughtful and nonthoughtful answers, or creative/noncreative answers. The amount of written material in the book has deliberately been kept terse to allow more time for thought. In effect, we postulate a Gresham's Law of Study: Faced with a choice of reading about something versus thinking about it, people will choose reading. Reading drives out thinking. Reading is a well-defined technology at which most of us are relatively competent; it provides easily recognized benchmarks of progress and completion, and it can be accomplished with certainty in some easily predicted time period.

Reducing the necessary reading time is only part of the solution, though. We also need to make thinking more attractive and rewarding. One way to do this is the formation of small problem-set groups. Each group meets outside of class to discuss the problems and ultimately turns in a single answer to them. The stimulation of small-group discussion provides the immediate rewards, and the common problem provides structure. Such problem-set groups seem to work well as measured by either student satisfaction or quality of answers turned in. One hazard lies in defining a grading system that assures each student a fair grade. One solution—used at the end of the course—has been to have an evaluation by each student in the group of the contribution of the various group members over the length of the course. Problem-set grades are then allocated on the basis of these evaluations. (Group members had very high internal agreement concerning the identification of "creators" versus "parasites.") This system also has the advantage of reducing the number of papers to be graded and hence allows more detailed comments on each paper.

Note that Problems 1–4 emphasize predictions from a given model. Problems 5–8 involve model building and prediction in a structured context. Problems 9–12 are the most general model-building exercises.

1. The model developed in Section 2.4 says that opinions change as a result of the interaction of two variables: (1) the amount of power and responsibility a person has and (2) the amount of exposure to alternative opinions. In the text some of the predictive implications of varying amounts of power and responsibility were explored. Use the same model to do the following. (Be sure the logical connection between the model and your predictions is explicitly stated and that any assumed facts concerning the world are explicit.)

   (a) Pick some type of decision maker and show what the effects would be if his exposure to opinions varied.

   (b) Make some predictions with respect to real world situations.

   (c) Draw some implications for the organization of democratic governments.

2. Suppose that a study of the opinions of congressmen showed that members of the House of Representatives who serve on the House Committee on Education and Welfare (which considers welfare matters) generally have more extreme views (pro or con) on welfare matters than the average member of Congress; that members of the Senate Foreign Relations Committee generally have more extreme views on foreign policy than the average member of the Senate; and that the same pattern seems to be true of other committees in Congress. (Remember that congressmen have some choice about their committee assignment and presumably select the committees that interest them most.)

   (a) Do these results contradict the model outlined in Section 2.4? Explain why or why not.

   (b) If the data *do* contradict the model, how would you revise it?

   (c) If the data *do not* contradict the model, are there any data that might?

3. The morning newspaper has a story concerning the governor's new plan to aid the children of minority families. Your friends have offered two possible explanations for the governor's behavior: (1) The governor has just become aware of the problems faced by minority children; he is a genuinely humane man and so has decided to do something about it. (2) It is a political act; the governor is trying to buy votes.

A description of four different worlds follows. Discuss the compatibility of each world (viewed as a result) with the two explanations. You might say, for example: The facts of World A are clearly compatible with the humanistic explanation and incompatible with the vote-buying explanation because . . .

World A
The latest Gallup poll shows that the governor is supported by 65% of the voters; the state has a one-term limitation on how long a governor may serve; he has a long prior history of charitable activities in church and community associations.

World B
It is two months until the next election, and the polls show him to be running 5% behind his opponent; the aid program is quite cheap, and he has only discussed it in his speeches in ghetto areas; he has always been known as a hard-headed, practical, unsympathetic person.

World C
It is two months until the next election, and the polls show him to be running 5% behind his opponent; the aid program is expensive; he has a long prior history of charitable actions.

World D
At the same time he announced the aid program, he also announced that he was retiring from politics; he has always been known as a hard-headed, practical, unsympathetic person.

4. Consider four well-known and widely believed theories of socially deviant aggressive behavior (for example, criminal behavior, revolutionary behavior, rude behavior):

Theory I
Deviant aggressive behavior is learned from experience. Individuals in a society learn to do those things for which they receive rewards and to avoid those things for which they receive punishment.

Theory II
Deviant aggressive behavior is a symbolic expression of hostility toward personal authority figures. When an individual is frustrated in his personal life, he becomes angry toward parents, bosses, or

public officials. He will express this anger by deviant aggressive behavior.

Theory III

Deviant aggressive behavior is the rational action of oppressed individuals. Social rules systematically discriminate among people. People who are most hurt by the rules are least likely to profit from conforming to them and thus do conform less.

Theory IV

Deviant aggressive behavior is a social role. Individuals are socialized into the role through contact with a deviant subculture.

Answer the following questions:

(a) What social policy would be appropriate to reduce aggressive deviant behavior if Theory I were correct? Theory II? Theory III? Theory IV? Explain why.

(b) During the past decade, American society has been running a series of "experiments" with deviant aggressive behavior. Take any one of these experiments (for instance, college unrest, violence in the cities, hard-hat demonstrations) and discuss what we have learned about the four theories from this series of experiments.

5. *Basic Observation.* In the 1920s the typical heroine portrayed in stories in women's magazines was a career girl. In the 1960s the typical heroine was a housewife.

(a) The following explanatory model was produced by a student: "The kinds of stories women like to read have changed over time." Using Rule 1 of the Three Rules of Thumb, try to put some sense of process into the model. Why does a woman find a story interesting in the first place? Why has this changed over time, and what could have caused the change? Do not necessarily try to give specific answers to these questions. They are meant only to help you build a better model.

(b) Using the third rule of thumb, produce another model that is a more general version of the model you produced in (a).

(c) Using the model from (b), make at least three interesting predictions. Use the second rule of thumb, look for natural experiments to which the model may be applied, and then say what the model predicts for those situations. Depending on how your model has evolved, you may or may not find some of these natural experiments useful: other situations in which women may express their preferences; other things that should have changed over time; situations involving products that men buy or choices they make; other kinds of decisions made by magazine editors; changes in social relationships, and so on. Be sure that the logical connection between your model and your predictions is clearly *stated*; and if you are using some facts about the world, state them explicitly. (Treat them like assumptions—they need not be documented, but they must be stated explicitly so that your derivation can be understood by others.)

(d) Produce an alternative general model to explain the basic observation and make two interesting predictions from it.

6. *Basic Observation.* Over the past 30 years the minimum education requirements set by employers have increased significantly. In particular the proportion of jobs "requiring" a college degree has greatly increased.

(a) The following explanatory model was produced by a student: "The reason for this is that college graduates are smarter." Using Rule 1 of the Three Rules of Thumb, try to put a sense of process into the model. What are employers looking for in the first place? Have their goals changed over time, and if so, why? Have the people seeking jobs changed in some way over time? How would this change interact with employers' wishes to produce the increased education requirement? Do not focus on specific answers to these questions. They are intended only to help you build a better model.

(b) Using the third rule of thumb, produce another model that is a more general version of one you produced in (a).

(c) Using the model from (b), make at least three interesting predictions. Use the second rule of thumb, look for natural experiments to which the model may be applied, and then say what your model predicts for those situations. Depending on how your model has evolved, you may or may not find some of these natural experiments useful: instances involving other kinds of potential employee characteristics such as age, sex, race, strength, technical skills; other kinds of decisions made by employers such as product quality, where to locate new plants; predicted changes in the educational system or training programs; other kinds of changes in the characteristics of those seeking employment, and so on. Be sure that the logical connection between your model and your predictions is clearly *stated;* and if you are using some facts about the world, state them explicitly. (Treat them like assumptions: They do not have to be documented, but they do have to be explicitly stated so that your derivation can be understood by others.)

(d) Produce an alternative general model to explain the basic observation and make two interesting predictions from it.

7. *Basic Observation from one of our students who works as a part time waitress.* When I smile at my customers, I get better tips.

(a) The following explanatory model was produced by another

student: "The customers are pleased by her good service, and so they reward her with bigger tips." The process is clear in this model, but its general scope is too narrow. Use the second rule of thumb to broaden this model. Make a more general statement about the character of human interactions, or the ways in which we indicate pleasure, or the ways in which we give rewards, or the kinds of behavior people engage in to receive rewards. Do not try to deal specifically with these suggestions. They are intended only to help you build a better model.

(b) Using your model, make at least three interesting predictions. Use the second rule of thumb. Look for natural experiments to which your model may be applied, and then say what the model predicts for those situations. Depending on how your model has evolved, you may or may not find some of these natural experiments useful: local coffee shops that have a regular clientele; restaurants near vacation beaches that have a highly transient clientele; the behavior of waitresses in truck stops along the highway, which cater to both transient tourists and regular truckers; other situations involving interactions or the giving of services, and so on. Be sure that the logical connection between your model and your predictions is clearly *stated;* and if you are using some facts about the world, state them explicitly. (Treat them like assumptions: They do not have to be documented, but they must be explicitly stated so that your derivation can be understood by someone else.)

(c) Produce an alternative general model to explain the basic observation and make two interesting predictions from it.

8. *Basic Observation.* There has been a substantial increase in the rate of divorce over the past decade.

(a) The following explanatory model was produced by a student: "The rise of the women's liberation movement has resulted in changing attitudes toward divorce." This model has a feeling of process in it, though it is not clear just what the process is or how it works. Using Rule 1 of the Three Rules of Thumb, try to make the explanatory process clearer. Why do people get married, and what holds them together afterward? What ideas or orientation of the women's liberation movement might have changed these things, and how did it change them? What kinds of attitudes promote stability of marriages, and how have they been changed? Do not try to give specific answers to these questions. They are only meant to provoke thought. But do build a better model.

(b) Using the third rule of thumb, produce another model that is a more general version of the model you produced in (a).

(c) Using your model, make at least three interesting predictions.

Use the second rule of thumb. Look for natural experiments to which your model may be applied, and then say what the model predicts for those situations. Depending on how your model has evolved, you may or may not find some of these natural experiments useful: other situations in which women have traditionally had subordinate roles such as parent/child or boss/employee; historical situations before women's liberation in which women might have had financial or social independence; instances of male/female relations other than marriage, and so on. Be sure that the logical connection between your model and your prediction is clearly *stated*; and if you are using some facts about the world, state them explicitly. (Treat them like assumptions: They do not have to be documented, but they must be explicitly stated so that your derivation can be understood by someone else.)

(d) Produce an alternative general model to explain the basic observation and derive two interesting predictions from it.

(9–12) Following are four basic observations that you might use as a starting point for your model building. They are distinct and unrelated. For whichever observation you are assigned, do the following:

(a) Ask yourself *why* the observation might be true and write down your explanations.

(b) Generalize the explanatory model—that is, induce the most general, abstract model you can produce that still has the original observation as a consequence.

(c) Induce an alternative model that also has the original observation as a consequence.

(d) For each of the two general models—one from (b) and one from (c)—derive two interesting predictions (that is, a total of four predictions). Be sure the logical connection between your model and your predictions is explicitly stated and that any assumed facts concerning the world are made explicit. (You might want to reread the rules of thumb first.)

9. People often do things at the last minute (students turning in papers, professors grading exams, and so on).

10. Terminating conversations, leaving parties, getting off the phone and so on, is difficult to do, at least in this culture.

11. Professor Socialman once tried having problem-set groups with 17 members instead of the traditional 4. The results were dreadful because, as Professor Socialman is now fond of saying, "People in large groups can't get anything done."

12. A casual set of observations over several years suggests the following empirical generalization: Automobile drivers rarely smile. If you study the faces of drivers as they pass, you will see an unrelieved series of somber people.

chapter three

the evaluation of speculations

3.1 INTRODUCTION

In Chapter Two we asked you to consider which of several models for the dumb football player was "best." It is a tough question. Possible complications in evaluating models fill large sections in libraries. This is a short book and, as a consequence, we clearly will not do justice to the complexity of scientific methodology. As a further consequence, we are free to present a somewhat personal interpretation of the evaluation of models.

The construction and contemplation of models are aesthetic experiences. Like other aesthetic experiences they become richer and more enjoyable with an appreciation of their nuances. The dicta of methodology are nothing more mysterious than rules of thumb for improving the artistry of speculations. What we present here are some rather simple points of view about truth, beauty, and justice that we, and others, have found helpful in heightening the pleasures and usefulness of model building in social science.

3.2 TRUTH

Some of the pleasures of social science come from the difficulty of discovering models that are *correct*. Because this is hard work we devote a good deal of imagination and effort to discovering how one model might be more correct than another. The skills and techniques we use are similar to those of a clever and thoroughly responsible detective—"clever" because we need some imagination in inventing theories of what is happening and fitting them to the facts; "thoroughly responsible" because we need to find not only one explanation of the facts but the best possible explanation among many.

We can start by asking how we assess the correctness of any single model. How do we determine whether a model is consistent with reality? In order to assess truth value, we must be able to compare assertions of the model with observations of the real world. In short, a good model must be testable; it must make assertions that can be verified or disproved.

An introductory social science class was asked to make models that might explain protests and riots by college students during the late 1960s and to explain how their models might be tested.

STOP AND DO IT. Determine what kind of answer you would give. Make up at least one model; then describe how you would test it.

Following are three poor answers that were submitted by the students. Read them critically. Try to figure out what makes them poor.

Answer 1

Model. "People resent being told what to do and will express this resentment if they get a chance. College students are told how to run their lives by both their parents and college authorities and both parents and authorities use various kinds of threats to prevent the expression of resentment; the recent change to permissive regulations at colleges gives students a chance to express resentment."

How to Test the Model. "Distribute a questionnaire among college students and ask them if they resent being told what to do. You could also ask parents if they use threats to control behavior."

STOP AND THINK. Can you see what is wrong with this answer? It could be either the model, the testing procedure, or both that are at fault.

Although the model in Answer 1 is potentially testable, the testing procedure is weak. The proposed test is an attempt to examine the model's assumptions by interviewing the people involved. To test a model you generally want to test the truth of its derivations, rather than the truth of its assumptions. Assumptions are a part of your model, and you would probably prefer them to be true rather than false. Our reasons for suggesting that you test derivations rather than assumptions are mostly tactical. First, many good models are based on seemingly unreasonable assumptions, and we do not want you to reject potentially fruitful ideas too rapidly. Second, testing assumptions is likely to be uncommonly difficult because they are often assertions about things that cannot be observed directly. Third, leaping to test assumptions is likely to keep you from trying to figure out what derivations the model has. Learn to exercise the model before you start testing it. The trick is to test the whole model, including all its derivations.

In addition, Answer 1 has lazy testing procedures. The mistake is asking the people involved why something has happened. There is nothing wrong with this as a way of getting some ideas. But even if all students claim that parents use threats to control behavior, this does not make the statement true. You must still find out whether what the students believe (or answer) is the correct theory. Interviewing is an important technique in research, but the circumstances under which respondents are good theorists are limited.

When we look for interesting derivations to test, we note that the key variables involved in the process are the degree of threat and people's sensitivity to the threat. So you look for natural instances in which these two key variables vary.

Some colleges have stricter regulations and harsher penalties for student infractions than other colleges. The model says that there will be fewer riots on the stricter campuses. On any given campus some students are more sensitive to administrative threats than other students are. Students nearing graduation have more to lose through suspension than freshmen do. Students without definite career plans and those who have only marginal needs for a degree also have less to lose through suspension. Hence we can make some predictions about the relative likelihood that different students will take part in riots.

Answer 2

Model. "People become unreasonable when they are frustrated. Attempts by college students to make changes at the college are usually ignored or postponed by college administrators."

How to Test the Model. "Examine the record of student riots on many campuses to see if the model is true."

STOP AND THINK. Can you see what is wrong with this answer? It could be either the model, the testing procedure, or both that are at fault.

The model given in Answer 2 is good, but again the testing procedure is not. What would you look for and how would you interpret it? There is too little information given to judge the adequacy of the test. A reasonable test of the model might be as follows: The model predicts that there should be much less student unrest on those campuses where student attempts at change were successful. Examine the recent history of many colleges and divide them into two groups—those in which student attempts at change were successful and those in which they were not. If the model is valid, the successful group should have a lower incidence of student unrest.

Answer 3

Model. "The taxpayers make great sacrifices to provide free education for students. Students, therefore, owe it to the taxpayers not to abuse this freedom."

How to Test the Model. "Find out what percentage of the state and federal budgets goes to support higher education. Determine if there are other things that taxpayers would rather spend the money on."

STOP AND THINK. **Can you see what is wrong with this answer? It could be either the model, the testing procedure, or both that are at fault.**

Answer 3 is weak on several counts. First, it is obvious that the test proposed is a test of the model's assumptions rather than of its predictions. A more fundamental difficulty is that the model has no process; it has nothing to do with predicting student behavior. It is not a statement about how people actually behave, but rather a statement about how people ought to behave. It is not an explanation of the causes of student protest but simply a condemnation of them.

With these comments in mind the student reformulated Answer 3 as follows:

Model. "The taxpayers make great sacrifices to provide free education for students. People only value what they pay for.

Since students do not pay for their education, they are willing to disrupt it by protesting."

The student also derived some predictions to test the model:

"1. Taxpayers will place a higher value on education than the people who are getting it and will be more upset than students when it is disrupted.
2. Those students who are working to pay for their education will be much less inclined to participate in disturbances.
3. Raising tuition so that more students will be forced to work will decrease the number of protest incidents."

This is a very good answer (though this is not to say that it is necessarily correct). The model is well formulated, and the predictions are interesting. Testing the first and second predictions is comparatively easy. The third prediction will require some ingenuity to test, since we may have to wait for "nature" to perform the experiment.

There is elaborate debate in the social sciences on the question of what it means to say we "understand" or "explain" human behavior. We do not intend to entangle you in the debate. You should know, however, that one school of thought equates the ability to predict with the ability to understand; according to another school of thought, prediction per se is less critical. We propose a somewhat less doctrinaire rule: A model that has empirically correct derivations is better than a model that does not unless you have other strong reasons for thinking it is unsatisfying. When you think you understand some type of human behavior but your predictions keep turning out wrong, and you keep having to add more special exceptions to your model, you should check to see how much of your "understanding" was only self-delusion.

3.2.1   CIRCULAR MODELS

Think about the following model: When the Rain Dance ceremony is properly performed, *and all the participants have pure hearts*, it will bring rain.

STOP AND THINK.   Is this a testable model? Why?

As ordinarily used, the model is not testable. It cannot be disproved. If the ceremony occurs and it does rain, then the model is verified; but if the ceremony occurs and there is no rain, then the model is also verified because we take the lack of rain as evidence that some of the participants must have had evil hearts. No matter what happens, the model can account for it; it is always "correct" because it is circular. For our purposes it is a bad model because it does not satify the fundamental requirement of testability.

Circular models can take other forms as well. Consider, for example, statements of the following general form: "People pursue their own self-interests." We used such a statement in one of the models in Chapter Two. There is a rather elaborate literature and an even more extended history of cocktail-party conversations on the question of whether this statement is true or false.

STOP AND THINK. What do you believe? How did you decide? What are the issues?

If you answered that the statement is true, you may well have meant either of two things:

1. Whatever people do must be in their self-interest or they would not do it.
2. Models that include a self-interest assumption turn out to make correct predictions.

Either of these meanings is perfectly sensible, but they are fundamentally different. The first is a definition of an observational procedure. It says that we can discover something about a person's values by observing his behavior—if he does X instead of Y, it is probably because he values X more. However, we can easily get into trouble if we take this first meaning to be an assertion about human behavior as well, for we will be liable to the circularity of inferring someone's values from their behavior, and then predicting the same behavior from the values we have just defined.

The second meaning says that self-interest assumptions are often useful in our models; they help produce correct predictions. However, we must be careful that the observational procedures used to test a model's predictions are carefully specified in advance, for again it is easy to fall into the circularity of allowing a loose definition to confirm any possible empirical result.

The possible circularities in either meaning of self-interest are, of course, no more defensible than the beliefs about rain and evil hearts.

3.2.2   *CRITICAL EXPERIMENTS*

So far we have considered the case of testing a single model. Although such situations arise, we generally prefer to *compare alternative models* rather than accept or reject a single model. Suppose we consider the models produced to explain the dumb question in Section 2.3. What do we need to do to examine the comparative correctness of these models? Recall that we had three alternative models, each of which was consistent with the observation that a football player asked a dumb question.

> **Model 1.**   Being a good athlete requires large amounts of practice time; being smart in class requires large amounts of study time. The amount of free time is so limited that we cannot both study and practice well.

> **Model 2.**   Everyone wants to feel successful. Achieving success in any one area, for example, athletics, is enough to make most people content.

> **Model 3.**   We tend to be jealous of success in others. When we are jealous of someone, we attempt unconsciously to lower his apparent success in class by interpreting his questions as "dumb."

To choose among different models, each of which explains the same event, you must find some new question to which they give *different* answers. Such a question defines a "critical experiment," that is, an observation that will allow us to choose among alternative reasonable models. For example, when the football season is over the first model predicts that football players will have extra time to study and their questions will improve. The second and third models predict that the behavior will be unchanged, since recognition presumably extends beyond the football season.

STOP AND THINK.   Suppose we obtain some new data: Football season has ended, and the classroom questions of football players have improved substantially. Given this new information, which of the three models is correct? Why? Why are these new data critical?

Up until now the three models looked equally good—each provided a clear explanation of the original observation (the dumb question). The new data are critical because the three models do not provide equally good explanations of it. In fact, only Model 1 explains (is consistent with) the new data. Models 2 and 3 are contradicted by it.

Another possible critical experiment occurs in schools that de-emphasize athletics. Suppose that athletic success is a matter of indifference to a student body, but scholarly success is valued very highly. Model 1 predicts that athletes will still ask dumb questions during football season because of the time constraints on them; Model 2 predicts that athletes will work hard to get their recognition in the academic area and will tend to ask better questions than Model 1 predicted; Model 3 predicts that the questions asked by athletes would appear better than in Model 1.

We have now found two situations in which Model 1 makes different predictions from Models 2 and 3. Can we find any situation that differentiates between Models 2 and 3?

Yes, we can. One possibility is the following: Suppose we distinguish between football players who are easily recognized as football players (for instance, by the sweaters they wear, by their size, by their language, and so forth) and other kinds of athletes (for instance, fencers, soccer players, and so forth) who are not easily recognized as athletes. Then Models 1 and 2 predict that both groups will ask dumb questions; Model 3, however, predicts that they will not.

So we can construct Table 3.1. Now you can collect the appropriate data and decide which model is best (although you may find that none of them is very good).

In order to have a critical experiment, you need at least two different models. It is obviously more work to figure out two possible explanations than to figure out one, but there are substantial benefits associated with this extra bit of work. If you have two possible explanations, you will be forced to decide which is better. You will have to look for some situation in which they predict different outcomes so that one model may be supported and the other contradicted. The process of figuring out what might be such

TABLE 3.1   Truth Table for the Dumb Question Models

QUESTION	MODEL 1 Limited Time	MODEL 2 Need Success	MODEL 3 Jealousy
Will athletes ask dumb questions "out-of-season"?	no	yes	yes
Will athletes ask dumb questions in schools that de-emphasize athletics?	yes	no	no
Will athletes who do not look like athletes ask dumb questions?	yes	yes	no

a critical event will clarify your explanations. You will have to sharpen the models, define them more precisely, and clarify their underlying processes before you can discover critical events. Doing your speculative thinking in this way will generally help you develop more interesting predictions.

3.2.3   THE IMPORTANCE OF BEING WRONG

You may have noticed the difference between the fundamental logic of model building and the fundamental logic of debate. The difference lies in the indispensability of being wrong. That is, having tried as hard as we can to define a true model, we are then (contrary to any reasonably normal human behavior) expected to delight in finding out what is wrong with it. The problem is to avoid "falling in love" with our own models, or prejudices. We must evaluate them rather than simply defend them. Most of us have difficulty doing this.

In our experience there are three major ways in which we can protect ourselves from the insidious tendency to defend, rather than destroy, models. The first of these is to think as much as possible in terms of *alternative models*. We have already suggested that such thinking sharpens the models and defines the kinds of critical observations to which we should devote our observational effort. At the same time, it is a powerful emotional aid. By testing alternative models in a critical experiment, we are, at least in principle, guaranteed to have one model succeed as the other fails.

A second way to make the pursuit of truth more possible is to make it less important. One of the reasons for considering alternative criteria for evaluating models in social science is to relieve the pains of failure with respect to discerning truth. Even if beauty and justice were not important in their own rights, belief in them would still provide a basis for admitting failures with respect to the truth criterion.

A final protection from the danger of believing too fervently in a theory is to be intellectually *playful*. Model building is a serious pastime with serious consequences. For this reason it should not be done "seriously." The importance of the work and our own pride in it guarantee that we will not ignore information about correctness. Playfulness about ideas in general blurs our commitment to any specific ones and increases our willingness to recognize when they are wrong.

3.3 BEAUTY

Truth is an important quality that is emphasized in most treatises on the evaluation of models. Many people consider it the most important quality, at least when writing about the activity of model building rather than doing it. It is the least ambiguous quality. But truth is not the sole criterion for evaluating our efforts.

Models are art. Their contemplation should produce aesthetic pleasure. Many wise words have been written on the general problems of aesthetics, and several gifted theorists have described the importance of beauty in their own work. Such commentary should be savored directly rather than summarized. We will simply call your attention to three important aspects that seem significant to us in our own understanding of the pleasures of beauty.

3.3.1 SIMPLICITY

A beautiful model is simple. A theory that has a small number of assumptions is more attractive than one having a large number of assumptions. For example, suppose we have the map of a village shown in Figure 3.1. All of the people in the village live along the shore of the lake, and a visiting anthropologist has noticed that they can be divided into four groups:

Group A
Lives on the north end of the lake. A-type people generally travel clockwise to the store and counterclockwise to the church.

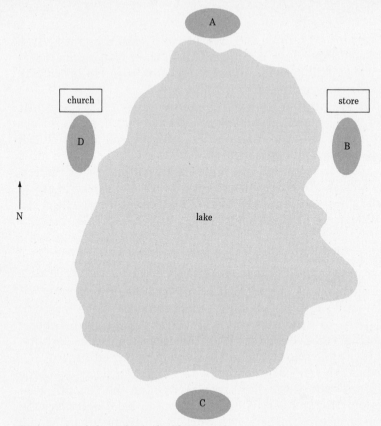

Figure 3.1: A hypothetical village.

Group B
Lives on the east shore of the lake. B-type people generally travel in a counterclockwise direction regardless of where they are going.

Group C
Lives on the south shore of the lake. C-type people generally travel clockwise to the church and counterclockwise to the store.

Group D
Lives on the west shore of the lake. D-type people generally travel in a clockwise direction regardless of where they are going.

We might propose the following model as an explanation of the observed behavior:

Individuals have innate preferences for walking in a clockwise or counterclockwise direction. Among a group of neighbors these preferences will be shared. Group A prefers to go clockwise to shop and counterclockwise to pray. Group C prefers the opposite. Group B prefers always to go counterclockwise. Group D prefers the opposite.

Such a model does, in fact, produce the observed facts as an implication. Compare it, however, with the following model:

Humans try to accomplish their goals with the least possible effort.

Quite aside from its other attractive properties, the "least effort" model has the beauty of simplicity.

Or consider the following observation: Most parliamentary democracies outside the Anglo-Saxon world utilize some form of proportional representation. That is, the election system is designed to produce an assignment of parliamentary seats to the various parties such that each party has about the same proportion of votes in parliament as it received in the last election. Most Anglo-Saxon electoral systems are not systems of proportional representation. How might we explain this difference?

There are many possible explanations involving a variety of variables, including national character, socioeconomic conditions, historical development, class structure, and political maturity. One simple model, however, is as follows:

Assume that a democratic political system acts to satisfy the following constraints on the rules that assign seats to parties on the basis of votes received:
1. The labels attached to the parties should be irrelevant. No party should be discriminated against.
2. Party legislative strength should depend only on its voting strength. It should depend neither on considerations other than the vote nor on the way the rest of the vote is distributed among other parties.

It can be shown that these assumptions imply proportional representation for any country having more than two parties. For a country having only two parties (a frequent condition in Anglo-Saxon countries) the model predicts a large number of possible systems (including the one observed in the United States and the United Kingdom). Thus we can predict the relative frequency of proportional representation in two-party and multiparty countries from nothing more than the assumption that the system is constrained by our two requirements.[1]

On the whole, the social sciences have had difficulty in keeping models simple. Partly, this is because the world is complex but it is also because we are too close to its complexity; we are frequently overly concerned about the adverse consequences of abstraction and not sufficiently attentive to the elegance of simplicity. We can list a small set of precepts for increasing the simplicity of speculations:

1. Do not try to say everything you know every time you speak. Some things will be omitted. This is in fact your goal.
2. Do not worry about counterexamples to your assumptions. The object is to interpret behavior, not to describe it.
3. Remember your listeners have less time to devote to this problem than you do, and they may not be too much smarter than you.

3.3.2 FERTILITY

A beautiful model is fertile. It produces a relatively large number of interesting predictions per assumption. For example, think about the following model:

When Mr. Jones is angry, he kicks his cat.

The model is not very attractive because it is too limited. It applies only to one person (Mr. Jones); even so, it only describes his reaction to one kind of emotion (anger) and to one kind of being (his cat). A more fertile model would be:

People kick pets when they feel bad.

This model applies to more people, more kinds of emotions, and more kinds of animals. It is still limited to animals though. A still more fertile model would be:

Unhappy people vent their feelings on objects that cannot retaliate.

This is obviously a more fertile model than we started with. It produces a wide variety of specific predictions—for example, the conditions for wife beating.

To be fertile a model must be general. As we suggested in Chapter Two and further illustrated here, the problems of generality are susceptible to some elementary devices that should not be secrets. They involve nothing more profound than using your knowledge of language to make both nouns and verbs somewhat more general. For example, assumptions in a model are often stated as sentences in the form: *A person of type P will do behavior B in situation S*. Thus: Little men often start an argument in the presence of a big man. We wish to make this assumption more fertile by making P, B, and S more general. We look for nouns and verbs that include our original nouns and verbs as "special cases."

Consider the following development of our original statement:

Little men often start an argument in the presence of big men.

Little *people* often start an argument in the presence of big *people*.

Little people often are *verbally aggressive* in the presence of big people.

People who are *physically disadvantaged* often are verbally aggressive in the presence of *physically advantaged* people.

Among people, *inequalities* in one domain lead to aggression in another.

The device of substituting more general words has helped us to build a more general model.

This specific chain is not the only possible way in which the original observation could have been made more fertile. But from an original, very narrow assertion, we now have another rather general addition to our "theory" of aggression. It predicts, for example, that a person will be more sharp-tongued about intellectual matters in the presence of others who are sexier than he (or she) than in the presence of others who are about equal in sexiness; and that a person will be more aggressive sexually in the presence of others who are intellectually more adept than he (or she) in the presence of intellectual equals.

We find fertility also by looking for a more general model, a process that implies our first set of ideas. For example, suppose we have confidence in the truth of the following model:

> Commuters choosing between alternative ways of getting to work will give strong preference to the fastest mode of transportation.

This model has some important implications (deductions) about the possibility of ever getting commuters to give up their cars and use public transit. But it is a very restricted model. It only applies to certain kinds of decisions (What kind of transportation should I use?) by certain kinds of people (commuters). So we work backward and see whether we can find a more general model that implies this model as one of its deductions as, for example:

> People try to minimize the amount of time spent on unpleasant or unproductive activities.

This second model clearly has the first model as one of its deductions (if we assume that commuting is regarded as an unpleasant or unproductive activity). But is it otherwise fertile? To check its fertility we ask if it can make interesting predictions about the world. It can. If the second model were true, it would imply:

1. In urban areas where walking is regarded as a means of getting between two points and hence as unproductive time, people will make straight-line paths; in parks, on the other hand, where walking is an end in itself, the paths people make will tend to meander.
2. If low speed limits are posted in a scenic area, they will tend to be ignored by local residents, who have learned to take the scenery for granted and to view travel as just a means of getting around; tourists, on the other hand, who find the view pleasant and productive, will obey the speed limits.
3. Time-related occupational specialties should arise in societies whose people are described by this model. These will include inventors who try to discover faster ways of doing things; efficiency experts who try to find faster ways of producing the

inventor's products; and finally advertising men who write jingles about the "new, *time-saving* miracle ingredient, Super XZ Plus."

3.3.3   SURPRISE

A beautiful model is unpredictable. It produces some interesting implications that are surprising to us and that are not immediately obvious from the assumptions. Suppose, for example, that any system of international relations must satisfy these four axioms of alliance:

1.   Friends of my friends are my friends.
2.   Friends of my enemies are my enemies.
3.   Enemies of my friends are my enemies.
4.   Enemies of my enemies are my friends.

Assuming that such a tendency toward consistency holds and that each country has feelings about every other country, what are the possible patterns of alliances within an international system consisting of 50 countries?

> **STOP AND THINK ABOUT IT.**   **Can you predict the pattern of alliances from this set of assumptions?**

In fact, it can be shown that according to this model there are 562,949,953,421,312 possible patterns of alliances. But each of them is characterized by one simple property—it is *bipolar*. The model predicts that the world will always be divided into no more than two groups of countries. Each of the countries within a group will be a friend of every other country within that group and an enemy of every country in the other group. (The model may become slightly more hopeful if you note that included among the 562,949,953,421,312 possibilities is one in which all countries belong to the same group and are friends—that is, one of the two bipolar groups has no members.) Thus polarization in a system of international alliances can be derived from what appear to be rather innocuous assumptions. The model has the beauty of surprise.

Or consider the following model:

Suppose we have a society with two clans (A and B). A is much larger than B. Intermarriage between the two clans is discouraged but occurs at a rate that is proportional to the frequency of contact. Contact between the two clans is limited but occurs at a rate that is proportional to the product of their relative sizes (that is, [size of A] × [size of B]). Children whose parents are both from the same clan also belong to that clan. Children whose parents are from different clans are raised as members of Clan B. Birth rates are the same in each clan.

What can we expect to see happen over time?

STOP AND THINK. Can you say anything about the implications of such a model? What about future marriage patterns or the relative growth of the two clans?

You might have noted the following interesting, possibly nonobvious, implications of the model:

1. Clan B will grow larger over time. In fact, Clan A simply will grow smaller and smaller until it vanishes.
2. The proportion of marriages within each generation that are *interclan* (that is, that involve spouses who are from different clans) will increase up to some point and then decrease. That point will be reached when the two clans are equal in size.
3. The proportion of Clan B members who are involved in interclan marriages will be relatively high early in the time period studied but will decline steadily thereafter. The proportion of Clan A members who will be involved in interclan marriages will be relatively low early but will rise steadily later. At the same time, the proportion of members of Clan B who will have one parent from the other clan will be relatively high early in the time period but will decline steadily later.
4. All of these phenomena are true regardless of the degree of limitation on contact between the clans or on intermarriage (so long as some occurs). However, the *rate* at which changes take place depends on the contact and intermarriage rates.

STOP AND THINK. Go back over the model and the derivations. See if you can reconstruct how they were

derived. Can you discover any others? Can you think of any possible applications of such a model? Is there any similar situation in our society?

The description of a society with Clan A and Clan B is an abstract description, but it is not completely unrelated to some real world situations that might have occurred to you. For example, suppose that there were two religious groups in a society (for instance, Catholic and Protestant), that intermarriage between them was discouraged but did occur, that the children stemming from a marriage between members of the different religions were raised mostly as members of one of the groups (for instance, Catholics), and that that same group was initially much smaller than the other.

For an even more profound example, suppose that there were two racial groups in a society (say, black and white), that intermarriage between them was discouraged but did occur, and that the children of racially mixed marriages were defined to be members of one of the groups (say, black).

Each of these cases seems close enough to our abstract model to suggest that the surprises of the model may even be related to potential surprises in the world of our own experience.

Finally, consider the following examination of the consequences of parental preferences for male babies:

Suppose
    that each couple agreed
        (knowing the relative value of things)
    to produce children
        (in the usual way)
    until each couple had
    more boys
        (the ones with penises)
    than girls
        (the ones without).

And further suppose
    that the probability
    of each coupling
        (technical term)
    resulting in a boy
        (the ones with)
    varies from couple to couple

but not from coupling to coupling
for any one couple.

And
      (we still have a couple more)
that no one divorces
      (an Irish folk tale)
or sleeps around
      (a Scottish folk tale)
without precautions
      (a Swedish folk tale).

And
      that the expected sex
      (technical term)
of a birth
if all couples are producing equally
is half male, half female
      (though mostly they are one or the other).

Question:
      (Are you ready?)
What will be the ratio
of boys
      (with)
to girls
      (without)
in such a society?

Answer:
      The sweet truth is
      (given the supposings)
that we end up with
more girls
      (without)
than boys
      (with).

      (That's beauty, baby.)

STOP AND THINK. The conclusion is that there will be more girl children than boy children despite the explicit contrary desire. In fact, there will be more girls than boys *because* of the contrary desire. Try to figure out why this is true if you can. It is not tricky, but it is difficult.

Think about possible birth sequences that might occur in the absence of any desire to regulate the sex ratio. For example:

1. M, M, M, M, M, M, M, M, . . .
2. F, F, F, F, F, F, F, F, . . .
3. M, F, M, F, M, F, M, F, . . .
4. F, M, F, M, F, M, F, M, . . .
5. F, F, F, M, M, M, M, M, . . .
6. M, M, M, F, F, F, F, F, . . .
7. and so on.

In the absence of any general decision rule, all possible sequences can occur up to some point at which individual couples stop having children. But once you adopt the rule "stop having children once boys outnumber girls," you produce a surprising result. Sequences in which males might dominate are cut off early (many of them after only one child). Since the model assumes variation in the propensity of couples to produce boys or girls, those couples who are more likely to produce boys tend to have smaller families than other couples. Thus the result is that society ends up with more girls than boys, while most couples end up with more boys than girls! General theorem: Simple rules sometimes have surprising consequences, and justice is sometimes served by mistake.

One thing that may have occurred to you is that the unpredictability of many models comes primarily from the fact that they are stated in a way that allows for some relatively powerful tools of analysis. Perhaps, surprisingly (!), precision and surprise go hand in hand. So long as we are restricted to the analytical language of everyday discourse, the beauty of surprise is largely denied us. We are limited to the less pleasing device of saying outrageous things that may surprise others. By using some analytical power, however, we can shift to the beauty of discovering an unanticipated implication of an ordinary set of assumptions.

We can illustrate the reality of the advantages of even very elementary technical precision by a simple example pointed out originally by Bertraud de Jouvenal. It involves one of the most brilliant of modern philosophers, Jean Jacques Rousseau. His writings heavily influenced both modern political thought and modern political institutions. One of his concerns was population problems.

He formulated a simple model of population growth for eighteenth-century England. His model contained three assumptions:

1. The birth rate in London is lower than the birth rate in rural England.
2. The death rate in London is higher than the death rate in rural England.
3. As England industrializes, more and more people leave the countryside and move to London.

> ***STOP AND THINK.*** **Assume that all three of these assumptions are true and will continue to be true over a long period. What will happen to the *total* population of *England* over time? Will it increase? Decrease? Wobble?**

Rousseau reasoned that since London's birth rate was lower and its death rate higher and since rural people continued to move there, that the population of England would eventually decline to zero.

> ***STOP AND THINK.*** **Is Rousseau's conclusion correct? Does it follow his three assumptions?**

Rousseau was a brilliant philosopher, but he was unaccustomed to thinking in numerical terms. This particular problem needs numerical thinking. As de Jouvenal has observed, Rousseau's derivation is false. To explain why it is false we need to define some quantitative concepts. "Birth rate per thousand" can be defined as the number of children that would be born to 1000 typical people during one year. Thus if the birth rate is 35, we know that a city with 1000 people in it would have 35 new children during the year, and a city of 100,000 would have 3500 new children. "Death rate per thousand" can be defined as the number of deaths that will occur among 1000 typical people during one year.

If the birth rate is 35 and the death rate is 20, then the population is increasing at the rate of 15 people per 1000 (1000 at the beginning of the year + 35 new children − 20 deaths = 1015 people at the end of the first year; 1030 by the end of the second;

1046 by the end of the third; and 2000 after about 45 years). So long as the birth rate is greater than the death rate, population will increase. If the differences between the two rates is large, then population will grow rapidly; if the difference is small, then population grows slowly.

Now consider Rousseau's model. Suppose that the birth rate in rural England were 35 and the birth rate in London were only 30. Thus we satisfy Rousseau's first assumption. Suppose the death rate in rural England were 20 and the death rate in London were 25. This satisfies his second assumption. Suppose that his third assumption were also true. Now what happens? The rate of population growth in rural England would be 15 per thousand ($35 - 20 = 15$), and in London it would be 5 ($30 - 25$). Thus Rousseau's prediction is incorrect; the English population would continue to grow. It is true that the population of London would not increase as fast as the rural population, but it would increase—it must do so provided the birth rate exceeded the death rate.

The result is not surprising perhaps, but it would have surprised Rousseau (and, in our experience, most people). What appeared to be obvious turned out to be not only not obvious but also not true. By using some analytical power we discovered an unanticipated implication of an ordinary set of assumptions.

Thus we add one final precept on the production of beauty: Play to your analytical strength. Do not be afraid of twisting a phenomenon around a bit to make it fit into an analytical scheme that can derive some implications for you. Do not hesitate to look for phenomena that can be examined usefully with the models and techniques you have. The warnings you have had against letting technique dominate substance are all right in their place. Here, however, they usually seriously underestimate the importance of beauty in social science.

3.4 **JUSTICE**

Not only should we like to be correct and beautiful, but we should also like to be just. We should like to be able to say that our models contribute to making better, not worse, worlds. The idea is a quaint and complicated one. As in the case of truth and beauty, a major consideration of the concept of justice is beyond the scope of both this book and these authors. All we will attempt to do is to remind you of the importance of justice in the construction of social science theory and to outline some possible elementary approximations to its pursuit.

Like truth and beauty, justice is an ideal rather than a state of existence. We do not achieve it—we pursue it. In this pursuit we accept some responsibility for the social myths by which we live. Our models are not neutral. They establish our perception of the world, and they condition our attempts to act. We use them to describe others as well as ourselves. Though we need to be suitably humble about the prospects for justice and our contributions to it, we do not need to be shy about trying to pursue it.

Suppose, for example, that a nation contains people from two different cultures and that one of the culture groups makes up a clear majority of the population. Members of the minority culture do not do as well in school as members of the majority culture. Their grade averages are lower, and they are less likely to go on to college and graduate school. Suppose some social scientists observe the situation and come up with two possible explanatory models.

Model 1. The two cultures are quite different from each other. They have different habits of speech, different home circumstances, and different values. Schools are controlled by the majority culture and correct education is defined to be consistent with the values and habits of the majority culture. Thus the poor school performance of the minority students is due to judging members of one culture by the standards of another.

Model 2. Members of the minority culture are inferior to members of the majority culture. They do badly in school because their average intelligence is inherently lower.

When the two models are evaluated on the truth criterion, the results are sometimes ambiguous. IQ tests given to members of each culture may indeed show that members of the minority have lower average scores, but the tests were designed by the majority culture and embody its values and language habits. It is in fact quite difficult to judge the comparative truth values of the two models.

The justice implications of the two models are radically different, however. Government policy based on Model 1 would concentrate on new techniques of schooling, better early education, and multicultural education. Government policy based on Model 2 might simply be that since the minority is inferior, there is nothing to be done other than creating enough simple, menial jobs to keep the minority employed.

Independent of the truth value of the two models, they have quite different justice values. They produce different actions, and the social consequences of those actions do not depend entirely on the degree to which the models are correct. Nor is this problem solved in any significant way by combining our alternative models to produce a more correct one. Correctness is not the problem here. In a world in which we never have complete knowledge two equally correct models may have radically different action implications. In the present case Model 1 is better than Model 2; it leads to better behavior.

The problems of justice in models of social science are no where more conspicuous than they are in our models of individual human behavior. These models are the myths we use in dealing with other people and with ourselves as well. If the models impute unattractive features to people, we are likely to do the same in our ordinary life.

Consider, for example, the following model of interpersonal behavior:

> Power is the ability to induce other people to do something you want in a situation in which they would not ordinarily do what you want; and the ability to do what you yourself want in a situation in which other people want you to do something else. Human beings aspire for power and direct their behavior primarily toward gaining a favorable power balance with respect to other people. Power is secured by offering resources, or promises of resources (for instance, support, money, respect) in exchange for acquiescence.

Such a model has some interesting features. It is simple; it predicts some important aspects of behavior. But it makes a series of predictions about human behavior that are unattractive as a basis for dealing with other people. For example, it predicts that:

> Most favorable statements made in an interpersonal situation are probably lies. This is particularly true of statements reporting supportive behavioral intentions or positive feelings with respect to other people. The probable truthfulness of an insult is much higher than the probable truthfulness of praise.

Insofar as we come to believe such a series of assertions, we almost certainly make our daily life less pleasant and ourselves less attractive as human beings.

Consider similarly the following assertion common to a rather large number of models of individual behavior:

> Adult human behavior is understandable in its basic forms as stemming primarily from experiences of early childhood.

Such an assertion seems eminently plausible. It may even be true. Yet, if believed, it has at least two curious side effects. First, it leads parents and children to believe that parents should accept primary credit (and blame) for a child's beliefs, character, and general intellectual and moral performance. School report cards become more important to parental self-respect than to the child's; parents are valued in terms of their children's behavior. As a consequence, parent-child relations combine the worse features of juvenile blackmail (children threatening to behave in such a way that parents will lose respect) and parental repression (parents determined to manage their children).

Second, belief in the model seems likely to create a retrospective and static bias in personal self-analysis and development. Individuals who believe the "formative years" hypothesis seem quite likely to consider the problem of personal identity to be a problem of discovering a preexisting real self rather than one of creating an interesting self. The idea of discovery is biased against adult change. A person who believes his basic character has been formed at an early age can have little serious expectation of being able to modify his style of life as an adult. He is protected by his model of personality development from the dangers and pleasures of continuous personal change.

Consider finally the following assertions, which form a part of a relatively large number of familiar models of individual behavior:

> Things are not what they seem. Human beings are guided by a number of unconscious motives that affect their behavior in subtle ways.

Such assertions seem reasonable. They may be true often enough to warrant consideration as useful models of human behavior. What makes them unattractive from the point of view of justice is the basic ambiguity a belief in them introduces with respect to human action. We are led to ask: What does he *really* mean? Indeed, we are led to ask: What do *I* really mean? By introducing substantial elements of affective ambiguity into interpersonal communications, we undermine trust as a basis for dealing with people. We each become a little more paranoid.

> What do I mean
> When I say
> I love you?
>
> Is it a convention,
> Like "Good morning"?
> Or "How are you?"
>
> Or a wage
> That you earn
> With praises, or money, or smiles?
>
> Or a cover
> For my distaste
> Meant to conceal it,
> Barely?
>
> What do I say
> When I mean
> I love you?[2]

It is not easy to define a simple set of rules by which we make life better through speculation. Certainly the injunction to seek justice demands more than that we merely dress our prejudices up and call them theories. It requires some subtle choices between interpreting behavior offensively in order to change it and interpreting behavior positively in order to provide a new perspective for ourselves. It requires a sweet appreciation of the limitations of human wisdom. We are probably incapable of meeting the demands of justice; but better worlds are made by elementary attempts.

In particular, we may want to ask ourselves about any proposed model:

> If we come to accept this model as a good interpretation of behavior by individuals, groups, or institutions, will our own behavior become more human and our commitment to each other more profound?

3.5   THE SEARCH

That, in brief is something of the nature of the search for truth, beauty, and justice. It involves a continuous interplay among the real world, the world of aesthetics, the world of ethics, and the model world. To make a speculation about human behavior you begin by working backward. You explain an observed fact by imagining what kind of process would, if it were true, produce such a fact. Then you assume your imagined process is correct and infer some additional facts that should be observable. Then you check those predictions in the real world. At the same time, you assess the justice and the beauty of your speculations. At this point you usually have to start over again.

Such a description, of course, makes the procedure sound much more orderly than it is. The previous paragraph is, in fact, a model of model building rather than a description of it. It avoids mentioning the many complications in imagining processes and in comparing truth, beauty, and justice. As you come to appreciate the model, you will also come to appreciate both the complications and the interesting idiosyncracies that distinguish individual artists and specific performance within the general frame and to develop your own style in such a way that both the composition (model) and the individual performer (you) are recognizable.

References

Graham Collier, *Art and the Creative Consciousness* (Englewood Cliffs, N.J.: Prentice-Hall, 1972).

John Rawls, *A Theory of Justice* (Cambridge, Mass.: Harvard University Press, 1971).

Eugene J. Webb, Donald T. Campbell, Richard D. Schwartz, and Lee Sechrest, *Unobtrusive Measures* (Skokie, Ill.: Rand McNally, 1966).

Notes

[1] It should be noted that most students of election systems would probably argue that the electoral system affects the number of parties at least as much as the number of parties affects the electoral system.

[2] It may have occurred to you that one of the persistent sources of problems with respect to justice arises from the variety of possible models. Thus amateur psychologists can select among the alternative models and choose the model that places them in a favorable light relative to the person behaving, as: "You are being defensive" or "You are only playing a game with me." This can be an easy way to make your friends uncomfortable, but we do not consider it an interesting or productive use for models in social science.

Problems

1. A simple childhood theory of personality says that a person's basic personality and character are formed between the time he is born and age five and that this basic personality and character remain substantially unchangeable for the remainder of his life. A simple conditioning and growth theory of personality says that a person's basic personality and character are formed continuously by his daily experience. Hence, he may change over time in response to changing environment, and it is possible to change adult personality and behavior radically.

  (a) Make up two facts (that is, derive two specific predictions) that, if they were true, would tend to confirm the childhood theory.

  (b) Make up two facts that, if they were true, would tend to confirm the conditioning and growth theory.

  (c) Make up a critical fact that, if it were true, would simultaneously contradict one theory and support the other. It should be an observable fact in a natural experiment.

  (d) Examine the relative *justice* of the two theories, assuming they are equally correct.

2. It has frequently been observed that students coming into a lecture hall will tend to fill up the rear of the hall first. Here are two possible explanatory processes that predict this kind of behavior.

  Process I
  People try to minimize effort; having entered at the rear of the hall, they sit there rather than walk to the front.

  Process II
  General student norms say that it is undesirable to be deeply involved in school work. Sitting in front would display interest in the class, whereas sitting in the rear displays detachment.

  (a) Make up two facts (that is, derive two specific predictions) that, if they were true, would tend to support the model in Process I. Then do the same thing for Process II.

(b) Make up a critical fact that, if it were true, would tend to support one theory while contradicting the other.

(c) Propose a third theory to explain student seating results and explain how you might test it against the other two theories.

(d) Comment on the relative beauty of the three theories.

(e) Comment on their relative justice.

3. In 1950 a study was made of 712 undergraduates at a large Eastern university. The study measured personal values and occupational preferences. Each student was classified as having either "people-oriented" values or "nonpeople-oriented" values. Similarly, each student was classified as choosing either a people-oriented occupation or a nonpeople-oriented occupation. The cross-classification of values and occupational preferences showed the following result:

		VALUES		
		People-oriented	Nonpeople-oriented	Total
Occupational choice	People-oriented	266	86	315
	Nonpeople-oriented	166	231	397
	Total	392	320	712

The same study was repeated in 1952 with the same students. In 1952 the cross-classification showed the following results:

		VALUES		
		People-oriented	Nonpeople-oriented	Total
Occupational choice	People-oriented	226	86	292
	Nonpeople-oriented	154	266	420
	Total	380	332	712

Summarize the basic results in the table. Outline a model that might be consistent with them. Are there any other data that might be useful to you to test your model? How would you evaluate the model?

4. In a study in 1948, voters were asked two questions about three months before the presidential election:

Question I

For whom do you intend to vote for President?

Question II

Which party do you think does best for people in your social class?

On the basis of answers to these questions, the respondents were divided into four groups:

Type A

People who believe the Republicans do best for their class and who intend to vote Republican (286 people).

Type B

People who believe the Republicans do best for their class and who intend to vote Democratic (10 people).

Type C

People who believe the Democrats do best for their class and who intend to vote Democratic (161 people).

Type D

People who believe the Democrats do best for their class and who intend to vote Republican (73 people).

In a follow-up poll in November the same people were asked how they voted, with the following results:

	%VOTING DEM.	%VOTING REP.	%NOT VOTING
Type A people	6	81	13
Type B people	50[a]	30[a]	20[a]
Type C people	76	3	21
Type D people	21	48	31

[a] Note the small number of cases involved.

   (a) Summarize the basic results in the table.
   (b) Produce two different models that would explain the results.
   (c) Suggest how you would decide which model is better.
5. Recent efforts to reduce the birth rate in India have included the introduction of intrauterine devices (I.U.D.s) for preventing conception. In one test 10 villages of approximately comparable social characteristics were used. In each village 8 women chosen at random (there were about 50 married women of childbearing age in each village) were provided with I.U.D.s and instructions for their use. Over the following 6 months 2 counts were made: (1) How many of

the 8 women reported pain or other difficulty in using an I.U.D.? (2) How many of the other women in the village requested information on I.U.D.s or reported trying an I.U.D.?

The scatter diagram below shows the results. Each asterisk in the diagram is a different village.

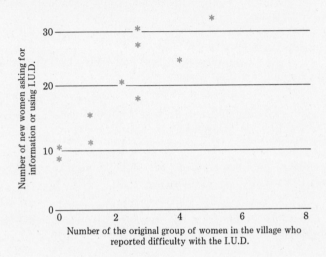

Number of the original group of women in the village who reported difficulty with the I.U.D.

You are to do three things:

(a) Summarize the basic results in the diagram.
(b) Outline *two* plausible models that would account for the results.
(c) Suggest how you would decide which model is better.

6. In these statistics from a recent sociological survey half the people had previously been diagnosed as mentally ill. The other half were not diagnosed as mentally ill. They came from three different income levels: extremely poor, very poor, and poor. The results of the survey appear in the following table. The numbers are the percentage of people who answered "yes" to the question "Do you think you will ever get a better job?"

	EXTREME POVERTY	*VERY POOR*	*POOR*
Mentally Ill	55	56	63
Other Group	35	44	49

(a) Summarize the basic results in the table.

(b) Outline two plausible models that would account for the results.

(c) Suggest how you would decide which model is better.

7. The football team has just lost a game. When the reporters interview the coach afterward, he explains. "I'm sorry. The problem was that our players didn't have enough fighting spirit, enough will to win." Is the coach's statement a good or bad model of his team's loss? Explain why.

8. Some psychiatrists have cited insufficient love as the principal cause of marital instability. Is this a good model? If so, how would you use it? If not, how would you make it useful?

(9–15) Problems 9 through 15 are basic observations that you might use as starting points for your model building. They are distinct and unrelated. For whichever observation you are assigned do the following:

(a) Make up two *abstract* models that would account for the observation.

(b) Generate a *total* of three interesting predictions from the two models and identify which model each prediction is derived from.

(c) Find some critical fact/situation/observation/prediction that will distinguish between the two models. It should be *observable*, and you should make it clear how you would observe it. It should involve a *natural experiment*. Please be very explicit as to why it *simultaneously confirms* one model while *contradicting* the other.

9. A few years ago, Detroit had a six-month newspaper strike that closed down all its newspapers. During the strike, Detroit's suicide rate fell very sharply (that is, there were far fewer suicides), but returned to its usual rate when the papers resumed publishing. (This is true, by the way.)

10. A group of women medical students reported that during the period of time when they had been trying to make up their minds about going to medical school, their parents had tried to argue them out of going to school. But once the girls had actually made up their minds to go to school, their parents became supportive of the decision.

11. No matter what kind of parents they have, children tend to think their own parents are among the worst. Very often, children and young adults can be heard to say to their friends: "You certainly are lucky to have such nice parents. Mine are terrible." Also, most children like their grandparents better than their parents. (*Hint:* Some possible natural experiments to consider are: communes, kibbutzim, children raised by their grandparents, adopted children, stepparents, orphanages, the difference between being raised as an only child and being one of many children.)

12. On a visit to the Smith family you notice that their three sons behave quite differently. John, the oldest, always does his chores

quickly and obeys his parents. George, the second oldest, obeys most of the time. Robert, the youngest, never obeys his parents.

13. Sociological evidence suggests that most people have more respect for doctors than for lawyers.

14. It has been observed that football players rather than scholars receive more attention and interest from other students.

15. The number of labor-saving home appliances has increased incredibly; the number of labor-saving, preprocessed foods has increased; and average family size has decreased. Yet the number of housework hours per week done by the average (nonworking) wife has not decreased very much over the past 50 years.

chapter four

choice

4.1   INTRODUCTION

In the remainder of the book we will illustrate a number of basic models that are commonly used by social scientists. Our purpose in doing so is twofold: First, since the models are rather basic, you will probably be able to include all, or parts, of them into your own models. Second, we wish to illustrate in greater detail the complexity and richness of social science.

Chapters One through Three are the fundamentals of the analytic method in science, humanities, and art criticism and should prove useful to you in any of those fields. Chapters Four through Seven are devoted more specifically to social science; they are designed to give you some flavor, a small taste of what has already been done in social science. They are in no sense a catalog of the knowledge contained in the various social science disciplines, though they are illustrative of that body of knowledge.

This chapter considers some of the common social science models of the way in which people make decisions. These could be relatively mundane decisions like "Should I go home via Main Street or should I try the shortcut?" Or they could be relatively consequential decisions like "Should I drop out of school for a year?" The model actually arose over 200 years ago as a solution to a gambling problem, but it turns out to provide insight into people's choices in a wide variety of situations. In particular, our examples will be taken from such dissimilar areas as voting, crime, emigration, and use of foreign products. Thus we are focusing on the decision-making process, wherever it may occur. For example, consider the following instances:

1. During national presidential elections, the number of people who decide to get to the polls and vote seems to depend on the closeness of the contest between the two candidates and the difference between their platforms and programs.
2. An examination of the backgrounds of bank robbers and other criminals shows a very small proportion of educated people, college graduates, or people who come from upper middle-class homes.
3. Emigration occurs most often among the poorer members of society and frequently results from a decrease in their fortunes, as during a famine.

4. In international Grand Prix racing there was originally
   a very strong tendency for drivers to be on the teams of
   their home country and use the racing products of their home
   country. Today one finds Swiss driving for the English and
   English driving for the Italians, and so on.

This collection of examples is not merely a random assort-
ment of situations. As social scientists interested in developing and
applying a model, we have assembled situations with a property in
common. Each situation involves an individual making a decision:
Should I take the trouble to vote? How about a career in crime?
Is it time to pack it up and try to find a better life in a new land?
Should I race for the home country or for the other guy?

A second property these situations share is that the person
making the decision cannot be certain about the outcome of the
decision. Thus the voter does not know whether his candidate will
win, and, perhaps more importantly, he does not know whether his
single vote will be crucial to the outcome. The criminal does not
know whether he will be caught; the emigrant does not know
whether he will improve his lot; and, finally, the racer may win or
lose, even using the foreign car, though he may think he has improved his chances of winning by forsaking his own country's team.

Notice the expression "improved his chances" in the preceding sentence. This is an important notion. If patriotism means a
lot to the driver (but the foreign-built car is better), then his
chances of winning will have to be improved a lot to entice him
into using the foreign car. On the other hand, if the glory of
winning and the prize money are very valuable to him, a relatively
small increase in his chances of winning will suffice to overcome his
patriotism. How much is "a lot"? To keep ourselves honest (that is,
consistent) we shall have to be more precise about these expressions. To do so we shall eventually turn to numerical values, but
for the moment we continue in ordinary language.

Just as the racer considers his chances of winning, so the
criminal considers his chances of getting away with his crime and
the probable size of the haul. He may also consider the "size" of
the possible punishment. These comments apply to a decision between two possible "jobs" as well as to the choice between crime
and no crime. The criminal, like the racer, is considering the *value*

to himself of the various results possible from different courses of action and the likelihood, or *probability*, of these results actually occurring.

SLOW DOWN. Try to answer these questions. Give some thought to the emigration example given previously. Who is the decision maker? What are his possible choices? What are the consequences—that is, the possible outcomes, or results—associated with each choice? How likely are the possible consequences associated with each choice? Which consequence (outcome) would the decision maker value most highly? Which consequence would he value next most highly, and so on? (That is, compare the value or desirability of the outcomes.) Look at any one consequence resulting from any one choice. Suppose the connection between the choice and the outcome were strengthened. How would this influence the decision maker?

It is actually useful, and even interesting, to answer the previous questions. The practice will certainly make it easier to answer the next question, which is the important one.

STOP READING. Do the following: Write down one or more general statements that you could call "principles of decision making" and that might apply to some or all of the preceding examples. Give it a try; actually write down some principles.

The decision-making model we will present involves concepts like "probability" and "expected value" and a certain amount of numerical calculation. Before making an explicit statement of the model, we can work through a simple, and specific, example of decision making to give you a better intuitive feel for what will follow.

Imagine that you are in a gambling casino playing the following game: (1) You choose a coin from your pocket, flip it and allow it to fall on the floor. (2) If it comes up heads, we will pay you $4; if it comes up tails, we will pay you $1. (3) You get to keep your coin. (4) The catch is that you must pay us $2 for the privilege of playing the game. You may play it as many times as you wish, but it costs you $2 each time. The question is, should you pay your $2 and play the game?

STOP READING. Think about it for a moment. Would *you* play? Why or why not?

You can analyze the situation and see what you should have done (assuming you are willing to gamble at all). Obviously, if the coin comes up heads, you win money; if it comes up tails, however, you lose money; and there is no way of predicting exactly how the coin will land on any one play of the game. But you can compute what you *expect* it to do over a large number of plays. Suppose you play the game 100 times: You would expect heads to come up about 50 times, thus producing an income of $200 (that is, $4 × 50); and you would expect tails to come up about 50 times, thus producing an income of $50 (that is, $1 × 50). So your total expected winnings would be $250. We said it costs you a $2 entry fee to play the game; so your expenses over 100 trials would be $200, and hence your net profit would be $50; or, on an average, your expected net profit is 50 cents per game.

The 50-cents-per-game net profit is the expected profit of playing the game. You will not earn this every time you play. In fact, you will either make $2 or lose $1 each time. Fifty cents, however, is the expected result of playing enough games. It is dependent on both the payoff associated with each outcome ($4 for head outcome, $1 for tails outcome) and the likelihood, or probability, that each outcome will actually occur.

4.2 A MODEL OF INDIVIDUAL DECISION MAKING

We have deliberately delayed the introduction of our model so that you would have the opportunity to think about the sample situations yourself. If you have done so, you may have ideas that are different from ours, and you may have criticisms of the model we are about to introduce. You are hereby encouraged to criticize the model, which follows, but also to understand it fully.

An individual makes a decision *as if* he were going through these steps:

1. Examine all possible plans of action and see what possible outcomes can result from each.
2. Judge how desirable each outcome is and how likely it is to occur as a result of following the particular plan of action.
3. Choose the plan of action with the highest expected value.

We must now elaborate some of the concepts used in this model. We begin with the concept of probability.

4.2.1 PROBABILITY

Probability theory is concerned with the likelihood of future events occurring in certain situations. To illustrate such situations imagine a few simple experiments. (1) A coin is flipped, and we are concerned about our chances for having heads show up. (2) A die is rolled, and we are concerned about the chances for having a 4 appear on top. (3) A man is asked to vote, and we are concerned about the chance of his voting for a particular candidate. In any of these three situations we cannot predict exactly what the outcome will be. It is indeterminate. Instead we talk about the probability that some specific outcome will occur. But what does "probability" mean?

Intuitively, when we talk about probability, we are using the notion of relative frequency. When we say the probability of a head appearing is 0.5, we mean that if you flipped the coin many times, a head would show up about ½, or 50%, of the time. When we say that the probability of hearing anything interesting in a lecture is 0.75, we mean that if you went to a large number of lectures, something interesting would be said in about ¾, or 75% of them. The relative frequency of occurrence is 75%.

From the relative frequency notion, it should be clear that probabilities must all be within the range 0 to 1. The statement "The probability of a head occurring is 1.3" does not make sense. It would mean that you expect heads to occur 130% of the time—that is, in 100 flips of the coin, you would expect to see 130 heads. Clearly, this is no easy trick.

STOP AND THINK. George claims that the probability of a head is —0.4. Is this possible? What does it mean?

Using the relative frequency notion of probability, we can interpret George's statement to mean that in 100 flips of the coin, heads did not occur 140 times. This is nonsense. Thus we rule out probabilities greater than 1 and less than 0. Probabilities of either 1 or 0 are possible though. They designate, respectively, something that is certain to occur and something that is certain not to occur.

Notation. Generally, we use capital P as an abbreviation for probability. $P(\text{head}) = 0.5$ means the probability of heads occurring is 0.5; $P(\text{voting for Dr. Spock}) = 0.74$ means that the probability of voting for Dr. Spock is 0.74. We often use lower case p, q, and r to stand for some *unknown value* of probability for some event. For example, $P(\text{rain}) = q$ means that we do not know the probability of rain, but we assign it a value of q to stand for that probability.

If you add together the probabilities of all the possible outcomes associated with some situation, they must equal 1.0 (provided the outcomes are mutually exclusive). That is to say, out of all of the things that might occur, at least one of them will occur. For example, suppose that Sally cuts class one day in order to tune up her Volkswagen. Upon questioning by you, Sally says that there are only three possible outcomes: The car works much better $(P = 0.8)$; the car works the same $(P = 0.05)$; or the car blows up $(P = 0.05)$. The sum of these three probabilities is 0.9, which means that 90% of the time one of these three things will occur. But what about the other 10% of the time? Since Sally has claimed that these are the only three possible outcomes, there is something wrong. Either there must be other possible outcomes or the probabilities are not correct. The sum of all the probabilities must equal exactly 1.0.

How do we know the probability of an event? In the case of a fair coin we know that there are only two outcomes, heads or tails, and (we assume) that the two outcomes are equally likely. Hence we can say that the probability of a head is ½. In the case of a fair die we have six possible outcomes, 1, 2, 3, 4, 5, 6, and because we know they are all equally probable (if it is a fair die), we say that the probability of a "5" is ⅙.

In many real life situations you have to estimate the probability of some event by using your past experience. In effect, you have some notion of the relative frequency of an event occurring, as observed in the past, and you assume that circumstances will be the same in the future. For example, you go to the door and call your dog. In the past he has come about 70% of the time, so your guess about his future behavior is that the probability of his coming when you call is 0.7. Farmers commonly do the same thing with the weather. They know how often it has rained in October in the past, and they use this knowledge as a measure of the probability of rain in October next year.

John has just bought a raffle ticket. If he wins the raffle, he gets a new car; if he loses, he gets nothing. The ticket cost him $1. John's analysis of the situation goes like this: "There are two possible outcomes: I can win the raffle, or I can lose it. So my probability of winning is 1 out of 2, or 50%. The ticket only cost me $1 and so I bought a 50% chance of winning a car for only $1, which is a pretty good bet." What do you think of John's reasoning?

STOP AND THINK. John is obviously wrong, but do you know why? Try to explain his error.

One of the most common errors people make when they estimate probabilities is to assume that because there are two possible outcomes, the probability of each of them is ½. This works fine for coins because the two outcomes are *equally likely*. But all two-outcome situations do not have equally likely outcomes. For example, every time you drive you may have an accident or not have one, but this does not mean the probability of having an accident is ½. In the raffle-ticket example, John apparently assumed that the two outcomes "win" or "do not win" are equally likely. In fact, if 10,000 tickets are sold, John has only a 1/10,000 probability of winning and a 9,999/10,000 probability of losing.

4.2.2 EXPECTED VALUE

The expected value of some situation is the *average* payoff you would receive if you played the game a large number of times. Imagine a situation like this: A die is rolled; if it comes up with a "5," you win $12; if it comes up with any other number, you win nothing. What is the expected value of this game? What is the average result you would expect if you played the game a large number of times?

Suppose we play the game 600 times. We throw the die 600 times in succession, and keep track of how much we win in total. What would we expect to be the overall result (aside perhaps from a sprained wrist)? Since there are 6 sides to a die and each is equally likely to occur, there is a ⅙ chance that a 5 will occur. In 600 throws we would expect the 5 to come up 100 times, (that is, ⅙ times 600) and so you would win $1,200 (that is, $12 × 100). For the other tosses you would receive nothing. Thus your total expected winnings are $1200 for the entire series of tosses, or $2 per game. This $2 per game is the average payoff, the expected value of the game.

> **STOP AND THINK.** **If you played the game just once, would you receive the expected value ($2 in this case)? Why or why not?**

Since the outcome of playing this game can be only $0 or $12, there is no way of winning the expected value of $2 in a single game. We are using the word "expected" in a probability sense to designate an average amount of winning. You always win either $0 or $12 on any given toss of the die, but on the average your winnings will be $2 per toss. In the game just described you can never win the "expected" amount on any given trial. (Though this may seem to be a peculiar use of language, bear with us for the moment. It turns out to be useful and, in any event, is standard in probability discussions.)

Now that you understand expected value in an intuitive way, we will give a more formal, algebraic definition:

1. We shall designate the possible outcomes of the game by their values and use V as a symbol for them. We can use subscripts to designate different outcomes: Thus V_1 is the value of outcome number 1; V_3 is the value of outcome number 3, and so on. In the game last described there were two outcomes, which we designate:

$V_1 = \$12$ (outcome number 1 is the occurrence of a "5")

$V_2 = \$0$ (outcome number 2 is the occurrence of any other number)

2. We shall designate the probability of each outcome using P:

$P_1 = \frac{1}{6}$ (the probability of outcome number 1 is equal to $\frac{1}{6}$)

$P_2 = \frac{5}{6}$ (the probability of outcome number 2 is $\frac{5}{6}$)

3. If we designate the expected value as EV we can now write the formula for expected value as:

$$EV = P_1V_1 + P_2V_2$$

Or in the dice example just given we would have:

$$EV = \frac{1}{6}(\$12) + \frac{5}{6}(\$0)$$

$$EV = \$2 \qquad + \$0$$

$$EV = \$2$$

If there are more than two outcomes, then we just add more P_iV_i terms to the formula, and we have the general expression for the expected value of an alternative having n possible outcomes:

$$EV = P_1V_1 + P_2V_2 + \cdots + P_nV_n = \sum_{i=1}^{n} P_iV_i$$

4.2.3 DECISION TREES

The examples so far have been simple. When we turn to more complicated situations, it will be useful to represent them graphically. It is possible to draw pictures of these decision situations, and we call the pictures "decision trees" because they have branches and involve decisions. The decision tree for the dice game is shown below.

We use boxes to designate events or outcomes; the lines connecting the boxes in the figure show *all* the possible connections, or relations, between the boxes; the number beside each line is the

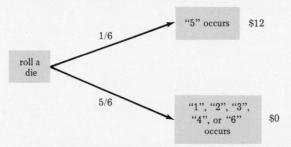

probability that the path will be followed; the dollar values at the right hand side of the figure show the value associated with each possible outcome. You read the tree from left to right; the die is rolled, and each of the outcomes branches from that point and ends in a value associated with a final outcome.

Example

Now we can try a more complicated game.

Game A. You roll a die. If it comes up "1" or "2," you win $6; if it comes up "3," you win $18; if it comes up "4" or "6" you win nothing; and if it comes up "5," you win $12.

Each of the six sides of the die is equally likely to come up, and hence each has a probability of ⅙ of occurring.

> **STOP AND THINK.** First of all, what is the probability that you will win nothing if you play the game? *Hint:* there are two possible outcomes, 4 or 6, that could cause this to occur.

We know that the probability of any given number occurring is ⅙, and we know that there are two possible ways to win nothing. To find their combined probability you simply add the two separate probabilities together. Thus the probability of winning nothing is ⅙ + ⅙ = 2/6 , or ⅓. The decision tree that follows describes Game A. *Be sure you understand all the probabilities on its branches.*

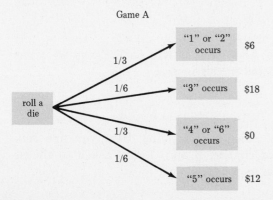

Game A

There are six numbers that might turn up on the die, but there are only four outcomes (in our sense of the word) because some of the numbers on the die produce the same result.

To find the expected value of the game we simply multiply the probability of each outcome by its value and add up all the results. Since there are four outcomes, there will be four terms in the equation:

Outcome 1

"1" or "2" occurs.

Outcome 2

"3" occurs.

Outcome 3

"4" or "6" occurs.

Outcome 4

"5" occurs.

$$EV = P_1V_1 \ + P_2V_2 \ + P_3V_3 \ + P_4V_4 = \sum_{i=1}^{n} P_iV_i$$

$$\begin{aligned} EV &= \tfrac{1}{3}(\$6) + \tfrac{1}{6}(\$18) + \tfrac{1}{3}(\$0) + \tfrac{1}{6}(\$12) \\ &= \$2 \quad + \$3 \quad\ + \$0 \quad + \$2 \\ &= \$7 \end{aligned}$$

This can also be written as $EV(\text{Game A}) = \$7$; that is, any given time we play Game A, we might win as little as $0 or as much as $18, but the expected payoff is $7.

Example

Upon entering the Social Sciences Gambling Den, you are confronted with two games of chance, B and C, and asked to choose which of them you wish to play.

Game B.   Flip a coin. If it comes up heads, you win $0. If it comes up tails, you get to roll a die.

If the die comes up as "1," "2," or "3," you win $0.

If the die comes up as "4," you win $4.

If the die comes up "5," you win $5.

If the die comes up as "6," you win $6.

Game C.   Draw a card from a regular 52-card deck. If it is a club, diamond, or spade, you win $0. If it is a heart, you get to roll a pair of dice.

If the dice come up as a "12" you win $288.

If the dice come up as "1" to "11," you win $0.

You may play either game as many times as you wish, but which game should you choose to play? First, you should draw the Game B decision tree.

This tree is more complicated because it has branches radiating from the end of other branches, but the basic rules are still the same. Notice that the sum of the probabilities *radiating from any one point* is 1.0 (for instance, $\frac{1}{2} + \frac{1}{6} + \frac{1}{6} + \frac{1}{6} = 1.0$).

Game B

STOP AND THINK.   Does this have to be true? *Why?*

Remember that we defined a decision tree as a *complete* picture of the world, one that shows all possible outcomes. Each of the boxes in a tree is one possible outcome, and if that one outcome can possibly lead to other outcomes, *all* of them will be shown branching off toward the right. If all of the possible branches are shown, then one of them must occur. (The principle is exactly the same as that in the discussion of probability at the beginning of the chapter.) The sum of the probabilities must be 1.0 because the branches must be a complete description of the world.

What is the expected value of playing Game B? One easy way to answer this question is to divide the problem into two parts. First you should figure what it would be worth if you were already at the point where you get to roll the die. Suppose the tree *only* consisted of the portion to the right of the outcome "roll die." The expected value of that tree is:

$$EV \text{ (roll die)} = \tfrac{1}{2}(\$0) + \tfrac{1}{6}(\$4) + \tfrac{1}{6}(\$5) + \tfrac{1}{6}(\$6)$$
$$= \$0 \quad + \$4/6 \quad + \$5/6 \quad + \$6/6$$
$$= \$15/6 = \$2.50$$

STOP AND THINK.   Take another look at this calculation. Do you know why the first line of calculations looks the way it does; that is, could you have set it up to figure out the expected value?

Since we now know that the expected value of being able to roll the die (of getting to that outcome on the tree) is $2.50, we can redraw the tree for Game B in simplified form like this:

Game B (simplified tree)

In the new diagram we have replaced all the branches to the right of "roll die" with a single number, their expected value. The same procedure can be used on any tree, no matter how complex it is. Just start at the right side and successively reduce the complex branches to single numbers. Thus you successively simplify the tree until the final calculation involves a tree with a single set of radiating branches.

From the simplified diagram of Game B we can now calculate the expected value as:

$$EV \text{ (Game B)} = \frac{1}{2} (\$0) + \frac{1}{2} (\$2.50)$$
$$= \$1.25$$

Now we can draw the decision tree for Game C and show how it can be simplified and analyzed. The entire tree looks like this:

Game C

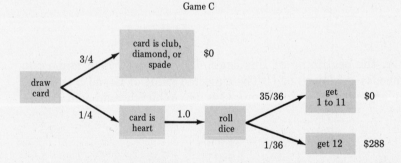

How did we calculate the probabilities for each branch? A deck of cards has equal numbers of clubs, diamonds, hearts, and spades so that there is 1 chance in 4 of drawing a heart and 3 chances in 4 of drawing some other card. What about the dice? There are 36 ways to roll a pair of dice, that is, 36 possible outcomes (try listing them) but only 1 outcome (a 6 and 6) can give a total value of 12 points. So there is 1 chance in 36 of getting a 12; and there is a 35/36 chance of getting something else.

We begin by looking at the part of the tree to the right of "roll dice." The expected value is:

$$EV \text{ (roll dice)} = \frac{35}{36} (\$0) + \frac{1}{36} (\$288)$$
$$= \$0 \qquad + \$8$$
$$= \$8$$

So we can now redraw Game C in simplified form by replacing the right-hand branches with a single outcome, their expected value.

Game C (simplified tree)

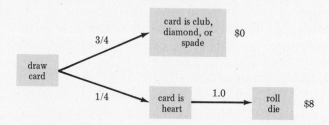

And we can now calculate the expected value of Game C as follows:

$$EV \text{ (Game C)} = \tfrac{3}{4}\,(\$0) + \tfrac{1}{4}\,(\$8)$$
$$= \$0 \quad\ + \$2$$
$$= \$2$$

At the beginning of this example we asked which game you would choose to play, B or C. The expected value of Game B is $1.25, and the expected value of Game C is $2. Which would you choose to play?

STOP READING. Answer *each* of the following questions.
1. In which game would you win most often?
2. In which game *could* you win the most on any one try?
3. Which game would you play if you were allowed to play as many times as you wished?
4. Which game would you play if you could play only once? Be sure you can give some explanation for each of the foregoing answers. (This question is especially worthy of thought.)

It is obvious that you would have some sort of dollar payoff more often in Game B than in Game C. In Game C you are out of the action 3 times out of 4 after the first branch; and even if you get beyond the first branch, you have only a $\tfrac{1}{36}$ chance of winning anything at all.

The most money you could ever win on one try of Game B is $6, while you could win $288 on a single (lucky) try in Game C.

If you were allowed to play as often as you wished, you should play Game C because its expected value is higher. Even though you win less often, when you do win it is for much more money.

Question 4 seems more difficult to deal with than Question 3, but the conventional solution is identical and you should still choose Game C (except under the unusual circumstances outlined in the next paragraph). The fact that you are only going to play once does not change the probabilities or the payoffs. The expected value of Game C is still higher. There is another way of looking at this argument. Over your lifetime you will be confronted with *many* one-play choice situations; actually your whole life situation is really like playing a kind of supergame in which you constantly choose among simpler alternative games. Even though the alternatives change each time you play, you will maximize expected value over the *series* of decisions by always choosing the alternative with the highest expected value.

There are two very special circumstances in which the answer to Question 4 might be to maximize the chance of winning anything, rather than maximizing expected value. What we are really interested in is maximizing happiness. We have been assuming that maximizing dollar payoffs will maximize happiness. But suppose we are advising some individual who puts a very high value on winning and really hates to lose. He might choose Game B instead of Game C because the fun of winning frequently makes up for the lower expected value. Or consider the following hypothetical situation: You are dead broke yet too proud to borrow from your roommate. You have nothing to hock, sell, or barter, and you will get your next check in two days. Meanwhile you must eat. Under these specialized circumstances it might be quite rational to choose Game B. You cannot afford to wait for the highest expected value; you are hungry and want to eat now, so you play the game that has the best chance of giving you immediate money.

Such special circumstances are infrequent though, and so you will probably wish to choose the maximum expected value solution in almost all cases. However, in the next paragraph we outline a way to incorporate these special circumstances into the expected value theory. Since the idea is a common one in the literature, we mention it here. We will return to it in Section 4.4. You might wish to skip this the first time you read this section.

We will propose a name for happiness; we will call it "utility," and we will speak of comparing alternatives by measuring how many "utils" of happiness are associated with them. Suppose you are choosing between the two part-time jobs: Job A pays $3 per hour but is relatively dull; Job B pays $2 per hour but is more fun. Which should you choose? The problem is to measure the dollar payoff and the boredom payoff in similar units so the two jobs may be compared (otherwise it is the old problem about whether two apples or three oranges is "more"). Utils provide the common measure unit. Conceivably, you might examine your values and decide that $1 (the money difference between the two jobs) is worth 10 utils of happiness, whereas the boredom difference between the two jobs is 14 utils. So now you can look at the total utility gained from each job (utils from money plus utils from fun) and choose the job that gives you maximum utility. In this case that would be Job B. Since it is possible to convert any kind of payoff into utility units—for example, the fun of winning or the necessity of immediate money to buy food—you can easily handle the two special cases we discussed in the preceding paragraph. We would simply measure all payoffs in utils and hence always choose the solution that maximizes expected utility. In most of the situations dealt with in this chapter we ignore nonmonetary payoffs and concentrate on maximizing expected dollar payoffs instead. Since there are many situations that involve major nonmonetary payoffs, such a device will often mislead you considerably. But we did not promise a world without temptation.

4.2.4 EXPECTED VALUE AND PROBABILITY (ROUND II)

The method we have used to simplify complex decision trees makes the solution simple and intuitive. In this section we show a more direct way of calculating expected values.

Look at the decision tree for Game C again. Instead of calculating the results in two steps, through successive simplification, we can do it in one step. The principle is simply to multiply the numbers along each branch in a continuous fashion. For Game C we would get:

$$EV \text{(Game C)} = \tfrac{3}{4}(\$0) + \tfrac{1}{4}[1.0 \times \tfrac{1}{36}(\$288)]$$
$$= \$0 \quad + \$2 \quad + \tfrac{1}{4}[1.0 \times 35/36(\$0)]$$
$$= \$2 \quad + \$0$$

This is, of course, the same result obtained from the two-step process. Notice that the calculation involved three strings of multiplications, one for each of the outcomes.

An alternative way of looking at this is to ask: What is the probability of getting to the end of any one branch. We have redrawn the tree as follows to show how these probabilities can be calculated.

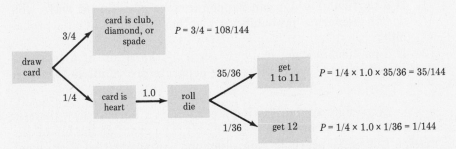

Next, we redraw it and simplify it. (*Note:* the 144 on the bottom of the fractions is the result of multiplying $\frac{1}{4} \times \frac{1}{36}$. We convert $\frac{3}{4}$ to $\frac{108}{144}$ so that all the fractions may be in the same units.)

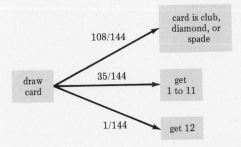

Notice that each of the possible outcomes from the original Game C ("card is club, diamond, or spade"; "get 1 to 11"; "get 12") is shown. If all of the possible outcomes are shown, then the sum of their probabilities must equal 1; and this is true here because they add up to $\frac{144}{144}$. Notice that you can also calculate expected values directly from such trees. For example:

$$EV\,(\text{Game C}) = \tfrac{108}{144}\,(\$0) + \tfrac{35}{144}\,(\$0) + \tfrac{1}{144}\,(\$288)$$
$$= \$0 \qquad\quad + \$0 \qquad\quad + \$2$$
$$= \$2$$

In probability terms, we can say that there is 1 chance in 144 of getting any payoff at all and 143 chances out of 144 of getting no payoff. Notice that there are two ways of losing (the top two branches) and we can simply add their probabilities together. There is a general rule for manipulating probabilities implicit in this example.

1. If a particular event can happen in *several* different ways, you *add* the separate probabilities together to figure out its probability.
2. If a particular event can only occur as the result of a *sequence* of prior events, you *multipy* the separate probabilities together.

For example, in drawing a card from a normal deck there is 1 chance in 4 of drawing any given suit. The event at the top of the Game C tree is "card is club, diamond, or spade," so that event (getting into that box) can occur as a result of 3 possible draws; and the sum of their separate probabilities is $3/4$.

The event at the bottom of the Game C tree is "get 12," and you can only get to it through a sequence of prior events—draw a heart, *and* role the correct number. So we multiply probabilities.

You can use these rules and the tree idea to calculate complex probabilities in an intuitive way. For example, what is the probability of rolling a 10 with two dice? We draw the partial tree as follows:

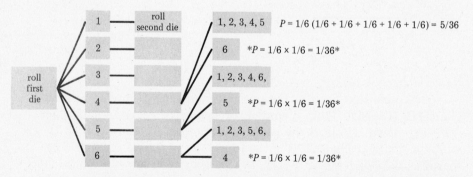

Only the starred outcomes will add up to 10; and so we know there are 3 possible ways to roll a 10. Their sum is $3/36$ or $1/12$, so $P(\text{"10"}) = 1/12$.

Example: Automobile Troubles

One morning you go out to drive to school but discover that "Old Paint" simply will not start. You tinker with it for a while but without luck. Fortunately, though, your sister is in medical school at the same university; she happens to be pretty good at diagnosing car innards too, and she makes house calls (for close relatives, anyway). She examines the patient and discovers that all of the spark plugs seem to be heavily covered with thick, black crud. "That's your problem," she says. "Those plugs can't possibly fire. I'll bet you've been using lots of oil lately." You nod. "That missing oil is getting into the combustion chamber and fouling up the plugs." This sounds sensible to you because you had to put in another set of spark plugs only a thousand miles ago.

You could simply put in new plugs and go on driving. That would mean using up lots of oil and spark plugs over the next year, as well as lower gas mileage and lots of smoke coming from your exhaust pipe. It is probably the cheapest solution, but you are concerned about the environment and do not want to create more air pollution. So you decide either to junk the car or to repair it. But you need more information to make a rational choice between these two alternatives, namely, the probable repair costs. Your sister asks you some questions about the car's history and then says that there is about a 60% chance that the problem is just bad valves (which are cheap to fix) and a 40% chance that the problem is worn piston rings (which are expensive).

You call a local mechanic, who confirms her diagnosis and says that he will do a valve job for $100 or the rings for $250 or $400, depending on the amount of other work required; that is, once he gets inside the engine, he will know whether it is a simple ring job ($250) or whether the bearings need replacement also ($400); and there is an 80% chance that both the rings and the bearings are bad.

Okay, should you fix "Old Paint" or junk it? It is an old car, and you only need one more year of transportation from it. (By the end of that time you will have graduated, gone to work, and earned the money to buy something sportier.) Your roommate has an old car in reasonably good shape that he will sell you for $175. Your guess is that if your current car were repaired, it would be about as reliable, mechanically, as your roommate's car. What should you do? The following list summarizes the facts:

1. Cost of roommate's car = $175.
2. Simple repair (valve job): cost = $100, probability = 0.6.
   Complex repair: probability = 0.4.
   Fix worn piston rings: cost = $250, probability = 0.2.
   Fix worn rings and bearings too: cost = $400, probability = 0.8.

STOP AND THINK. What would you do? Sketch a possible decision tree and figure out the expected cost of your alternative actions.

There are a number of possible ways to draw the tree and work out the expected costs. You have two major alternatives—fix or junk the car—and you should draw a tree for each of them. The tree for one alternative looks like this:

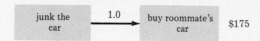

Expected cost (junk the car) = $175

The tree for the other alternative looks like this:

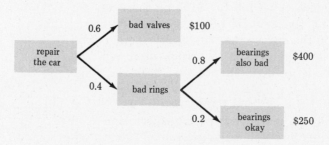

$$\begin{aligned} \textit{Expected cost (repair the car)} &= 0.6(\$100) + 0.4\,[0.8(\$400) \\ &\qquad\qquad\qquad\qquad + 0.2(\$250)] \\ &= \$60 \qquad + 0.4\,[\$320 + \$50] \\ &= \$60 \qquad + \$148 \\ &= \$208 \end{aligned}$$

Thus the expected cost of the repair alternative is $208, and the expected cost of the other alternative is $175. So you should junk the car.

After thinking about the problem some more, however, you remember that there is a diagnostic testing center for cars nearby. You call the center and determine that they can accurately diagnose the difference between bad rings and bad valves, but the tests cost $15. That is, for $15, you can buy an accurate forecast of what the repair work will cost you. Should you test the car?

STOP AND THINK. **Should you buy the diagnostic test for the car?** *Hint:* **What would you do if the test pointed to one alternative or the other?**

To begin we draw a decision tree involving the diagnostic test:

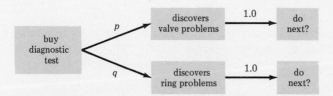

Remember, all you are buying is a prediction of what is wrong with the car. The test does not change any of the probabilities—it only recognizes them. Therefore, the probability that the diagnostic test will discover valve problems (p) is identical to the probability that there are valve problems in the first place; that is $p = 0.6$. Likewise $q = 0.4$. If the test discovers that there are valve problems, what would you do next? You could fix the car or junk it; but since you know that a valve job will only cost $100, compared to $175 for another used car, you should fix the car if you wind up on that branch. Now what would you do if the test discovers ring problems? This time the cost of repair ($250 to $400) is much higher than the cost of replacement—so you would junk the car. The complete new tree is shown as follows:

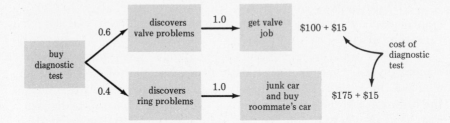

Two things are especially important about this tree: (1) The test does not change the underlying probabilities but only recognizes them. It does not control which branch you will end up on. (2) Your decision about what action to take will be contingent on which branch you end up on: If you end up on the top branch, you will fix the car; if you end up on the bottom branch, you will junk it. The expected cost of this new tree is:

Expected cost (test alternative) $= 0.6\,(\$100 + \$15)$
$$+ 0.4\,(\$175 + \$15)$$
$$= \$69 \qquad + \$76$$
$$= \$145$$

Hence this new alternative is superior to your best previous alternative (junking the car no matter what). That is, the diagnostic test can act as a guide to your actions and will save you money in the long run.

4.3 EXPLORATIONS OF DECISION TREES

We have presented a model of rational decision making that is somewhat different in spirit from the models in the first three chapters. Those models are all descriptive models; this rational choice model has a strong normative aspect. A normative model is one that tells you how to do something, how to behave in order to achieve a goal. A descriptive model is one that tells you what people do; it enables you to predict behavior. Normative models give advice, whereas descriptive models predict behavior. For example, a descriptive model might tell you that people will speed on the freeway when a cop is not around. Such a model does not say that it is good to speed. It merely says that people will do so. The golden rule is a normative model. It tells you how you should behave, but it does not predict that people will actually behave that way.

A given model might give good advice but bad predictions, or bad advice and accurate predictions. Some models do both well while others do neither. The rational choice model is a normative model that tells you how to make a choice decision. Given some difficult choice problem, the model tells you how to evaluate alternative courses of action so as to produce one kind of optimal decision. But the rational choice model also has descriptive uses and can be used to predict what decisions people will in fact make.

We have created a model of a rational man. We know that people do not always behave rationally, but to the extent that they do, the model predicts their behavior. Although there are conspicuous exceptions, we might speculate that the more important a decision is, the more likely it is to be made rationally. We might also suspect that the easier it is to compare outcomes in numerical terms, the more likely it is that the decisions will be made rationally. Thus, for example, many business decisions can be predicted by the model.

We can also make use of *aggregation*. Suppose you are trying to apply the model to predict the decisions of people in choosing between mass transit or private automobiles, or to predict the decisions of people choosing among alternative careers. The decision of any one person is likely to combine both rational and irrational elements. Thus it is difficult to predict accurately the decision of any given person. However, it will be much easier to predict the behavior of groups of people, provided the irrational elements are random and hence tend to cancel out in a large population. Thus the model sometimes does a relatively good job of predicting the average behavior of a large number of people.

In this section we elaborate the model to explore some implications of how people *should* behave and how they *do* behave. We will shift from one mode to the other. You should keep in mind the conditions under which such a shift is justified and keep asking yourself whether the situation meets those conditions.

4.3.1 DECISION MAKING UNDER RISK

Since you now understand the basic probability and expected value concepts, let us try out your new knowledge on a practical decision-making problem. The basic situation in the following description is a true, real world example. The numbers are simplified somewhat to make the example easier, but the essence of the decision making remains the same. We have also added a general story to the situation. It is complete with plot, intergenerational conflict, human interest, and an ecology angle.

Basic Facts.   Almost all U.S. raisins come from grapes grown and dried in the San Joaquin Valley of California. You make raisins by picking the grapes, putting them in trays, and allowing them to dry in the sun. If the grapes are rained upon once, they lose half their value (due to molds, and so on) ; if they are rained upon twice, they are completely ruined. It takes 20 days of drying to produce raisins. The rainy season starts in September; it has never rained earlier than that in the valley, and the first rainfall is usually not until the last part of September. So every year the farmer plays a game of chance against nature. The longer he leaves the grapes on the vine to grow, the bigger and more valuable they become, but the greater the probability of their being rained upon (because of the delay in picking). It is a tough decision to make, and the farmer's livelihood depends upon it. He has a number of alternatives.

The farmer can decide to play it safe. That is, he can pick the grapes on August 11 so there will be a certainty of enough rain-free drying time. This gives him revenue of $300 per acre.

The farmer can decide to take a chance. That is, he can wait until September 1 to pick the grapes, hoping for 20 days of dry weather. If there is no rain, he gets $400 per acre.

There is also one alternative use for the grapes: Instead of drying grapes to make raisins; the farmer can sell them to the local winery for crushing. This gives revenue of $260 per acre (or $130 per acre if they have been rained upon once; or $0 if they have been rained on twice).

Now we begin the story.

You are a poor, but proud, social science major, working your way through college. Your parents are grape growers (union) in the San Joaquin Valley who have been paying half your expenses. Upon visiting them over Christmas vacation (you hitchhiked across the country to save money), you find that they have used up all their savings and will not be able to keep you in college anymore.

You wonder whether your background in social science can be used to make the farm more profitable so that you can stay in school. Since the problem seems to involve decisions about when to pick the grapes, you decide to draw decision trees for each of the alternative actions. Maybe you can figure out a better set of actions for your father to follow.

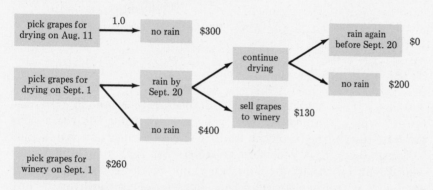

The first and third tree offer certainty about the payoffs. The second tree has the biggest potential payoff, but the actual outcome is uncertain. Your father explains that what he currently does is to follow the first alternative because it is obviously more profitable than the third. That clearly is the correct decision when choosing between one and three; so the only way to improve on his decision is to analyze the second tree to see whether it offers higher profits. Unfortunately, the second tree has no probabilities on it.

STOP AND THINK.   Can you think of a way to figure out the probabilities in a real situation like this?

Fortunately, your education has not been in vain. You head over to the local library and look up the weather records for the past 50 years. You discover that during that time it stayed dry from September 1 to September 20 in 70% of the years and rained at least once in 30% of the years. Furthermore, in those years when it had already rained once before September 20, the probability of rain occurring a second time before September 20th was 40%. Now you have the information you needed to add to the tree.

Examining the new tree, we see that 70% of the time you will get a $400 payoff and 30% of the time it will rain. If it does rain, you have a decision to make: Sell grapes to the winery immediately for $130 or continue drying them and take a chance that

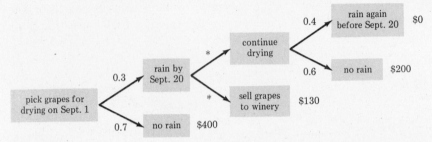

it will not rain a second time. If it does rain a second time, the grapes will be ruined; if not, you will get $200 for them. The probabilities on the branches leading up to this decision are labeled "*" to indicate that you make a decision at that point and follow one branch or the other. You can think of these points as being similar to a railroad switch. You can set the probabilities to any values you wish, provided they add up to 1.0.

If it does rain once and you are at the switching point, which decision should you make? (*Note:* We assume you want to make your choice by setting one probability equal to 1.0 and all others equal to 0. Why?)

STOP AND THINK. Which decision would you make at the switching point? Why?

The expected value of immediately selling the grapes to the winery is $130. The expected value of continued drying is 0.4 ($0) + 0.6 ($200) = $120. So the best decision at that point is to quit drying and sell to the winery. Now what about the expected value for the entire tree?

$$EV \text{(pick and dry September 1)} = .3 (\$130) + 0.7 (\$400)$$
$$= \$319 \text{ per acre}$$

So you inform your father of what his proper course of actions should be: "Allow the grapes to grow until September 1 and then pick them for drying. If it rains before they are dry, sell them immediately to the winery. You used to get revenues of $300 per acre (and almost all of that was taken up by expenses); you will now have revenues of $319 per acre, with no additional expenses. So profits will be $19 per acre higher. Since you have 1000 acres of land, that is $19,000 extra profit, enough to raise wages, pay my tuition, buy me a new Jaguar, and get Mom that electric skillet she always wanted." Your father is amazed and thankful, and you feel pleased.

Think back for a moment and review how the problem was solved. Step 1 was to examine the problem carefully and thoughtfully, to find all of the possible alternative courses of action and what kinds of outcomes were associated with each. *This is always the most important step*, whether you are solving problems in this course or real problems in your own life. Too many people make bad decisions because they narrow a problem artificially; they define a problem as choosing among two or three possibilities and ignore the existence of superior, but less obvious, alternatives. (In fact it seems likely that such artificial narrowing of a problem will be the source of many of the bad decisions you will make during your own lifetime.) Step 1 creates a series of decision trees, and in Step 2 you attach probabilities to each branch and decide on the value of each outcome. The trees are now complete. In Step 3 you calculate the expected value of each tree and choose the one having the highest expected value.

4.3.2 THE VALUE OF INFORMATION

It is a year later, and you are home again, this time temporarily in charge of the farm yourself. The federal agricultural agent drops by to tell you about a new weather forecasting service that is about to be started by the government. It seems that government meterologists have discovered enough to be able to make accurate 20-day weather forecasts. The process involves putting a weather satellite directly over the valley, the full-time services of a large computer, plus associated programmers and scientists. In short, it is an expensive operation. Since the new President has declared that there shall be no more giveaway programs, you will have to pay for the new service if you want it. The government will charge each farm $30 per acre for the service. If you do buy the service, you agree to keep the information to yourself ($1000 per acre fine if you are caught reselling the forecasts to other farmers); the government guarantees that the forecasts will be 100% correct. (*Note:* There are actually long-term, accurate weather forecasts available, but they are not 100% accurate. They do provide useful information for farmers, but the decision tree becomes more complex because it must take into account the chance that the forecast may be wrong. Since a good example should illustrate the basic principle without getting mired down in side issues, in our example we have made the assumption of 100% accuracy.)

Should you buy the forecasts? The first question you ask is whether the forecasts would ever change your farming behavior? If knowledge of the future weather would not change your actions, it cannot have any value.

> **STOP AND THINK.** Look back at the basic decision tree. Is there ever a time when knowledge of the weather might change your decision? How? There is both an obvious answer and a subtle one. Try for both.

Obviously, knowledge of weather conditions would change your behavior if you were at the switching point. It has already rained once and you must decide whether to continue drying your grapes or sell them for wine. A perfect forecast at this point would often tell you to continue drying rather than crush (our former action). Thus you would usually (60% of the time) be able to continue drying and make $200 instead of $130. There is also a less obvious alternative action (*remember Step 1 deserves a lot of thought*): If on September 1 you know that it will rain during the coming 20 days, you should immediately sell the grapes to the winery and make $260. So the alternative tree "buy forecast" looks like this:

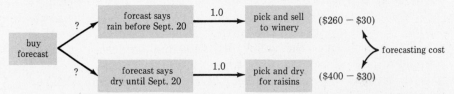

You cannot calculate the expected value of this alternative yet because you are missing one set of probabilities. Remember, the government will not be controlling the weather, it will only be forecasting it. How often then are they likely to forecast rain?

> **STOP AND THINK.** What are the two missing probabilities in the tree? How often will the government meteorologists forecast rain or dry?

Since the government is not changing the weather but only recognizing it, the natural frequency of rain and dry spells will remain the same. It will still be dry 70% of the time and rain at least once 30% of the time. So the probability of a dry forecast must be 0.7. The expected value of this alternative tree is

$$EV \text{ (buy forecast)} = 0.3 (\$260 - \$30) + 0.7 (\$400 - \$30)$$
$$= \$69 \qquad\qquad + \$259$$
$$= \$328$$

Since your best alternative before only earned $319 per acre, you should buy the forecasts. In fact, you should be willing to pay up to $39 per acre for the forecasts. Why?

Up until this section your choices have been relatively simple. You were given a number of alternatives and asked to choose among them; you were only allowed to choose which game you wanted to play, nothing more. Real decisions are more complex than this. In particular, it is often the case that you can obtain more information before making the decision. This extra information generally comes at some price, either monetary or in terms of the time it takes to gather it. For example, a businessman faced with the problem of locating a new plant in one of three cities can make decisions on the basis of his past experience alone, or he can take the time to look up published information on each city, or he can actually pay to have expensive surveys made of the relevant characteristics of each city. The more information he has, the more he reduces the uncertainty about the result of locating in a particular city. Should he therefore try to obtain complete information about each? He has a trade-off to make. More information costs more money, but it also reduces risk.

Our numerical example has been in terms of weather forecasting. Obviously, there are many more types of information that might be useful in any given decision. The principles for using the information remain the same though. First, is there any way that the information might change your actions? Second, what is the expected value of the new actions? Third, is the information worth what it will cost to obtain? In general, *the value of some kind of information* is the difference between the expected value with information and the expected value without information.

4.3.3 THE VALUE OF CONTROL

Time goes on, the farm is prospering, and your father sends you occasional checks in the mail out of gratitude for the wise decisions you have provided for running the farm. Still, you wonder if things might be done even better. You reason that the basic problem is still the variability in the weather. You now have accurate forecasting available, but this only tells you how the weather is going to vary. Is there some way you might gain control over the actual variability or control the weather itself? No, this does not seem too promising. How about controlling the effects of the weather? This seems like a more promising line of speculation. You might try to develop a new grape that dries more quickly; you might try to devise an artificial drying process; or you might try to protect the grapes while they are drying in the sun. This last idea seems most promising, and you get to work and design a new type of drying tray that can still be used for sun drying but that can also protect the grapes in the event of rain. You check with a number of manufacturers and find that the best price you can get on the new trays will amount to an extra $60 per acre. These new trays can only be used once; permanent trays would be much more expensive to manufacture. So every year you will have to buy new trays.

What is the expected value of using these new trays to control the weather? You reason that every year you would buy a set of the new trays, and every year you would gain the maximum price of $400 as a result. No more uncertainty. The tree looks like this:

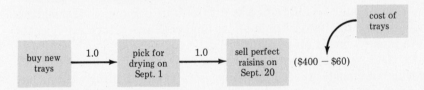

Since your best alternative before was to buy the weather forecasts, whose expected value was $328, you are $12 per acre better off with the new trays. You congratulate yourself and tell your family about the new idea.

STOP AND THINK. The preceding calculations are correct, and the proposed alternative is better than the weather forecast alternative. But it is not the best alternative. Look

for more alternatives. Can you think of a better way of using the new trays? *Hint:* **Must you always buy the new trays?**

Your younger sister has been going to college meanwhile and has had the wisdom and good sense to major in social sciences. In fact, she has been reading this book. She says, "The good book talks about overlooked alternatives as the most frequent cause of bad decisions. I think we ought to take that advice seriously. Now you have devised a clever way to gain control over the variability in the weather and hence decided to throw away your old decision about yearly purchase of the forecast information." Then she proposes, "I think we can combine your new trays with the weather forecasting information and have an even more profitable alternative. Weather forecasts are relatively cheap, but the trays are relatively expensive. How about buying the weather forecasts first and then deciding about the new trays? That way you would only have to buy the expensive trays 30% of the time." She then draws a new decision tree like this:

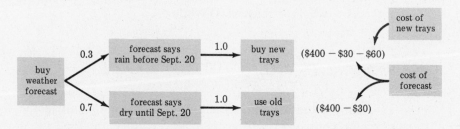

$$EV \text{ (sister's strategy)} = 0.3 (\$400 - \$30 - \$60) + 0.7 (\$400 - \$30)$$
$$= \$93 \qquad\qquad\qquad + \$259$$
$$= \$352$$

So her proposed alternative is $12 per acre better than yours. As penance for your error, you agree to reread this book and loan her your Jaguar on weekends.

Summary. As before, the first step in figuring the value of control is to decide whether control would change your actions in any way; and you try to think *very carefully* about all the new alternatives that might now be available. Then you calculate the expected value of the new actions and decide whether they are worthwhile. In general, *the value of control* is the difference between the expected value of your best alternative with control and the expected value of your best alternative without control.

Our example has been in terms of a specialized kind of farming. Most farmers worry about getting enough rain to produce a decent yield. They are also playing a game against nature. They too calculate the expected value of their best alternative. If it is high enough, they play the game; if it is not high enough, they sell their farms and go to the city. For these kinds of farmers, buying control over the weather means such actions as digging wells and putting in irrigation systems.

There are many other situations in which you may effectively buy control over a chance event. For example, buying a reliable new car instead of a cheap old one so that the chance event of your car breaking down and your being late to work occurs less often. Or a businessman may decide to buy his own trucking fleet instead of relying on commercial carriers so that he can be sure of always having delivery equipment available when he needs it. Control over chance events is obviously desirable, but sometimes it costs more than it is worth. You have to calculate the expected value first in order to know whether it is worthwhile.

4.3.4 THE VALUE OF INSURANCE (OPTIONAL)

There are many situations in which it is possible to gain some information or control over the basic uncertainty inherent in a situation; and people do commonly buy information or control in such situations. There is still a third way that people deal with chance events. Consider automobile accidents as an example. They are clearly chance events. To some extent information is useful in dealing with them. It helps, for instance, to know how to steer out of a skid, or when the peak accident hours are, or what the most dangerous roads are. To some extent you can also buy control over automobile accidens by driving a safer car, wearing seat belts, or commuting by bus.

The third way that people use to deal with uncertain events involves one of the largest and oldest industries in the United States —the insurance business. Insurance is another way of gaining some control over chance events. An insurance policy can be thought of as a bet between you and the insurance company. You are both gambling on the likelihood of some event occurring. Insurance companies are profitable businesses, which suggests that they win most of the bets. Yet people continue buying insurance. Why? Are they being irrational? Perhaps another example might shed some light on the question.

A new farmer has just come into the valley. He has spent all his money on the farm next door to your family. He seems like a nice guy, and you are trying to help him decide how to run his farm. His biggest problem is that he has put all of his money into a down payment on the farm and has almost nothing left over. He wants to find a harvesting strategy that gives him the greatest amount of money, but it must be absolutely safe.

When you talk to him, you discover that he intends to follow the strategy of buying the new trays every year, which gives him an expected value of $340 per acre. He defends his decision this way: "It's true that the strategy combining the new trays and weather forecasting would have a higher expected value, $352, but I cannot take a chance on it. Seven years out of ten, when it was dry, I would make $370 per acre (that is, $400 — $30), which is great. But, in three years out of ten, when it was wet, I would only make $310 per acre (that is, $400 — $30 — $60), which would wipe me out."

> **STOP AND THINK.** Be certain you understand what the new farmer has said so far. How did he arrive at the number $370 and $310? How do these two outcomes produce an expected value of $352?

"My problem is that I must earn at least $320 per acre to meet the mortgage payments and my expenses. One of those wet $310 years would be a disaster, since I have used up all my money and would have no savings or other cash resources to fall back on. The resulting $10-per-acre loss would be enough to put me out of business. Now it's true that I could gamble on its being a dry year, and 70% of the time I would be all right, but that 30% chance of being wiped out seems like too much of a risk to me."

His argument is correct, but it seems that there should be some way to help him earn more money. Suppose you give him a personal guarantee that he will always earn $325 per year no matter what happens (the reasons for choosing this amount, rather than \$320, will become apparent in the next paragraph); and he should follow the strategy of buying forecasts plus the new trays (if needed). How much would it cost you to make such a guarantee? The tree looks like this:

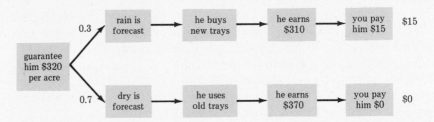

If it is a dry year, the guarantee will cost you nothing. If it is a wet year, the guarantee will cost you \$15. So the expected cost to you of the guarantee is \$4.50, (that is, \$15 × 0.3).

All of your clever decisions over the years have made you relatively rich, and you now have lots of loose dollars lying around. You decide to go into the insurance business. For a yearly insurance premium of \$5 per acre you will guarantee the farmer that he always earns at least \$325 per acre. Thus he earns the needed minimum of \$320 (that is, \$325 revenue − \$5 insurance cost) no matter what. This insurance arrangement would work well for you because you get \$5 income against an expected loss of \$4.50. (It's true that in some years you will have to pay out \$15 to your friend, but you have enough extra cash to be able to survive such years.) The insurance would also work well for your friend: Without your help he will have an expected revenue of \$340 per acre (straight control strategy); with your help he can have an expected revenue of \$351.50 (forecast with control and insurance strategy). So he expects to earn \$11.50 more per acre even after paying for the \$5 insurance policy. So you both have a good deal using this insurance option, and you all live happily ever after.

STOP AND THINK. Do you understand how the expected value of \$351.50 was obtained?

To make sure you understand the example, what would happen if the farmer decides to buy enough insurance to guarantee himself revenue of at least \$340 per acre. You decide to sell him a policy for $10 cost. From your point of view then you would now be incurring a 30% chance of paying out $30, which is an expected loss of $9, against your insurance fee income of $10. From the farmer's point of view the expected value of the new forecast-control-insurance strategy is $351 (that is, [0.3 × $340 + 0.7 × $370] —$10) compared to $340 for the straight control strategy. Thus he is $11 better off with the insurance. Notice that when he only wanted a $325 insurance policy, the net increase in his expected profits was $11.50; when he wants a $340 insurance policy, the net increase in his expected profits is only $11.00. He gains a little more certainty (regarding his lowest possible yearly revenue) at the cost of a little lower expected profit.

This is the essence of the insurance business. On one side are the insurance companies, which are comprised of people with lots of money, gambling small (to them) amounts in situations with positive expected values. Since they only gamble a small amount at a time, there is virtually no chance of their going broke; and since they only gamble in situations in which the expected revenue is greater than the expected cost, they keep getting bigger and bigger. On the other side are people like us who are faced with large (to us) risks that we wish to be protected against; we are willing to pay insurance premiums that are actually larger than our expected losses because the consequences of a loss are too dangerous. To the extent that such insurance allows us to pursue more profitable (but riskier) ventures, or protects us against large (to us) risks to our existence, it is a valuable service for us. This certainly does not mean that all insurance is good though. Let us see why.

Some universities are "self-insured"; that is, they have no insurance to protect them against stolen office and lab equipment, for example, or vandalism or minor injuries to employees. If an electric typewriter is stolen from a self-insured university or a piece of electronic equipment burns up, the university simply buys a replacement out of its own funds. Self-insured universities have no insurance protection against such events.

STOP AND THINK. **Is this rational behavior? Explain why or why not.**

Remember that an insurance company must set its premiums high enough to protect it against expected loss and still be able to make a profit. So on relatively small losses like those just mentioned (they are small compared to the size of the university budget), the university does without insurance. The yearly insurance premiums would be higher than the expected loss, and the losses are not large enough to threaten the existence of the university. This is called self-insurance. On the other hand, the university often buys insurance to protect itself against major losses such as destruction of an entire building or a large computer. They choose some critical value, say $1 million and decide they will be self-insured for losses below this and will buy insurance for amounts above this. The bigger a university is, the higher the critical value will be.

These same principles apply to your own purchases of insurance. Even though it is much lower than $1 million, there is obviously some critical self-insurance value for you as well. One of the authors had to make a decision about automobile insurance a few years ago. Let us examine his reasoning. "The car involved was only worth about $200. The insurance policy had a variety of options available. Basic liability coverage protects you against the possibility of very large damage suits resulting from accidents that were judged to be your fault. Comprehensive coverage pays up to the value of the car in case your car is stolen, destroyed by fire, or vandalized. Collision coverage: Pays up to the value of the car in case it is damaged in an accident. I decided to buy the first two options, liability and comprehensive, and not collision protection. I reasoned that collision insurance was unnecessary because the possible loss of a $200 car would not ruin my budget." This is a true story. Unfortunately, the decision was not quite correct.

STOP AND THINK. Can you spot the error in this decision? What is the correct decision?

One of our nagging bits of wisdom concerns bad decisions that result from failure to consider all the alternatives. In the example the alternative of buying only liability coverage was not considered. After all, if someone can afford the loss of a $200 car through collision, then he can afford its loss through theft, fire, or vandalism. Liability coverage is still needed, since a $50,000 damage suit would be a disaster; but coverage against a $200 loss is not needed. If you happened to own a $3000 car, your decision might be different.

Life insurance provides another interesting example. It does not actually protect your life, which would be worth a great deal; it only agrees to pay somebody else a lot of money if you die. Suppose you are married and have one child. Your death would leave your wife and child in real financial trouble—so you buy life insurance. What you are buying is peace of mind. But suppose you have no dependents or your spouse has a very good job? Is life insurance still necessary?

4.4   MAXIMIZATION OF EXPECTED UTILITY

Before you begin this section you should reread the long paragraph set off at the very end of section 4.2.3. When we discuss the utility of some outcome, we mean its value to some individual. The utility value is an overall measure of the happiness or usefulness of that outcome. In effect, we are defining a new system of measurement, a happiness scale, and measuring value along this new scale. There are two reasons why we need to define this new utility scale: (1) It allows us to analyze outcomes that involve nonmonetary rewards; and (2) it allows us to deal with seemingly paradoxical behavior in gambles involving only money.

It is obvious that the outcomes on many decision trees involve both monetary and nonmonetary components. For example, suppose you are comparing two alternative ways of getting home for vacation. One way costs $200 and takes six hours; the other way costs $100 and takes three days.

STOP AND THINK.   Which of these two ways would you prefer? Explain why.

Some people would prefer one alternative, and some of course, would prefer the other. As long as you believe that values are subjective, there are no correct or incorrect answers to this question, only thoughtful and unthoughtful ones. Some people value their time more highly than others, and the same person might value his time differently at various points during the year. For example, many people would give more to save an hour in the week before final exams than they would in the week afterward. Thus during finals week you might observe a student hiring a typist to get a paper done, rather than doing it slowly himself. After finals week, however, you might see the same student "wasting" half a day on the bus in order to save money, instead of taking a plane.

To deal with nonmonetary payoffs, we need some common measurement scale that we can use to express the value of both monetary and nonmonetary outcomes. Although not all social scientists prefer it, utility is the common concept. For example, take some complex reward such as "you getting to marry the handsome prince, getting the benefit of his father's money, plus the problems of being a good ruler and living with the prince's irascible mother." The utility associated with this reward is the combination of all these different monetary and nonmonetary factors, advantages and disadvantages. Given this all-inclusive definition of utility, you will always prefer the outcome having the greatest utility, and it is utility maximization that is basic to good decisions, not dollar maximization.

Utility, as a concept, is often difficult to use. *You* have to decide on the overall utility of two different outcomes; there is no objective yardstick or meter you can use to measure the utility of some outcome. It will be easy to do this in some situations and almost impossible to do it in others. In the situations in which it is difficult, you may not be able to calculate actual expected utilities for yourself; but even in these situations it will generally prove worthwhile to draw out the decision trees and try to compare outcomes. The very process of trying to compare outcomes will help your decision, and you will also probably discover some alternatives you had not thought about. We give some examples of this in the next section.

The second reason we need something like the utility concept is to help in the analysis of seemingly paradoxical behavior. It seems obvious that most people are not intrinsically interested in money, but rather that they are interested in the things for which money can be exchanged. That is, you desire not the money itself, but the utility you can buy with it. If utility and money are proportional to each other (for example, doubling the amount of money would double your utility), then the decision that maximizes expected dollars will also be the decision that maximizes **expected** utility.

It seems reasonable to expect that utility and dollars should be proportional over small ranges, but what about over very large ranges? For example, is the utility associated with $1 million exactly a million times greater than the utility associated with $1? There are some observations that suggest that utility and dollars are not proportional over large ranges like that. For example, many countries and some states, for instance, have a lottery in which you pay some small amount, roughly 50 cents, in order to have a chance of winning some very large amount, say, $100,000. If you calculate the probability of winning the lottery, you will find that the expected value of playing this game is much less than 50 cents. Why do people play it then? One possible answer is that money and utility are not proportional over that large a range. For a relatively poor person 50 cents may not represent very much additional comfort, but $100,000 may represent the chance to get out of a life of poverty. In fact, in many instances such a lottery may be a poor person's *only* chance of escaping the cycle of poverty. Therefore, he values the lottery payoff disproportionately higher than dollar calculations might indicate. Its utility is much greater than its expected monetary value.

This sort of disproportionate utility can also occur when monetary circumstances cause some minimum-need situation. Suppose you are confronted with a 50% probability of earning $20 versus a 100% probability of earning $8. And suppose that you had broken your glasses and desperately needed $8 to repair them. Under these circumstances you would probably take the $8 situation even though its expected value was somewhat lower.

All of this should, however, leave you somewhat nervous about our model of choice. By introducing the concept of utility we "explain" why people make decisions that do not maximize expected monetary reward. But, in effect, what we are saying is that our model is correct; we have only redefined the values involved in a decision to include nonmonetary, as well as monetary, rewards. If we are not careful, we violate an important rule about models: They must be capable of being proved wrong, and we must be eager to find them wrong. The concept of utility runs the risk of being used in order to save the model. We are often better off simply saying the model is wrong, particularly if we have no good way of measuring its utility. Maybe people do not maximize the expected value of anything.

STOP. Review the discussion in Chapter Three about circularity in models. Can you see the danger in the idea of utility? Can you see other concepts in social science that are similar? Is there any way to keep utility from becoming useless?

4.5 TREES WITHOUT NUMBERS

Many decisions have substantial nonmonetary components. Sometimes these components are measurable in other numerical terms. For example, we can talk about the expected time to complete a task using alternative procedures. Sometimes it may be fruitful to introduce some ideas about subjective utility as a way of converting values to a common numerical basis. Sometimes, however, we are left with outcomes that cannot be handled in any of these ways. Nevertheless, decision trees can still be a fruitful approach.

4.5.1 TRAFFIC ROUTES AS CHOICES

Harry is a city planner working on the problem of traffic distribution. The city council is concerned about traffic congestion on Main Street, and it wants him to do something to reduce it. Harry thinks about it for a while, talks to the local engineers, and comes up with a plan for widening Main Street. It will cost $2.5 million and take six months of construction time, but it will effectively solve the congestion problem. The city council reads his report and rejects it overwhelmingly: "We want to reduce traffic on Main Street but not at that cost. We are paying you to be smart. Can't you find a better way?"

Harry goes back to his office and recalls his social science training. It occurs to him that what he really has is a choice problem. Many people now choose to use Main Street instead of some alternative route. If he knew why they made that decision, he might be able to influence their choice and get them off Main Street. Naturally, he begins by drawing a tree (remember that the asterisks designate a decision point):

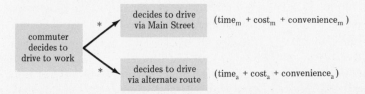

Presumably, the combination of time, cost, and convenience produces a certain amount of utility on each possible route, and the commuter chooses the route that maximizes his utility (or that minimizes his disutility). Harry does not have to calculate what that utility is for each route. It is sufficient to realize that if he changes the characteristics of a route (time, cost, convenience), he will affect people's decisions and hence affect the amount of traffic. Now what can he do?

STOP AND THINK. **Think of some actions that Harry might take to affect relative time, cost, or convenience.**

How could he affect relative cost? He could put up toll gates along Main Street and charge for its use. No, the city council would never buy that idea. But, what can he do to affect time and convenience? He decides to install 10 new stop signs along Main Street. The inconvenience of constant starting and stopping will now divert traffic onto alternative routes—a neat, cheap solution. The city council gives Harry a raise and some new responsibilities (plus a shovel and 10 stop signs).

It is now your turn to be social scientist. Harry has used choice notions to devise an interesting solution. You take over and figure out what kinds of people will be affected most by his solution.

STOP AND THINK. **What kinds of drivers will continue to use Main Street and what kinds will switch?**

Obviously local traffic will still tend to use Main Street, whereas people with more distant destinations will find it easier to find acceptable alternative routes. Likewise, the ratio of strangers to locals should increase along Main Street, since the strangers are unaware of alternative routes. Types of cars will be affected as well. People driving automatic-shift cars will be more likely to continue using Main Street than people with manual-shift cars because the inconvenience of stop-and-go driving is less for them. To the extent that manual-shift cars tend to be tired old heaps or else noisy new high-performance cars, the traffic remaining on Main Street will seem more civilized and middle class. Since the traffic diverted onto side streets will be noisier, Harry can definitely count on letters of complaint from residents of parallel streets. And, finally, since strangers will tend to see only Main Street, they will come away with an impression of a higher-class town than they would have otherwise.

We discovered a whole series of relatively interesting predictions from a relatively simple tree—and without even having to calculate numerical utility values.

4.5.2 *COLLEGE AS A CHOICE*

Becky is trying to decide where to go to college. She has been accepted at Podunk University and Famous University. Which should she choose? She has read all about decision trees and tries to represent her problem this way:

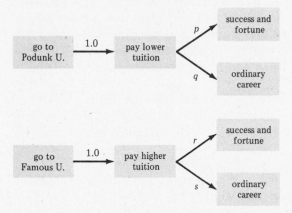

Famous University charges much more tuition, but its graduates have a greater chance of success (that is, p is less than r). Since she does not know what the difference in probable success is, she cannot work out an exact solution. After talking to a number of people in her major field, she decides that it would make a 15–25 percentage point difference if she goes to Famous. She is very ambitious, and it seems to her that the added chance of success is large enough to justify the extra cost. She will simply have to do more part-time work and borrow more money to pay the extra cost.

Becky is not only ambitious, she is very smart, and so she decides that a decision of this importance is worth extra thought.

She will think about it for a few more days, and if she cannot figure out a better alternative to achieve success, she will go to Famous University. She uses the decision tree as an aid to thinking about the problem and begins by asking herself questions about it. Why do graduates of Famous University have a greater chance of success? Is it because they are better educated? Well possibly, but as far as she can tell the main difference is in the prestige value of the different degrees. Does this suggest any interesting alternatives?

STOP AND THINK. As originally formulated, the problem is too narrow. Try to think of some overlooked alternative.

Becky decides that the real problem is how to get a Famous degree, and she knows that she does not have to go to Famous University for four years to do this but only needs to graduate from there. Like other universities, Famous University loses a lot of freshmen and sophomores for various reasons; hence it is willing to accept junior and senior transfers from other schools. So one additional alternative is to go to Podunk for the first two years of college, transfer to Famous Unversity, and then graduate from there. This alternative is cheaper than going to Famous for four years, and its outcome is just as good. She can realize her ambitions at a lower cost.

One other principle is of use in dealing with trees that have substantial nonmonetary effects or that have some missing probabilities. It is often possible to *simplify* the trees until they are solvable. For example, you may end up trying to compare two branches whose monetary outcomes are different but that both involve moving to New York. It is hard to evaluate the utility of such a move; but you do not have to do so. Since the same unknown utility appears on both branches, its net effect will be zero; you can ignore it.

Sometimes trees become very complex. It is often possible to prune them a little. For example, some very complicated set of branches may begin with a very low probability branch, or there may be some very low probability branch connecting it to the outcome. Unless the outcome of that branch is *very* large (compared to the other outcomes), you can simply forget the whole branch. Prune it, erase it: Multiplying the low probability by the outcome will produce a very small number that is not likely to affect the overall decision. Obviously, if the low probability branch is connected to some relatively large outcome (say, loss of life), you would not use this technique.

Example: Voting as a Choice (Optional)

Democratic societies provide citizens with opportunities to vote. Citizens vote in national, regional, and local elections for public officials; they vote in union elections for officers; they vote in elections in voluntary organizations; they vote in schools. Political participation—as represented by a vote—is a major individual right in a free society. Some societies enforce a rule that everyone must vote. Most democratic societies and most organizations, however, provide individuals with the right to vote but do not require that the right be exercised. Some people vote, and others do not.

Suppose we consider the decision of whether to vote as a choice, rather than as an absolute social duty. How could we evaluate that choice?

STOP AND THINK. **What are the alternatives? What are the possible outcomes? What are the values of these outcomes?**

The alternatives are simple enough, or we can make them simple enough: I can vote, or not vote. I want to evaluate the expected value of voting and compare it with the expected value of not voting.

In order to make such an evaluation I need to identify what can happen as a result of my vote in combination with the votes of everyone else. I might notice that the outcome of an election, if I assume only two candidates, must be one of three things: (1) My candidate wins. (2) There is a precise tie between the two candidates. (3) My candidate loses. Thus I have a tree that looks like this:

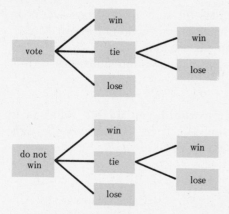

Notice that we have added "win-lose" branches to the tree after the ties. We assume that any election procedure specifies some rules for dealing with a tie and converting it into either a win or a loss. According to our tree, there are only two possible outcomes, win or lose. Within our model, therefore, we need to be able to specify the value for winning and the value for losing.

STOP AND THINK. **How would you do this? What is the difference to you whether your candidate wins or loses?**

There seem to be four general items of "value" in this situation. The first is the value to me of my candidate's being elected. This might include the value to me of his policies; it might also include the psychic value to me of having someone "like me" prove himself successful; it might include anything that I value that is associated with the election of my preferred candidate. The second item of value to me is that of the other candidate's being elected. We need to reflect the fact that even if my less preferred candidate is chosen, I still obtain some benefits. Some of his policies, for example, may be policies I support. The third item of value involved in the decision to vote is the value to me of the costs of voting. Voting involves the expenditures of time and energy; it also involves some social costs if the society has attitudes about the appropriateness of someone like me being allowed to vote. Similarly, the fourth item of value to me is the costs of not voting.

In order to use such values in our model, however, we need some way of representing them. Since we do not know exactly how to assign specific numbers to the various values, we will need some way of assigning nonnumerical values to our outcomes.

STOP AND THINK. How would you do it? What is a general way of representing the four values even though you do not know their exact sizes?

We need to define four values:

$V_1 =$ the value of a victory by my candidate.
$V_2 =$ the value of a victory by the other candidate.
$V_3 =$ the value of the act of voting.
$V_4 =$ the value of the act of not voting.

We will see what we can do without knowing exactly what these values might be.

We need something else. We need to be able to associate probabilities with each of the branches on our tree. It seems reasonable to assume that if there is a precise tie, the probability of winning is $\frac{1}{2}$ and the probability of losing is $\frac{1}{2}$. In fact, one standard way of deciding the outcome of a tie election is by tossing a coin. But what probabilities should we associate with "win," "tie," and "lose" in the first place?

STOP AND THINK. What values would you assign? What is a general way of representing these probabilities?

The probability of winning depends on my vote. If I do not vote and my candidate ties, I know that he would have won had I voted. If I do not vote and my candidate loses by precisely one vote, I know that he would have tied had I voted. Thus I need to know the probability of four events *if I do not vote:*

$p_1 =$ the probability of winning without my vote.
$p_2 =$ the probability of tying without my vote.

$p_3 =$ the probability of losing by precisely one vote without my vote.
$1 - p_1 - p_2 - p_3 =$ the probability of losing by more than one vote without my vote.

Since I do not know the exact values for the four probabilities, I will use the letter values on my tree:

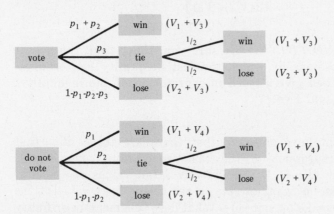

We now have a complete decision tree with very few actual numbers in it. Can we determine whether I should vote?

With the information contained in the tree, I cannot say whether I should vote or not. However, I can determine the conditions under which I should vote. The procedure is the same as the procedure when the actual numbers are available. First, we determine the expected value of the choice to vote:

$$EV \text{(vote)} = (p_1 + p_2)(V_1 + V_3) + p_3(V_1 + V_3)/2 + p_3(V_2 + V_3)/2$$
$$+ (1 - p_1 - p_2 - p_3)(V_2 + V_3)$$
$$= V_2 + V_3 + p_1(V_1 - V_2) + p_2(V_1 - V_2)$$
$$+ p_3(V_1 - V_2)/2$$

Next we find the expected value of the choice not to vote:

$$EV \text{(do not vote)} = p_1(V_1 + V_4) + p_2(V_1 + V_4)/2 + p_2(V_2 + V_4)/2$$
$$+ (1 - p_1 - p_2)(V_2 + V_4)$$
$$= V_2 + V_4 + p_1(V_1 - V_2) + p_2(V_1 - V_2)/2$$

Our rule is that we will vote when the expected value of voting is greater than the expected value of not voting. Thus we will vote if:

EV (vote) $> EV$ (do not vote)

$$[V_2 + V_3 + p_1(V_1 - V_2) + p_2(V_1 - V_2) + p_3(V_1 - V_2)/2]$$
$$> [V_2 + V_4 + p_1(V_1 - V_2) + p_2(V_1 - V_2)/2]$$

This simplifies to a basic concluding statement that we will vote if:

$$[(p_2 + p_3)(V_1 - V_2)] > [2(V_4 - V_3)]$$

> ***STOP AND THINK.*** **Be sure you understand the simple algebraic steps by which the last inequality has been obtained. Then give a word interpretation of the inequality: When should I vote?**

You might have observed that there are three important values in the expression of the basic conclusion: $(p_2 + p_3)$, $(V_1 - V_2)$, and $(V_4 - V_3)$. Relatively large values of the first two tend to make me want to vote; a relatively large value of the last one tends to make me not vote. What does this mean in ordinary terms? If we refer back to the meaning of p_2 and p_3, we observe that $(p_2 + p_3)$ is the probability that the election will be very close. The closer I expect the election to be, the more likely I will be to vote. $(V_1 - V_2)$ is the difference (to me) between the two candidates. If my candidate is much better for me than the other candidate, I am more likely to vote than I would be if both candidates were very similar. Finally, $(V_4 - V_3)$ measures the net cost of voting. V_4 is large if there is a good deal of effort associated with voting, and thus a good deal of value to nonvoting. V_3 will be large if there is a good deal of social credit given for voting or if my psychic sense of well-being for having voted is considerable.

If I want to decide whether to vote in a particular election, I might conceivably make such an analysis. I might also want to see what such an analysis tells me about actual voting. Can I predict anything about elections from this model of rational choice?

> ***STOP AND THINK.*** **What is the problem you might have in using this model to predict an individual's behavior?**

Although our model is formally a model of individual behavior, we rarely use it to predict individual behavior. Instead, we use it to predict the behavior of groups of people. If we are interested in applying our model of choice to consumer behavior, for example, we do not try to say what each individual consumer will do in the face of a price change. Rather, we try to say what the aggregate movement of consumers will be.

> **STOP AND THINK.** Why would such a strategy make sense? Can you think of any reason why a model of individual behavior might be better at predicting aggregate behavior than individual behavior? Go back and reread page 109 and the traffic route problem, Section 4.5.1.

There are two slightly different reasons for this phenomenon.

Explanation 1. Suppose that there are many factors involved in the decision to vote, including the ones in our model. Suppose that different people have different factors and weigh them differently. But suppose that the factors in our model are a small part of everyone's decisions (or a major part of a few people's). And suppose that the other factors are so heterogeneous that they end up canceling each other out when we look at the behavior of many people. If all of these assumptions are almost correct, then the predictions of the model will be correct even if they account for only a small part of any individual's behavior. (In practice, the assumptions are used more often than they are correct simply because they are convenient and powerful.)

Explanation 2. You will recall from the basic algebraic conclusion, a few pages back, that the chance of voting depends on the size of $(p_2 + p_3)$. That is, the closer the election (which makes p_2 and p_3 large), the greater the chance of the individual voting, *other things being held equal.* The prediction would not apply across a pair of situations like this: (1) The election is very close, but George's car breaks down on election day; it is ten miles to the poll, and it is snowing, and he is supposed to be finishing up a vital report. (2) The election is *not* at all close, but Henry has nothing to do that day and is bored with loafing; the sun is shining, and the polls are next door to his house. That is, it is very obviously inaccurate to take the basic conclusion that the closer the election, the greater the probability of someone's voting and then predict:

Since George's election is close, he will vote. Henry's election is not close, so he will not vote.

Now suppose we had not known anything at all about the personal situations of George and Henry but had only known that one was a voter in a tight race, while the other was a voter in an apparent landslide. We would then have made our erroneous predictions. What do we do? This is a serious problem in social science. Some social scientists try to avoid the problem by studying every situation in minute detail: "Get *all* the facts." It is obviously difficult to do so, however, since the number of possibly relevant facts is very, very large. Nonetheless, it is possible, and after a sufficiently exhaustive study of George and Henry these social scientists might be able to predict their (George's and Henry's) behavior with respect to voting on that particular day. But this is a lot of work to do in predicting the behavior of only two people, and we obviously need a better strategy for questions of more general interest such as the voting behavior of an entire population. Fortunately, we have such a better strategy available: the use of models. They are simplifications of the real world that concentrate on a few, potentially easily measurable variables. These models will undoubtedly make erroneous predictions about the behavior of some specific individuals, but they will do very well with respect to the behavior of whole populations. That is, George's special circumstances may lead him to stay home even though he is voting in a tight race, but all the other voters in George's district will not have the *same* special factors affecting them. Some will have special factors that make it even more likely that they will vote (such as, someone with a situation like Henry's but who lives in George's district). Thus some of the people in George's district will be even more likely to vote than we predict, and some will be less likely. In the aggregate these effects tend to cancel out because they compensate for each other. Thus we can make an accurate prediction that tomorrow's election will bring a 73% turnout but will have difficulty identifying exactly which specific people will vote. Just as in the example of the stop signs on Main Street, it was easy to predict that traffic would be diverted but hard to predict which specific people would be diverted.

You should understand the logic of the move from individual models of individual behavior to predictions of aggregate behaviors. It underlies much of modern social science. We can take advantage of such assumptions in our voting model. We wish to predict variations in voting turnout in an aggregate of voters.

STOP AND DO IT. **Use the model to predict variations in voter turnout. Look at the basic algebraic conclusion and try to predict variations in turnout as a function of the variables in the model.**

Our model predicts the following:

1. The closer the election, the greater the turnout.
2. The greater the difference between the candidates, the greater the turnout.
3. The greater the difficulty of voting (for instance, weather, distance), the smaller the turnout.
4. The greater the social legitimacy of nonvoting, the smaller the turnout.

These simple predictions are, for the most part, consistent with actual results. A rational model of voting participation predicts variation in voting turnout among different groups of voters, different offices, and different candidates.

4.6 ALTERNATIVE DECISION RULES (OPTIONAL)

The formal model of choice that we have presented in this chapter is one that assumes the following things:

Assumption 1
The individual has a list of alternatives from which he chooses. (The list is assumed to exist and to be complete. Although the model can be used informally to generate new alternatives, the formal model assumes that the alternatives are given in advance.)

Assumption 2
The individual can draw a map of the consequences of each alternative. (This map, in the form of a tree, shows all of the possible consequences that might stem from each alternative. The tree terminates in a number of final outcomes.)

Assumption 3
An individual can attach a value to each outcome. (The value reflects his preferences and has the property of being a cardinal

number or a symbol representing a cardinal number. We have reflected this assumption by showing the monetary, or utility, or other value of each outcome.)

These assumptions are quite general to rational models of choice. The specific (expected value) model with which we have been concerned adds two additional assumptions to the list:

Assumption 4

An individual can specify the probability of any particular outcome, given the choice of any particular alternative. (We have reflected this assumption by associating a probability to each branch on a decision tree.)

Assumption 5

An individual chooses among the alternatives given to him by maximizing expected value. (That is, he multiplies the value of each outcome that might possibly occur by the probability of that outcome and chooses the alternative with the highest expected value.)

Some formal models of choice use the first three assumptions, but they introduce a different way of moving from them to a decision. We can illustrate some of these alternative models by examining a simple situation. Consider a football team preparing for a game. For convenience we will assume that this team has precisely four plays, which are:

Alternative 1. Pass short.

Alternative 2. Pass long.

Alternative 3. Power sweep.

Alternative 4. Quick slant.

The opposition is known to have three defensive formations: Attack (A), Bandit (B), and Cat (C). Our team is interested in gaining yardage, but the yardage gained on any given play depends on the defensive formation. In fact, the coaches know that the possible outcomes can be represented by the following table:

		IF MY TEAM CHOOSES PLAY			
		1	*2*	*3*	*4*
AND THE OPPOSITION	A	10	20	−15	2
USES DEFENSIVE	B	14	−20	3	5
FORMATION	C	0	0	12	3

The entries in the table are the number of yards gained. For example, if I choose play number 2 and they use defense A, I will gain 20 yards; had they chosen defense B, I would have lost 20 yards. What offensive play should I select?

STOP AND THINK. How would you decide? What is your model?

In order to use the model we have presented in this chapter, we would need to know one additional piece of information: the probability that the opposition will use formation A, B, or C. Suppose the probability of A is 0.1, the probability of B is 0.3, and the probability of C is 0.6. We can calculate the expected values:

$$EV\,(\text{play 1}) = (0.1)\,(10) \quad + (0.3)\,(14) \quad + (0.6)\,(0) \quad = 5.2$$
$$EV\,(\text{play 2}) = (0.1)\,(20) \quad + (0.3)\,(-20) + (0.6)\,(0) \quad = -4.0$$
$$EV\,(\text{play 3}) = (0.1)\,(-15) + (0.3)\,(3) \quad + (0.6)\,(12) = 6.6$$
$$EV\,(\text{play 4}) = (0.1)\,(2) \quad + (0.3)\,(5) \quad + (0.6)\,(3) \quad = 3.5$$

If we want to maximize expected yards gained, we would choose the third alternative, the power sweep. This famous result in football theory is known as the Lombardi-Shula theorem. (In fact, you may be interested to know that professional football teams devote considerable time and expense to estimating the probability that their opponents will do one thing or another under certain conditions and to calculating optimal strategies given that information.)

Suppose, however, that we did not know the probabilities of the various outcomes. Then we would have to construct a new model by specifying a new decision rule that did not require knowledge of the probability of any particular outcome. Such situations can occur easily.

STOP AND THINK. Can you think of what other decision rules might be? Look at the football example. If you did not know what the likely opposition strategy was, how would you choose yours?

A standard situation in social behavior is one in which you have two rational actors confronting each other (say, across a collective bargaining table). Each tries to act intelligently; each knows that the outcome depends not only on his own choices but also on the choices of the other. In such a situation we cannot assume easily that there is some fixed probability for one actor against which the other actor behaves. We need a different conception of what a rational choice might mean.

Considerable effort has been devoted to trying to specify some alternative decision rules that might be described as "rational" or "intelligent." By focusing our attention on the expected value decision rule, we would not want to give the impression that it is the only possible model. There are others, depending upon what basic information you have available to you.

An optimistic decision rule: We might say that an individual should (or would) choose among alternatives by looking at the best outcome that could possibly result with each alternative. Such an optimistic view of the world produces the following maximum values (that is, the best outcome that might occur for any given play):

Max (play 1) = 14
Max (play 2) = 20
Max (play 3) = 12
Max (play 4) = 5

(Be sure you understand how these numbers are derived.) If we want to maximize the maximum possible value (*maximax*), we would choose the second alternative, the long pass. We can predict that such a decision rule might be used by a basically optimistic person. This decision rule also has some normative value in certain situations. Suppose it is late in the game, your team is behind, and you want to maximize your chances of winning. Since you are already behind, conservative play will not win it for you. You must give yourself the best chance of making some *big* gains. Since you cannot predict what the opponent will do, then assume the best possible actions from him and maximize accordingly. Maximax is the way.

A pessimistic decision rule: We might say that an individual should (or would) choose among alternatives by looking at the worst thing that could possibly happen to him if he selects each alternative. This pessimistic world view yields the following minimum values (that is, the worst outcome that might occur for any given play):

Min (play 1) = 0
Min (play 2) = −20
Min (play 3) = −15
Min (play 4) = 2

(Be sure you understand how these numbers are derived.) If we want to maximize the lowest possible value (*maximin*), we would choose the fourth alternative, the quick slant. We can predict that such a decision rule might be used by a basically pessimistic person. This decision rule also has some normative value in certain situations. Suppose that your team is ahead. You want to preserve your point margin, take no chances, and play in a conservative way. You assume the most harmful possible defense will occur and plan accordingly. Maximin is the way.

A minimum variation decision rule: We might say that an individual should (or would) choose among alternatives in terms of the range of possible outcomes and wish to keep the range to a minimum. That is, he might want to minimize surprise. The range of possible surprise (that is, the best outcome minus the worst outcome) for our alternative plays is:

Range (play 1) = 14
Range (play 2) = 40
Range (play 3) = 27
Range (play 4) = 3

(Be sure you understand how these numbers are derived.) If we want to minimize surprise (*minirange*), we would choose the fourth alternative, the quick slant. We can predict that such a decision rule might be used by someone with a strong bias in favor of certainty. He wishes to minimize the chance of error in his prediction. Normative uses of this decision rule are harder to imagine. Perhaps one of your friends has a weak heart and you are interested in producing a nice, tame, unexciting game for him. Mini-range is the way.

   A *minimum regret decision rule:* Finally, we might say that an individual should (or would) choose among alternatives in terms of the possible regret he could experience. Regret here refers to the observation that if I had known what defensive formation was going to be used, I might have chosen a different offense and done better. The difference between what I achieve and what I could have achieved with perfect advance knowledge is a measure of my regret. For example, I decide on play number 1. What could happen? If the defense uses formation A, then I actually gain 0 yards. *But* if I had only known that they were going to use A, then I would have chosen to use play number 3 and gained 12 yards. The difference between 0 and 12 is the amount of regret I feel in the situation. Likewise, suppose I decide to use play number 2 and the defense uses formation B—then I lose 20 yards. *But* if only I had predicted he was going to use B, then I would have known to use play number 1 and gained 14 yards. The difference between these two possibilities establishes my potential regret of 34 yards. The maximum regret (*maxregret*) for each alternative play is:

Maxregret (play 1) = 12
Maxregret (play 2) = 34
Maxregret (play 3) = 35
Maxregret (play 4) = 18

(Be sure you understand how these numbers are derived.) If we wish to minimize the maximum regret (*minimax regret*) we would choose the first alternative, the short pass. We can predict that such decision rules might be used by someone with a particular kind of individual psychology. He is the sort of person who lies awake at night reviewing the day's mistakes—"If only I had done. . . ." It is also possible to find normative uses for this decision rule. Suppose that the coach is concerned about keeping his job and that the board of trustees contains some self-styled football experts. The coach is very much concerned about the possibility that one of these trustees will say to him: "Why it was obvious that they were going to use defensive formation B. I could just feel it in my bones. And you were so unperceptive that you went right ahead and used play number 2 instead of number 1. You're fired." With such after-the-fact experts as his boss, the coach might well minimax regret on crucial plays.

STOP AND THINK. Do you understand how each of the decision rules works? Notice that it is quite possible for different decision rules to produce quite different rational decisions. What does this mean?

In effect, we have produced five different choice models by varying the decision-rule assumption. Each of the five models has been used in the literature; each has some claim to legitimacy. There is no one choice model. There is not even one rational choice model. You will need to choose among models in terms of the usual trinity of truth, beauty, and justice. If you know the basic probabilities and the utilities associated with each outcome, then you probably should choose the expected utility model. Without this information you may want to try the maximax, maximin, minirange, or minimax regrets model, depending upon the circumstances. There is still another model, game theory, which we do not explicate here, which is also useful for these information-deficient situations. Though they are all minor variations in terms of the differences in assumptions, they often produce substantially different results.

References

Sheen Kassouf, *Normative Decision Making* (Englewood Cliffs, N.J.: Prentice-Hall, 1970).

R. Duncan Luce and Howard Raiffa, *Games and Decisions* (New York: Wiley, 1957).

Howard Raiffa, *Decision Analysis* (Reading, Mass.: Addison-Wesley, 1970).

Problems 4.2

1. In each of the following situations draw the decision tree and indicate which choice a rational person would make.

   (a) *Alternative 1*
       Write down the name of a day of the week on a piece of paper.

If it is the same day as George's birthday, you win $5; if it is the same day as Mabel's birthday, you win $10.

Alternative 2
You are paid $2.

(b) *Alternative 1*
Choose two children at random from the first grade. If the two are of the same sex, you win $4. If the children are of different sexes and the boy is older, you win $2. Otherwise, you *lose* $8.

Alternative 2
You are paid nothing; you lose nothing.

(c) *Alternative 1*
Marry Mary. She has a million dollars but is about to gamble it all in Canadian uranium stocks. Such stocks have a 10% chance of doubling and a 90% chance of becoming worthless.

Alternative 2
Marry Sally. She has scrimped, saved, gone without shoes and lunches, and managed to put $50,000 into U.S. government bonds.

(d) *Alternative 1*
Stay at home. You lose a sale ($40), but if it snows, you save the cost of a new fender ($150).

Alternative 2
Go out. You make a sale, but if it snows, you lose a fender. (You may either assume that the chance of snow is 50%; or you may wish to solve for the probability where one alternative becomes better than the other.)

2. A recent study for the Republican party indicates the following effects of a face-to-face contact during an election campaign.

   i. If a Republican precinct worker contacts a registered Republican, he increases the probability that the Republican will vote at all from 0.5 to 0.6 and the probability that he will vote Republican from 0.8 to 0.9.

   ii. If a Republican precinct worker contacts a registered Democrat, he increases the probability that the Democrat will vote at all from 0.4 to 0.6 and the probability that he will vote Republican from 0.25 to 0.3.

   (a) You have the registration lists, so that you know the party affiliation of everyone. Would a rational Republican precinct worker contact Democrats, or Republicans, or both?

   (b) You have no registration information about voters. Hence when you knock on a door, you have no advance knowledge about the person inside. How large does p, the probability of contacting a

Republican, have to be in order to make Republican precinct work profitable?

3. The transmission on George's car breaks down. He has to decide whether to fix it or junk the car and replace it with another used car. He knows that Friendly Al's Used-Car Lot will charge him $90 for a shiny new used car and will guarantee it for a year. He knows that a garage will charge him $30 to pull his transmission and inspect it. If the inspection shows that the problem is minor, it can be repaired for an additional $30; if the problem is major, it will cost an additional $150 to repair. Any repairs are guaranteed for one year. The probability of a minor problem is ⅔, of a major problem, ⅓. (*Assume:* George is only interested in getting the cheapest possible transportation for one year; that if the transmission is fixed, nothing else on the car will need repairs for one year; and that George is the type of driver who will ruin either car in one year of driving so that there will be no resale value at the end of the time.) What course of action should George follow?

4. You are a telephone sales agent for a socially useful product. You are provided with a list of potential customers and their telephone numbers. For each sale that you make you receive $20 commission. The company requires that you make all telephone calls station-to-station (that is, you are charged no matter who answers) and that you pay the costs of the calls. Each call you place costs $1. Your experience is that you are successful in reaching the individuals on the list 3 times out of ten, and you are successful in selling the product to 2 out of every 10 contacted persons.

   (a) Draw the decision tree. What is the expected value of each telephone call?
   (b) The telephone company also offers a person-to-person telephone service at higher cost. In this service you pay the charge only if you actually reach the person being called. How much more would you be willing to pay per call for such a service if your employer would allow you to use it? Explain.

5. Suppose seat belts cost $30 and that they cut the probability of being killed in an auto accident by half. Suppose also that last year in the United States 50,000 people (out of a population of 200 million) would have been killed in these accidents if they had not worn seat belts.

   (a) How much does a rational man's life have to be worth before he will buy a seat belt?
   (b) Suppose a new seat belt is being introduced. It reduces the probability of a fatality to one-third its original value and sells for $120. Who would buy it?

(c) Discuss what relevant considerations are omitted in this formulation of the problem.

6. If Paul Revere wished to minimize effort, under what conditions would he say "two if by land and one if by sea" rather than "two if by sea and one if by land"?

7. (This problem is difficult.) The Royal Institute for Ulcer Detection is developing a two-test diagnostic procedure for detecting stomach ulcers along with treatment procedures.

Test A
This test costs $100 to administer. A patient will exhibit a *positive* response on Test A about 60% of the time.

Test B
This test costs $150 to administer. A patient will exhibit a *positive* response on Test B about 70% of the time.

Furthermore, it is known that if a patient has a positive response on Test A, the probability is $5/6$ that he will have a positive response on Test B; if he has a negative response on Test A, the probability of a positive response on B is $1/2$. Similarly, a patient with a positive response on B has a probability of a positive response on A of $5/7$; if he has a negative response on B, the probability of a positive response on A is $1/3$. There are three treatment procedures:

Treatment I
No treatment. This will "cure" the patient (with certainty) only if the response on both tests is negative. This treatment is free.

Treatment II
Diet. This will cure the patient (with certainty) if the response on no more than one test is positive. This treatment costs $200.

Treatment III
Drugs. This will cure the patient (with certainty) regardless of the test outcomes. This treatment costs $1000.

Assume that a doctor wishes to ensure that all patients will be cured and minimize the expected cost of curing them. What is the best test and treatment procedure (that is, what tests and treatment should be given) to satisfy the doctor?

8. (This problem is difficult.) Captain Chou is in command of a company of Chinese regulars in combat along the northern border. Each day he must decide whether to issue ammunition to his troops. If he does not issue ammunition and the enemy does not attack, he and his men sleep peacefully through the day. Over the past few weeks, he has

observed that when he prepared for the enemy, but the enemy does not attack, his men kill about four of their own comrades. On the other hand, when he fails to prepare and the enemy attacks, he loses about 46 men killed (compared with about 10 men killed when he is prepared and the enemy attacks). Captain Chou wishes to act to minimize expected deaths under these circumstances.

(a) On any given day will Captain Chou issue ammunition or not? Why?

(b) Suppose Captain Chou could establish an intelligence communications system that could send a signal about enemy intentions using either of the following predetermined codes:

Code 1
Signal means enemy will attack. No signal means enemy will not attack.

Code 2
Signal means enemy will not attack. No signal means enemy will attack.

Chou knows that if the signal is sent by his men but detected by the enemy (the probability of detecting a sent signal is ½), he loses two men in his intelligence unit; but the enemy does not alter his plans.

Under what circumstances should Chou establish such a system? Why?

(c) How would the answers to (b) be affected if the signal technology were such that a signal got through only about half of the time? (*Note:* You must figure out the probability that a signal was sent *given* the fact that none was received; this is different from the probability that a signal will be received *given* the fact that it was sent.)

Problems 4.3

1. You are the owner of Honesty First electrical contractors. Today there will be a luncheon meeting of the local contractors. You know that only at 10% of these meetings are important issues ever dis-

cussed—that is, which of the contractors is to submit the low bid for some future contract. (There are only four other contractors in the area. You settle the problem of who is to be low bidder by rolling a fair, five-sided die.) You know that submitting the low bid and winning a contract is worth $100,000 to you on the average. Alteratively, you can decide to spend the afternoon playing golf at the local club. From past experience you know that there is a 50% chance of meeting someone important there and that, on the average, meeting important people has resulted in obtaining $6000 worth of business for you.

Considering only maximum gain for your firm:

(a) Should you go to the contractors' luncheon or play golf?

(b) What would it be worth to you to know in advance whether your friends were going to discuss important issues today?

(c) Smiling Ralph (the businessman's friend) has offered to give perfect forecasts of what kind of business will be discussed and also to substitute a loaded die to guarantee that you will win the contract bid. How much will you be willing to pay for Ralph's services (ignore [b])?

2. You are the production manager of the Fraud Motor Company and are concerned about the effects of sloppy production on your profits. You hire some students for the summer to do some research for you. Their report gives the following information: *Ten percent* of the auto frames produced by the shop are defective; half of these defects are serious and half are minor; there is a quality control program, but it is so crude that it can only detect serious defects, and even then it only has a 0.6 probability of detecting them. Thus most defects are not caught until the car is fully assembled and road tested. Fixing a minor defect before assembly costs $10, but it costs $100 to fix after the car is completely assembled. Fixing a serious defect before final assembly costs $100, but it costs $1000 to fix after the car is completely assembled.

(a) What is the expected cost, per car produced, of the sloppy frame production?

(b) General Inspection, Incorporated, has a new device that detects 100% of all minor defects. (It only works on minor defects.) What is the maximum price you should pay for their services?

(c) The Laguna Chanting Society has examined your problem, and it simply offers to cure all defects *right at the source* in the auto frame shop. Assuming that General Inspection, Inc., is no longer in the picture, what is the maximum value of the society's service to you?

3. Herman Smith wants to sell hot dogs at the President's inauguration. He already has the franchise. He knows that he can make $1 net profit

per hot dog sold. He estimates that he can sell 10,000 hot dogs if a Republican is being inaugurated; only 8,000 if a Democrat (unless he is an Easterner—in which case Smith can sell 15,000 hot dogs). He assesses the chances of the Democratic hopefuls as follows if a liberal Republican is the opposition:

	CHANCE OF BEING NOMINATED	CHANCE OF BEING ELECTED IF NOMINATED
Western Democrat	½	⅕
Eastern Democrat	⅕	½
Southern Democrat	³⁄₁₀	⅘

If the Republican nominee is conservative, Smith believes the Republicans are certain to win. All Republicans are either liberal or conservative.

(a) Which kind of Republican candidate will Mr. Smith prefer if his objective is to maximize his expected earnings from this franchise? Show calculations.

(b) Suppose someone offered to guarantee the nomination of whichever *Democratic* candidate Smith wanted. How much should Smith be willing to pay for this service? Why?

(c) Suppose someone offered to guarantee the nomination of whichever *Republican* candidate Smith wanted. How much should he be willing to pay for this service? Why?

(d) How much should Smith be willing to pay for a perfect prediction of the nominations and elections? Why?

4. In November there will be a major circus parade in downtown Monterey. Herman Smith has obtained (for $50) the exclusive rights to sell sunhats and raincoats at the parade. Under the terms of his contract, he must sell sunhats at 75 cents and raincoats at $2; but he can determine the number of hats and coats that he stocks.

From past experience with parades like this one in California, Smith knows that his sales will depend heavily on the weather. If the sun shines, he can sell 260 sunhats and 15 raincoats. If it is raining, he can sell 170 raincoats and 115 sunhats. If it is cloudy, he can sell 50 sunhats and 75 raincoats. In November the Monterey weather is fairly predictable. It rains about one day out of six; it is cloudy (but does not rain) about one day out of three; the sun shines the rest of the time.

Smith can obtain sunhats in 100 piece lots, and raincoats in 50 piece lots at the following prices:

Sunhats		Raincoats	
100	. . . $40	50	. . . $15
200	. . . $70	100	. . . $30
300	. . . $90	150	. . . $40
		200	. . . $45

At these prices the suppliers will accept no returns; any unsold merchandise must be dumped.

(a) Assuming that Smith is rational, how many sunhats and how many raincoats will he stock?

(b) The Fair Weather Forecasting Service can predict the November weather with certainty. The service provides such predictions for a fee. If Smith is rational, how much should he be willing to pay for such a service?

(c) A second forecasting service offers a cheaper but less precise service. Although they are perfectly accurate, they can only predict whether the day will have rain or not. They cannot tell whether it is going to be cloudy or sunny. How much should Smith be willing to pay for this service as an alternative to the one in (b)?

(d) The Medicine Man Corporation can control the November weather with certainty. How much should Smith be willing to pay for such a service (ignoring [b] and [c])?

5. There are three stages in bringing a new product to market:

Stage I
Constructing the prototype.

Stage II
Testing it.

Stage III
Putting it into full-scale production.

Out of every 10 such products 7 die during Stage I. Of the survivors, only 10% perform well enough during tests to warrant going to Stage III. Only 1 out of every 5 products that reaches this stage is a success. The costs associated with each stage are $100,000, $20,000, and $200,-000 respectively for a new tape deck. If the tape deck is successful at every development stage, the anticipated profits are $60 million.

(a) What is the expected value of trying to build a new tape deck? Should the effort be made? Why?

(b) For $15,000 a consulting firm will predict (they are always right) whether or not a prototype that makes it through Stage I will perform well enough in tests to justify going to Stage III. Are their services worth it? Why?

(c) The same firm, for a modest $20 million per tape deck will take over the entire process—including costs—and guarantee that the probability that their tape deck will make the profit is ⅖. Are their services worth it? Are they worth more than the prediction? (Show tree.)

(d) Suppose that by hiring a particularly skillful engineering technician you could reduce the mortality rate in the first stage from 70% to 60%. How much would such a technician be worth to you, assuming that all of the opportunities outlined in (b) and (c) are still available to you?

6. The *Wall Street Journal*, March 27, 1967, published a description of a simple get-rich-quick scheme called the Federal Land Lottery. Every month the government puts up 100 parcels of land. For fifty cents per acre you may buy a mineral rights option on one of these pieces of land. If the land turns out to have oil on it, you can immediately sell it to an oil company for $100,000. In order to be "fair" about who gets the land, the government holds a lottery for each piece of land. For $10 you may file an entry for a particular piece of land and be included in the lottery. The government actually puts all the entries into a barrel and draws one out at random to determine who will be awarded the mineral rights for that parcel of land. If you win the lottery, you have to purchase the mineral rights option. (The average parcel of land is 2000 acres.) You then look around to see whether an oil company wants to buy your land. Each month an average of 10 parcels of land turn out to have oil on them. And each month an average of 1000 people enter the lottery for a particular piece of land.

(a) Should you pay your $10 and file an entry?

(b) The *Wall Street Journal* also reports that there are geological consulting firms that examine the land before the auction to see which parcels are most likely to have oil. They will sell you a list of recommended parcels for $10 per recommended parcel (that is, two "hot tips" cost $20). Their recommendations are not perfect: On the average they forecast correctly with a probability of 0.4. Should you buy their services?

(c) What would you be willing to pay for perfect forecasts of which parcels had oil on them?

7. Prove that the ability to control an outcome can never be worth less than the ability to predict the outcome (from the point of view of expected value theories of rationality).

Problems 4.4

1. Matilda Smith has $1000 that she wants to invest. She knows that any investment has some risk and that she cannot be sure what it

will return. She has, however, retained an investment adviser. The adviser has indicated what he thinks are the probabilities of gains of various amounts to be realized from the several investment opportunities Matilda is considering. He has advised Matilda that it would be a good idea to spread her investment over several different opportunities rather than concentrate all of her money on one.

(a) Matilda quickly fires her adviser, commenting that she wants to maximize expected value. Explain.

(b) Is it possible that Matilda acted too quickly? Explain a rationale for the adviser that would make his advice consistent with maximizing expected value.

2. Insurance is a profitable business. The only way that insurance can be a profitable business is if insurance is a "bad gamble" from the point of view of expected value. On the average a person spends more on insurance than he receives in benefits (particularly if you include the lost opportunities to invest that money in alternative ways). Outline a rational model of insurance buying and then, using the model, answer the following questions:

(a) Why might the rates charged for any form of insurance tend to rise over time?

(b) Why might rich people buy insurance against major risks but not minor ones; why might poor people buy insurance against minor risks but not major ones?

(c) Why might the same person purchase insurance from an insurance company *and* purchase stock in the same company?

3. If citizens were rational, who would commit robberies? How would a rational society organize criminal justice differently from the way we do?

Problems 4.5

1. Some universities and colleges operate under honor codes with respect to cheating. Honor codes normally require that an individual not cheat on examinations and that he not permit another person to cheat.

(a) Outline a model of rational student behavior and use it to predict when an individual would cheat and when he would permit cheating.

(b) Use your model to predict any differences you would expect in honor code violations between men and women, good students and poor students, resident students and commuters, freshmen and sophomores.

(c) If you wished to strengthen the honor code, what policies would you suggest to the college on the basis of your model?

2. Many American states support community colleges, state colleges, and state universities from general tax revenues. This support permits qualified students to attend the institutions at tuition costs that are substantially below the costs charged at comparable private institutions.

   (a) Would a rational citizen of a state support such a scheme?
   (b) If you wished to organize a political coalition to require higher student charges at state-supported institutions, what groups would you seek as allies?
   (c) What demographic and social characteristics would you expect to see in citizens of states in which state institutions of higher education require substantial tuition as compared with citizens of states in which tuition is low?

3. When would a rational police officer ignore the commission of a crime he has witnessed? What predictions can you make about differential rates of ignoring crimes? Stemming from differences among police officers? From differences among criminals? From differences among crimes? From differences among situations? From other factors?

4. Develop a rational theory of the politics of women's liberation. Which women would you expect to find most strongly supportive of the movement? Which men? Under what circumstances would you expect political progress? What other predictions can you make? Be sure your predictions come from the analysis.

5. Show, by applying a model of rational choice, why you agree or disagree with the following statements:

   (a) According to a rational model of language, irregular verbs will, on the average, occur more frequently in ordinary speech than regular verbs.
   (b) According to a rational model of individual behavior, good teachers will be less likely to support educational reform than will poor teachers.
   (c) According to a rational model of mobility, American states having small populations will grow in population faster than large states (everything else being equal).
   (d) According to a rational model of choice, graduate students in English will take longer to earn their doctorates than will graduate students in physics.

6. Consider the following three alternative systems of health care:
   Alternative I
   A fee-for-service system in which individuals pay for any services they receive.
   Alternative II
   An insurance system in which individuals may either pay for services or purchase insurance that pays for services received.

Alternative III

A national health system in which the government uses general revenue sources to pay for services.

According to a rational model of behavior, would the choice of system affect the utilization of health services, the quality of health care, or the distribution of health care resources to different health problems?

7. What would a rational theory of language predict about natural languages? In your answer you should do the following things:

(a) Show how you would define a rational code for communication and illustrate your definition by solving a simple problem in the selection of code for communicating in a particular situation.

(b) Develop a series of predictions about natural languages that can be derived from the assumption that natural languages are designed rationally.

(c) Discuss the current controversy in education over the extent to which educational institutions should insist on proficiency in standard English regardless of any proficiency the child may have in another language (for example, Spanish, Black English, Chinese). In your discussion be sure to link your points clearly to the model you have developed.

8. Develop a rational model of marital choice. Then use it to address the following questions:

(a) Who will get married to whom and when?

(b) Who will get divorced from whom and when?

(c) What social policies could be adopted to encourage (or inhibit) marriage?

(d) What social policies could be adopted to encourage (or inhibit) divorce?

(e) To what extent do the answers to the questions depend on some general social norms in our society? What would happen if those norms changed?

Problems 4.6

1. Whenever there is a political campaign, political leaders face a series of difficult decisions. One of the most interesting is the problem of deciding whom to support (and when) in a primary campaign. Suppose that a particular party leader faces a decision in a primary election. He can support Smith or Brown or he can avoid a commitment, simply declaring himself neutral in the primary. The consequences stemming from these three alternatives depend, of course, on whether it is Smith or Brown who wins the nomination. Let us sup-

pose that our leader is mostly concerned about the number of patronage jobs that will be allocated to him and that the following table reflects the actual situation:

	IF SMITH WINS	IF BROWN WINS
If I am neutral	10 jobs	15 jobs
If I am for Smith	28 jobs	0 jobs
If I am for Brown	5 jobs	25 jobs

(a) What would the party leader do if he wants to maximize expected value and the probability of Smith's winning is equal to p? Show tree.

(b) What would he do if he maximizes the maximum return (maximax)? Show table.

(c) What would he do if he maximizes the minimum return maximin? Show table.

(d) What would he do if he minimizes the range (minirange)? Show table.

(e) What would he do if he minimizes the maximum regret (minimax regret)? Show table.

(f) If you were Brown, what could you do to improve your position?

2. Outline a theory of choice for a situation in which two individuals (or groups, or organizations, or nations) independently choose among several alternative actions and the outcomes for each depend on the joint choices. (*Example:* You choose whether to go to the beach or to the library. I choose whether to go to the library or to the movies. The pleasures we receive depend not only on our own choices but also on the choices of each other.)

(a) Use your theory to explore any one of the following situations:

   i. Labor-management negotiation.
   ii. International relations.
   iii. Cops and robbers.

(b) Show how your predictions in the model depend on the assumptions you make about the kind of decision rule used by the participants.

(c) Discuss the circumstances under which you would expect a *maximin* decision rule rather than an expected value decision rule.

chapter
five

exchange

5.1 INTRODUCTION

Situations in which exchange is either necessary or desirable appear rather pervasive in a world of many, often conflicting, goals. Our major concern in this section is with developing a generalized model of economic exchange. We will then see that the model is related to the choice models examined in Chapter Four and, not surprisingly, that choice behavior and exchange behavior are related. Like the model of rational choice, the model of exchange is a way of looking at behavior; it is not the behavior itself. For example, when we say "Trust is an exchange relationship," we mean that we choose to think about trust as though it were an exchange: I give you my trust in return for your being trustworthy. We can then examine the model and ask whether it correctly predicts behavior, whether it is aesthetically pleasing, and whether it leads to good worlds. Like all of the other models in this book, the exchange model is often an attractive way of thinking about things, but (also like the others) it is not perfect. It has major limitations. It is not always true, not always beautiful, not always just. It is only a set of ideas, not a religion. The exchange model grew out of observations like the following:

1. A woman in a store is seen exchanging money for a cart full of groceries. How did she decide on the goods in the cart, on the type and amount of each?
2. Manufacturers of cheese in Switzerland export more of their premium grade of cheese to the United States and keep more of their lower grades for sale to their home markets. How do they decide which cheese to export and which to keep?
3. Children in a playground are seen trading baseball cards (or bottle-cap sports figures, or bubble-gum cards, or candy-bar pictures). You observe that a child with a lot of one particular type of card is willing to trade four of that card for only one card of a type that he does not have. What determines these exchange ratios?
4. The Yir Yoront tribe of Australia is an essentially Paleolithic society—they are aboriginals. In this almost Stone Age society a complex trade pattern is observed. These people use stingray tails for spear points and special flat stones for ax heads. The stingrays can be caught locally. The ax heads are made by another tribe and come from 400 miles inland. There are many

tribes between the Yir Yoront and the inland tribe. These intermediate tribes trade spear points in one direction and ax heads in the other. In the Yir Yoront village people can exchange 12 stingray spear points for one ax head. The spear points apparently become more valuable as they move inland. A hundred and fifty miles inland of the village the exchange ratio is one spear point for one ax head. And presumably (the anthropologist was not able to travel to the point of origin) farther inland one spear point could be exchanged for several ax heads.

What accounts for this change in comparative values? What kind of model could you make to explain these observations? First of all, what common properties do the situations have? All of the preceding observations involve some kind of exchange. They all involve giving up some of one thing to get some of another. Some of the exchanges were internal exchanges, or trade-offs—for example, the woman in the grocery store not only exchanged dollars for food (an external exchange), she also had to decide which foods to buy. She made some kind of implicit trade-off of one kind of food for another. She had to answer the question "Would I like to have two more pounds of hamburger or another pound of steak?" (an internal exchange).

Secondly, all of the preceding observations seem to involve elements of choice and decision making. This leads you to suspect that some variant of the decision tree model might be of use. But there are some differences between the exchange data and the kinds of problems we considered in Chapter Four. Decision trees have a limited number of specific alternatives and uncertain consequences. Exchange behavior is characterized by an infinite number of alternatives (2 pounds of hamburger and 1 pound of steak, or 1.5 pounds of hamburger and 1.2 pounds of steak, and so on), and there is *no* uncertainty about whether you will get the one you choose. Thus our model will be similar in form to the decision tree model, but it will focus on a different set of questions and use a different basic format.

5.2 INTERNAL EXCHANGE

Internal exchange concerns choice behavior. We assume that the world is offering us a series of opportunities (such as the chance to buy certain commodities at given prices) that we may react to. In the process of choosing among these opportunities we act as though we were mentally exchanging them inside our minds, trading some of one for some of another. Our thinking looks something like this: "I really want to go to the concert on Saturday, but I would have to give up lunches for the rest of the week to pay for it. Am I willing to exchange the lunches for the concert?"

5.2.1   UTILITY (AGAIN)

In Chapter 4 we discussed utility (the value or usefulness of some commodity) and the maximization of expected utility. Utility maximization is also a major concern here, and we will begin with the following problem: Given a certain weekly budget, how do you spend it so as to maximize utility?

> **STOP AND THINK.** **This question and its variants are fundamental to the entire chapter. Please give it a few minutes thought now.**

Let us talk about a particular college student, Albert the scholar. Al's highest goal in life is knowledge. He lives in a sleeping bag near the library, and he wears castoff clothing; because he does this he is able to devote his entire weekly budget to buying books and hamburgers (he eats to keep up his reading speed).

Table 5.1 shows the utility that Al would receive from consuming various amounts of hamburgers or books. We measure this in utils. Consumption of 0 hamburgers yields 0 utils; consumption of 4 hamburgers yields 84 utils of happiness, and consumption of 4 books yields 106 utils of happiness.

Notice that the more he consumes, the happier he is—12 books would be worth 210 utils of happiness, whereas 7 books would only be worth 160 utils. But you should also notice that his total utility is growing at a slower and slower rate; his increase in utility is more rapid at first when he has very few books.

We need a new term to describe this change. The increase in utility that results from having one more unit of some commodity is called the *marginal utility*. If Al already had 6 books (and hence 144 utils of happiness), 1 additional book would increase his

TABLE 5.1   *The Amount of Utility That Al Gets from Consuming Hamburgers or Books*

HAMBURGERS		BOOKS	
No. of units consumed	Total utility	No. of units consumed	Total utility
0	0	0	0
1	24	1	34
2	46	2	60
3	66	3	84
4	84	4	106
5	100	5	126
6	114	6	144
7	126	7	160
8	136	8	174
9	144	9	186
10	150	10	196
11	154	11	204
12	156	12	210

happiness to 160 utils. The change in happiness is 16 utils, and we say that the marginal utility of the seventh book is 16 utils.

> *STOP AND THINK.* **Suppose that Al already had 11 books. What is the marginal utility of the 12th book? (This one is easy.)**

The value of having 1 more unit of some commodity ordinarily depends on how much of it you already have. When you have no hamburgers, then the marginal utility of having another hamburger is very large. But when you already have 10 hamburgers per day, the marginal utility of one more hamburger is very small.

Suppose that Al already has 7 hamburgers and 2 books. Which would he value more: an additional hamburger or an additional book? (Look at Table 5.1) He would place a higher value on having an additional book, since the marginal utility of an additional book would be 24 utils, whereas the marginal utility of an additional hamburger would be only 10 utils.

Thus we say that the value of some commodity (its marginal utility) is not fixed and that it depends on how much of that commodity you already have.[1]

5.2.2   INDIFFERENCE CURVES

We are now going to perform an experiment to discover something about Al's relative preferences for food and books. He has volunteered to participate. To begin the experiment we *give* him 1 hamburger and 6 books   (1H and 6B)   as payment for his participation.

Part A.   We now show Al a bundle of goods containing   2H and 7B,   and we offer to swap this for his existing bundle   (1H and 6B).   Will Al make the swap? (Would you?) Al accepts the swap. He reasons, "The new bundle has more hamburgers and more books. Of course I'm willing to make the trade."

Part B.   So Al now has 2H and 7B, and we ask if he is willing to give this up in exchange for a bundle that contains   3H and 6B. Will Al accept this offer? He reasons, "The new bundle has 1 less book but 1 more hamburger. Since I don't have very many hamburgers I'm willing to give up a book in order to get an extra hamburger. I'll do it."

Part C.   Al now has 3H and 6B, and we make him a new proposition. We will *trade* 7H and 3B for his existing bundle. Al now says, "I'd be giving up 3 books to get 4 more hamburgers. It seems to me that the loss of happiness from giving up 3 books and the gain in happiness from getting 4 hamburgers are equal. I have no preference for one bundle or the other—I'm indifferent between them."

Analysis of the Experiment.   First we list the results from the three parts of the experiment.

Part A.   2H and 7B   are preferred to   1H and 6B.
Part B.   3H and 6B   are preferred to   2H and 7B.
Part C.   3H and 6B   are equal to   7H and 3B.

From A we might conclude that more is better. When offered a bundle with more of everything, Al definitely prefers the bigger bundle. B is interesting because it shows that he is willing to make trades in which he gives up some of one commodity to get more of the other. The extra hamburger more than compensates for the book he has to give up. And finally C shows that it is possible to have two different bundles that are perceived as being equally good. Is it possible to have more than two equivalent bundles? Suppose we continue the experiment in search of other combinations that Al considers equal to the bundles in C.

TABLE 5.2   *"Equivalent" Combinations*

BUNDLE	COMBINATION
A	0H and 12B
B	1H and 9B
C	3H and 6B
D	4H and 5B
E	7H and 3B
F	10H and 2B

Table 5.2 lists six of these bundles. They are all equivalent (from Al's point of view); he is indifferent among them. (The original bundles from Part C are labeled C and E.) The bundles are equally appealing to him because although each contains less of one good than the previous bundle, it also contains more of the other good. Having less of one thing but enough more of the other to compensate is a trade that leaves Al neither happier nor sadder.

Figure 5.1 shows the 6 bundles (A–F) as dots on a graph. Each dot (like each bundle) represents a specific combination of

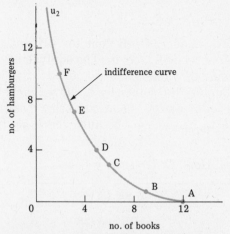

Figure 5.1: Indifference curve. Each point on the curve represents a combination of books and hamburgers. All points on the curve produce equal happiness for Al.

books and hamburgers. We might question Al about other combinations of books and hamburgers that give him equivalent happiness to these points, and if we filled in all the resulting dots, we would have a continuous curve that joined together the original 6 points.[2] Such a curve is shown on Figure 5.1 and labeled u_2 to stand for utility level number 2. Any point on the curve represents a combination of books and hamburgers, and any one of these combinations makes Al equally happy. Because u_2 is a curve of constant utility, Al is indifferent between any two points on it, and we call u_2 an indifference curve.

We plotted the curve u_2 by discovering which combinations Al thought were indifferent to 3H and 6B. We might have used a different starting point, for example, 1H and 2B. Such a bundle is clearly inferior to the other bundles along u_2; it represents a lower level of happiness or utility. We could question Al and discover other bundles that he thought were equivalent to 1H and 2B. These equivalent bundles are shown on the left side of Table 5.3. They also lie along an indifference curve, and we shall label this new curve u_1.

We could repeat this process one more time, starting with an initial bundle of 6H and 10B.

STOP AND THINK. **Is this new bundle superior or inferior to the original 3H and 6B bundle? Explain why.**

By searching for bundles that Al considers equivalent to 6H and 10B, we could discover a curve that we will label u_3. The equivalent bundles are shown on the right side of Table 5.3.

Figure 5.2 shows these bundles as points on a curve, each curve representing a different level of utility. There are other possible indifference curves besides u_1, u_2, and u_3 because there are

TABLE 5.3   Equivalent Bundles Along Other Utility Levels

BUNDLES AT LEVEL U_1		BUNDLES AT LEVEL U_3	
G	0H and 3B	J	5H and 12B
H	1H and 2B	K	6H and 10B
I	4H and 0B	L	8H and 8B
		M	10H and 7B

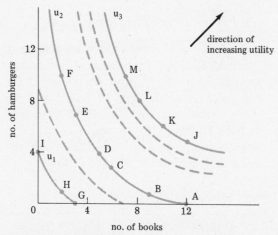

Figure 5.2: Indifference map. Though there are indifference curves in all parts of the graph, only six are shown here.

other possible levels of happiness. Some of these other possible indifference curves are shown in Figure 5.2 as dotted lines. The farther toward the northeast an indifference curve is, the higher the level of happiness that it represents. The various indifference curves are like the successive contour lines on a topological map. Each line (contour) represents points of similar height, or in this case, similar happiness.

We call this set of indifference curves an *indifference map*. This particular map represents Al's preferences. Anyone else would probably have a different indifference map because his relative preferences for hamburgers and books would be different from Al's. Thus the indifference map is a picture (or model) of Al's preferences. The indifference map for anyone else, such as yourself, would be different. However, it would have a *roughly* similar shape. Your indifference curves would probably also be convex as viewed from the origin (the 0 point on the graph). And moving upward and to the right would represent greater utility for you. Thus although everyone's preferences are somewhat different, they have some significant similarities that will allow us to make predictions without knowing the preferences in detail.

You would like to be on the highest indifference curve you can reach. What is it that limits you, that keeps you from going out as far as you wish? The next section shows how the constraints on your decision are determined.

5.2.3 CONSUMPTION POSSIBILITY LINE

Suppose that Al has a budget of $20 per week to live on and that hamburgers cost $1 and books cost $2. If Al spends all of his money on hamburgers, he would buy 20 hamburgers and no books. If he spends all of his money on books, he would buy 10 books and no hamburgers (and end up as a skinny guru). He might also buy combinations of the two, such as 10 hamburgers and 5 books or 4 hamburgers and 8 books. Some examples of the possible combinations of hamburgers and books that use up his budget follow:

Various Possible ($20) Combinations of Hamburgers and Books

COMBINATION	NO. OF HAMBURGERS	NO. OF BOOKS
T	0	10
U	4	8
V	10	5
W	16	2
X	20	0

The table shows a number of possible combinations of hamburgers and books that all cost exactly $20. We can plot these data as points on a graph, which is shown in Figure 5.3. The line connecting the dots together shows *all* the possible combinations of

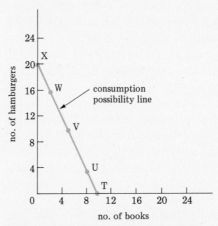

Figure 5.3: Consumption possibility line. Given Al's budget, only points on the line or to the left of it may be purchased.

hamburgers and books that Al might buy that cost exactly $20, that is, all of the bundles that have equal total cost. We call this line the *consumption possibility* line, or *budget* line.

5.2.4 MAXIMIZATION OF UTILITY

At this point we have developed a way to represent graphically the constraints on Al's decision (his consumption possibility line) and to represent graphically his preferences (his indifference map).[3] In this section we will combine the two graphs to show how he can choose the bundle of goods that maximizes his utility, subject to his budget.

Figure 5.4 shows both the indifference map and the consumption possibility line on the same graph. (This is easy to do since both graphs had the same dimensions on their axes). We know that Al may consume any bundle of goods along the budget

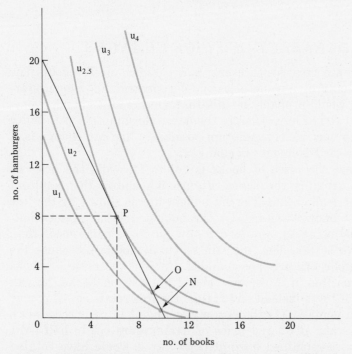

Figure 5.4: Maximization of utility. The greatest utility is obtained at point P; it is the highest indifference curve that Al can reach given his budget constraint.

line itself or any bundle of goods to the left of the budget line. He has enough money to afford any of these combinations. How should he spend his money? Which of the possible bundles of goods will make him happiest?

The bundle of goods represented by point N is not the best possible. Bundle O is clearly better than N because O is on indifference line u_2, and N is on indifference line u_1, and we know that u_2 represents a higher level of satisfaction than u_1. In fact, point P is the best combination of goods (given the size of Al's budget). Point P touches a higher indifference curve than does any other point along the budget line. It is the "equilibrium point." We call it an equilibrium point because once Al has discovered point P, he will (not rationally) move away from it because any other combination of goods will feel inferior. The equilibrium point, the point of maximum utility, occurs where the budget line is tangent to an indifference curve (in this case, an indifference curve that lies between u_2 and u_3). Thus Al will end up buying 8 hamburgers and 6 books per week, if our model is correct.

5.2.5 EFFECT OF PRICE CHANGES

Al's indifference curves represent Al's personal preferences. The indifference map of anyone else would represent his own preferences and so would probably be different. On the other hand, everyone with $20 would have exactly the same consumption possibility line. The only way the consumption possibility line can change is if prices change or the budget is changed.

Suppose the price of books is cut to $1 while the price of hamburgers remains the same. Figure 5.5 shows the resultant change in the budget line. The old budget line is shown by the line AB. The new budget line is AC. The budget line has pivoted outward (around point A), and Al can now purchase more goods than he could have before. The line still starts at point A because the price of hamburgers was not changed. Cutting the price of books in half means that if Al spends all of the $20 on books, he can now buy 20 of them instead of 10; thus the line rotates until it now goes through point C. (If the opposite change had occurred—price of books constant at $2 and price of hamburgers cut in half—the line would have remained fixed at point B but would have rotated away from point A until it became even steeper.) Note that because

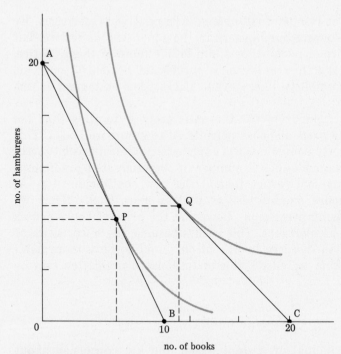

Figure 5.5: Effect of a price change. Halving the price of books causes a change in the budget line and a change in the equilibrium point.

the budget line shifted we now have a new equilibrium consumption bundle at point Q. At Q the budget line is again tangent to an indifference curve.

Why did Al's consumption of books and hamburgers change? What is an explanation for the shift from P to Q? Here are two possible explanations (one of which is wrong):

1. "The reduction in the price of books changed Al's preferences. He now values books more highly because they are cheaper, and so he buys more of them."

2. "Al's relative preference for books and hamburgers is still the same; but the reduction in the price of books allows him to buy more."

STOP AND THINK. See if you can decide which statement is correct.

The lower price did not change Al's relative preferences. He still values books and hamburgers in the same way as before, but the cheaper price of books allows him to buy more of them. Notice, in Figure 5.5, that his indifference curves did not shift; only his consumption possibility line moved. The second statement is the correct one.[4]

So our explanation for the shift from P to Q is that the reduction in the price of books permits Al to buy more books. This seems like a pretty common-sense explanation, almost trivial; actually, though, the model has a number of unanticipated predictions hidden in Figure 5.5. Notice that at the new equilibrium (Q) Al is consuming more hamburgers as well as more books. Thus we have the surprising prediction: Lowering the price of books causes Al to eat more hamburgers. This occurs because the lower price of books acts like an increase in Al's income, and he buys more hamburgers out of this increase.[5] This unanticipated prediction may be applied to other areas as well.

Example: Lunch Subsidies for Slum Schools

You are the principal of a slum school and are concerned about the physical well-being of your students. You believe that many of the students are not getting a proper diet. You know that some of them are given a daily lunch allowance by their parents, and you have observed that much of this money seems to be spent on candy bars and cigarettes, rather than in the school cafeteria. You reason that the students' "unhealthy" spending habits are caused by the high prices in the cafeteria. Yet the cafeteria is already operating at a slight loss, and you cannot order it to cut prices and lose even more money. So you journey to Washington, at your own expense, and talk with bureaucrats and congressmen and eventually get a federal grant for your cafeteria to subsidize its lunches. Using the federal subsidy you are able to reduce greatly the price of hot lunches in the cafeteria, making good food much cheaper to students than it used to be. Now they can spend their money on a good diet. The problem is solved. You feel a warm glow inside because you have really done something for your students.

Then at the end of the first week of the new low lunch prices one of your assistants comes to you with the news that cigarette and candy consumption has actually increased. What went wrong with your plan?

Figure 5.6 illustrates the situation for a typical student. He

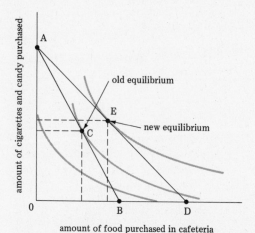

Figure 5.6: Price change in cafeteria. Consumption patterns before (C) and after (E) the federal subsidy.

has some daily allowance to spend on food. If he spends it all at the cafeteria, he could buy OB amount of food. If he spends it all on cigarettes and candy, he could buy a quantity equal to the distance OA. Given his consumption possibility, line AB, and his indifference map, he reaches maximum utility at point C, spending some of his money on food and some on cigarettes and candy. When you cut the price of lunches, it meant that the student could now buy as much as OD amount of food, and so his consumption possibility line shifted outward. Given his new consumption possibility line, he now reaches maximum utility at point E. Notice that a point E he is consuming more of everything. Hence the seemingly strange result. You were partially successful: Students *are* now eating more good food in the cafeteria, but they are also buying more cigarettes and candy.

You were only partially successful because you did not make good food more attractive—you only made it cheaper. (You left the indifference map unchanged and only moved the budget line.) Suppose that instead of using the federal money to subsidize prices, you had used it to subsidize quality (as perceived by the students). That is, you bought more expensive ingredients and spent more on proper cooking but left the prices unchanged. This would have acted to make the food more desirable and hence shifted the indifference map rather than the budget line. Figure 5.7 shows the original indifference map with solid lines and the new indifference map with dotted lines. Notice that the new equilibrium is shifted to

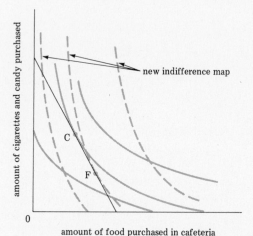

Figure 5.7: Effect of change in values. The indifference map shifts because of a change in food quality, and there is a new equilibrium point.

point F, where students are now consuming more good food and *less* cigarettes and candy. It may very well cost much less to subsidize quality than to subsidize price. So this second plan could be better than the first (as a way of reducing consumption of cigarettes and candy). Manufacturers too face the same kind of problem: how to increase the sales of their products.

STOP AND THINK. Suppose you are a manufacturer of bicycles. What two things could you do to sell more bicycles?

You can increase sales by cutting prices or by improving the quality of your product. You have to decide which of these alternatives will give the greatest effect for the lowest cost. In addition you have a third alternative—advertising. If you can devise a good advertising campaign, you can convince consumers that a product has been greatly improved even when it is still essentially the same. If the product is one that is difficult for consumers to evaluate, such as toothpaste, deodorant, fertilizer, or education, then it may be much cheaper to advertise an imaginary new secret ingredient than it is to actually discover and produce one.[6]

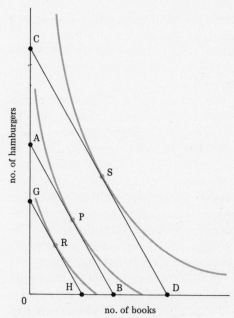

Figure 5.8: Effect of budget change.

5.2.6   EFFECT OF BUDGET CHANGES

From the point of view of the consumer another major change that can effect buying decisions is a change in the amount of money he has to spend. Figure 5.8 shows Al's original budget line, AB, based on the original prices for goods, and a $20 budget.

If we now double his budget to $40, the slope of the budget line remains the same (because prices are still the same), but it makes a parallel shift outward to CD. If his budget had been reduced, the line would have made a parallel shift inward to some line such as GH. Note that his point of maximum utility shifts from R to P to S as his income is successively increased.

5.2.7   SUMMARY OF UTILITY MAXIMIZATION GRAPHS

An indifference map represents a person's particular values and preferences. Normally, we would expect that an indifference map would change very slowly, if at all, since people's values do not change very rapidly. On the other hand, different people will probably have different indifference maps because values do differ among people. You might expect, though, that the indifference maps of one group of people, say college students, might be roughly similar to each other and quite different from the indifference maps of some other group of people such as parents.

The consumption possibility (budget) line of someone represents the constraints on his spending. The line is determined by two things: relative prices and personal income. Relative prices determine the *slope* of the budget line; personal income determines its *position*. Since all consumers face the same relative prices, they all have budget lines with the same slope. But since consumers have different incomes, the actual position of their budget lines will differ.

The budget line is responsive to changing economic circumstances but is independent of changing tastes and preferences. The indifference map is responsive to changing tastes and preferences but is independent of changing economic circumstances. There are, however, two possible exceptions to these statements: (1) If *enough* people change their preferences, it can ultimately affect the price of things and hence affect the budget line. (2) If the income of someone changes by a large amount, it will affect the kinds of people he has daily contact with, and exposure to their values may ultimately change his values and hence his indifference map.

5.3 EXPLORATIONS OF INDIFFERENCE CURVES

5.3.1 TRADE-OFFS

Let us briefly examine the characteristics of the model we have just been discussing to see if it can be used in other, noneconomic situations. Al had a fixed amount of money ($20); he could buy various amounts of books and hamburgers; and he wanted to discover the combination that gave him the most happiness. Or, to generalize the characteristics: The model involves a *fixed resource* (for instance, Al's income), *a set of alternative actions and the preference ranking between them* (for instance, indifference curves), *and a decision rule* (for instance, maximize utility). Al allocated his fixed resource among his alternative actions in such a way as to maximize the satisfaction received.

This problem (a fixed resource to be allocated among competing alternative uses) is common to many other situations as well; but it is often not apparent to the decision makers that this is true.

Example: Strategic Air Command Versus the Navy

About 10 years ago, in Washington, D.C., you could have seen a very famous general, the head of the Strategic Air Command, making a statement before Congress about America's military needs. It went something like this: "There is only *one* way to deter our enemies, and that is the manned bomber. We *must* have at least 1000 more manned bombers on our nation's defense lines, and nothing else can do their job."

Had you stayed around Washington for a few more days, you could have heard the Navy testifying something like this. "Polaris submarines are our *only* hope. We *must* have a minimum of 40 of them if we are to protect our nation's historic interests. At least 40 submarines are required; no less can do the necessary job."

Further listening in Washington could have uncovered equally single-minded statements from the chiefs of the other armed services and their subordinates ("Without a minimum of 975 more gun-bearing lighthouses we shall not be able to sleep well at night").

All of these people seem to believe that there is only one way to solve a problem—their way. How might a social scientist analyze their competing claims using this exchange model? First he would have to decide what the basic goal was. *This is often the most important step*, since it involves taking a fresh look at the situation, broadening it, and discovering the real underlying problem and goal. In this case the basic goal is defense or deterence. Apparently, there is some minimum level of defense that everyone is interested in. Is there a fixed resource that influences the decision making? In this case it is again a budget constraint. Congress did not have enough money to meet all of the conflicting demands. The alternative actions in this case would be different numbers of bombers, submarines, and so on that you might purchase,[7] and the preference ranking among them will be given later. The decision rule is to obtain the acceptable amount of defense for the lowest cost.

To simplify the problem, initially, let us begin by considering only the decision about manned bombers versus submarines. Figure 5.9 shows the analytic situation. The number of bombers or submarines you might purchase is shown on the vertical and horizontal axes. The lines that look like indifference curves are "equal deterrence" lines. Each is a curve of possible combinations of bombers

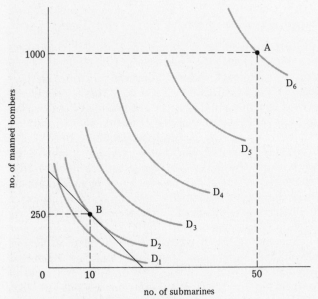

Figure 5.9: Strategic deterrence.

and submarines that yield the same defensive potential. The curves assume that there is some trade-off between different kinds of nuclear weapons carriers, that a nuclear warhead can be delivered either by an airplane or by a Polaris missile fired from a submarine. The curves represent successively higher levels of deterrence. Curve D_1 represents the smallest amount of deterrence, and curve D_6 represents the greatest amount.

We are concerned with some minimal level of security, and so we must find the combination of weapons that gives us this level most economically. Suppose we put all the relevant experts together, and they decide that our minimum level is D_2 First of all, notice that if we give both the Air Force and the Navy what they think are their minimum requirements, we will be at point A on D_6, with much more defense than we actually need. We really only need to be high as D_2. What is the cheapest way to get to D_2? The price of bombers is $25 million each, and the price of submarines is $500 million each, and thus we can determine the *slope* of the budget line.

STOP AND THINK. **How would you determine the slope (not the exact location) of the budget line in this case?**

One simple way to find the slope is to assume some arbitrary total budget, say, $10 billion. We know this amount of money could buy the combination (20 submarines and 0 bombers) or the combination (0 submarines and 400 bombers); so this locates the end points of the $10 billion budget line. We then move a line of this slope up and down until we make it exactly tangent to D_2. We thus discover that point B, 250 bombers and 10 submarines, is the cheapest way to purchase the minimum required amount of deterrence. Note that the analysis has saved substantial money as well: Point A costs $40 billion to attain ($20 billion for the Navy "minimum" plus $25 billion for the Air Force "minimum"); Point B costs only $11.25 billion.

An alternative approach would be to first decide how much money we wish to spend for defense, draw this onto the graph as a budget line, and then select that combination of weapons that yields the greatest potential deterrence.

The example of generals, admirals, and defense is a real one; but it is not the only case of such behavior. Consider the budget requests of different scientists, different educators, different mayors, or different children. They all tend to be cheerfully unconcerned with the question of alternative ways of accomplishing what they plan to do. There are many reasons for the lack of concern on their part; but you generally should examine the possibility that an indifference curve analysis might do better.

Thus the point of the story: There is more than one way to attain an objective. In practice you do this by first broadening your objective until it represents the general goal you are trying to achieve. (Thus we broadened the objective "need 1000 bombers" into the general goal of "minimum acceptable level of defense.") Then you look around to see what other ways there are to achieve the same goal. (Submarine-based missiles could also defend the country.) Very often the alternatives will be more attractive than the original method, or else some combinations of them will prove to be better than using one method alone.

Once you start to broaden the goals associated with a particular problem, you will generally discover that there are trade-offs involved in the solution. The concept of trade-offs is fundamental to indifference curve analysis, and it is extremely important in real world situations. It says that no commodity is uniquely necessary and that resources can be substituted for each other. Thus with the general goal of obtaining happiness, Al discovered that there was a trade-off between consumption of hamburgers and books. Similarly, with the general goal of obtaining defense, we discovered that there is a trade-off between the purchase of submarines and bombers.

Some other examples of the goal-broadening/trade-off-generating process follow:

Diplomacy. You are the chief diplomatic troubleshooter for the United Nations, and you have just received word that North Aram is preparing to attack South Aram. You immediately fly to North Aram and arrange to see its president. After some hours of verbal fencing he admits that he really is preparing to invade South Aram. Yet he appears to be a humanitarian person who is genuinely regretful about the possible destruction and loss of life. He justifies his plan as follows. "My first duty is to my own people. There are too many of them to live off the meager land area of our country. We simply cannot grow enough food. There is already some starvation now, and it will become worse. South Aram has much unused land, enough to feed my people for generations to come. Fighting is bad, but starvation is worse. We must have more land."

He seems to have a reasonable solution to the problem as he has defined it, but possibly his definition of the problem is too narrow. His goal is to obtain more land. Can you think of a way to broaden this goal and find some peaceful solutions?

STOP AND THINK. **Try to broaden his goal. Is more *land* really necessary?**

Actually what the president of North Aram wants to do is obtain more food, not necessarily more land. It is true that more land would bring more food, but that is not the only way. Food production per acre of land varies enormously among countries, and hence there must be resources other than land that affect output—for instance, more fertilizer, better irrigation, better seed, or more labor will produce more food. Any of these can be substituted for land. Therefore, land is not uniquely necessary. From the standpoint of increasing food production, there is a trade-off between more land and more of these other things. By broadening the original goal you discover these trade-offs.

So you advise the president of North Aram that war is not

necessary and send in a team of agricultural experts to help him increase his food output. If you have correctly represented his goal (more food) and you can solve any political, social, or personal problems that the model has ignored so far, then you have helped maintain peace.

Berlin, 1949.   Although West Berlin is part of West Germany, it is actually located about 100 miles inside of East Germany. One major highway connects the city to West Germany, and this is how West Berlin obtains much of its food and fuel. In 1949 the East Germans closed this highway in order to put diplomatic pressure on the West. There were high-level strategy conferences in the Pentagon, and many plans were formulated to "liberate" the highway. Of course, these plans involved some danger of war, but how else would it be possible to open the highway?

> *STOP AND THINK.*   Broaden the perspective here. Are we being excessively preoccupied with the highway? What function does the highway serve?

Fortunately, someone was smart enough to broaden the goal. The problem was not "How do we open the highway?" but "How do we supply Berlin with food and fuel?" Once looked at this way, it becomes obvious that other forms of transportation should be considered, and so the Berlin Airlift was begun. The highway was not uniquely necessary because airplanes could do the same job. And, from the point of view of the United States, there was some trade-off between spending more money to use air freight and the alternative of risking war over the issue of access to the highway.

Sex Appeal.   Your roommate John is unhappy and depressed. "I never get to meet any girls. I sure wish I was better looking." John wants to look different than he does, a rather difficult goal. Since you like John and good roommates are hard to find, you decide to apply your social science wisdom to his problem. What would you suggest?

> *STOP AND THINK.*   How would you solve this problem? Try broadening the goal. Can anything be substituted for appearance?

John has defined his goal as changing his appearance. But his real goal is to be more attractive to women; he has narrowed the goal too much and is simply preoccupied with his appearance. But appearance is not uniquely necessary; there are many substitutes for it. Personality, for example, is one substitute, that is, simply being the kind of person who is fun to be with—cheerful, funny, complimentary, interesting, and so on. Being successful at something—sports, government, the band, and even (fortunately) scholastic success—is another substitute. In this case we would say that, from the point of view of a woman, there is a trade-off between appearance and other qualities when it comes to deciding whether a particular man is desirable or not.

5.3.2 THE SQUEAKY WHEEL THEORY OF VALUES

What determines the relative values of different objects? Why is one thing worth more than another? This is an old and difficult question, of great interest and concern to theology, philosophy, and social science. Indifference curve analysis provides a partial answer to the question as well as a number of interesting predictions.

We will begin by examining indifference curves in greater detail. Figure 5.10 represents Al's u_2 indifference curve from the beginning of the chapter. We know that all the points along it represent an *identical* level of happiness but that each point is a *different* combination of goods. We can learn about Al's values by examining the substitutions that produce the different combinations along the curve.

Bundles C (3H and 6B) and D (4H and 5B) are on the same indifference curve and hence must have the same value to Al. To get from C to D, Al gives up one book in exchange for an extra hamburger. Bundle C represented a certain level of utility to Al; hence when he gave up one book, he suffered a loss of utility. What he lost was the marginal utility associated with the sixth book. Likewise, we can discuss the gain in utility of receiving one more hamburger; we call this the marginal utility associated with the fourth hamburger. If bundles C and D are at equal levels of utility, then the marginal utility of the sixth book and the marginal utility of the fourth hamburger must be equal. The loss of one marginal utility is exactly compensated by the gain of the other.

Now look at bundles E (7H and 3B) and F (10H and 2B).

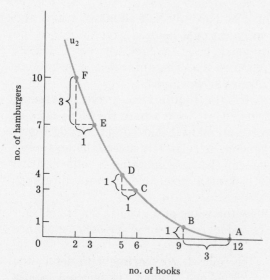

Figure 5.10: Relative utility of hamburgers and books. The slope of the indifference curve shows the relative values to Al.

Since they are on the same indifference curve, the loss of marginal utility from giving up one book must be exactly compensated by the marginal utility of gaining three hamburgers.

Going from C to D, Al's swapping ratio was one book for one hamburger, and so we would say that he values books and hamburgers equally. Going from E to F, his swapping ratio was one book for three hamburgers, and so we would say that he values hamburgers only one-third as much as he values books (because it took three hamburgers to compensate for the loss of one book).

STOP AND THINK. What caused this great change in the relative value of hamburger? Why does Al value hamburgers much less at E than he did at C?

At the beginning of this chapter we explained how the marginal utility of having one more unit of something depended on how many units you already had. We observed that if you only had a few units of some good, then one additional unit might be worth a great deal; but if you already had many units of the good, then one additional unit would not make much difference to you. When Al is in situation E, he has more than twice as many hamburgers as at C, and so the marginal utility of an additional hamburger is lower. Likewise at E he has only half as many books, and so the marginal utility of an additional book is greater. Since the relative scarcities of the two goods have changed between C and E, their relative values have changed too. The difference in swapping ratios reflects the difference in relative values.

Notice that the slope of the indifference curve represents the relative values of the two goods: At A, where the slope is relatively flat, Al is willing to give up many books to get an additional hamburger; at E, where the slope is relatively steep, the swapping ratio is reversed. Thus we can learn something about relative marginal utilities by simply looking at the slope of the indifference curve.

From this point of view the value of a good is not its market price in dollars. Instead its value is measured by what you are willing to give up in order to obtain it.

Suppose we perform the following experiment to determine people's values: A group of 20 college students is selected totally at random from the entire student body and asked to participate in a short experiment. Each student fills out a questionnaire, which says: "Six items follow. We want you to decide which of these six is the most valuable. You have two votes. Please vote for the two items that you think are the most valuable to your life and well-being." The results of the students' voting are shown in the following list. We do not list the specific items that were in the questionnaire (they were all common, ordinary items that everyone encounters daily) but simply designate them by letters. Notice that the first three items received almost all the votes. Apparently, the overwhelming feeling is that these three items are the most valuable.

Which Three of These Items Do You Consider Most Valuable to Your Life and Well-Being?

ITEM	NO. OF VOTES RECEIVED
A	12
B	11
C	13
D	1
E	1
F	2

The students are each paid $5 at the end of the experiment (in marked $1 bills). There are two local banks, and each has agreed to watch out for the special money and keep track of which stores are depositing it. Thus we will have a rough record of what kinds of things the students spend money on. Now we list the original six items from the value questionnaire and the amount of money that was spent on each by the end of the week. (The total is only $86 instead of $100 because some of the money was spent on items other than A–F or else had not yet been spent.)

ITEM	*($) AMOUNT SPENT ON IT*
A	2
B	3
C	2
D	24
E	21
F	32

Notice that almost all of the money has been spent on the last three items.

How can we make sense of these results? When students were asked to vote on which items they considered the most valuable, they were almost unanimously in favor of the first three. Yet when they spent their money (in effect, they were casting "dollar" votes), they were equally unanimous in preferring the last three items. What is going on here? When the President of the United States makes a speech favoring brotherhood and education and then proposes a national budget that concentrates spending on defense and highways, many students would say that the President is a hypocrite. When the governor declares he is extremely proud of the states's universities and then vetoes a bill for their expansion, many students would say that the governor is a hypocrite. The six items on the value questionnaire were: A—clean air, B—good water, C—plants and animals, D—gas stations, E—the student union, F—grocery stores. Students claimed they valued the first three but spent their money on the last three. Are they hypocrites?[8]

STOP AND THINK. Can you explain the behavior of the students? *Hint:* Recall the discussions on total utility, and decreasing marginal utility.

Remember that any indifference curve represents some *total* utility level. Let us look closely at one of the 20 students, George.

Suppose that George is currently on his 100,000th util indifference curve. How did he get there? What is it that gives him the 100,000 utils of happiness? In George's case 90,000 utils of his happiness come from his general environment—clean air, good water, and pretty trees and healthy animals—and only 10,000 utils come from other goods. Thus George can truthfully say that he values items A, B, and C the most; they make the greatest *total* contribution to his current level of happiness.

But why does George not spend his $5 on those three items if he values them most? Remember the principle of decreasing marginal utility: George's first quart of water is really marvelous; he could not get along without it. His second quart of water is still very good but not quite as good as the first quart. By the time George is receiving 50 quarts per day, he values an additional quart so little that he will even use it to wash his car. The marginal utility gained by consuming an additional quart keeps getting smaller and smaller; it never falls to zero, though, so an additional quart of water always adds something to George's total happiness, but just not very much.

Thus when George is already at his 100,000 util level of happiness and we give him an extra $5 to spend, he will not spend very much on water, air, and plants and animals, since he already has a great deal of them. Rather he will spend the money on something that is still scarce, something whose marginal utility is still high. Hence he spends most of his money on items D, E, and F.

Returning to the original question, we see that there is no hypocrisy involved in the students' behavior. Within our model there is *no necessary* connection between behavior and *total* utility; there is only a connection between behavior and *marginal* utility. It is marginal utilities that determine behavior most of the time. The governor may really believe that the university is necessary and truly be proud of it. Yet when it comes to allocating an additional million dollars of tax money, he may feel that he obtains a greater *gain* in utility, more marginal utility, by spending it on traffic signals or the construction of public buildings.[9]

We are distinguishing between two kinds of values: the values associated with general questions of happiness and well-being and the values associated with behavior. One kind of value is concerned with the philosophical question "What is responsible for my overall state of happiness?" The other kind of value is concerned with the question "What do I desire and want more of?" This book is mostly concerned with the latter definition, and this is how the word "value" has been used up to now. It is obviously the more useful definition if our concern is the prediction of human behavior, but it is not the only possible definition.

Our definition of value turns out to be quite useful in solving one of the oldest paradoxes in economics: "Why is it that diamonds have a greater value than water, when diamonds contribute very little to man's welfare, whereas water is actually essential to life?" There were many books written about this paradox in the nineteenth century, with little result. However, you now know enough to solve it.

STOP AND THINK.   Can you solve the paradox?

Our present model tells us to ignore the determinants of total utility and concentrate instead on the marginal utility of *changes* in the existing situation. After all it is quite difficult to distinguish among all of the things that are said to be "essential" to man's welfare. In the paradox it would have been easy to substitute the words "land," "air," "sunshine," "animals," or "plants" for "water." They are all essential too in the sense that we cannot exist without them. But our present theory of value says that we should take these things for granted because they are abundant and that we should concentrate our attention on those things that are scarce. Notice that since clean air and pure water have recently become less abundant, they are beginning to acquire higher behavioral value to people; that is, people are now willing to give up more of other things in order to get more of them.

According to a proverb, "It's the squeaky wheel that gets the grease." The idea is that a driver, for example, ignores those parts of his car that are functioning properly (or things that are abundant) and concentrates his attention on those parts that are not working. Thus we also call our theory the squeaky wheel theory of value.

There are a number of interesting consequences of this theory of value, one of which we call the *Connoisseur Corollary*. The Connoisseur Corollary states that when a person is placed in a situation that has a relative abundance of some commodity, he will take that abundance as a given and will then start making finer and finer discriminations among the attributes of that commodity. Some examples follow:

Intellectuals. Al and Hank both have intellectual interests. Unfortunately, they are both at a surfing/football-oriented high school. They spend a lot of time together and are good friends. They both decide to go to Scholarly University, where *everyone* has intellectual interests. After being at S.U. for two years, they no longer spend much time together and each is now involved with separate groups of friends. When asked why they no longer associate with each other, Hank says: "Our political beliefs are too different, and Al is materialistically oriented. My new friends even read the same sort of novels that I do." In the relative scarcity of their old high school anyone with two brain cells to rub together (to produce sparks of knowledge?) was a treasured friend. In the relative abundance of Scholarly University they now discriminate among many different kinds of intellectual interests, with the result that they have drifted apart.

Friendship. Suzy has never been popular and longs for a lively social life. She wants a friend, any kind of friend. When her social life finally does improve significantly, she will begin making finer and finer distinctions among friends. She will become a connoisseur and will be unhappy with friends who would have formerly pleased her; she will raise her standards of what is minimally acceptable.

Clubs. Spike wants to get into a fraternity, any fraternity. When he finally does become a member and learns to take his membership for granted, he will begin distinguishing between "good" and "bad" fraternities, citing distinctions that are not at all obvious to non-fraternity members.

Cars. Some of you do not have a car and wish that you did have one, any sort of car. Those of you that do own a car take it for granted and wish that you had a "better" one.

The squeaky wheel theory of value says that people ignore the commodities that they already have and concentrate their attentions on improving utility by making marginal readjustments to obtain more of those things that are scarce. And one of the ways in which people do this is by making finer discriminations, by becoming connoisseurs. The average person in the United States is incredibly well off by the material standards of 100 years ago; yet he devotes his attentions to getting still more material goods, and he concentrates on those things that he does *not* have. Once a need is satisfied, he begins to make still finer distinctions and hence discovers new needs. Heaven may someday arrive on earth, but no one will ever recognize it.

5.3.3 MEN AND WOMEN

It is possible to treat the relation between men and women as a problem in indifference curve analysis. In order to do so, we must treat men as commodities (sex objects?) when examining the behavior of women and women as commodities when examining the behavior of men. Since the relation between men and women is often more complicated than our abstraction—or possibly even fundamentally different—we can take a more than usual delight in discovering all of the ways in which the model makes erroneous predictions. Alternatively, of course, we may want to consider the possibility that, to the extent that the model makes good predictions (no matter how much we disagree with it), the model provides some insight concerning the way we think about each other.

Example: Marriage

Bill would really like to spend time with Janet. She agrees to go to the movies with him, and their relationship begins. Bill values Janet very highly (because he has so little time with her) and hence behaves well toward her. He brings flowers, takes her to interesting places, listens carefully, and so on. And he will continue this good behavior as long as his time with her is limited in some way. (One of the interesting characteristics of Western courtship behavior is that it does impose a limit on the amount of time he can spend with her.) Suppose they eventually get married and start spending a good deal of time together. Although their fundamental value for each other (their total utility) is not affected by this extra time, their behavior-value (marginal utility) for each other will decrease. Gradually, they begin treating each other more casually, even callously. Enough of such callous treatment can eventually feed back to their estimates of each other's fundamental value, and hence divorce occurs.[10]

This seems a grim prospect. What can Bill do, for example, to retain his value? Basically, he needs to be rationed in some way. He might start working late at the office or do more traveling or take up golf. Any one of these would act to make him more scarce and hence more valuable. Janet faces the same problem. How can she manage to keep her value? One of the side effects of child raising is that it takes so much time. Hence having many children means less of Janet's time is available to Bill, and she stays scarce and valuable. (Obviously, if scarcity is overdone, it can create discontent too.)

All time is not of the same quality. An hour spent with a boring person is obviously less valuable than an hour spent with a stimulating one. This implies that instead of simply rationing her time with Bill, Janet could diversify her "time appeal." That is, she might acquire a *range* of interests, skills and ways of interacting. By diversifying she creates a relative scarcity of the different kinds of time. This suggests that women with interesting jobs will be more fun to interact with than housewives; hence the former will have a greater chance of staying married.

Possible predictions from this theory are: (1) The longer the courtship, the less the chance it will end in marriage. There is more time for casual, callous behavior to appear. (2) There will be an upsurge in divorces after children become old enough to leave home. Janet then has more time to devote to Bill. (3) The longer hours a man works, the more stable the marriage. (4) There will be an upswing in dissatisfaction at retirement because Bill will become more available. (5) The children of mothers who work away from home will value time with their mothers more highly than will the children of housewives (holding constant the number of children).

Example: Love

Suzy has been asked to accompany Mike to the concert this Friday. Should she accept? How could you use an indifference curve model to help her decide?

Broaden the Goal
"Well," says Suzy, "my goal is to decide whether or not to date Mike." *But why is this a problem?* "Because if I date Mike, then I cannot date Byron; besides, I have homework to do too." *Well then, your goal is to use your time in the way that makes you most happy. Agreed?* "Yes. That's true."

List Alternatives
What are the alternatives involved here? "Happiness gained through getting homework done, Happiness gained through dating Byron. Happiness gained through dating Mike."

Rank Alternatives
Do you have a preference ordering among combinations of the alternatives? "Yes."

Limited Resources/Constraints
Why can't you do all the alternatives? "My time is limited."

The problem is now set up and ready for solution. But notice that the problem would have been much different if we had defined Suzy's broadest goal as simply to get to the concert. Then if her constraint had been money, she might have considered the alternative of giving up lunches to save money for the concert. Or if her constraint had been transportation and she really was not too enthusiastic about Mike, she might have considered the bus or thumbing a ride.

Let us look at two of the alternatives to begin with, study time versus social life; and once we find out how much time to devote to social life, we can then figure out how to allocate it between Mike and Byron.[11] The indifference curves in Figure 5.11 show Suzy's preferences for time spent studying versus time spent socializing. Any point along a given indifference curve represents a certain number of study hours and a certain number of hours spent socializing. All the points on this curve yield equal happiness. The axes are calibrated in number of hours. Suzy says that after doing all those things that "absolutely must be done" (you might want to examine this statement more closely), she has 62 hours per week to allocate between studying and socializing. This 62-hour

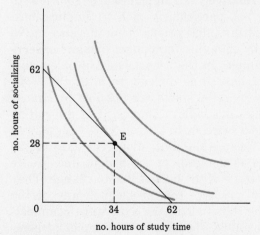

Figure 5.11: Allocation of Suzy's free time.

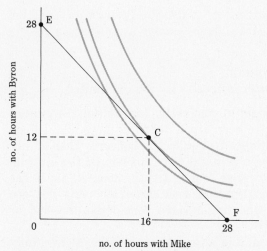

Figure 5.12: Allocation of social time.

time constraint is drawn in as a budget line in Figure 5.11 and her point of maximum happiness is at E, where she is spending 34 hours studying and 28 hours on socializing.

Now she must decide how to allocate her social time between Byron and Mike. So she draws another indifference map, puts time with Mike on one axis, time with Byron on the other axis, and then draws in a 28-hour budget line, line EF on Figure 5.12. Her point of maximum happiness occurs at C, where she is spending 16 hours per week with Mike and 12 hours per week with Byron.

So far we have a relatively straightforward solution to Suzy's problems, but it is not particularly rich in implications. What can we do? The interesting implications of indifference curve analysis are often obtained by changing the budget line and observing the results (as, for example, in the school lunch problem discussed earlier). But in this case it is difficult to alter the *slope* of the budget line (although parallel shifts are possible by changing the total number of hours available). That is, it is difficult to create a change analogous to a price shift.

The difficulty arises because the units along the axes of the graph (hours) are the same as the units of the budget line. Hence there is no way to cause the slope of the budget line to change. They are locked together. We did not have this problem in any of the earlier examples because the items along the axes were commodities of various kinds. For instance, We measured "number of hamburgers" consumed rather than "number of dollars spent on food."

Look at Figure 5.11 again. What could we do with "hours of study time"?

STOP AND THINK. What commodity could we put along the horizontal axis? What is the study time meant to obtain? What commodity does it "purchase"?

Presumably the study time is not an end in itself. Suzy studies to increase her knowledge. We might measure this knowledge in terms of GPA, or number of new ideas, or pages read, or papers written, and so on. So we make knowledge the commodity along the horizontal axis. Now what is the commodity that is obtained from hours of socializing?

STOP AND THINK. How would you convert hours of social life into something else? What do hours of socializing purchase?

Although there are many possible names we would give to the vertical axis, suppose we call it affection. We might measure it in terms of number of compliments received, feelings of warmth and happiness, and so on.

Now to draw a budget line we need to know the exchange rate between hours and affection, and between hours and knowledge. That is, how many units of knowledge can Suzy "purchase" with an hour's study time? We will now assume some particular values for these exchange rates, draw the resultant budget line, and then show the consequence of a change in the rates.

Assume
1 hour of study time produces 3 units of knowledge.
1 hour of social time produces 2 units of affection.

We can now produce Figure 5.13, and reanalyze the question of how Suzy divides her 62 hours between studying and socializing. If Suzy devotes the entire time to studying, she will receive 186 units of knowledge (that is, 62 hours × 3 units/hour) and no affection. Or if she devotes the entire available time to socializing, she will receive 124 units of affection and no knowledge. Since we

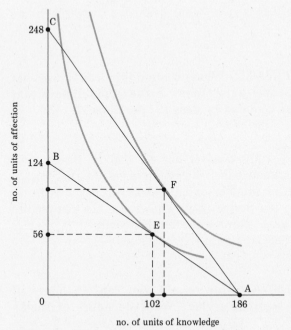

Figure 5.13: Allocation of Suzy's free time.

have the two end points for the budget line we can now draw it in. Given budget line AB, Suzy's optimum combination is at point E, where she is receiving 102 units of knowledge and 56 units of affection. We can convert these figures back into hours if we divide by the appropriate time-prices, and hence we discover that Suzy spends 34 hours of her time budget on knowledge (that is, 102 divided by 3 units/hour) and 28 hours of her time budget on affection. This, of course, is the same solution we calculated in Figure 5.11.

Now suppose that Suzy makes herself more attractive (by means of any of the standard remodeling processes available to men and women). She will now receive more units of affection from each hour of social time. In terms of the model, the time-price of affection will decrease. Suppose she now receives 4 units of affection per hour of social time. She can now purchase as much as 248 units of affection (that is, 62 hours × 4 units/hour). This is shown on Figure 5.13 as point C. The budget line remains fixed at point A, and hence it pivots about A until it reaches C. The line AC is the new budget line, and point F is the new equilibrium. Suzy is now receiving more affection *and* more knowledge. How can that be?

STOP AND THINK. Do you see why? If necessary, review our earlier discussion of the school lunch problem.

The increase in Suzy's attractiveness has permitted her to increase her consumption of both goods. But the surprising thing (if you do not agree that it is surprising, ask someone to predict what would happen) is that when Suzy becomes *more* attractive, she spends *less time* on her social life.[12] Since the time-price of affection has been reduced, she finds more time to study. Conversely, if we teach Suzy to study more efficiently, we reduce the time-price of knowledge, and she will spend more time on her social life.

We can now go on to budget Suzy's social time between Mike and Byron in the same way, putting units of affection from Mike on one axis and units of affection from Byron on the other. And the budget line need no longer be a 45-degree line as it was in Figure 5.12. We could also assume different time-prices of affection for the two men and work out the corresponding consequences.

Furthermore, we could also allow more realistic budget lines within this new framework. For example, it seems likely that the first hour devoted to studying yields a higher knowledge payoff than the sixty-first hour. So the budget line would no longer be straight. It would be concave (as viewed from the 0 point on the graph). It is still possible to find the point of utility maximization with such a concave budget line, and a bit of experimentation with the time-price assumptions can yield still further interesting implications.

Example: Love's Contradictions

Having solved Suzy's problems let us see if we can use this analysis to shed some light on two pieces of ancient folk wisdom: (1) "Absence makes the heart grow fonder" and (2) "Out of sight, out of mind." They appear contradictory. Which (if either) is correct?

Suppose that Mike transfers to another school and that commuting between his new school and Suzy is so long that he can only afford to spend 10 hours per week with Suzy. Mike is now out of sight most of the time. What happens to Suzy's allocation of social time? In Figure 5.14 the line AB shows the maximum possible time Suzy can spend with Mike (that is, 10 hours $\times$ 2 affection units/hour = 20). None of the points to the right of AB

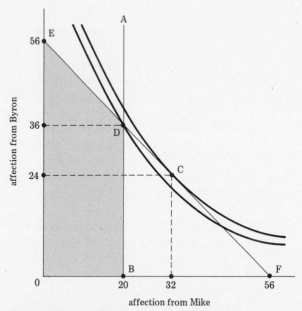

Figure 5.14: Allocation with two constraints.

is possible because each requires more than 10 hours per week of Mike time. Only points to the left of AB satisfy the 10-hour constraint. Otherwise the old time budget line EF still applies; therefore, only points below EF meet Suzy's total time constraint. So Suzy's area of choice must be below EF and to the left of AB. This area is shaded on the figure. Since she would never want to choose a point that is actually inside the boundaries of the shaded area (why?), her choice points lie along BDE. The highest indifference curve she can reach is the one that intersects point D, where she is receiving 20 affection units from Mike and 36 from Byron; that is, she spends 10 hours per week with Mike and 18 with Byron. If we compare the old equilibrium, point C on Figure 5.14, with the new equilibrium, point D, we can see that she now spends fewer hours per week with Mike and more hours per week with Byron. (Again, remember that our model only analyzes the effect of changes in *one* factor, and we assume that all the other factors that affect interpersonal relationships are held constant.)

Now since Suzy increased her time with Byron when Mike left, we conclude that "out of sight, out of mind" is correct. However, notice that at point D the slope of the indifference curve is steeper than it was at C. The steeper slope means that Suzy's swapping ratios have changed; her relative value for time with Mike has increased. At C she valued an extra minute with Mike or an extra minute with Byron equally. At D she places higher value on an extra minute with Mike—therefore, we conclude that "absence makes the heart grow fonder." So (at least in our model) both bits of folk wisdom are correct; one refers to total time, the other to the marginal value of the time.

One interesting aspect of this analysis is to notice that Suzy is not naturally monogamous. Under almost any budget conditions she is going to end up *dividing* her social time between Mike and Byron. Furthermore, this is likely to happen in spite of her best intentions to remain true to one or the other. For as she gets closer and closer to full time with one of them, say, with Mike, the marginal utility of an extra minute of time with him will become less and less. Meanwhile, the new scarcity (created by her) of Byron will make the marginal value of an extra minute of time with Byron become greater and greater.

Suzy might be monogamous if a really unusual man, like Al, came along. Figure 5.15 shows her preference for affection from Al versus another person, "X." Her preference for Al is so strong that the slope of the indifference curve is still very steep even when she already is spending lots of time with him. Since the slope of the budget curve is less steep than the slope of her indifference curve, she will end up at a "corner solution," point B, because this gets her to curve u_5, which is the highest level she can reach with

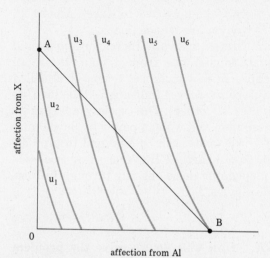

Figure 5.15: Strong preference for Al.

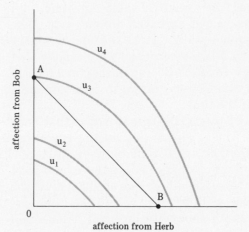

Figure 5.16: Janet's preferences.

her budget constraint. The same result could be obtained if the time-prices of affection from the two men were extremely unequal.

Is there any type of woman who is naturally monogamous? Figure 5.16 shows the indifference curves of another girl, Janet, for her two boy friends, Bob and Herb. Notice that Janet reaches a corner solution at point A, where she is spending all of her time with Bob, and obtains a level of happiness corresponding to curve u_3. Given the shape of her indifference curves, Janet is going to be naturally monogamous, no matter what the slope of her budget line—hence the famous theorem (which we owe to Karen Anderson, a former student) : Concave women are monogamous.

Concave indifference curves indicate increasing marginal utility—the more affection a woman has from a man, the more she values additional affection. In less technical terms, it is called "falling in love." Steep indifference curves indicate a "true love"— one man completely dominates all others. Our society appears to regulate the relations between men and women partly by developing beliefs in falling in love and true love. Such beliefs tend to produce monogamy (as well as broken hearts). However, few societies interested in encouraging monogamy do so entirely through falling-in-love and one-true-love ideologies.

STOP AND THINK. **How else do we solve the problem of keeping people monogamous?**

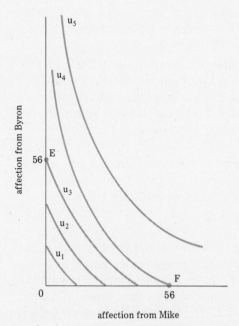

Figure 5.17: Effect of all-or-nothing choice.

One solution is to pass a law such as: "Thou shalt be faithful to thy spouse or thou shalt be thrown into jail." Another (and nearly equivalent) solution is the all-or-nothing threat. Suppose that Byron and Mike decide that they are no longer willing to share a girlfriend, and each says something like this to Suzy: "I really love you, but I can't stand the thought of your seeing someone else. If you can't give me all your love, I'd prefer to have none of it, and I'll have to stop seeing you. It's just too painful for me." Figure 5.17 shows this situation. Suzy no longer has a budget line, since combinations are not possible. Rather she has only two choice points, E and F. She must choose one of these two choice points. Since F has a higher level of utility, she will choose it and will spend all her time with Mike.

5.4   A FORMAL MODEL OF INTERNAL EXCHANGE

In this section we develop a more formal, axiomatic model of indifference curves. Aside from its logical interest, the material is useful for understanding why indifference curves have the shape and properties we have been discussing. It is also useful for drawing indifference curve solutions for the problem assignments.

Assumption 1.   The most fundamental assumption is that the consumer has some set of preferences and knows what they are. Thus for *any* two bundles of goods, A and B, a particular consumer will either prefer A to B or prefer B to A, or he will be indifferent between them. This assumption says that he *can make choices*

Assumption 2.   We further assume that the consumer's preferences will be "transitive." Thus if he prefers bundle A to bundle B and if he prefers bundle B to bundle C, then he will also prefer A to C. This assumption says that his choices will be *consistent.*

Assumption 3.   We also assume that for the economic goods under consideration the consumer will always prefer more goods to fewer goods. Thus if bundle A contains more of one kind of good than bundle B and if it has equal amounts of the other kinds of goods, then bundle A will be preferred to B. In other words, *more is better.*

   Now, let us see how far we can get with these three assumptions. Figure 5.18 shows two possible indifference curves, u_1 and u_2, which pass through commodity bundle A. Are they both "legal" indifference curves in terms of our three assumptions? Compare bundle A and bundle B on indifference curve u_2. Since they are both on the same curve, they must be seen as equally good by that consumer.

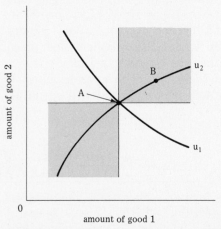

Figure 5.18: Possible indifference curves?

STOP AND THINK. **Is u_2 a legal indifference curve? Is there one assumption that would forbid A and B from being on the same indifference curve?**

First, we notice that bundle B has more of each kind of good than bundle A. Since it has more of everything, Assumption 3 says that *it must be preferred* to A; therefore, both points cannot be on the same indifference curve. In fact, any bundle in the shaded quadrant to the upper-right of bundle A must be preferred to A; even if the bundle were on one of the boundary lines of the quadrant, it would still have more of one good and an equal amount of the other. Conversely, bundles in the shaded quadrant to the lower left of bundle A must be inferior to A because they contain fewer goods. Thus an indifference curve, passing through bundle A, could never enter either of the shaded quadrants.

We now know that any legal indifference curve through bundle A must lie in one of the unshaded quadrants. Can we specify anything more about its shape? Figure 5.19 shows three possible indifference curves. Are they all legal?

STOP AND THINK. **Do any of the curves in the figure violate any of the three assumptions? If not, do the curves make sense? Can you describe behaviors that would produce each of the curves?**

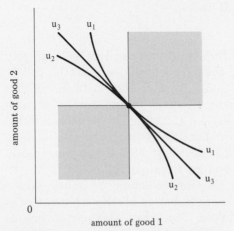

Figure 5.19: Possible indifference curves?

None of the curves in Figure 5.19 violates our three assumptions, but u_2 and u_3 imply some rather peculiar real world behavior. We examine them in greater detail in the next paragraph and then add one last assumption to make them illegal.

In Figure 5.19 curve u_2 is concave (as viewed from the origin), and we have already seen the effect of concave curves in Figure 5.16. We know that they produce corner solutions where a consumer is buying only one of the two possible goods. We know that such concave curves could not be typical of the real world, since consumers do not concentrate all their spending on a single item but instead typically purchase *combinations* of goods. The only curve shape that can produce noncorner solutions is a convex curve, like u_1. Straight lines, like u_3, will produce either corner solutions or else no definite solution at all (when the budget line and the straight-line indifference curve lie on top of each other). So we add one final assumption to our model.

Assumption 4. Indifference curves must be *convex* (toward the origin). In Figure 5.19 only u_1 is a legal indifference curve in these terms.

Is there anything else we can say about the shape of indifference curves? In Figure 5.20 we show two curves, u_1 and u_2, on the map of a single person. Are they simultaneously legal?

STOP AND THINK. **Can the indifference curves for some person ever intersect? What would it mean if they did? *Hint:* Compare bundles B and C.**

Suppose someone claims that u_1 and u_2 can intersect. If you believe the drawing is correct, then the consumer must be indifferent between bundle A and bundle B, since they both lie on the same indifference curve. Likewise, he must be indifferent toward bundle A and bundle C. And finally we know that to be consistent he must also be indifferent between bundles B and C. But this last statement is clearly impossible because bundle C contains more of each kind of good than B; bundle C cannot be equal to B—it must be preferred. To resolve the contradiction we must either throw out the assumption that more is better or else we must rule out intersecting indifference curves. Since the assumption has a great deal of intuitive appeal and intersecting curves have nothing

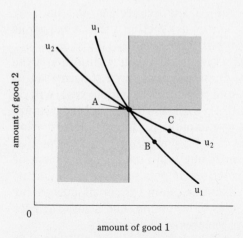

Figure 5.20: Possible indifference curves?

intrinsic to recommend them, we will keep the assumption and rule out intersections.

Suppose in Figure 5.20 that the two indifference curves belonged to two different people. In this case it would be quite legitimate for them to intersect. The fact that one curve is steeper than the other merely means that the preferences of the two people are different. (The person associated with curve u_1 has a stronger relative preference for Good 1.)

5.4.1 HOW TO DRAW INDIFFERENCE CURVES

The first questions that students generally ask when they are trying to analyze choice situations are: "How do I know what shape to draw for the indifference curves? Should I actually try to measure the indifference curves of a real person?" We will answer the last question first.

It is possible to discover the indifference map of a real person. In Section 5.2.2 we discussed an experimental process for such measurements, but it is almost never used. In part this is because we are generally interested in predicting the behavior of groups rather than of some specific individual. But the main reason for ignoring actual indifference curve measurements is that they are unnecessary when it comes to solving most of the problems of interest to us in this chapter.[13] That is, provided there is some arbitrary set of indifference curves that conforms to the four assumptions discussed in the previous section, the conclusions reached in the various analyses will be correct.[14]

How then should you draw the curves when trying to analyze one of your own problems? The answer is that any arbitrary set of curves (which are both convex and nonintersecting curves) will do provided that they are compatible with the three basic assumptions and also compatible with any explicit preference information given in the problem. In other words, you simply draw a set of arbitrary convex curves and work out your analysis in terms of them. Specific preference information, if you have any, should be incorporated. Figure 5.21, for example, shows a set of curves for Spike, who strongly prefers cookies to ice cream, and a set of curves for Henry, who strongly prefers ice cream to cookies.

> **STOP AND THINK.** Which set of indifference curves depicts a strong preference for cookies? Why? *Hint:* A and B yield equal happiness. What do you give up, and what do you gain when you move from A to B?

We know that A and B represent different combinations of ice cream and cookies, and we know that A and B are on the same indifference curve; therefore, the two different combinations must be seen as being equally good. Now look at the left-hand graph: a movement from A to B involves giving up a lot of cookies in order

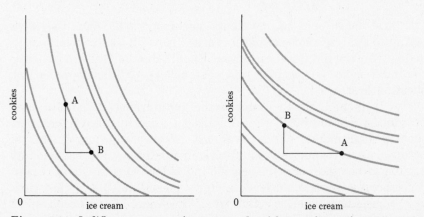

Figure 5.21: Indifference curves for two people with opposite preferences.

to get a little bit of ice cream. Clearly, you would only make this trade if you had strong preferences for ice cream; thus the left-hand curves must belong to Henry. Now look at the right-hand graph: a movement from A to B involves giving up a lot of ice cream in order to get a few cookies. Clearly, you would only make this trade if you had a strong preference for cookies; thus the right-hand curves must belong to Spike.

Another consideration in drawing a set of curves is whether they should intersect the axes. The speed with which they approach the axes depends upon your willingness to give up the last unit of some commodity. If they approach steeply, then the equilibrium point is likely to be a corner solution, as in Figure 5.15. If they approach gradually, then the equilibrium will involve consumption of both commodities.

5.5 · EXTERNAL EXCHANGE

We now turn to the problem of explicit trades among people, what we originally called external exchanges. Analysis of external exchange will involve simple extension of the internal exchange models developed previously.

Exchange of goods and services is one of the most widespread and easily observable phenomenon in all societies. In our society, money is used as a convenient intermediary good. For instance, one first exchanges his services for money and then exchanges the money for food, but the process is still basically an exchange of services for food. We will look at two different classical ways of analyzing external exchange: the Edgeworth box and supply/demand analysis.

5.5.1 THE EDGEWORTH BOX (OPTIONAL)

Suppose that the world has only two kinds of goods, food and clothing, and two people, Jim and Dan, who divide all of the goods between them. Figure 5.22 shows their indifference maps for food and clothing. This time we have labeled the indifference curves as J_1, J_2, and so on, to stand for Jim's indifference curves, and D_1, D_2, and so on, to stand for Dan's indifference curves.

Figure 5.23 shows Dan's indifference map again, but this time it is flopped over and turned upside down. It is still the same

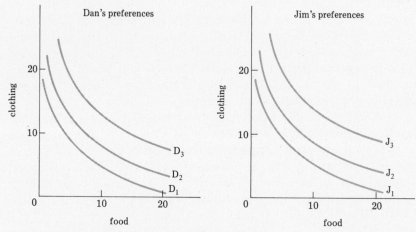

Figure 5.22: Indifference maps for Dan and Jim.

map, but now food quantity increases going to the left, and clothing quantity increases going downward. Likewise, Dan now increases utility by moving in the southwest direction. We have shown his indifference curves as dotted lines to make them look more distinctive.

Now let us suppose that these two people, Dan and Jim, have different amounts of food and clothing. Dan starts with 20 units of food and 6 of clothing, and Jim starts with 8 units of food and

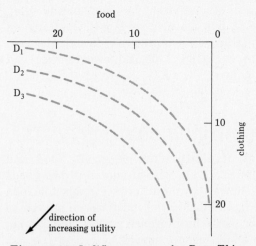

Figure 5.23: Indifference map for Dan. This is the same as Figure 5.22 but is rotated half a turn.

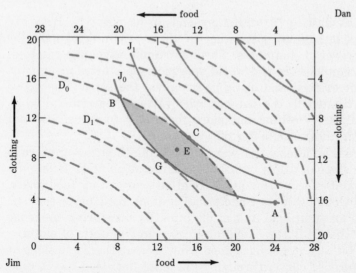

Figure 5.24: Edgeworth Box.

14 of clothing. Can we say anything about what kind of trade they
might engage in? To do so we need a device that can simultaneously
look at the indifference maps of both of them. Figure 5.24 shows
such a device. It is called an Edgeworth box. It is made by combining Dan's upside down indifference map (Figure 5.23) with the
normal indifference map for Jim.

Dan's indifference curves are shown as dotted lines increasing to the southwest, and Jim's indifference curves are shown as
solid lines increasing toward the northeast. The dimensions of the
Edgeworth box, 28 food by 20 clothing, represent the total amount
of available food and clothing. And any point in the box represents
some division of the total quantity of food and clothing between
Dan and Jim. For example, point A allocates 4 units of clothing
and 24 units of food to Jim and also 16 units of clothing and 4
units of food to Dan. Similarly, point B represents the initial distribution of food and clothing mentioned previously: 8 food and
14 clothing possessed by Jim, and 20 food and 6 clothing possessed
by Dan.

Given the starting point B, can we predict how trading will
occur? Jim is now on indifference curve J_0 and would like to move
toward the right. Dan is now on indifference curve D_0 and would
like to move toward the left. Notice that any point within the
shaded area between J_0 and D_0 will make both Jim and Dan better
off than they are at B. Suppose, for example, that they trade com-

modities back and forth until they end up at point E. Both are happier, and it has not cost either of them anything to gain the new higher level of happiness. Through simple exchange the total amount of happiness in the world was increased, even though the total amount of food and clothing remained the same. The goods were redistributed to the persons who valued them more highly. Jim now has less clothing but more food. Dan has less food but more clothing. Both are better off.

There is an alternative way of analyzing the trading process. Look at the slope of Jim's indifference curve at point B. It is quite steep and implies that Jim has a relative scarcity of food there. That is, he would value an additional unit of food more than he would value an additional unit of clothing. By measuring the slope we discover that at B Jim is willing to give up two units of clothing in order to get an extra unit of food. Now look at Dan. The slope of Dan's indifference curve, through B, is quite flat. Dan has a relative scarcity of clothing; he would value an additional unit of clothing more than an additional unit of food. By measuring the slope at B, we discover that Dan would be willing to give up three units of food in order to get an additional unit of clothing.

Jim would be willing to swap 2 clothing for 1 food; Dan would be willing to swap 3 food for 1 clothing. Is trade between them possible? Obviously it is. In fact they will happily exchange goods until they end up at some final point where their swapping ratios are equal. Happiness can be increased because each of them may trade a good he considers relatively abundant for one he considers relatively scarce.

We know that Jim and Dan will end up in the shaded area—can we tell where? Assume that Jim is a "nice guy" who agrees to give all the benefits of trading to Dan. In other words, Jim says that he will move to any point along J_0 that Dan chooses. Dan chooses point G, the point where the shaded area is tangent to his highest attainable indifference curve, D_1. At point G Jim is as happy as he was at point B and Dan has received all the benefits of the trading. The corresponding point where Jim has received all the benefits of the trading and Dan is just as indifferent as at point C.

We can show that they will trade in such a way as to end up somewhere on a line between G and C (the line being all the points of tangency between two indifference curves). Where they end up between C and G presumably depends on the relative bargaining powers of the two men. But neither man need ever accept an exchange position outside of the shaded area. As long as trade is voluntary, there can be no exploitation of one person by the other through trade. The worst that can happen is that one person manages to obtain all the benefits of trade for himself while leaving the other in a position indifferent to the one he started from. Obviously, this is not to say that the two individuals end up about "equal." They may differ substantially in the initial resources they start with.

Who should get the benefit? This is a difficult, emotionally loaded question. In its simplest form you might consider the question of how to distribute the benefits from trade between Jim and Dan. Or suppose a new highway is being planned and there are alternative routes that it might follow. Each possible route gives benefits to different people, but which route is best?

We intend to duck this question because it involves value judgments that we all do not share. We can give some guidance, though, as to when some changes or redistributions should be done. Suppose that a change (call it C*) is contemplated that will benefit at least one person but harm no one. If our objective is to make individuals happier, such a change should be made. Now suppose a different change (C**) is contemplated that will benefit some people but harm at least one person. Here we can give no easy guidance. To clarify the difference we must define some terms:

Pareto[15] *Optimal Change*
A change that makes at least some people happier while hurting no one. (For example, change C*.)

Pareto Optimal Point
A point, or state, or distribution that we cannot move away from or change without hurting someone. (For example, the preexisting situation, *before* change C**, was a Pareto optimal state.)

In Figure 5.24 any of the three possible end points shown (G, E, C) are Pareto optimal points. But point B is not. The change from point B to point G, E, or C is a Pareto optimal change. When you start at some point like B, you know that trade will go on until a Pareto optimal point is reached. Once this occurs, voluntary trade must stop. A Pareto optimal point is a point where two indifference curves are tangent to each other. There are many such points between C and G, but only one of them, E, is shown. Figure 5.25 shows all the Pareto optimal points in the Edgeworth box (all the points where two indifference curves are tangent). Starting at point B you can only get to points on the line between C and G. You cannot get to F.

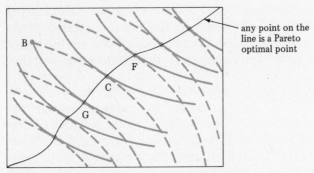

→ any point on the
line is a Pareto
optimal point

Figure 5.25: Location of Pareto optimal points.

STOP AND THINK. Why can voluntary trade between Jim and Dan, which starts at point B, never end up at point F?

The trading of axes and stingray tails among the Yir Yoront aborigines, described at the beginning of the chapter, is a good example of the type of behavior predicted by the Edgeworth box analysis. Similar trading behavior was observed among prisoners of war (P.O.W.s) in World War II: Every month or so Red Cross parcels would be passed out to all P.O.W.s. Each parcel was *identical* and contained items such as cigarettes, chocolate, and canned snacks. Yet because of the *difference* in tastes among the prisoners a very active trade in commodities arose and eventually they even made their own currency to facilitate the trading.

The ability to move people to Pareto optimal solutions is one of the most prized properties in the evaluation of markets or political systems. Though it is important, it is sometimes misunderstood. The following points about Pareto optimality are important:

1. In any situation there is not just one Pareto optimal point; there are many. And they can be radically different in their equity consequences.
2. Given that you are *not* at a Pareto optimal point, there is *some* set of Pareto optimal points that you can reach; but many Pareto optimal points are not reachable. It makes a difference where you start.

In short, mutually beneficial exchange is a powerful way of improving life, but it cannot "solve" inequities due to differences in initial resources. In this sense, then, it is conservative.

International trade among nations provides another example. The United States compared to Zambia has a relative abundance of consumer goods and a relative scarcity of copper. So the two countries agree to trade: Copper goes to the United States while consumer goods go to Zambia. Both countries are better off than they were before. Likewise, we trade for raw materials from many other underdeveloped countries, and again both sides gain from the trade. Why then is there so much controversy about this trade? Why do many critics claim that we are exploiting the Third World? Remember how we started at point B in Figure 5.24 and traded until we reached some point on the line between C and G. At C all the gains from trade went to one person, whereas at G all the gains went to the other person. Critics claim that because of its enormous power, the United States manages to negotiate trading contracts that give this country most of the gains from trade; that the underdeveloped countries do benefit from the trade but not enough. You might give some thought to ways of disproving or defending these claims.[16]

5.5.2   SUPPLY/DEMAND ANALYSIS (OPTIONAL)

The Edgeworth box analysis in the previous section is a demonstration of the common-sense proposition that mutual trade between two people or two countries can make *both* of them happier. In the example given we discussed direct exchange, barter, between people. We know that there is a good deal of exchange behavior in the world and that it is not usually done through barter. Instead, money is used as an intermediate, general-purpose good. Instead of direct exchange, we first trade one of our relatively abundant goods for money; then we take the money to someone else and trade it for some good that is relatively scarce. Thus instead of direct exchange (involving only two people), we have an indirect exchange (involving at least three people) through the use of money.

Are there any advantages to using money as an intermediate good? Or should we try to build an ideal world without money, one in which exchange is somehow simpler and more direct?

STOP AND THINK. Give this some thought. Should we try to build a system in which only direct, person-to-person exchanges are permitted ?

Imagine the world without money: Zacharia grows organic tomatoes and has a relative abundance of them. What he wants is a new pair of sandals, which are made in the commune across the mountain. He cannot transport tomatoes very easily, so he trades the tomatoes to local farmers for wheat, trades part of the wheat for a horse, and then transports the wheat across the mountains where he trades it for 20 pairs of sandals. He takes the sandals home and then trades them to a local hunter for meat. Meanwhile, he is still growing tomatoes and wonders how he is going to live this winter. Since he cannot store tomatoes, he trades more tomatoes for more wheat, and then trades wheat for lumber to build a storage shed for the wheat. When winter comes, he can eat some wheat and trade the rest for other items.

Money makes trading easier and more flexible. Money permits trade to take place over longer periods of time. Thus I can trade something for money now, then hold onto the money for a few months until I find some item that I wish to trade it for. Likewise, money permits trades to take place over longer distances. Thus I can trade something for money in one area and take the money to a distant area to buy something there. And money permits trades to take place over longer, more complex chains of people.

In our own world, of course, money is the intermediate trading good that we commonly use. The main question that concerns us in this section is how prices are determined. Who determines the exchange rate between money and goods? This particular exchange rate is of great personal interest: How many dollars do I have to exchange for an apartment, or a book, or a bag of groceries?

This section discusses the interaction of supply and demand. It is this interaction, working with a price signaling system, that society uses to make the kind of trades that the Edgeworth box analysis predicts. Supply/demand analysis is one of our most useful analytic tools. It can be applied to a wide variety of social problems with quite useful, though often controversial, results. We will eventually discuss its analysis of our farm subsidy program and of pollution control as two possible examples. But first, what is supply/demand analysis?

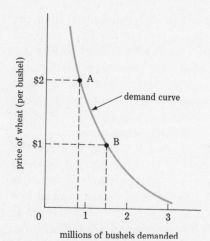

Figure 5.26: Demand curve for wheat. The amount of wheat consumers are willing to buy at a given price.

To begin we need some way of depicting the demand for some commodity. Suppose we are considering the demand for wheat at the Chicago Commodities Exchange. We know that wheat buyers are more interested in buying wheat when it is cheap and less interested when it is expensive. We can show this relationship between price and quantity demanded with a demand curve, as in Figure 5.26. First notice that the figure has price on one axis and quantity on the other. The demand curve shows the relation between the price of some particular good and the amount that people, as a group, are willing to buy. At a price of $2/bushel consumers are willing to buy a total of 0.8 million bushels of wheat. This is shown as point A on the demand curve. If the price of wheat were lower, consumers would be willing to purchase more. Thus point B shows that at a price of $1/bushel, consumers would like to purchase 1.5 million bushels of wheat.[17]

The demand curve is a schedule of consumer intentions. It shows the amount they would like to buy as a function of the price. It slopes downward because consumers are willing to buy more at lower prices. Notice that the demand curve only concerns one commodity at a time (whereas indifference curves concerned two commodities at a time); that there is only one demand curve for that commodity (whereas there was a whole family of indifference curves); and that the demand curve generally shows the desires of an entire group of consumers (whereas the indifference curve was only for a single person). Finally, remember that the *demand curve* is only a curve of *consumer intentions*. They may not be able to carry out these intentions. Consumers intend to buy 1.5 million bushels if the price is $1/bushel, but they may not be able to buy that much if producers are not willing to sell that amount of wheat. All anyone can say for certain is that consumers would not purchase any more than 1.5 million bushels at a price of $1 and that they may have to settle for less than that amount.

Figure 5.27 shows the supply curve for wheat. It gives the relationship between the price of wheat and the amount that farmers are willing to supply. The supply curve slopes upward because farmers are willing to supply more wheat at high prices than at low prices. The *supply curve* is a schedule of *producer intentions*. It shows what producers would like to do, not what they actually do. Thus if offered a price of $2/bushel for their wheat, farmers would be willing to supply as much as 3 million bushels of wheat but no more than that.

Suppose that the year is 1925, when the government did not interfere in the wheat market. How were prices set? Who decided how much wheat was produced? Since we already have a curve of consumer intentions and a curve of producer intentions, it seems reasonable to combine them so that we can examine them simultaneously. (This is easy to do because both curves have the same dimensions on their axes.) Figure 5.28 puts together the supply curve (ss) and the demand curve (dd).

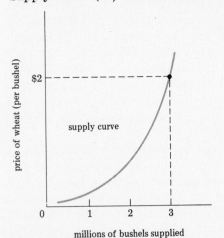

Figure 5.27: Supply curve for wheat. The amount of wheat farmers are willing to produce at a given price.

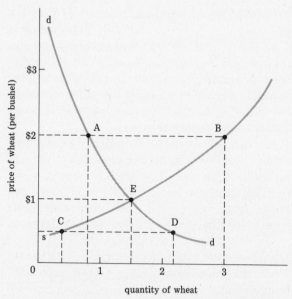

Figure 5.28: Determination of market equilibrium.

Point E is the equilibrium position where consumer intentions to purchase and farmer intentions to produce are simultaneously satisfied. It corresponds to a price of $1/bushel and sales
of 1.5 million bushels. Suppose that someone tries to increase the
price to $2/bushel. What would happen? This new price corresponds
to point B on the supply curve, meaning that farmers would wish
to grow and sell 3 million bushels. At $2/bushel consumers will be
at point A on the demand curve and would be willing to buy as
much as 0.8 million bushels. If farmers grow 3 million bushels and
consumers only buy 0.8 million, however, there is going to be a
surplus of 2.2 million bushels. If you were a farmer stuck with
excess wheat, in today's world, your first thought would probably
be to write your congressman and insist that the government purchase the surplus; but since this is 1925, you would use your second
alternative, namely, cut prices to clear out your surplus. Once a
few farmers start cutting prices, the others will have to follow and
the price will be driven back down toward the equilibrium price.
Thus competition between farmers acts to keep prices from rising
above the equilibrium.

What keeps prices from falling below the equilibrium? Suppose the price were to be set at 50 cents/bushel. This would be
point C on the supply curve and point D on the demand curve. At

this low price consumers would try to purchase more than farmers were willing to supply. The gap between amount supplied and amount demanded (D — C) would be seen as a shortage of wheat. Since some consumers are willing to pay more than 50 cents/bushel, they would offer more money in order to get wheat. This process would continue until consumers had bid the price up to $1 again. It is only at $1 that the amount consumers wish to buy and the amount that farmers wish to sell are equal.

Suppose the demand for wheat increased, either because of advertising ("Wheat makes you sexy") or because new uses are found for it (a new antibiotic that will only grow in wheat mush as a cultural medium). The increase in demand would shift the demand curve to the right, from d_1d_1 to d_2d_2 in Figure 5.29, indicating that at any given price there would be a higher level of consumption.

Suppose automation lowers the cost of production. This would cause an increase in supply, the shift from s_1s_1 to s_2s_2 in Figure 5.30. Any shift in the supply or demand curves will cause a corresponding shift in the market equilibrium price and quantity.

This analysis was for the wheat market in 1925. Since the Great Depression the government has adopted a number of measures designed to help farmers. One of the most commonly used devices is the system of price supports. Suppose that farm state congressmen convince the government that the price of wheat really ought to be $2. The government then decides to support prices at that level by becoming a buyer in the wheat market. Every time the

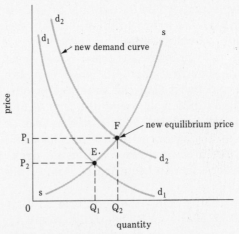

Figure 5.29: Effect of a shift in demand.

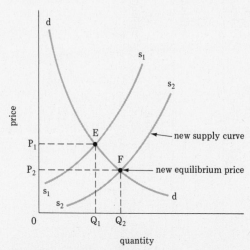

Figure 5.30: Effect of a shift in supply.

price of wheat starts to drop below \$2 the government buyers start buying wheat to push the price back up. Refer again to Figure 5.28 to see what effect this will have. At \$2 farmers will produce 3 million bushels, but consumers will only buy 0.8 million bushels. The 2.2 million bushels of unbought wheat must be taken by the government to keep the price at \$2.

Table 5.4 summarizes the effects of the price-support program. The first row shows the situation before price supports, and the second row shows the situation with price supports. Notice that farm income rises from \$1.5 to \$6 million (3 million bushels times \$2) ; that the amount of wheat received by consumers is decreased; that it actually costs consumers more money to obtain the lower quantity; and that the government now owns a lot of wheat.

This newly acquired wheat is a problem for the government. It is expensive to store, difficult to sell abroad without hurting the wheat sales of our foreign friends, and difficult even to give it away. (If the government tries to give it to a country, that country's own wheat farmers complain because the free U.S. wheat undercuts their local markets.) So the government now uses a program according to which it pays farmers to take agricultural land out of production. Figure 5.31 shows that this shifts the supply curve to the left ($s_2 s_2$) and gives a new equilibrium at point F. Consumers pay higher prices and receive less wheat (compared to E) ; farm income is increased (compared to E) because farmers get paid for not growing wheat; the amount of labor required in wheat

TABLE 5.4 *Price-Support Program for Wheat*

	PRICE OF WHEAT	AMOUNT CONSUMERS SPEND	NO. OF BUSHELS CONSUMERS RECEIVE	AMOUNT THE GOVERNMENT SPENDS	NO. OF BUSHELS GOVERNMENT RECEIVES	TOTAL INCOME OF FARMERS
Before Price Supports	$1	$1.5 million	1.5 million bushels	0	0	$1.5 million
With Price Supports	$2	$1.6 million	0.8 million bushels	$4.4 million	2.2 million bushels	$6 million

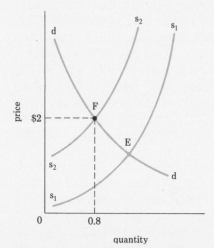

Figure 5.31 : Effect of Acreage Restrictions.

farming is changed; and the government no longer has a wheat surplus to worry about (compared to a system of price supports).

There are a number of alternative suggestions for replacing the current system of farm subsidies (one of which is discussed in the problem set), but they all have one central characteristic in common. They all involve a transfer of income from one group of people to another; they take money away from taxpayers to give it to farmers (In other words, they do not accept the initial distribution of income as equitable.)

Government farm policy in the United States (and in most European countries) is a standard illustration of the problems that develop when the workings of the supply/demand system are modified. It is worthwhile to discuss the classical operation some more. There is a market for almost all commodities, and it functions in such a way as to set coordinated prices and quantities—"coordinated" in the sense that there are neither surpluses nor shortages of the product at the given price. No one has to intervene in the market or plan the coordination because the forces of the market process do the coordinating. If public demand for some commodity increases (shifting the demand curve to the right), the price of that commodity increases, and the higher price encourages manufacturers to produce more. Note that this happens without any kind of official intervention; consumers do not have to write to their congressmen to have a federal memorandum sent to the manufacturers. Prices themselves are the only necessary means of communication. When prices go up (because of an increase in demand), manufacturers know that it is time to increase production. This same process occurs in the labor market as well. In the late 1950s there was an increase in demand for medical research, causing a shortage of biologists and health sciences personnel (B and HSP), and accordingly, the salaries of B and HSP started increasing. Because the price of B and HSP increased, more college students decided it would be worthwhile to go to graduate school in these fields; and so the production of B and HSP rose in response to the increased demand.

Thus consumer buying is something like voting in an election, except that instead of voting with "Xs" you vote with dollars. You cast your dollar votes for the products you like; and manufacturers who are smart enough to produce products that you like are rewarded accordingly. Your dollar votes influence prices, and prices in turn act as the master signaling system to keep the economy coordinated. This, incidentally, suggests why people who are poor might prefer government intervention in the economic system: They have a larger proportion of the political votes than of the dollar votes. Conversely, this suggests why rich people might oppose governmental participation in economic decisions.

The supply/demand price signaling system is never viewed as a perfect system. We choose to have the government intervene in a number of markets in order to modify their results. Many modern arguments over economic planning, price systems, and political systems concern the circumstances and methods for using a supply/demand price signaling system rather than a centrally planned political regulation of supply, demand, and price. Virtually no one believes that a supply/demand system should be used for all situations; virtually no one believes it should never be used. Between these bounds, however, there is enough disagreement to support at least two major schools of political/economic thought and considerable messianic fervor.

Example: Pollution (Optional)

Pollution, a difficult problem, is obviously also a problem of broad public concern. Accordingly, it seems appropriate to use the analytic tools developed in this chapter to take a closer look at it.

Imagine the kinds of problems faced by the president of a large manufacturing company. There has been much public protest about industrial pollution. He receives angry letters from customers, stockholders, and the public. The president of the company is probably a fairly smart person, and regardless of what you may think of his values it is interesting to see how he deals with the problem. The president decides to tackle the problem systematically, and he begins by writing something like this:

Step 1
What is the problem? We need to do something about pollution.

Step 2
Can I broaden the definition of the problem? Actually, what I mean to accomplish is to calm all those angry people.

Step 3
What are my alternatives? This broader definition of the problem seems to provide me with two alternative actions:
1. I can do something about pollution.
2. I can simply claim that I am doing something about pollution (that is, advertise).

Step 4
What are the constraints on my actions? The constraints are mostly monetary. We have only so many dollars to spend on better technology or on advertising.

Step 5
Can I find the best alternative? The natural thing is to make an indifference curve analysis.

The result is somewhat like Figure 5.32. The horizontal axis shows the amount of money spent on advertising; the vertical axis shows the amount of money spent on actual pollution reduction. The lines that look like indifference curves are lines of equal public satisfaction: The farther out you go, the higher the level of public satisfaction.

The president calls in his public relations people, and they determine that satisfaction level s_3 is the desirable level. The president knows the cost of advertising and the cost of new pollution reduction equipment, so he can determine the slope of his budget line; and he can also discover where a budget line having that slope is tangent to curve s_3. Thus he knows how much money to allocate to equipment ($E) and how much to allocate to advertising ($A), and his problem is solved.

All goes well for a few years until a Ralph Nader type of

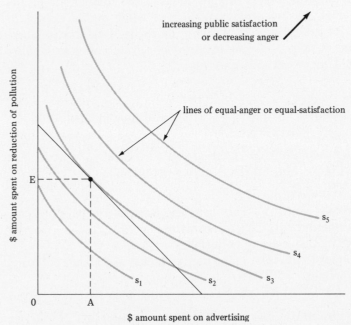

increasing public satisfaction
or decreasing anger

lines of equal-anger or equal-satisfaction

s_5

s_4

E

s_1 s_2 s_3

0   A

$ amount spent on reduction of pollution

$ amount spent on advertising

Figure 5.32: A pollution solution?

individual comes along and raises public consciousness over the effects of pollution. This changes the shape of the curves in Figure 5.32 and shifts them outward. Satisfaction level s_3 is now shifted farther to the northeast. Angry letters start coming in again; the neighbors do not talk with the president of the manufacturing company anymore; and small children throw stones at his car. So the president talks with his board of directors, gets a bigger "pollution" budget, and then shifts his budget line outward to find a new least-cost solution in which he is spending more on both advertising and technology.

Thus a major result of increased public consciousness about pollution is an increase in so-called public service advertising explaining how virtuous the manufacturers are. (You will probably recall that this was in fact one of the first noticeable effects of the ecology crusade.)

Such an outcome may not be completely satisfactory. Suppose you want to do something about pollution, not simply talk about it. What should you do? Most of us (including the authors) tend to think that one key problem is how to obtain the political power to do what we want. Once we have such power, however, we still need to know what kinds of laws we want. We might pass, for instance, a law saying that all manufacturers must reduce their current pollution level by 50% over the next year. How would such a law work in practice; what would its effects be?

Figure 5.33 shows the relationship between pollution reduction and cost for a typical manufacturer. The vertical axis shows the amount of pollution emitted by some manufacturing process. The horizontal axis shows the cost of controlling pollution output. The curve shows the relation between control expenditures and amount of emissions. With no control, expenditures emissions are high; the more money spent on controls, the lower the emissions. The curve is determined by the existing technological knowledge about pollution reduction, and real curves for actual plants often have this particular shape.

> **STOP AND THINK.** Why is the shape of this curve important? What does it say about the cost of reducing the first increment of pollution (say from 100 tons to 90

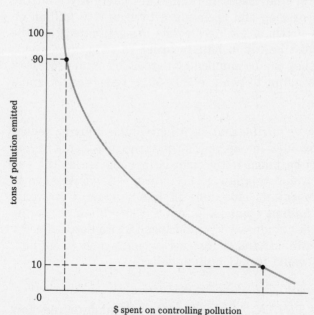

Figure 5.33: Cost of controlling pollution.

tons) versus the cost of reducing the last increment of pollution (from 10 tons to 0)?

It is a fact that it becomes more and more expensive to remove each successive increment of pollution. All industries will not have this same identical curve, but most will have curves of the same general shape. Table 5.5 shows the relation between emission and cost of control for five hypothetical industries. For example, industry A now emits 100 tons of glop and spends nothing on controls. They could reduce their emissions to 50 tons by spending $1 million. Industry B is already spending $10 million on controls and is emitting 100 tons of glop; the expenditure of an additional million dollars would reduce its emissions by only 15 tons (compared to the 50-ton reduction in A).

Figure 5.33 and Table 5.5 show that it is increasingly expensive to have higher and higher increments of cleanliness. Zero pollution would be incredibly expensive. Fortunately, zero pollution as a goal is not necessary on most kinds of emissions, since the environment has an ability to handle and clean up certain amounts of pollution by itself. In Table 5.5 the five industries, according to the first line across the table, are currently emitting a total of 500 tons of glop and spending a total of $10 million on emission control. A group of local ecologists has estimated that the emission of glop must be cut in half in order to reduce emissions to the point where they can be handled by natural cleanup processes.

How are we going to achieve this 50% reduction in emissions?

Plan 1. Pass a law requiring that each individual industry reduce its output of glop by 50% in one year's time; the presidents of any offending firms will be jailed if the firm is in violation at the end of the year. What would this law cost? Industry A would have to spend $1 million to cut its emissions in half; industry B would have to spend $35 million (that is, an extra $35 million above the amount it now spends); industry C would spend $1 million; industry D would spend $2 million; and industry E would spend $2 million. The combined cost would be $41 million dollars.

STOP AND THINK. First, be sure you understand how these numbers are derived. Then consider the following

TABLE 5.5 Cost of Emission Control for Typical Industries

INDUSTRY A		INDUSTRY B		INDUSTRY C		INDUSTRY D		INDUSTRY E	
Tons of Glop Emitted	$ Cost of Controls	Tons of Glop Emitted	$ Cost of Controls	Tons of Glop Emitted	$ Cost of Controls	Tons of Glop Emitted	$ Cost of Controls	Tons of Glop Emitted	$ Cost of Controls
100	0	100	10	100	0	100	0	100	0
50	1	85	11	50	1	70	1	70	1
20	2	73	12	30	2	50	2	50	2
10	3	69	13	15	3	33	3	40	3
5	4	67	14	5	4	19	4	35	4
1	5	60	30	0.1	5	8	5	—	—
0.01	6	50	45	0.01	6	2	6	0.01	95
—	—	0.01	250	—	—	0.01	7	—	—

(*Note:* Costs are in millions of dollars.)

questions: Is there anything unfair about this solution? Furthermore, is it the cheapest possible solution? Why?

We have already discussed the nature of the emission reduction curve. Industry B is already spending $10 million and hence is already on the flatter portion of its curve; if it had been spending nothing at all on controls (and emitting, say, 300 tons of glop), then it would have cost the industry less than $10 million to comply with the new law. Instead, because industry B was already on the flat portion of its control curve, it must spend an additional $35 million. The other industries, on the other hand, which have been spending nothing, will have to spend relatively little (only $6 million among them) because they are still on the steep portions of their control curves. This situation hardly seems fair.

Furthermore, Plan 1 is certainly not the cheapest possible solution to the problem. It achieves a 250-ton reduction at a combined cost of $41 million. (The total amount being spent for pollution controls is $51 million: the $10 million that was already being spent by industry B plus the additional $41 million necessitated by the new law.) If you examine Table 5.5 carefully, you will see that it is much cheaper to reduce emissions in some industries than in others. For example, $4 million spent in industry A gives a reduction of 95 tons; $4 million spent in industry C gives a reduction of 95 tons; and $3 million spent in industry D gives a reduction of 60 tons. (Be sure that you understand these figures.) This total reduction of 250 tons (which was your goal) has a combined cost of only $11 million. In fact, there are even cheaper solutions than this if you examine the table carefully. We conclude, therefore, that Plan 1 is not only unfair but also unnecessarily expensive.

It is worth analyzing the consequences of the pollution-control expense. Plan 1 would have increased pollution control costs by $41 million; the solution in the preceding paragraph would have increased costs by only $11 million. Does the difference matter? Why do we, as consumers, care that one solution costs manufacturers more money than another? First, the money spent on pollution controls is used to buy goods and services (for example, better smokestack and masons to build them). The amount of goods and services produced by the total economy at any one time is limited; otherwise we would all have as much as we wanted. The more of these goods and services that are devoted to pollution control, the less that are available for other uses that we might like, such as consumer goods and better schools. Therefore, we want our solution to the pollution problem to be the least total cost, the most efficient solution. Second, there is an alternative way of looking at the cost argument. Figure 5.34 shows the supply and demand curves for a typical product. The initial supply curve, s_1, and the demand curve, d, intersect at E_1 to determine the equilibrium price and quantity for that product. Now obviously the supply curve for the product is dependent upon the cost of manufacturing, and an increase in manufacturing cost must shift the supply curve upward.

If a manufacturer spends more money on pollution control, his manufacturing costs go up, giving the new supply curve, s_2. The curve s_2 is parallel to s_1, but it is higher by the amount of the cost increase. Notice the two points G and H: The vertical distance between them represents the per-unit cost of increased pollution controls. The new supply curve produces a new equilibrium at E_2, where consumers are paying higher prices and buy less of that good. The consumer price increase, $P_2 - P_1$, must be less than the manufacturer's cost increase unless the demand curve is perfectly

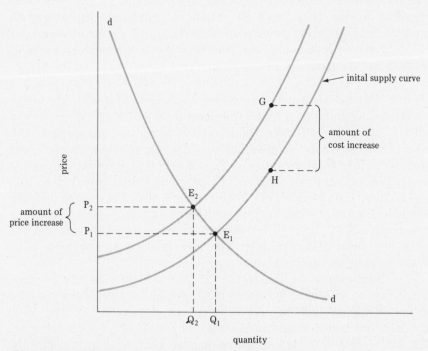

Figure 5.34: Effect of cost increase for a typical product.

vertical. The consumer price increase would be smaller if the demand curve were flatter, but unless it becomes horizontal, there must be some consumer price increase. Thus we can see that part of the cost of increased pollution control must be borne by consumers; therefore, consumers should be interested in having the controls operate as cheaply and efficiently as possible.

Now that we are convinced that efficiency is important, we devise another plan.

Plan 2. Hire a crew of pollution engineers to go to every plant in the area and determine its individual curve of pollution reduction cost. Figure out the combination of emission reductions by each plant that gives the desired total reduction for the least total cost. Pass a law that specifies the amount by which each individual plant must reduce its emissions.

There are some problems with this plan, however. We must hire many technicians to get the basic information and then administer it. Each plant has a strong incentive to misrepresent its potential pollution reduction cost (if they can convince the planners that it would be very expensive for them to change, then they will have to do less changing). It would be continually necessary to modify the legislation to keep up with changing circumstances.

Let us propose another plan that keeps the efficient parts of Plan 2 and discards its disadvantages.

Plan 3. Put a sealed metering device on the smokestacks or sewage outlets of all industries and have monthly meter men go around to each plant to record their pollution output figures (essentially the same setup as electric companies now use, except that we meter an outflow rather than an inflow). Pass a law that charges industries a certain amount per unit of pollution emitted, payable to the government. Make no other requirements. That is, industries are not obligated to any particular pollution reduction goals or to telling the truth about their pollution reduction curves (in fact, do not even ask them about them). They are free to do anything they want so long as they pay their pollution meter bill.

What would be the results of plan 3? Suppose the government tax on pollution is set at $50,000 per ton. We examine the situation facing industry A: It is emitting 100 tons of glop, and its pollution meter would indicate a tax bill of $5 million (that is, 100 times $50,000). It can go on paying this amount indefinitely if it wishes, but presumably somebody in accounting would figure out that industry A could cut its tax bill in half for a cost of only $1 million. That is, the industry could spend $1 million on control equipment to reduce emissions by 50 tons and hence save $2.5 million in taxes. This is certainly a good investment. In fact, spending an additional million dollars would reduce emissions by another 30 tons (that is, put the industry at the 20 ton/$2 million point on its pollution reduction curve) and hence save industry A an additional $1.5 million in taxes. This is another good investment.

Another way of describing what happens is this: The initial 50-ton reduction had a marginal cost of $1 million and marginal tax savings of $2.5 million. The marginal cost of the next 30-ton reduction was also $1 million, and the marginal tax saving was $1.5 million.

STOP AND THINK. We have demonstrated that industry A will find it financially advantageous to reduce its emission down to at least the 20-ton level. Will they have any incentive to reduce emissions still further? Is it financially advantageous to reduce to the 10-ton level?

A reduction to the 10-ton output level would be another 10-ton reduction in emissions (from an output level of 20 tons of glop to a level of 10 tons). This would save industry A $0.5 million in taxes (10 times $50,000) and would cost $1 million for additional control equipment. Since the marginal cost is greater than the marginal tax savings, the industry will not reduce to the 10-ton output level.

The same obvious line of reasoning will occur to the managements of the other industries as well: B will continue at its present level; C will reduce to the 30-ton output level; D will reduce to the 50-ton output level; E will reduce to the 50-ton output level; and we already know that A will reduce to the 20-ton output level. Thus we have reached our original target of a 250-ton reduction. The dollars spent on reduction will be: A—$2 million; B—no additional spending; C—$2 million; D—$2 million; and E—$2 million. Thus the combined cost of Plan 3 will be only $8 million dollars.

Plan 3 is not only the cheapest way for society to reduce total emissions, it is also the easiest to administer. We simply set a level for the pollution tax and then allow natural, high incentive, cost-cutting behavior of manufacturers to do the rest. Since they have the most knowledge of their own plants and processes, they will know the most efficient ways to cut pollution output. We do not tell them exactly what they should do; we merely give them an incentive. If a particular tax level does not produce enough emission reduction, we simply raise the tax level.

Notice though that the final outcome of Plan 3 does not involve equal pollution output per industry. Some industries will be polluting more than others. Hence there are many people who might say:

> "This solution is inequitable. There should be equal sacrifice by each industry. They should all be equally clean. It is unjust to allow some industries to pollute a lot just because they are rich enough to afford the higher taxes from their pollution."

The contrary argument from most economists would be

> "It is true that some industries will be contributing a greater share of the "acceptable" pollution level. This happens because some industries are bigger or are producing inherently messy products or because their products are so costly that the pollution tax is only a small fraction of their total production cost. Equal "sacrifice" is a myth: It would be difficult to define it in the first place and impossible to administer if you could define it. Our goal was to reduce total pollution to an acceptable level, and we did that in the fashion that was cheapest, and easiest to administer. If you want a still lower level of pollution, then raise the tax."

STOP AND THINK. You will probably encounter both arguments yourself in the future: with friends, in the media, or in congressional discussions. Which argument do you think is correct? (No answer is supplied here. You must consider the question yourself.)

Society faces many situations in which it wishes to change human behavior. Legislative coercion is one way of doing so. There are laws that say what you should do and not do. Changing incentives is another way of changing human behavior. Thus with regard to the agricultural surplus problem, you might either forbid farmers to grow more than a certain amount of wheat or give them financial incentives for reducing output by changing the prices that they can receive. Or with regard to the goal of producing more low-cost housing for the poor, you might either have direct government intervention through direct programs of government building or simply make low-cost loans or low-cost materials available to anyone who wanted to build that type of housing. Or with regard to the problem of decreasing wasted materials in a production process, you might either circulate a memo setting specific goals or institute an employee profit-sharing plan allocating, say, 50 cents out of every dollar saved on the production line for wage bonuses.

The general question is that of direct, centralized *controls* versus a system of indirect, decentralized *incentives*. A common first reaction to solving almost any problem is to choose coercion— pass a law or issue an order. Yet because the world is more complex than we realize, this direct solution will often be inefficient, or it may not work at all. Restructuring the incentives in a situation is sometimes a better solution, even though it has the psychological disadvantage of seeming indirect and circuitous.

Restructuring the incentives in a situation—indirect intervention—allows people more individual control over their own actions and is often a good way to solve a problem. In what instances would you use indirect intervention? As you answer, you might speculate on the following observations: Conservatives seem to favor indirect intervention in the economic sphere but direct control in the moral/social sphere. Modern liberals seem to favor direct central intervention in the economic sphere and an indirect intervention strategy in the moral/social sphere.

5.5.3 DERIVATION OF SUPPLY AND DEMAND CURVES (OPTIONAL)

Most of the problems we work on can be analyzed with only a general knowledge of the shape of supply and demand curves. Occasionally, we need precise knowledge about the curves. This can be obtained by a complex statistical analysis of existing economic data (and economists devote a great deal of time to these analyses). We can also obtain a demand curve from indifference maps. This is not practical in a real situation but is fun to do as a theoretical exercise. An example follows:

Figure 5.35 is Henry's indifference map for wheat versus "all other goods," that is, every other commodity that Henry might buy. So any movement along an indifference curve represents a trade-

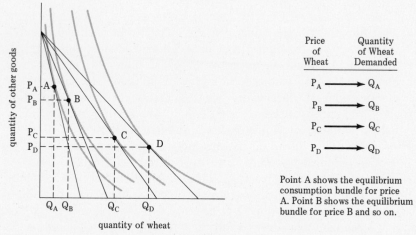

Figure 5.35: Derivation of Henry's demand curve.

off between wheat and all the other goods that Henry might buy. At the existing price of wheat, P_A, the slope of the budget line is such that Henry reaches an equilibrium at point A and buys Q_A amount of wheat. If the price of wheat is lowered to P_B, the budget line will rotate counterclockwise and produce a new equilibrium at B and a new equilibrium quantity of wheat Q_B. By drawing the budget lines associated with different wheat prices we can discover the amount of wheat that will be bought at different prices. This can then be plotted as Henry's individual demand curve for wheat,

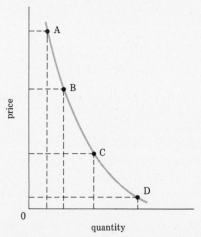

Figure 5.36: Henry's demand curve for wheat.

Figure 5.36. We could make such an individual demand curve for everyone and then add up all the individual demand curves to obtain society's demand curve for wheat.[18]

References

Robert Dorfman, *The Price System* (Englewood Cliffs, N.J.: Prentice-Hall, 1964).

Richard G. Lipsey and Peter O. Steiner, *Economics* (New York: Harper & Row, 1969).

George C. Homans, *Social Behavior* (New York: Harcourt Brace Jovanovich, 1961).

Richard L. Simpson, *Theories of Social Exchange* (Morristown, N.J.: General Learning Press, 1973).

Notes

[1] Technical Point: It is also dependent on how many units of other things you already have. For example, the marginal utility of the second hamburger is quite high when you have no other food and quite low when you have a whole refrigerator full of goodies. Thus marginal utilities are interdependent, and you cannot simply add up the two columns in Table 5.1 to calculate the total utility associated with various combinations of books and hamburgers.

[2] This assumes that it is meaningful to talk about fractional numbers such as 1.2 hamburgers.

[3] An indifference curve shows all points of equal happiness and is a curved line. A consumption possibility line shows all points of equal total cost and is a straight line. Why is one curved and the other straight? The curvature of an indifference curve reflects your *changing* relative preferences. As you move along the curve and obtain more of one good, the marginal utility associated with gaining one more unit of that good declines because of its growing abundance. Hence at the extremes of the curve you are willing to trade quite a bit of the relatively abundant good to get a little more of the relatively scarce good. The straightness of the consumption possibility line reflects the *constant* trading ratio between the two goods in the market. Even when one good becomes relatively abundant to you, its market exchange ratio (how much of one good you can trade to someone else for some of the other good) remains constant. The line reflects constant external trading ratios in the marketplace. It is, of course, possible that a consumption possibility line will be curved or that an indifference curve will be straight. We leave experimenting with such cases as an exercise.

[4] In this model of exchange (it is the one used by almost all economists) preferences are assumed to be fixed; they are not influenced by price changes in the short run. Of course, alternative models are conceivable.

[5] It is also possible to draw indifference maps where this effect does not occur.

[6] At the time of this writing the Federal Trade Commission is finally beginning to ask that advertisers prove their claims.

[7] *The important point* about the preceding military testimony *is that neither the Air Force nor the Navy believed that there were any alternative actions.* They each had a fixed, minimum, necessary way of providing defense. *The essential step in our analysis* involved broadening the definition of the problem. We went from "what is the minimum number of Xs that, all by themselves, could carry out the X role" to the more general statement of "how we can achieve the minimum level of defense."

Although we do not do so here, it would be interesting and productive to broaden the goal even more: What we want is not defense but security from attack. This new goal points to alternatives like international negotiation, initiation of friendship offenses, and so on.

[8] There are four different ecology organizations and a biology club on campus. All of the campus political parties—Young Republicans, Democrats, Socialists, and so on—have taken strong pro-ecology positions. Students could spend money on the first three items by contributing to these organizations or by more direct purchases. As it turns out, the $8 spent on the first three items came from $6 in contributions and one purchase of bottled water.

[9] There are, of course, a wide variety of other theories for why people say one thing and do another. The phenomenon is a common one. See Irwin Deutscher, *What We Say/What We Do: Sentiments and Acts* (Glenview, Ill., Scott Foresman, 1973).

[10] Note that we are playing with a model here. We are not claiming a complete analysis of all the factors affecting interpersonal relations. Our model only deals with one of these factors; hence we are implicitly saying: "If all the other factors that affect courtship/marriage/divorce behavior are held constant and we only allow relative scarcity to vary, then the result will be. . . ."

[11] In fact, if you are interested in finer details, you could do it all in one step on a three-dimensional graph, using separate axes for study time, Byron time, and Mike time. The simplication here is all right to establish some general properties, however.

[12] Since she is purchasing more knowledge (the dotted vertical line from F lies to the right of the dotted vertical line from E) and the time-price of knowledge has not changed, then she must be spending more time on it.

[13] However, there are situations in which social scientists need to make specific numerical predictions. For example, about five years ago a number of social scientists were arguing that long-distance phone rates were too high. Their claim was that a large reduction in rates would increase phone usage by more than enough to compensate for the lower revenue per call. That is, the lower rates would benefit both the public and the telephone company. The theory developed in this chapter shows that decreasing the price of some good will cause people to buy more of it, but this is too general a result. Specific numerical predictions were needed to justify the proposed new phone prices. The demand curve, discussed in Section 5.5.2, is the tool used to analyze such situations. And measurement of actual demand curves is done via statistical analysis of real world data.

[14] There are two exceptions: It would be possible to change some of the simple conclusions in the school lunch problem and the dating problem if you redrew the curves a certain way. But even in these cases the fundamental conclusions would remain unchanged.

[15] This is named after the Italian economist, Vilfredo Pareto, who worked about 70 years ago.

[16] Here is some additional perspective on the question: Most developed countries trade with other developed countries, not with the Third World—more specifically, 80% of the dollar volume of world trade is among developed nations, while only 20% of it is between the developed and underdeveloped nations.

[17] We are only discussing the relation between the price of some commodity and the demand for it. We realize that there are factors other than price that might affect demand, but for the moment we assume that these are held constant. Thus in the demand curves we assume that only the price variable moves while all other relevant variables remain the same.

[18] The easiest way to do this would be to construct a total demand table first. For example, at $2/bushel, George wants 5 bushels, Ed wants 7 bushels, and Henry wants 3 bushels. So the *total* wheat demanded is 15 bushels if the price is $2. Total the demand at other possible prices and then enter the sums in the table too. Finally, plot the data from the table to obtain society's demand curve for wheat. (In this example "society" consists of only George, Ed, and Henry.)

Problems 5.2

1. You are tired of staring at the walls and decide to take your two ex-boyfriends Spike and Al to the snack bar. Spike orders milk and remarks that he strongly prefers it to coffee. ("It's better tasting and *good* for you.") Al orders coffee, remarking that he strongly prefers coffee to milk. Rather than participate in such a fascinating conversation, you doodle on your napkin to see whether you can draw indifference maps for the two men that illustrate their strong relative preferences.

    (a) Draw the indifference maps.
    (b) If milk costs 15 cents, coffee costs 10 cents, and each man has $3 per week to spend on nonalcoholic beverages, show the equilibrium consumption point for each man and state how many cups of coffee and glasses of milk that point represents.
    (c) Do (b) again under the assumption that each man's budget is increased to $4.50 per week.
    (d) Do (b) again under the assumption that coffee is cut to 5 cents per cup.
    (e) Do (b) again under the assumption that the price of milk is increased to 20 cents.

    On all of these put milk on the vertical axis and coffee on the horizontal axis, draw a numerical scale along each axis, show each separate equilibrium point, and then state what consumption levels that point implies.

2. As part of a social science experiment you are spying on the consumption habits of your two roommates, Helen and Omar. Both of

them have been eating dinner at the Grease 'n Gravy Café every night. Dinner is always the same, and you have observed that each consumes 10 cheeseburgers and 12 orders of french fries per week. (Cheeseburgers cost $1, french fries 50 cents.) Under new management, the café cuts the price of cheeseburgers in half but leaves the price of french fries unchanged. The food is still the same. Helen now eats 16 cheeseburgers and 16 orders of french fries per week; Omar now eats 22 cheeseburgers and 10 orders of french fries per week.

(a) Draw an indifference map for each roommate showing each person's former and current equilibrium position.

(b) Give a *brief* written explanation of why lowering the price of cheeseburgers makes both roommates consume more of them.

(c) Give a *brief* written explanation of why lowering the price of cheeseburgers makes one roommate consume more french fries and the other roommate consume less.

3. A social scientist asked Jerry Juicer how much he valued various combinations of champagne and cognac. He got the following results:

COMBINATION	NO. OF BOTTLES CHAMPAGNE	NO. OF BOTTLES COGNAC	RESULTANT UTILITY (UTILS)
1	0	2	100
2	0	5	200
3	0	8	300
4	1	0	100
5	1	5	300
6	1	8	400
7	2	3	300
8	2	5	400
9	2	8	500
10	3	0	200
11	3	3	400
12	3	6	500
13	4	6	600
14	5	0	300
15	5	1	400
16	5	3	500
17	6	2	500
18	7	0	400
19	7	1	500
20	9	0	500
21	9	1	600
22	1	11	500
23	0	11	400
24	0	15	500
25	4	2	425
26	2	1	200

(a) Draw Jerry's indifference curves for champagne versus cognac and answer all of the following questions *with lines on the indifference curves*. (Put champagne on the horizontal axis, cognac on the vertical.)

(b) Suppose Jerry is at combination 11; which ambrosia does he prefer?

(c) Assume Jerry has a liquor budget of $30. What will he buy if champagne costs $5 a bottle and cognac costs $5 a bottle?

(d) Ernest Cutbubbler has invented a process that reduces the cost of champagne to $2.73 a bottle. What will Jerry do with his liquor budget now?

(e) Outraged, nature responds by destroying some of the grape crop; and the price of champagne jumps to $7.50 a bottle. What will Jerry do?

(f) In the world of (c) Jerry starts giving $15/week to charity and cuts his liquor budget to $15.

(g) Suppose Jerry is now at combination 12. How much cognac will it take to compensate him for the loss of one bottle of champagne? How much for the loss of one more bottle of champagne? How much for the loss of one additional bottle?

(h) Is there a trend in the numbers in (g)? What does it mean?

4. Assume that Joe has $4 to spend on beer and pretzels. Pretzels cost 20 cents a bag, and beer costs 40 cents a glass.

(a) Draw a graph with beer on the vertical axis and pretzels on the horizontal axis and draw in Joe's consumption possibility line.

(b) Assume that beer goes up to 50 cents a glass. Draw the new consumption possibility line.

(c) Do the same thing for a beer price of 20 cents.

(d) Assume Joe's budget doubles and that beer still costs 40 cents. Draw the consumption possibility line.

5. The United States has periodically used food stamps as a part of its welfare program. Food stamps are provided to poor people. They may be used as part payment for certain designated food.

(a) Recently, Senator Artichoke has uncovered a major scandal in the program. He charges that since food stamps were introduced in Midland, Ohio, the residents have been buying better cars. In fact, he has obtained data indicating that the average value of cars owned by poor people in Midland has risen from $500 to $700 in one year. He says, "This program was designed to put food into the mouths of the poor, not to put the poor into fancy automobiles." Comment on the charges from the point of view of indifference curve analysis.

(b) Professor Tuff Milton has lectured his students on the futility and stupidity of food-stamp welfare programs. He advocates direct income subsidies for the poor. Although he concedes that the political realities are such that Congress will support larger apparent subsidies in the form of food stamps than it will in the form of direct cash, he argues that the difference is illusory. He says, "The poor, not the fat cats in Washington, should decide how to spend their subsidy." Comment on the position from the point of view of indifference curve analysis.

6. It is often said that California wine growers export most of their good wines to New York and save most of their bad wines to sell in California. Here are some (hypothetical) sales figures available that bear on this assertion.

	CALIFORNIA	NEW YORK
Good California wine sold in	$ 4 million	$9 million
Bad California wine sold in	$11 million	$6 million

Is all this part of some subversive plot against the people of California? Use the indifference curve analysis shown in this book to examine the assertion. In California good wine costs $2 a bottle, and bad wine costs $1 a bottle. It costs $1 per bottle (whether the wine is good or bad) to transport wine across the country; thus in New York good wine costs $3 per bottle, and bad wine costs $2 per bottle. (*Assume:* Indifference maps for wine are the same in New York and California.) Use indifference maps and budget lines in your answer.

7. The University of New Hope is considering a number of alternative ways in which it might organize student activities on the campus. Three plans have been proposed:

Plan 1

Elect a student legislature. This legislature then imposes a student activities fee upon all students and uses the money to support various activities (for example, lectures, dances, concerts, professorial supplemental salaries, newspapers) that it deems important.

Plan 2

Elect a student legislature. This legislature imposes a student activities fee upon all students. This money is then returned to the individual students in the form of script that may be spent for any of the same activities possible under Plan 1. Any group of students that can amass a certain amount of script can organize an activity. Script not spent within the school year becomes worthless, and unspent money is turned over to the legislature.

Plan 3

No legislature is elected, and no fee is collected. Each individual student spends his money as he pleases.

Discuss these alternatives from the point of view of indifference curve analysis. What are the advantages and disadvantages of each? Which would be most attractive to student leaders? Can you devise any alternative that would be better than any of these?

8. Discuss, using some sort of exchange analysis, a proposal to replace the present system of providing public education (precollege) with a completely private educational system, each parent being provided with a government subsidy for education that he could spend at the schools of his choice.

9. One of the authors has two dogs that are given two large meals a day, in the morning and evening. Their food dish is left out between feedings, and the amount of food is sufficiently large that there is generally some left when the dish is picked up to have the next meal put in. (It is washed out first, of course.) Two kinds of food are available, one chicken flavored and the other meat flavored. They are alternated every day; two meals of chicken followed by two meals of meat.

Initial Observation

On days when meat is served, only about half of the food is eaten up by the time the next meal is to be served; on days when chicken is served, almost all of the food is eaten.

Initial Hypothesis.

The dogs have a strong preference for chicken over meat.

Alternative hypothesis

After a day of stuffing themselves, naturally the dogs have smaller appetites the next day; they have simply gotten into the habit of big meals every other day, and by accident that day coincides with chicken.

Second Observation

The dogs were given chicken two days in a row and then the alternation pattern was begun again; once the new routine was established, the dogs repeated their former behavior of eating more chicken than meat.

Third Observation

A new feeding pattern is started—two days of chicken followed by one day of meat, then repeat pattern—the dogs now eat almost equal amounts of both kinds of food.

Fourth Observation

A new feeding pattern is started—three days of chicken followed by one day of meat, then repeat pattern—the dogs now consume equal amounts of chicken and meat.

Can you explain their strange behavior? (*Hint:* the dogs are pulis [Hungarian sheepdogs] and are very intelligent—perhaps a human-based exchange model might work.)

Problems 5.3

1. You have examined the time allocation examples carefully and now want to see whether they can be of any real help to you. You decided that you have 20 hours a week to give to dating, and you know what your indifference curves are for the two possibilities, Jennifer and Suzy. But the solution is not obvious because you do not know how to handle your cash limitations: You have only $10/week spending money. This causes no problem with Jennifer as she is the sensitive, dreamy type who thinks that a quiet walk and an ice cream cone makes a fine evening, whereas Suzy craves bright lights and action. Your past experience tells you that it costs only about 25 cents/hour to keep Jennifer happy, while Suzy's upkeep is $1/hour.

   (a) Using indifference curves, show how many hours per week you spend with each girl. (*Assumption:* You have similar preferences for both girls; that is your indifference curves are symmetrical about a 45 degree line.)

   (b) Which girl do you spend the most time with, and which girl do you have the greatest relative value for?

2. Hiram has been offered a job at Sean's Kosher Restaurant and Psychedelic Lounge. He has the option of being paid *either* $100 per week *or* 250 pastrami sandwiches a week. He must accept one or the other; no combinations are permitted.

   (a) Show his consumption possibilities and his choice on an indifference map.

   (b) Hiram's girlfriend, Prudence, has been offered a job at Sean's also. Her indifference map is identical to Hiram's. Her job also pays *either* $100 *or* 250 pastrami sandwiches (whichever she chooses). She makes the same choice as Hiram (one or the other). Can you suggest an alternative decision that she and Hiram might consider? (Assume that they can trust each other.) Argue using the indifference map from (a).

3. You are David Ben Geste, heroic one-eyed commander of a lonely desert outpost. The enemy is attacking at dawn, and you must construct your defenses. You know that your men can string 100 feet of barbed wire per hour or that they can plant 50 mines per hour.

   (a) Using Figure 5.9 as an example, draw a set of deterrence curves for this situation. Put number of mines on the vertical axis and number of feet of barbed wire on the horizontal axis. In this case the deterrence lines (which look like indifference curves) will show the trade-off between mines and wire in terms of their relative enemy-stopping power. Thus, for example, your lowest deterrence curve might show all the combinations of mines and wire with an enemy-stopping power of 100 enemies; and your highest deterrence curve might show combinations with a stopping power of 500 enemies. In terms of scale the farthest point on the horizontal axis should be for about 1000 feet of wire; the highest point on the vertical axis should be for about 750 mines.

(b) There are 10 hours before dawn. What is the strongest defense you can produce? How much barbed wire does this use? How many mines?

(c) Suppose your scouts have discovered that there are less than 200 of the enemy. What is the minimum number of hours you can spend on defense construction and still be secure? How much barbed wire does this use? How many mines? *Be sure that you draw lines on the graph that justify your answers. Label the lines!*

(d) A clever private has figured out a way to plant 75 mines per hour. Redo (b) of the problem.

(e) Suppose that the more you do a job, the better you become at it. In this case the rate of mine planting or wire stringing gets higher and higher as you do more and more of it. What would happen to the shape of your time-budget line? Do not rework any part of the problem, simply explain the new shape.

Note. Problems 4 and 5 deal with different aspects of the same situation. One concerns society's decision and is in the form of the verbal models of Chapters Two and Three. The other presents an individual's situation in terms of the exchange model. When society, through its legislature, attempts to implement its values, one thing it may wish to do is to look at how individuals will act under various possible economic incentives. After doing these two problems, you should think for a moment about how they are interrelated.

4. Last year the County Board of Supervisors (where one of the authors lives) voted down a plan to provide free taxi service for pregnant women to and from periodic medical checkups. The League of Women Voters then issued a strong criticism of this decision. Formulate *realistic* arguments for and against this proposal, each in terms of a model. That is, give a model (set of assumptions) from which you can deduce that passage of the bill will be beneficial to society in the long run. Then give a different model from which it follows that the bill would have harmful effects in the long run.

5. Mary is pregnant and poor. The only way she can get to the hospital for free checkups is by a taxi ride, which costs $5 round trip.

(a) Draw some normal, convex indifference curves for Mary. Put the total number of taxi trips on the vertical axis. (Make 16 trips the top point.) Put total spending money on the horizontal axis.

(Make $50 the farthest point.) The indifference curves reflect the fact that Mary can derive happiness from taxi rides or else from spending her money on things other than taxi rides. Make the curves quite steep, and have them intersect the horizontal axis.

(b) Draw Mary's *consumption possibility line* and state *how many trips* she will take in each of the following circumstances. You may assume that no other considerations affect her decision. (*Note:* In one of these cases the consumption possibility line is actually *two* line segments.)

i. She has $30. ii. She has $30 and 4 free tickets for taxi rides. iii. She has $30 and a card that certifies that she is entitled to discount rides; so she pays only $2 per ride. iv. She has $50.

(c) In (b) think of case i as Mary's initial situation and the three other cases as various ways of subsidizing her. Which of the three makes her happiest? Next happiest? Least happy?

(d) On the same set of axes sketch in and label some indifference curves for Susan, who would be happiest in case iii.

(e) Does Susan value a trip of this kind more or less highly than Mary?

6. Pescadero Academy offers two courses, English and French. In each course yearly grades ranging from 0 to 100 are given. In each of the following questions, assume that you have been invited to provide the academy with expert consultation based on your knowledge of indifference curve analysis. Show the analysis clearly.

(a) A careful study of the students at the academy indicates that girls can increase their grades in English at a rate of ½ point for every hour they spend on English and can increase their grades in French at a rate of 2 points for every hour spent on French. Boys, on the other hand, can increase their grades at a rate of 1 point for every hour spent in either subject. Assuming that each student has a maximum of 150 hours to spend on English and French combined, show the possibilities open to academy boys and girls.

(b) If each student wishes to maximize his average grade, subject to the constraint that a grade of at least 50 is obtained in each course, what will a girl student do? A boy student? (Show the analysis clearly.)

(c) Suppose the French department doubles the difficulty of its course (that is, doubles the amount of time required to increase a grade by 1 point) for both girls and boys. How would your answer to (b) change?

(d) Given the situation in (c), what would happen if each student found he had a maximum of 200 hours to spend?

(e) In many schools in the United States grading in physics is systematically lower than grading in some other courses. Comment on what some of the consequences would be if grades in physics were made about comparable to grades in other courses (for equal amounts of work on the average).

7. The concept of cost is derived directly from the implications of elementary exchange analysis; the cost of undertaking an activity is the alternatives that are given up. For example, the cost of a movie to you is the value of some other item you gave up in order to consume the movie. (This may be money, generalized purchasing power, but money itself derives most of its value from its ability to purchase other things.) Do *one* of the following:

(a) Last week a local professor said, "Education is expensive, but nothing is more valuable." Draw the implied indifference curves and budget lines. Is the statement correct?

(b) Newport Beach is a free public beach; that is, there is no admission charge. Is this true? What is the cost and who pays it?

(c) The following was overheard in the snack bar last week: "I have a four-year, full-expense scholarship covering my tuition and fees, room, and board; so going to college doesn't cost me anything."

  i. Is this true? What is the real cost of going to school?
  ii. Compare the real cost of going to school with the expected value of not going.

(d) The all-volunteer army, it has been claimed, is too expensive. We should return to a draft system because that way we get the military personnel at a lower cost. What does the United States give up in order to use people in the army? (Assume the draftees are all taken away from existing civilian jobs and that there will be full employment with or without an army.) Is this cost different under a draft system? Are the people who pay the cost different under a draft system?

8. Develop an indifference curve analysis of the allocation of time to work and leisure. Use the analysis to make some predictions about who will work relatively long hours and who will work relatively short hours, about what the effect of increased productivity in a society will be on the amount of leisure time, about the kinds of leisure activities that will be preferred by different people, and about the future.

9. Develop an indifference curve analysis of the way in which individuals allocate time to politics and earning income. Use the analysis to answer the following questions:

(a) Who will spend more time on politics—wealthy people or poor people? Men or women? Black people or white people? Show how your predictions follow from the analysis.

(b) Suppose you wanted to increase political participation. What social policies could you undertake (according to the model)?

(c) One common observation about politics is that many people who seem to have political ability devote rather little time to politics. How do you account for this (within the model)? If you wanted to change it, how could you?

10. Some modern societies feel that they must decide how to allocate their national effort between two attractive social goods: (1) economic equality—that is, minimizing the variance in wealth and income among people; and (2) economic growth—that is, maximizing the average wealth and income in the society.

(a) Analyze this problem from the point of view of indifference curve analysis. What differences in actions would you expect among societies? Why? Under what conditions would you expect an increase in the willingness to trade growth for equality?

(b) What difference would it make if equality made a positive contribution to growth? Or if growth made a positive contribution to equality? Show the indifference diagram.

(c) It has sometimes been argued that a fundamental difference between American politics and the politics of some other countries is that the American working class traditionally has been much more enthusiastic about growth than about equality (relative to the working classes in other countries). Why might this be true (according to your model)? Under what circumstances would it change?

Problems 5.4

1. The world consists of two goods and two people: Herbie, who owns a few apple trees and many grapevines, and Jeff, who owns a few grapevines and many apple trees. At the beginning of every week Herbie starts out with 10 bushels of apples and 20 gallons of wine; Jeff starts out with 45 bushels of apples and 5 gallons of wine.

(a) Draw an Edgeworth box to represent the situation. Label its dimensions clearly, indicating numerical scales and starting point.

(b) Draw indifference curves that take account of the fact that Jeff likes apples more than wine and that Herbie likes wine more than apples.

(c) Show the area of possible, noncoercive trade.

(d) Show one specific point that they might end up at and show why they cannot move away from this point once they get to it.

(e) Suppose we change the initial distribution of wealth so that Herbie starts out every week with 20 apples/15 wine, and Jeff starts out every week with 35 apples/10 wine. Repeat (c) and (d).

2. Joe has 20 units of food and 7 units of clothing; Moe has 10 units of food and 8 units of clothing.

(a) Draw an Edgeworth box and show a point representing this division of food and clothing.

(b) In the same diagram draw a system of indifference curves representing the preferences of Joe and Moe, which would cause them to trade.

(c) Locate the path of Pareto optimal points for these individuals.

(d) Locate the points that Joe and Moe might reach through trade.

3. Suppose Jim has 10 units of food and 5 units of clothing, Dan has 5 units of clothing and 10 of food, and their indifference maps are exactly alike.

(a) Is mutual trade between them likely to occur?

(b) Suppose Jim and Dan each have 10 units of food and 5 units of clothing and that their indifference maps are not exactly alike. Is mutual trade between them likely to occur?

4. Use an Edgeworth box to discuss the following: "Barter is less effective as a system for allocating resources in a society in which there is substantial agreement on values than it is in a society in which there is disagreement on values."

5. Exchange occurs not only among members of the same nation but also among members of different nations. Let us refer to David Ricardo's famous discussion of England and Portugal, recognizing that "England" is shorthand for "residents of England" and that "Portugal" is shorthand for "residents of Portugal." The labor hours required to produce a unit of cloth and wine in each country are:

	CLOTH	*WINE*
England	100	120
Portugal	90	80

(a) Will trade take place? If so, who will trade what?

(b) If trade occurs, what will the swapping terms be?

(c) Assume the exchange ratio is one wine equals one cloth. Describe (in terms of labor hours saved) the division of the gains from trade.

(d) Do you suppose that mutually beneficial trade is possible between the United States and Japan even though the Japanese wage rate is much lower?

6. In Japan wheat costs 10 yen per bushel, and cameras cost 500 yen each. In the United States wheat costs $2 per bushel, and cameras cost $200 each. Suppose that neither country produces any other products and that the exchange rate is 10 yen for a dollar. Since Japan can undersell U.S. prices, our manufacturers convince Congress to ban all trade with Japan. You are Plato, the famous Greek shipping pirate. You talk with some Japanese importers who agree to buy American goods from you but only in trade for Japanese goods; that is, they will barter but not sell because they do not trust the value of the dollar. Likewise, you find some American importers who will barter American goods for Japanese goods. (In order to get around the U.S. trade ban, you have recently married a member of the ruling American family, and now the U.S. customs officials will allow you to load your ships, no questions asked.)

(a) Was your marriage for nothing? Is there any way you can barter goods between the two countries so as to make a profit?

(b) Your new wife has converted you into an altruist, and you now wish to use your ships to make the people of the two countries better off. Is there any way you could barter goods between the two countries so as to make the people in each country happier?

7. In our society the function of getting goods from the manufacturer to the consumer is performed by middlemen. There is no law or public regulation limiting the profits of middlemen. Is there anything in our economic system that controls how much they can extract from the manufacturers or consumers in exchange for their services? Explain.

8. A parent gives each of his two children some meat and some milk. The two children then exchange with each other, one drinking most of the milk and the other eating most of the meat. As a parent, would you permit them to make this exchange?

9. Imagine a society in which there are two social classes. Label the two classes in whatever way you wish (for example, rich and poor, industrious and lazy, crooked and honest, and so on). Suppose that the total wealth in the society is $10 billion, of which $9 billion is held by one class and $1 billion is held by the other. Suppose that the total number of soldiers in the society is 1 million, of which 900,000 are in the poorer class.

(a) Draw an Edgeworth box and show a point representing this division of wealth and soldiers.

(b) In the same diagram draw a system of indifference curves representing the preferences of the two classes that would cause them to trade with each other.

(c) Locate the path of Pareto optimal points for these classes.

(d) Locate the points that the two classes might reach through trade.

(e) Comment on any possible observations about society that you derive from the analysis.

10. Suppose that in a conversation an individual pursues two goods: the pleasures of hearing his own voice and the rewards received from other people as a result of listening attentively to them. Use an indifference curve analysis of conversation to discuss the following:

(a) How will an individual divide his time between talking and listening? Discuss the factors on which the division depends and make some predictions (from the model) about the behavior of different people (that is, people of different statuses, ages, ethnic identifications, and so forth).

(b) What happens in a two-person conversation? Represent a two-person conversation as an Edgeworth box. Label the figure carefully and show what implications you can find for such conversations.

(c) How will a husband and wife converse? Discuss the basic marital conversation and the variations you would expect in different marriages, over time, in a single marriage.

11. The farm problem has been with us for a long time and has caused many possible "solutions" to be generated. One of the more interesting was proposed by President Truman's Secretary of Agriculture. The Brannan plan worked as follows: There would be no direct interference with the market; the natural workings of supply and demand would prevail; there would be no "soil bank" program according to which farmers were paid to take acreage out of cultivation; instead, each year the government would decide on the support price for wheat and give each farmer a cash reimbursement for the difference between the market price and the support price. For example, if the market price is $1.25 (with a support price of $2) and the farmer sells 1000 bushels at that price, he then takes his sales receipt to the government, which then gives him a check for $750 (100 × 75 cents). Using supply/demand graphs compare the Brannan plan to the soil bank proposal (which is discussed in the chapter). Using graphs only, discuss how much wheat is produced, who gets it, the cost to the government, and the effect on farm income.

12. Assume that you were to work hard, practice smiling, learn to act, and some day become a state governor. Assume that your state has

15 departments, many people, and not enough money. Specifically, its income is 10% less than its planned expenditures. Popularity is very important to you and so you cannot raise taxes. How do you reduce expenditures? Your advisers suggest two possible ways: (1) Make a detailed examination of the budget of each department; cut out all those items that you believe are unnecessary. (2) Make an across-the-board 10% budget cut by simply instructing each department to spend 10% less money.

(a) Which would you do? (*Hint:* Use the analytic techniques discussed earlier to learn how to be a better governor.)

(b) Suppose you believed that the work of some departments was more important than the work of other departments; or else that even though the departments were all doing equally important work, that some were more efficient than others. Would this change your evaluation of the two methods for cutting expenditures?

13. In 1965 Congress passed Medicare. By 1968 the country was confronted with a shortage of hospital beds. Why? Use an indifference curve and supply/demand analysis to illustrate your answer.

14. You are economic adviser to a new Southeast Asian state. Its leader wishes to develop the country and so has "persuaded" a large number of peasant farmers to migrate to the cities to work in factories. Unfortunately, the new workers have to be fed, and the increased number of people in the city has greatly increased the price of food there.

(a) Using supply/demand diagrams, show why this might happen.

(b) The government proposes to solve the problem by putting a price ceiling on food (last year's premigration price). You are to advise them on this proposal. Using supply/demand analysis, show what the result of the proposal will be and explain its effect on the food problem.

(c) Can you think of a more effective way of dealing with the food problem? (*Warning:* This will require imagination.)

chapter six

adaptation

6.1   INTRODUCTION

In this chapter we will consider models of adaptation and learning. Like the past two chapters, this chapter will also be concerned with models of human choice behavior. But the models are quite different.

In the chapters on choice and exchange we assumed that the individual used information about the situation facing him to calculate, according to some rational process, the proper decision. In a general way we can describe such processes as models of *calculated rationality*. In this chapter the models involve the notion of adaptive behavior: An action is taken; the world responds to the action; and the individual infers something about the world and then adapts his behavior so as to secure desirable responses. That is, in this chapter we consider humans as *adaptively rational*. They are assumed to learn in a regular manner from trial and error.

A good deal of the work in developing these models has been done with animals (which are cheaper and easier to observe in learning situations) rather than humans. But fortunately the theories developed to explain animal learning seem to work often enough for humans to make them interesting. The theories we will consider were developed to explain observations such as the following:

1. A mouse is placed in a simple maze in which it has the choice of turning left or turning right. If it goes left, it receives a food pellet. If it goes right, it receives nothing. The mouse is placed in the same maze several times. The experimenter observes that rather rapidly it stops going right and always goes left.
2. A pigeon is wandering around its cage. Every time it wanders into the northeast corner, a food pellet drops into its cage. The pigeon is never touched or moved by the experimenter, but every time it is in the northeast corner, it receives a food pellet. Soon the pigeon is spending most of his time in that corner.
3. Betsy is feeling lonely. Her parents are talking to each other and ignoring her. By accident Betsy falls from her chair and bumps her head. Her parents stop talking and rush to comfort her. A few weeks later, in the same situation (loneliness), she accidentally burns her hand. Again her parents rush to comfort her. Over time this seems to happen more and more often. Betsy's parents describe Betsy as "exceptionally accident prone."

4. Herman Smith is a new professor at High Class University. Each morning when he wakes up, he must choose whether to go to his laboratory and do research or to go to the classroom and teach. Because most of the teaching in High Class University is poor, the students are inattentive and uninterested. Over time Professor Smith spends more and more time in his laboratory and reports that research is much more interesting than teaching.

What are the common factors that underlie these observations? All involve the *response* of a human or animal. In all of them the response seems to change over time. The responder appears to adapt on the basis of experience. We can imagine humans as experimenting with various alternatives and coming to choose some more often than others because of the pleasurable and unpleasurable consequences they have experienced following the choice. We expect these choice processes to increase the effectiveness of behavior in achieving individual goals. Thus behavior is adaptively rational. But we will note that some of the most interesting consequences of adaption models involve situations in which there is "false learning," that is, when people learning in an apparently intelligent way come to believe things that are not true.

6.2 *THE BASIC MODEL*

There are several possible adaptation processes that we might explore, but we will devote most of the chapter to just one of these processes: reinforcement learning. Our basic adaptation model is taken from the area of learning theory in psychology. The model seems to be a good description of some learning in both humans and animals.

We begin by observing the adaptive behavior of an animal in a maze. Figure 6.1 shows the experimental setup. It is called a T-maze because of its shape. At the beginning of the experiment a mouse is placed in the starting box at the head of the maze. It then wanders around, exploring until it eventually ends up in one of the two goal boxes. All of the doors are one-way doors: Once the mouse goes through them it cannot go back. Furthermore, the mouse cannot see what is in a goal box until it enters it.

At the beginning of this experiment we put some food in the right-hand goal box and leave the left-hand goal box empty. Alfred, our mouse, is placed in the starting box. He does not know that there is food in the right-hand goal box. At first Alfred explores the starting box, but he will eventually wander out of it and up the maze. He comes to the intersection. He cannot go both ways. Perhaps thoughts go through his fuzzy little head. All we can observe, however, is that eventually he turns left and continues through the maze. When he comes to the door, he again hesitates somewhat and then goes through it. We allow him to explore the goal box for a while and then remove him to his original cage.

Half an hour later we put Alfred in the starting box again. This time he leaves it more quickly, gets down to the intersection, where he must decide which way to turn. Maybe something like this occurs to him. "When I went to the left last time, nothing special happened, either good or bad. Maybe there is more action the other way." So (at some trial) he turns right and explores the right-hand alley. When he gets to the door, he eventually goes in and discovers the food. After he has eaten the food and remained in the box for as long as he was in the left-hand goal box, we remove him and put him back in his original cage.

Every half hour we put food in the right-hand goal box, put Alfred in the starting box, and observe his behavior in the maze. (We keep the portions of food small enough so that he does not become full or bored with eating.) We call each of these half hourly events a learning trial. During the early trials, Alfred will turn left occasionally, but as the experiment continues, he will

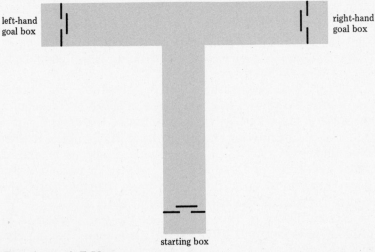

left-hand goal box   right-hand goal box

starting box

Figure 6.1: A T-Maze.

gradually turn right more and more often. Eventually, after many trials, he will turn to the right every time.

From Alfred's perspective he has learned to manipulate the world. He likes food, and he has found a reliable way of obtaining it: Turn right when put in one of those silly mazes. From our perspective he has adapted to the situation: His original behavior was, more or less, random; he learned that some kinds of actions bring pleasant rewards, and so he now performs those actions.

We could repeat this experiment with many different mice, perhaps rewarding some of them for turning left all the time, instead of right. What we would observe is that behavior (turning right or left) that is reinforced (rewarded) becomes more frequent whereas behavior that is not reinforced becomes less frequent. This generalization seems to apply to human learning as well. You might observe a mother teaching her child the alphabet, for example. She holds up a letter, and the child makes a sound. If it is the correct sound, the mother smiles; if it is incorrect, she does not. Here the subject is the child; the behavior is the sound the child makes; and the reward is mother's smile. Over a number of trials, the child will learn that he can get a reward from the world for making the proper sound for a given letter.

Suppose we build a description of these learning processes. The mouse had some initial disposition to turn right or left in the maze. We will call these dispositions.

$P_R(0) =$ initial probability of turning right before the first trial
$P_L(0) =$ initial probability of turning left before the first trial

The subscripts, R and L, designate the behavior of turning right or left. The number 0 in parentheses indicates that we are referring to the mouse's initial probability, that is, his probability before any training has taken place.

STOP AND THINK. Are $P_R(0)$ and $P_L(0)$ related? How?

The answer to this depends on how we define the possible outcomes in the T-maze. If we only observe the two outcomes—"ends up in right-hand goal box" or "ends up in left-hand goal box"—then the two probabilities must add up to 1. Either right or left must occur, and only one of them can occur on any one trial.

We are concerned about adaptation. In this model, adaptation means a change in the probabilities. Thus a model of the learning process must specify how these probabilities change over time. We know that if only the right-hand box contains food and the animal is capable of learning about his environment, over time P_R will increase and P_L will decrease. Thus

$$P_R(t+1) = P_R(t) + \text{increment}$$

That is, P_R at time $t+1$ is related to P_R at time t. The equation also says that $P_R(t+1)$ has increased and that the amount of this increase (the amount that has been learned as a result of the trial) is the increment. Describing the size of this increment and the factors that determine that size is a difficult problem, and many different learning models have been prepared to accomplish this task. We will examine two relatively simple ones here.

A Constant Increment Model. For the moment we will assume that Alfred happened to turn right initially, was rewarded, and that the learning increment for turning right is 0.2; hence we can write

$$P_R(t+1) = P_R(t) + 0.2$$

Thus if Alfred was originally neutral in his turning preference, that is $P_R(0) = 0.5$, and if he happens to turn to the right on the first trial, then

$$P_R(1) = P_R(0) + 0.2 = 0.5 + 0.2 = 0.7$$

So at the beginning of the second trial Alfred's probability of turning to the right is 0.7. Suppose he also happens to turn to the right on the second trial. Then we have

$$P_R(2) = P_R(1) + 0.2 = 0.7 + 0.2 = 0.9$$

And so after two trials Alfred has almost completely adapted to the situation—he has a 90% chance of turning correctly.

STOP AND THINK. **Suppose that on the third trial Alfred also turns to the right. Calculate his new probability of turning right. Is this a reasonable probability? Why?**

If we apply our adaptation equation to calculate $P_R(3)$, we find that the calculated probability is 1.1, which we know is impossible. Maybe the trouble is with our assumption that the learning increment is equal to 0.2; maybe 0.2 is too large. Well, we could make the increment smaller, say, 0.1; $P_R(3)$ would then equal 0.8 (that is, three correct responses with an increment of 0.1 each), which is a legal probability. But if Alfred continues to turn to the right, then we would eventually calculate $P_R(6) = 1.1$; making the increment smaller, therefore, will not solve the problem. What we need is a different adaptation equation, one that stays within the 0–1 probability range. Any model with a constant increment, no matter how small, must eventually produce illegal probabilities.

One possible modification is simply to say that when the model predicts numbers greater than 1 (or less than 0), we will interpret them as 1 (or 0). Such a strategy loses something in terms of beauty, but it is possible. The constant increment model, however, does not seem to be consistent with most data. We apparently need a model with a variable increment.

A Constant Proportion Model. The quantity $(1 - P_R)$ represents the amount that Alfred has yet to learn about his maze. If, for example, his current probability of turning right were 0.7, then the amount he would have left to learn would be 0.3; if his current probability of turning right were 1, then he would have nothing left to learn about this maze. To reformulate our adaptation equation we shall *assume that in each trial Alfred learns a constant proportion of the amount he has yet to learn.* If we call a the learning proportion (or rate), the increment will be $a(1 - P_R)$. For example, suppose that Alfred's initial chance of turning right is 0.5, and his learning rate, a, is 0.3; and suppose he turns right the first time. Using our new expression for the increment we have

$$P_R(1) = P_R(0) + \text{increment}$$

$$P_R(1) = P_R(0) + a[1 - P_R(0)] = 0.5 + 0.3(1 - 0.5)$$
$$= 0.5 + 0.15 = 0.65$$

That is, his initial probability of correct behavior was 0.5; he did make the correct turn, and so his probability of making a correct decision next time increased; the amount of this increase, the increment, was 0.15 (which is 30% of 0.5); and so his new probability of making the correct turn is 0.65. Suppose Alfred again makes a correct turn, to the right, on his second trial. Then he has learned something further about the world,

$$P_R(2) = P_R(1) + a[1 - P_R(1)] = 0.65 + 0.3(1 - 0.65)$$
$$= 0.65 + 0.105 = 0.755$$

That is, this time his learning increment is 30% of 0.35, which is 0.105. Assuming that Alfred continues to turn right each time (to keep the example simple), we can calculate his learning behavior as shown in Table 6.1. Notice that the learning increment is always positive, because he learns something from each trial; and the increment gets smaller and smaller as he gets closer to 100% correct behavior. For example, Alfred improved his probability of choosing correctly by 15 percentage points on the first trial, but he only made a 1.2 percentage-point improvement on the eighth trial. But also notice that his rate of learning remains constant: He always learns 30% of what is left to learn. In Figure 6.2 we plot Alfred's learning behavior over time. Notice that the amount learned (the change in P_R) is large at first but gradually becomes smaller and smaller as he approaches a probability of 1.

We have identified one general principle of learning—behavior that is reinforced tends to become more frequent, or probable—and have tried to formulate a model that embodies this principle. The principle implies that there is some increment in

TABLE 6.1   Adaptation Behavior

TRIAL NO.	P_R AT BEGINNING OF THAT TRIAL	LEARNING INCREMENT
1	0.500	$0.3(1 - .500) = 0.150$
2	0.650	$0.3(1 - .650) = 0.105$
3	0.755	$0.3(1 - .755) = 0.074$
4	0.829	$0.3(1 - .829) = 0.051$
5	0.880	$0.3(1 - .880) = 0.036$
6	0.916	$0.3(1 - .916) = 0.025$
7	0.941	$0.3(1 - .941) = 0.018$
8	0.959	$0.3(1 - .959) = 0.012$
9	0.971	$0.3(1 - .971) = 0.009$
10	0.980	

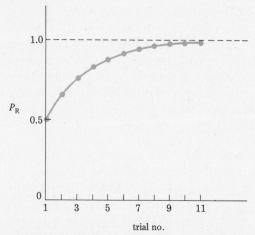

*Figure 6.2: Graph of Table 6.1, Alfred's
learning behavior.*

learning (an increase in the probability of the correct behavior)
that occurs during each trial, and we have explored two different
descriptions of the increment: a constant increment model, which
fails both because it implies probabilities outside the 0–1 range
and because it does not fit data well; and a constant proportion
model, which does produce acceptable probabilities and acceptable
predictions. Data from actual learning experiments with animals
and humans often yield learning curves very similar, in shape, to
Figure 6.2.[1]

6.3   THE ADAPTATION EQUATIONS

The basic idea of our model should be clear from the previous
section. We wish to assume that a human or animal chooses some
alternative; that following his choice he receives some kind of
reward or penalty; that in some way he notes the result and
attributes it to his choice; and that over time he reduces his
propensity to choose alternatives that have been followed by bad
consequences and increases his propensity to choose alternatives
that have good consequences. We wish to take these simple ideas
and develop a precise model of the change process. Specifically, we
wish to expand and clarify the constant proportion model developed
previously.

Our model makes six assumptions:

Assumption 1. Alternative Behaviors for the Individual. We assume that any individual has some set of possible alternative behaviors in which he might engage. The mouse may turn left or right. The pigeon may stand in the northeast corner, the southwest corner, the northwest corner, or the southeast corner. Betsy may have an accident or not. Herman Smith may go to the laboratory or to the class. Thus we start with a list of mutually exclusive (and exhaustive) alternative behaviors.

Assumption 2. State of the Individual. We assume that the individual is in some state with respect to the alternative behaviors at any point in time. Specifically, we will assume that the individual's state may be described by a set of probabilities, one for each of the alternative behaviors. Thus in the T-maze the mouse has a probability of going left and a probability of going right at any point in time. (These probabilities add up to 1.0 over the whole set of alternatives.) Initially, the mouse's probability of going left might be 0.5, and his probability of going right might be 0.5. This is the initial state of the individual with respect to the set of alternatives (go left/go right). As the adaptation proceeds, these probabilities might change so that at some subsequent point in time the probability of going left might become 0.8 and the probability of going right becomes 0.2.

Assumption 3. Alternative Responses of the World. We assume that the world (for instance, the experimenter) has a repertoire of possible responses to the behavior of the individual. These responses may include giving food, giving water, giving love, giving attention, giving an electric shock, biting, smiling, changing interest rates. Typically, we will attend, within a specific problem, to only a small number of the conceivable responses in the situation and focus on that small list (such as, give food or give nothing).

Assumption 4. State of the World. We assume that the world has some set of rules for its own behavior. These rules may take a number of forms, such as: Give food on the left in 70% of the trials and on the right in 30% of the trials. Or the rule might be: Always give food on both sides. These rules, along with the set of responses, describe the environment for our model individual.

Assumption 5. Set of Possible Events. In the first assumption we have identified the set of possible behavior alternatives by the individual (such as, go left/go right). In the third assumption we have identified the set of possible responses by the environment (reward/no reward). Taken jointly, these two assumptions provide us with a complete enumeration of all of the possible events that can occur within our model. For example, if we assume that our individual has only two alternatives (go left/go right) and the world is assumed to have only two possible responses (reward/no reward), then there are precisely four events that can occur:

Event 1. Individual goes left; reward is given.
Event 2. Individual goes left; no reward is given.
Event 3. Individual goes right; reward is given.
Event 4. Individual goes right; no reward is given.

Moreover, at any point in time, we know from our assumptions with respect to the state of the individual and the state of the world precisely how likely each of the events is. For example, if the individual has a probability of 0.6 of going left and a probability of 0.4 of going right and if the response rule is "always reward on the right and never on the left," then the probability of the various events is given as follows:

P(Event 1) = 0
P(Event 2) = 0.6
P(Event 3) = 0.4
P(Event 4) = 0

Assumption 6. Adaptation Equations. We specify for each of the possible events listed previously an equation that describes the assumed changes in the individual that follow the occurrence of the event. As we have seen, the model assumes that the individual is described at each point in time as having a certain probability of selecting each of the alternative behaviors. The model is basically a theory of how those probabilities change as a consequence of the occurrence of one of the possible events. And that "how" is portrayed precisely by a set of adaptation equations.

In this section we describe a specific set of adaptation equations for a simple two-alternative, two-response situation. In Sections 6.4, 6.5, and 6.6 we will use these equations to explore a variety of problems that can be viewed as two-alternative, two-response worlds. The structure outlined here, however, is considerably more general than the specific model we will discuss; and you should be sure that you understand fully the logic of the model before proceeding to the specific equations we will use.

6.3.1 *ADAPTATION EQUATIONS IN A T-MAZE*

The equations we will discuss are simplified from a theory of learning originally developed by Estes, Bush, and Mosteller and considerably elaborated subsequently by them as well as others. We will consider only a situation in which there are two alternatives for the individual and two possible responses by the world, reward and no reward. The two alternatives for the individual might be vote-Democratic/vote-Republican, go-left/go-right, buy/sell, or work/play. Indeed, they might be any action in which it is convenient to think of dividing the behavior alternatives into two broad classes that are mutually exclusive and exhaustive. Reward can be anything that might be viewed as pleasant—prosperity, love, success, and so on.

Using the subscripts L and R to designate his two alternative actions, the state of our individual is describable (at time t) in terms of two probabilities:

$P_L(t) =$ the probability of choosing alternative L (for instance, the probability of voting Democratic) at time t.

$P_R(t) = 1 - P_L(t) =$ the probability of choosing alternative R (for instance, the probability of voting Republican) at time t.

We are interested in the way in which $P_L(t)$ and $P_R(t)$ change to $P_L(t + 1)$ and $P_R(t + 1)$ depending on the event that occurs. Since we have two possible alternative behaviors by the individual and two possible responses by the world, we have four possible events: (1) L and reward; (2) L and no reward; (3) R and reward; (4) R and no reward.

In general, we would like our adaptation equations to reflect some intuitive notions of learning. The first of these intuitive notions is the direction of change. We would expect reward to increase the probability of the behavior that is rewarded. Thus for events E1 and E4:

POSSIBLE EVENT	=	INDIVIDUAL'S CHOICE	*plus*	WORLD'S RESPONSE	*produces*	INDIVIDUAL'S ADAPTATION
E1	=	L	and	reward	$\longrightarrow$	increase P_L, decrease P_R
E3	=	R	and	reward	$\longrightarrow$	decrease P_L, increase P_R

STOP AND THINK. **What does your intuition say about the results of no reward, that is, events E2 and E4? Can you construct a table similar to the preceding one for these two events?**

Some people would say intuitively that no reward would have the effect of decreasing the probability of the unrewarded behavior. Others would say that no reward would have no effect one way or another. We will follow the first of these two "intuitions," not because it necessarily is better, but because the second can be included as a special case of the first (by assuming that the amount of the decrease is zero!) Thus for all four possible events we have:

POSSIBLE EVENT	=	INDIVIDUAL'S CHOICE	plus	WORLD'S RESPONSE	produces	INDIVIDUAL'S ADAPTATION
E1	=	L	and	reward	→	increase P_L, decrease P_R
E2	=	L	and	no reward	→	decrease P_L, increase P_R
E3	=	R	and	reward	→	decrease P_L, increase P_R
E4	=	R	and	no reward	→	increase P_L, decrease P_R

A final notion that we might want to include is the idea that the learning impact of reward might be different from the impact of no reward. Thus we would want to allow the increase in P_L after possible event E1 to be different from the increase in P_L after possible event E4. Then we can include the case in which they are equal as a special case.

We are now ready to specify some specific equations for the adaptation following each event. We collect these in Table 6.2.

TABLE 6.2   Adaptation Equations

EVENT POSSIBLE	=	INDIVIDUAL'S CHOICE	plus	WORLD'S RESPONSE	produces	INDIVIDUAL'S ADAPTATION
E1	=	L	and	reward	→	$P_L(t+1) = P_L(t) + a[1 - P_L(t)]$
E2	=	L	and	no reward	→	$P_L(t+1) = P_L(t) - bP_L(t)$
E3	=	R	and	reward	→	$P_R(t+1) = P_R(t) + a[1 - P_R(t)]$
E4	=	R	and	no reward	→	$P_R(t+1) = P_R(t) - bP_R(t)$

$a =$ *the learning rate associated with rewarded behavior.* It is some number in the range 0–1. It shows the rate of response to reinforcement. Low values indicate slow learning; high values indicate fast learning.

$b =$ *the learning rate associated with nonreward.* Its range of possible values and its interpretation are identical to that of a.

Although the equations are written in terms of the alternatives L and R, they apply to any situation involving two alternatives. If you were predicting voting behavior, for example, you would simply rephrase the equations in terms of P_D, the probability of voting Democratic, and P_R, the probability of voting Republican.

There are two different learning rates, a and b, in the equations to allow for the possibility that response to reward might be different from response to nonreward. There is no necessary reason why one rate must be greater than the other, and a and b might even be equal if the individual learned as much from his failures (nonrewarded decisions) as from his successes. Suppose that Johnny only notices his successes but completely ignores his failures: Then b would be zero for Johnny. Or suppose that Richard is very suspicious of the world: He ignores his successes ("It was only luck") but finds his failures very significant. Then a for Richard might be almost zero while b would be large.

The four adaptation equations embody a few relatively simple principles:

1. Behavior that is reinforced becomes more probable, and behavior that is not reinforced becomes less probable.
2. Rewards cause behavior to change at the rate a; nonrewards cause behavior to change at the rate b.
3. The amount of adaptation on any trial is always a constant fraction (a or b) of the amount left to be learned.

The adaptation equations all have this same general logic to them, and they are actually quite simple.

STOP AND THINK. Suppose we are discussing a world in which going right is always rewarded and going left is never rewarded. That is, only events E2 and E3 can possibly occur. And suppose that a mouse turns right. Equation 3 in Table 6.2 tells how P_R will change. But how can you figure out the change in P_L?

It is *not* correct to use equation 2 from event E2 because event E2 did not occur. The mouse was rewarded, and so learning takes place at rate a. It is possible to write out a companion equation to equation 3 that would express the change in P_L, but this is not necessary if we keep in mind a simple principle: P_L plus P_R must equal 1. So we can simply calculate the new value for P_R and then subtract it from 1.0 to learn the new value of P_L.

To illustrate the use of these equations, we take one more look at Alfred the mouse in the T-maze before going on to situations involving people.

Problem. Alfred is in a T-maze, and we have decided always to reward left turns, never right turns.

STOP AND THINK. Which adaptation equations are we concerned with in this problem? That is, what are the possible events that can occur in this world?

Alfred can turn right and go hungry or turn left and be fed. Therefore, only events E1 and E4 can occur. There is no way that events E2 and E3 can occur. So we know which equations to use in describing the learning process. What else do we need to know before we can work an actual problem describing Alfred's behavior?

STOP AND THINK. You know which equations to apply, but what else do you need to know?

Please reread the first few pages of Section 6.3, the material about the six basic assumptions. Assumption 1 is clearly defined for this problem. There are two alternative behaviors that we will observe, turning left and right, and we will ignore any other behaviors that might occur (such as, "goes to sleep" or "escapes to freedom and a new life in Southern California").

Assumption 2 is unspecified so far. We have not been told anything about Alfred's initial state with respect to his alternative behaviors—that is, his initial probabilities of going either left or right. We will discuss the determination of such things in the next two sections. For now we might just accept the assumption that $P_L(0) = 0.5$ for Alfred.

Assumption 3 is well defined for this problem. The world's alternative responses are to give rewards or not, depending on what

Alfred does. And the initial state of the world, Assumption 4, is also clear. It always rewards going left and never rewards going right.

The possible events referred to by Assumption 5 are the four possible combinations of the responses of Alfred and the world. We have already decided that for Assumption 6 equations 1 and 4 are the relevant ones, but we still need the values of the two learning constants, a and b, before we can predict Alfred's behavior. Again we delay a discussion of how we might determine them and simply assume that $a = 0.3$ and $b = 0.2$ for Alfred.

We now have all the necessary information. What will happen when we put Alfred in the T-maze. We do not know with certainty what will happen on the first trial. All we have is the assertion that Alfred has a 0.5 probability of turning left. Suppose that he actually turns to the right on the first trial. This means that event E4 occurs. He tries and fails, but he learns something from the trial. We know that his probability of turning to the right next time will decrease as follows:

$$P_R(1) = P_R(0) - bP_R(0) = 0.5 - 0.2(0.5) = 0.4$$

and we know that $P_L + P_R = 1$; hence $P_L(1) = 1 - P_R(1) = 0.6$.

What will happen during the second trial? Again, we can only predict, and this time we predict a 60% chance of Alfred's turning to the left. Suppose he actually does turn to the left. This means that event E1 occurs. We know that his probability of turning to the left next time will increase as follows:

$$P_L(2) = P_L(1) + a[1 - P_L(1)] = 0.6 + 0.3(1 - 0.6) = 0.72$$

That is, after two learning trials Alfred has a 72% chance of making a correct response in the maze if he goes right first and then left.

Assume he turns to the left on the third trial, thus producing $P_L(3) = 0.804$, and also turns left from then on. It is informative to plot a graph of Alfred's behavior, Figure 6.3. Table 6.3 is also worth studying. For each point on the graph it gives the relevant information that produced that point. Notice that the table differentiates between the *probability* of a left choice, P_L, and the actual choice that was made. Sometimes Alfred is learning at rate a and sometimes he is learning at rate b, but the learning curve is always rising. The learning increments are large at first, when

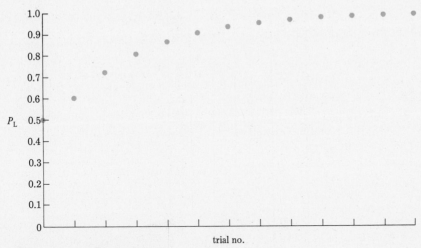

Figure 6.3: Alfred's adaptation over time.

there is still a lot to learn, and become smaller and smaller as adaptation becomes almost complete.

6.3.2 EXPECTED PROBABILITY

In Section 6.3.1 we considered how a single mouse, Alfred, learns according to our model. Now think about the following situation: We have ten identical mice in a learning situation; each mouse has the same value for a, b, and $P_L(0)$ as every other mouse; and we give each mouse two learning trials in a maze where left is always rewarded. At the end of the two trials each mouse will have a new probability of going left, $P_L(2)$. Will they each have the same probability of going left after two trials?

> **STOP AND THINK.** The ten mice have identical learning parameters [a, b, and $P_L(0)$] and go through an identical experiment. Will the probability of going left be the same for each of them after two trials? *Hint:* Will they all make the same choice on the first trial?

The question is an important one. For example, you might restate it in human terms to ask whether identical twins exposed to the same child rearing situation would exhibit identical behavior

TABLE 6.3 *Alfred's Adaptation over Time*

TRIAL NUMBER	0	1	2	3	4	5	6	7	8	9	10	11	12
ACTUAL CHOICE	—	R	L	L	L	L	L	L	L	L	L	L	L
REWARD?	—	no	yes	yes	yes	yes	yes	yes	yes	yes	yes	yes	yes
EVENT	—	4	1	1	1	1	1	1	1	1	1	1	1
P_L	0.5	0.6	0.72	0.804	0.863	0.904	0.933	0.953	0.967	0.977	0.984	0.989	0.993

preferences. In the case of our learning model, the answer is definitely not. Some mice (or people) will go left on the first trial, and others will go right. Those who go left will be rewarded and will increase their probability of going left to $P_L(1) = P_L(0) + a[1 - P_L(0)]$. Those who go right, on the other hand, will not be rewarded and will decrease their probability of going right to $P_R(1) = P_R(0) - bP_R(0)$. Unless a and b are equal, $P_L(1)$ will depend on what choice is made on the first trial. Clearly subsequent values of P_L will differ depending on the particular probabilistic choices that are made. Thus we cannot say exactly what value P_L will have for any one mouse after several trials. How do we deal with this indeterminacy?

What we identify is a kind of average probability of going left. Suppose that after two trials we had 3 mice with $P_L(2) = 0.6$ and 7 mice with $P_L(2) = 0.1$. Then we could say that the average probability was $(0.3 \times 0.6) + (0.7 \times 0.1) = 0.25$. That is, we multiply the probability of going left for each group of mice by the proportion of mice that are in that group. So long as we know what proportion of mice fall in each group, we can calculate an average.

Consider the situation involving ten identical mice in a single experiment. Suppose we have ten mice, all with $a = 0.5$, $b = 0.1$, and $P_L(0) = 0.3$. And suppose we have an experiment in which the reward is always on the left and only on the left. The possible behaviors of any given mouse can be represented by a tree, as follows:

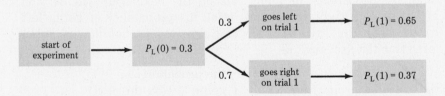

The tree shows everything that might happen to a mouse on the first trial. We do not know exactly what the mouse will do on the first trial but since $P_L(0) = 0.3$, we know there is a 30 percent chance it will go left, and a 70 percent chance it will go right. These probabilities are shown on the tree. Suppose the mouse does go left the first time, we know that the chance of going left again is

$$P_L(1) = P_L(0) + a[1 - P_L(0)] = 0.3 + 0.5(1 - 0.3) = 0.65$$

Suppose the mouse went to the right on the first trial, then the chance of going to the right again is

$$P_R(1) = P_R(0) - bP_R(0) = 0.7 - 0.1 \times 0.7 = 0.63$$

and hence $P_L(1) = 0.37$. Notice that if the mouse goes to the left on the first trial, its probability of a left response on the second trial is 0.65, while if it goes to the right on the first trial, its probability of a left response on the second trial is only 0.37. Clearly the probability varies greatly depending upon what happens on the first trial.

What is the average probability? Unfortunately, we cannot calculate the average, because we do not know exactly what proportion of the mice will go left on the first trial.

> **STOP AND THINK.** Be sure it is clear to you why we do not know exactly what proportion of mice will go left on the first trial. Could it be all of them? None of them?

We do not know exactly what proportion of the mice will go left on the first trial, but we do know the *expected* proportion. (Review the discussion in Section 4.2.4.) That is, we know that if we ran this experiment indefinitely many times with indefinitely many mice, 30 percent of the mice would go left on the first trial and 70 percent would go right.

In addition, we know that *if* a mouse goes left on the first trial, his probability of going left on the next trial will be 0.65 and *if* he goes right on the first trial, his probability of going left on the next trial will be 0.37. The *expected probability* of going left after the first trial is

$$\begin{pmatrix} \text{the expected proportion} \\ \text{of mice going left on} \\ \text{the first trial} \end{pmatrix} \times \begin{pmatrix} \text{the probability of} \\ \text{going left on the next} \\ \text{trial if you go left} \\ \text{on the first} \end{pmatrix} +$$

$$\qquad\qquad 0.3 \qquad\qquad\qquad\qquad\qquad 0.65$$

$$\begin{pmatrix} \text{the expected proportion} \\ \text{of mice going right on} \\ \text{the first trial} \end{pmatrix} \times \begin{pmatrix} \text{the probability of} \\ \text{going left on the next} \\ \text{trial if you go right} \\ \text{on the first} \end{pmatrix} = 0.454$$

$$\qquad\qquad 0.7 \qquad\qquad\qquad\qquad\qquad 0.37$$

To find the expected probability at the end of any particular trial, we simply extend the tree further. We originally asked what the probability would be of going left after two trials. We construct the next branches on the tree:

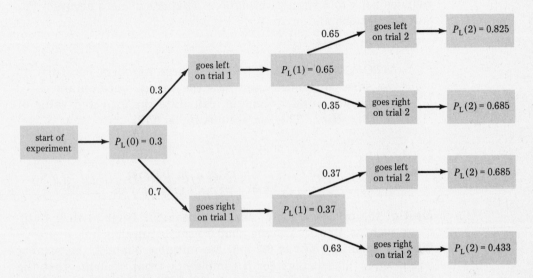

As before, we have calculated the new values for P_L by applying our learning equations (remembering that a left response is always rewarded and a right response never is). If a mouse goes left on the first trial and then left again, his probability of a left response after the second trial is 0.825. Similarly, a left-right pattern results in a probability of 0.685; a right-left pattern results in a probability of 0.685; and a right-right pattern results in a probability of 0.433.

To find the expected probability of going left after the second trial, we repeat the same kind of calculations we used to find the expected probability after the first trial. First, we find the expected proportion of mice that will follow each of the four paths through the tree. The left-left path has an expected proportion of mice equal to $0.3 \times 0.65 = 0.195$. The left-right path has an expected proportion of $0.3 \times 0.35 = 0.105$. The right-left path has an expected proportion of $0.7 \times 0.37 = 0.259$. And the right-right path has an expected proportion of $0.7 \times 0.63 = 0.441$. These expected proportions are multiplied by the appropriate value of $P_L(2)$, and the products are summed to obtain the expected value of $P_L(2)$:

$$E[P_L(2)] = (0.195 \times 0.825) + (0.105 \times 0.685) + (0.259 \times 0.685)$$
$$+ (0.441 \times 0.433) = 0.601$$

The exact arithmetic value of $E[P_L(2)]$ is 0.601168 which we have rounded back to 3 significant figures. This is sufficient accuracy for our calculations and yours.

> ***STOP AND THINK.*** **Review these numbers carefully to be sure you understand how the values were obtained. To check your understanding, calculate the expected value of** $P_L(3)$**.** *Hint:* **The correct answer is 0.727.**

6.3.3 THE MEANING OF PROBABILITIES IN ADAPTATION MODELS

Most of the problems about adaptive behavior begin with a statement such as this: "Assume that Herman Smith's initial probability of turning right is 0.3 and his initial probability of turning left is 0.7." This brings forth complaints from students that the assumption is arbitrary and meaningless. What does it mean to say that his initial probability of turning right is 0.3? Herman is a human being, not a set of dice. He makes some decision about what he is going to do and then does it. There are no probabilities involved.

The probability assumption is a simplification of the real world. We find it a useful simplification in terms of the results it produces, but it is also justifiable on more intuitive grounds. Think about the way you walk around between one place and another. There is one particular journey that you sometimes make by one path, sometimes by an alternative path. Your reasons for choosing one path over the other may be very rational and calculated; for instance, the low road is more pleasant in the afternoon, but it is wet in the morning, and the high road is dry in the morning; therefore, you always take the high road in the morning and the low road in the afternoon. If someone were observing you without any knowledge of why you made these decisions, all he could gather is that sometimes you went one way and sometimes you went the other. If he watched you for a while to count up the number of times per day you used each route, he could then make a statement such as: "Assume that X's initial probability of taking the low road is 0.6." Your observer could then go ahead and predict the effects on your behavior of "rewarding" one path or the other. For example, he might arrange that free concert tickets would be given away occasionally along the low road. He could then predict that your probability of taking the low road would increase. He would not have to know anything about your mental decision-making process—he only needs to know that behavior that is rewarded will occur more frequently in the future.

In such a case, the probability assumption is a useful simplification of the world's complexity. We do not have to know what is going on in people's minds; we only have to observe behavior. This does not mean that we believe that an individual's behavior is as simple as a pair of dice. We simply use probability as a sort of shorthand aggregation of the individual's complexity. The same considerations apply when we talk about the world's proability of rewarding a particular kind of behavior. The world may have any number of "reasons" for only rewarding an action occasionally. But from our point of view what matters is that the world's behavior does not appear to be constant.

6.3.4   THE SIGNIFICANCE OF a AND b

The adaptation equations we have specified include two parameters that influence the speed with which adaptation takes place:

a = the learning rate associated with rewarded behavior.
b = the learning rate associated with nonreward.

a and b are both numbers between 0 and 1. Small values for a and b produce relatively slow changes; large values produce relatively rapid changes. The two learning rates summarize many important features of adaptation. In fact, many of the most important results from the study of adaptation are (from the point of view of this model) statements about differences in the values for a and b. We will mention just three major ones.

Motivation. Suppose we had a learning situation in which the reward was water. Each time the correct response was made, we gave the subject some water. What would affect the value of a and b in this situation?

STOP AND THINK. Can you think of anything that would increase or decrease the rate of learning?

One likely determinant would be the amount of water we provided. A glass of water is more rewarding than a drop. Large rewards are more effective for learning than small rewards. Such a conjecture is supported generally by the research results, although there clearly are limits. An ocean of water is generally less rewarding than a glass unless you also provide storage capacity; and a glass of water may be less rewarding for a man who is expecting a gallon than a drop of water is for a man who is expecting nothing.

A second determinant, you might guess, would be the degree of thirst. How long has it been since the subject has had water? A cup of water is more important after being without water for a day than after being without water for ten minutes. This conjecture is generally supported by experimental literature. However, any kind of extreme deprivation is likely to produce not only a desire for the reward but also a variety of other psychological and physiological changes that reduce the effectiveness of information processing and thus reduce a and b. Despair, fatigue, anger, and illness do not ordinarily improve the rate of learning.

The term "motivation" is commonly used to summarize the attributes of a reward or the current state of the subject that make a given reward important to a given subject at a specific time. High values of a and b are associated with rewards that are highly valuable to the particular subject involved at the particular time involved. Since the model assumes that the values of a and b are constant, we are assuming that the kind of rewards offered and their value to the individuals involved do not change much during the course of a learning experience.

STOP AND THINK. How significant is this assumption? Can you think of some situations in which it would be erroneous? *Hint:* What might affect the level of motivation after repeated rewards?

Obviously, we need to worry about saturation effects (decreasing marginal motivation). After 20 glasses of water in 2 hours, the motivation associated with an additional water reward will decline and so will the learning rates.

Learning Ability.   Another factor that is summarized in the values of a and b is the ability of the subject to draw inferences and modify behavior on the basis of experience. We do not know exactly why it is that some people seem to learn faster than others, but it appears to be true that even if we establish equal motivation, there are differences.

> **STOP AND THINK.**   We are entering a domain of theory that is presently quite controversial. The question is "Why does Johnny not learn?" The data are that he does not. This indicates that a and b are different for Johnny than for others (if we accept a model roughly similar to ours) or that he has had different learning experiences. Some people prefer to assert that he has had different learning experiences (environment); some people prefer to assert that he has had different rewards or finds different things rewarding (cultural differences); some people prefer to assert that there are individual differences in the rate of learning (ability). You should be clear in your own mind both with respect to what difference it makes and with respect to how you would decide among the alternatives, or combinations of them, to produce a model that is true, beautiful, and just.

Differences among individuals in their learning ability would cause differences in their values of a and b . In fact, the estimation of a and b is essentially the same as the procedures we use to estimate learning in a classroom situation. We test at the start of some experience and again at the end. The magnitude of the change in knowledge is an estimate of ability. It is also the basis for an estimate of a and b. High values of a and b are associated with high ability in learning; low values are associated with low ability.

Notice that the model does not make a distinction between a highly motivated low-ability subject and a lowly motivated high-ability subject. We cannot, within the model, disentangle motivation and ability.

STOP AND THINK. Do you understand why this is so and what the implications are?

All we can say is that *when* there are variations in motivation that affect learning, they will influence the values of a and b; and *when* there are variations in ability that affect learning, they will also influence the values of a and b. Thus the learning rate parameters a and b *summarize* the net effect of a variety of variables. *If* ability or motivation vary from situation to situation, or from time to time, a and b will vary also. Since the form of the model we have used assumes a constant a and b throughout a learning experience, we essentially assume that learning ability, if it exists, does not vary much over time in any one situation, though we do not assume that it is constant over all situations.

STOP AND THINK. Can you specify a case in which the model would clearly be inappropriate because learning ability would be varying over time?

You might have noted the numerous ways in which learning ability is linked to physiology in the individual or efficiency in the organization. Fatigue changes the learning rate in an individual. Organizational overload changes the learning rate in an organization. The rate of learning depends on the ability to attend to the events taking place, on the ability to process information about them, and on the ability to recall history. Each of these varies over time as other aspects claim attention.

Novelty. A final factor that we might think would be reflected in the values of a and b is a subject's prior experiences. Some learning situations are new to a subject, while others are relatively familiar or have familiar components in them. This familiarity can have either positive or negative effects on learning speed. For example, if a mouse has had a great deal of experience with many *different* kinds of T-maze learning situations, then its learning speed in a new T-maze will probably be higher than if it had no prior experience. In effect, the mouse has learned how to learn. On the other hand, if the mouse has had a great deal of experience with one particular type of T-maze and is then placed in a novel one, its learning rate may be slower than if it has had no prior experience. It would insist on clinging to traditional solutions to this apparently familiar problem. Thus we might want to consider a and b as a summary of the degree of novelty in a learning situation.

STOP AND THINK. **Can you think of an alternative way of looking at prior experience in the model? That is, we believe that prior experience has an effect, and we have incorporated the effect by allowing it to influence a and b . What else could we have done to incorporate the effect into the model?**

A possible alternative approach would be to consider prior experience as affecting the initial probability of choosing one alternative or the other but as not affecting the rate of learning. Thus individuals with prior experience might have a strong initial propensity to do something in a new situation but would otherwise learn at the same rate.

By asserting that we will use a and b to capture some of the effects of novelty, we are implicitly recognizing that one of the strongest assumptions in our model is not quite correct. The model assumes that if I have a probability of, say, 0.7 of going left on any particular trial, then my probability of going left on the next trial depends only on which way I actually go on this trial and whether I am rewarded. *It does not depend on the whole history of my experiences by which I arrived at a probability of 0.7*. This is a strong assertion in the model.

To say that all of our learning history can be summarized by a single number (that is, we need no further knowledge of prior events) is wrong. As a result, we record a qualification for the model: We assume that learning history can be approximated by a single probability *in the short run*, for example, a series of learning trials. Over the long run we expect to capture some, but not all, of the effects of loss of novelty by allowing the values of a and b to vary depending on the long-run differences in level of experience among subjects. At the same time, we must be sure to check that the long-run predictions we make from the model would not be affected if the values of a and b systematically changed over time at a slow rate.

Motivation, ability, and novelty are three broad types of variables that are reflected in the learning parameters in our model. The model does not tell us anything about their interrelation. We can, however, use these interpretations of the parameters as a base for specific predictions from the model. For example, when the model predicts that individuals with high values for a and b do something different from people with low values, we will predict that people with strong motivation or high ability or relevant experience will do that same thing. This procedure of interpretation is an important tool of the modeling art.

> *STOP AND THINK.* **Can you think of other plausible interpretations of a and b ? As you develop additional interpretations, you make the model richer and more beautiful.**

6.4   *HOW THE MODEL WORKS*

We have now specified a model of how an individual or group adapts to an environment that rewards (or fails to reward) behavioral choices. An individual makes a choice; the environment responds; and then the individual modifies the propensity to repeat the action.

Our model gives the *probability* of a particular response at a particular trial. As long as that probability is neither 1.0 nor 0, either of the two responses *could* actually occur on a particular trial. Consequently, the model does not predict exactly what will happen to any given individual on any given trial, but it is effective regarding the behavior of groups. Why is this so, and how can we graph group behavior?

Figure 6.3 showed the hypothetical learning behavior of an imaginary subject. Suppose we create a new hypothetical subject having the same learning parameters in the same situation. We could plot his results and obtain a graph similar to Figure 6.3, though probably not identical to it. The graphs would have similar shapes and would asymptotically approach the 1.0 point. It would be useful to repeat the procedure a large number of times and then combine data from all the cases together. For each of the hypothetical subjects we would compute the probability of turning left after the first trial, then add all the probabilities together, find

their average value, and plot this as the expected value of $P_L(1)$. [2]
Do the same thing for the second trial to compute $P_L(2)$. The
graph of these average P_L values will give you a good idea of the
general learning tendency and speed of response for that particular
adaptation situation. (You might also want to make graphs showing
the distribution of responses on any given trial to see how repre-
sentative this average is.)

Because our model can produce a variety of different behaviors, it is useful to study the properties of any given learning
model in terms of the behavior of a large number of simulated
subjects. We program a computer to be a kind of mechanical mouse.
For example, suppose we wish to simulate the results of a learning
model with parameters $a = 0.1$, $b = 0.4$, $P_L(0) = 0.3$, reward
always on the left, never on the right. To find out what the mouse
does on the first trial the computer uses a random number probability generator like this: It randomly generates a number between
1 and 1000, then converts this number into first-trial mouse behavior by this decision-rule: If the number is between 1 and 300,
then the mouse goes left; if the number is between 301 and 1000,
then the mouse goes right. (Thus the mouse has exactly a 30%
chance of going left on the first trial.)

Suppose the computer randomly chooses the number 804.
This means the mouse turned right the first time and that $P_L(1)$
$= 0.58$. For the next trial the computer again picks a random
number between 1 and 1000, but this time it uses this decision-rule:
If the number is between 1 and 580, then the mouse goes left; if it
is between 581 and 1000, then the mouse goes right.

We might program the computer to do this 30 times to simulate the behavior of a single mouse over 30 trials in that particular
learning situation. Suppose we do this, ask the computer to store
the results, and then start all over again at the beginning of the
sequence of trials with a new hypothetical mouse. We could then
generate the behavior of this new mouse over 30 trials (and it
would undoubtedly be at least slightly different from that of the
first mouse), store those results too, and then simulate another
98 mice. We then ask the computer to plot average probabilities
(or the proportion of left turns) associated with any given trial,
and we have the simulation results of interest.

We will presently examine a number of such simulations.
They are a useful quick way of discovering the properties of any
given learning model. You should remember that the models are
not confined to the behavior of turning left or right and hence that

the simulation graphs can also show what the model predicts about, say, the average probability of voting Republican or the probability that there will be an increase in stock prices or the probability of violating some social norm.

The average probability on any particular trial is also the expected proportion of individuals that will respond in that way if each individual has been exposed to the same experiential situation. Individual probabilities will vary around the average. In some cases some individuals will deviate substantially from the average. This is not (according to the model) because those individuals are intrinsically different from the others but simply because the model is a probabilistic model and there is normally some variation in the exact experience individuals have even though they are in the same probabilistic environment. Where the model predicts individual deviations around the average that are particularly large, or particularly interesting, we will comment on them.

The results of a simulation depend on three *parameters* of the model: The learning increment associated with reward, a, the learning increment associated with lack of reward, b, and the initial probability of choosing one alternative rather than the other, $P_L(0)$. In each figure that follows the values assumed for these three parameters are indicated. In most cases we have assumed that $a = b = 0.2$ and that the initial probability of a left response is 0.5. As we noted earlier, higher values of a and b will result in more rapid learning. Figure 6.4 illustrates this by showing the learning pattern associated with two different sets of values for a and b. Notice what happens when the values of a and b are higher.

6.4.1   THE EFFECT OF REWARD SCHEDULES

The learning that will take place depends on the kind of environment that is faced. Specifically, it depends on the kind of *reward schedule* provided by the environment. We can illustrate this by showing the pattern of response to several standard kinds of environments.

Case 1: A Consistent Reward Schedule

The classic reward schedule is one in which one alternative is always rewarded and the other never is. Such schedules have been used extensively in experimental research; they are found often in the everyday world. If you simulate our model when faced with such a reward schedule, you obtain results such as those portrayed by Figure 6.4. The probability of a left response (if left is always rewarded and right never is) approaches closer and closer to 1. The approach is steady but occurs at a decreasing rate. The steepness of the approach depends on the values of the learning parameters.

Case 2: A Single Probability Reward Schedule

Instead of always rewarding on one side and never on the other, it is possible to reward with a fixed probability on one side and never on the other. We can, for instance, reward a left response with a probability of 0.8 and never reward a right response. The results of two such situations are portrayed in Figure 6.5. The

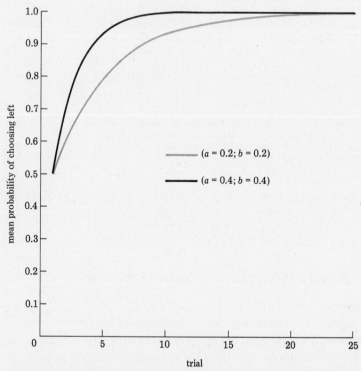

Figure 6.4: Simulation of 200 individuals in a learning model in which left response is always rewarded and right response never is. (Initial probability of left response is 0.5; a is 0.2, and b is 0.2 for all 200.)

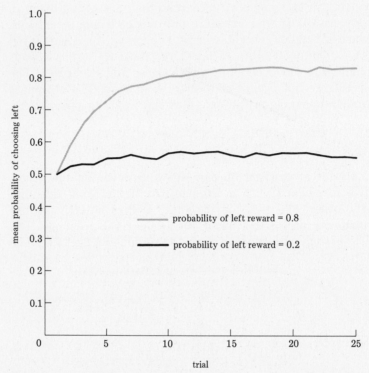

Figure 6.5: Simulation of 200 individuals in a learning model in which left response is rewarded with some fixed probability and right response never is. (Initial probability of left response is 0.5; a is 0.2, and b is 0.2 for all 200.)

average probability of responding left rises over time. The rate of the rise and the limit increase as the probability increases.

Case 3: A Double Probability Reward Schedule

It is possible for reward to be provided on one side with probability, p_1, and on the other side with probability, p_2. The probabilities can add up to 1, or not. The probabilities on the two sides can be independent, or they can exhibit various kinds of dependence. Figure 6.6 illustrates the outcome of double probability reward schedules for the situation in which the probability of reward on the left is 0.4 and the probability of reward on the right is either 0.2 or 0.8.

Case 4: A Patterned Reward Schedule

The model does not "recognize" patterns. Rather it assumes that events are defined in some terms. Those terms can be alternative patterns, and the choice in the model can be the choice of a pattern response. Thus we can present the model with a reward series that alternates from one side to the other on each trial as follows:

Trial Number	1	2	3	4	5	6	7	8	9	10
Rewarded Response	L	R	L	R	L	R	L	R	L	R

If we define the choice as being between an L and an R, the model will predict a response to such a reward schedule such as illustrated by the solid line in Figure 6.7. However, the reward sequence and choice sequence can also be described in terms of whether the choice (rewarded response) is the same (S) on this

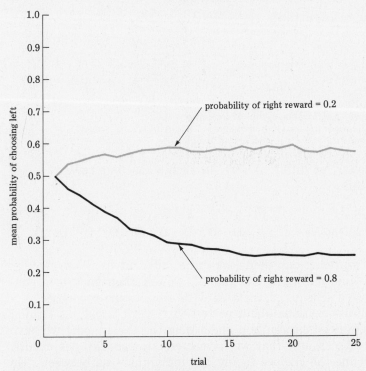

Figure 6.6: Simulation of 200 individuals in a learning model in which left response is rewarded with probability 0.4 and right response is rewarded with indicated probability. (Initial probability of left response is 0.5; a is 0.2, and b is 0.2 for all 200.)

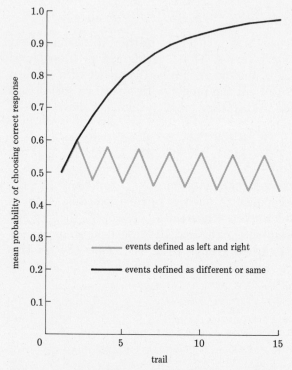

Figure 6.7: Two different definitions of events and their effect on predictions from a learning model faced with a simple alternating sequence of rewards. (Initial probability is 0.5; a is 0.2, and b is 0.2.)

trial as the last or different (D). In such a case our reward series looks like this:

Trial Number	1	2	3	4	5	6	7	8	9	10
Rewarded Response	—	D	D	D	D	D	D	D	D	D

The model's predictions then look quite different as illustrated by the dotted line in Figure 6.7. Indeed, we are then back to a consistent reward schedule associated with the pattern responses.

The observations about patterned reward schedules remind us of a suppressed assumption underlying the basic model we have presented: We assume that we have correctly specified the events. How we define the choices facing our individual—as between "Go left" and "Go right" or between "Go the same way as last time" and "Go a different way from last time"—may make a significant difference in some reward schedules. We may be able to make a poor model into a good one (or vice versa) by the imagination we use in defining the nature of the choice events.

These four cases define four different classes of environments. They have been studied in considerable empirical detail. One reason for believing that the simple model of adaptation we have presented might be a good one is that it fits the empirical results relatively well, even though the empirical world is more complicated and requires a variety of cautions.

6.4.2   *LEARNING LIMITS (OPTIONAL)*

You will notice that in each of the simulations presented in the previous section it appears to be true that the proportion of mice going left seems to approach some value. After a while, additional experiences in the T-maze have little effect on the average probability of a mouse's going left or right.

> *STOP.* **Go back and look at Figures 6.4, 6.5, and 6.6. See if you can guess what proportion of mice would go left after a million trials for each case.**

The conjecture that the proportion of mice turning left is, in fact, approaching some value in each case is correct. To prove this requires more mathematics than this book uses, so you will have to take our word for it.[3] We can also, using additional mathematics, prove what the value is. This value is called the *limit* for the proportion of rats going left as the number of trials increases indefinitely. There is a general expression for the limit in our model:

If $a = b$,

$\Pi_1 =$ the probability of reward on the left side,
$\Pi_2 =$ the probability of reward on the right side,

and Π_1 and Π_2 are greater than 0 and less than 1. Then the limit of the probability of going left is given by the following expression:

$$\text{limit } p_\text{L} = \frac{1 - \Pi_2}{2 - \Pi_2 - \Pi_1}$$

STOP. Use the expression to calculate the limits for each of the cases in the figures. In these cases, where the probability of reward is 0, you can assume that it is some very small number (for instance, 1/1,000,000); where the probability of reward is 1, you can assume that it is some number very close to 1 (for instance, 999,999/1,000,000). Compare your calculated limits with your earlier guesses.

You should have obtained the following values for the limits:

Figure 6.4.   The limits are 1.0 for both curves.
Figure 6.5.   The limits are 0.83 and 0.56.
Figure 6.6.   The limits are 0.57 and 0.25.

Our simulations and our derived expressions for the limits agree very closely.

6.4.3   EXPLORATIONS OF T-MAZES

Example: Behavioral Psychotherapy

"Bobby Jones is a dangerously withdrawn child," says his second-grade teacher. "We must do something to save him before he loses contact with the real world." In your capacity as Chief People Saver and Redeemer of the Central Unified School District, you sit in class for three days and observe Bobby's behavior. You notice that he spends most of his time alone at the side of the room. The teacher, trying to be supportive, frequently goes over to talk with him and praises his work projects. Sometimes Bobby wanders over to the group of children in the center of the room and joins the group. The teacher works with the center group without showing favoritism for any of the children.

In order to discuss Bobby in terms of our model, we will need to establish some relation between the real world and our model world. We can do this easily:

Bobby's Alternatives
S—play with others. (We designate this as "S," meaning social.)
A—play alone. (We designate this as "A," meaning alone.)

Bobby's Current State
Probability of S = 0.25 (or some other low number).
Probability of A = 0.75.

World's Alternatives
Reward—give much attention.
Not reward—give little attention.

State of the World
Probability of rewarding S = 0.1 (or some other low number).
Probability of rewarding A = 0.75 (or some other large number).

Set of possible Events
E1—play with others, rewarded.
E2—play with others, not rewarded.
E3—play alone, rewarded.
E4—play alone, not rewarded.

Adaptation Equations
Event Value for the Probability at the Next Trial
E1 $P_S(t+1) = P_S(t) + a[1 - P_S(t)]$
E2 $P_S(t+1) = P_S(t) - bP_S(t)$
E3 $P_A(t+1) = P_A(t) + a[1 - P_A(t)]$
E4 $P_A(t+1) = P_A(t) - bP_A(t)$

STOP. **Review this to be sure that you understand the model.**

Now we can (if we make some estimates of the values of *a* and *b*) see what will happen to Bobby as he continues in this environment and our model is correct.

STOP. **Suppose that** *a* = 0.2 **and** *b* = 0.2. **What will happen over the next few trials? Simulate the behavior. Then ask yourself what will happen if Bobby stays a long time in this classroom.**

From the previous section we know that Bobby will ultimately approach a probability of playing alone of 0.78. Since his present probability is 0.75, we can expect little change.

STOP. What can the teacher do to change things so that Bobby spends more time playing with others? Show what the consequences would be in the model.

Clearly, if we want to increase the probability that Bobby will play with others, we want to increase the frequency with which events E1 and E4 occur. The teacher must learn that her current way of "helping" Bobby is only making things worse. Therefore, she should change her conduct so that she gives him less attention when he is by himself but extra attention the moment he comes over and joins the group.

STOP. Suppose the teacher changed behaviors so that the probability of reward for playing alone is reduced to 0.3 and the probability of reward for playing with others is increased to 0.9. What will happen? What will happen in the next few trials and ultimately?

The basic facts here were taken from an actual case study, though the case study did not make use of numerical computations. The social scientists involved simply reported the change in reinforcement conditions (teacher to give attention only while Bobby was with the group) and the resultant change in behavior (Bobby gradually spent more and more time with the group and less time withdrawn by himself).

STOP AND THINK. Suppose you wanted to be sure that the results of the experiment were not just a chance accident. What could you do in this specific situation, with Bobby, to establish the fact that it was the change in reward conditions that caused the change in behavior? Think of an additional experiment.

One possibility would be to try the same therapy with other patients in the same situation to see if they also became less withdrawn. The social scientists actually conducted a somewhat stronger test of the theory. They asked the teacher to return to her original pattern of behavior. She was to give Bobby special attention when he was by himself but no special attention when he was with the other children. The theory predicts that Bobby should respond to the new rewards by returning to his former withdrawn behavior, which he actually did over several days' time. The teacher was then asked to reinstitute the new reward system. When she did so, Bobby promptly became social again. The changes of theoretical interest did cause a significant change in Bobby's behavior.

Conventional psychiatric theory says that human personality is formed at a very early age, perhaps by six or seven years old, certainly by late teens; that personality is formed as the result of important, perhaps even traumatic events; and that once formed, human personality is fixed and very difficult to change. Conventional psychiatric theory says that the symptoms that people try to cure in therapy—various traits of personal or sexual maladjustment—are the results of an underlying psychological sickness and that this sickness must be discovered and understood by the patient in order to effect a cure. It is a disease theory of mental illness.

As a result of adaptation experiments like those described early in this chapter, a new group of people called behavioral therapists has come into being. They believe that behavior is learned, and hence can be modified by changing the learning conditions; that the "symptoms" of mental illness can be treated as mislearned responses.

Which group of people is correct? Psychiatrists argue that one must cure the underlying illness in order to deal effectively with psychological problems; that merely changing behavior is like alleviating symptoms while ignoring the fundamental problems. Behavioral therapists argue that the fundamental problem *is* the behavior; that they can accomplish relatively quick changes in cases of severe malfunctioning.[4]

Example: Human Nature, Power, and Fate

One of the most interesting features of life as a social scientist is the way in which you consistently find most people "explaining" social events in terms of grand concepts that most serious students of those events consider of much more limited usefulness. For example, consider human nature theories of individual behavior or power theories of political behavior or fate theories of failure. You are continually asking yourself how it can be that intelligent people could learn to accept theories that you find unacceptably vague.

One possible answer is that social scientists are dumb, and people are smart. It is an answer that has been suggested rather frequently, though somewhat more frequently by nonsocial scientists than by members of the profession. The latter tend to accept an alternative answer: People are dumb and social scientists are smart. Both answers are consistent with the outcome, but we might want to search further for some explanation that suggests why smart people might come to prefer meaningless theories:

STOP AND THINK. **Do you have any ideas? Why might smart people acquire faith in bad theories?**

Suppose that people learn to prefer explanations of social events in the same way that they learn other things. They consider an explanation and see whether it fits their own experiences. If it does, they increase the propensity to express it. If it does not fit their experiences, they tend to reject it.

In addition, suppose that there are three different kinds of possible theories:

1. *Magic Theories.* A magic theory is a theory that cannot be proved wrong because any possible observation can be made to fit the theory (like the circular models in Section 3.2.1.)
2. *Perfect Theories.* A perfect theory is a theory that can, in principle, be proved wrong; but it is so good that it is always correct.
3. *Imperfect Theories.* An imperfect theory is a theory that not only can be proved wrong in principle but will be. It makes some erroneous predictions.

If an individual goes through life learning to prefer different theories on the basis of experience, he will clearly come to prefer theories that are either perfect or magic. Experience leads to a rejection of imperfect theories.

But perfect theories are quite rare. Indeed, most people would say that they are nonexistent. This leaves the individual with a learned preference for magic. Experience teaches a preference for theories that explain everything (but predict nothing). The faster a learner the individual is, the quicker his adaptation to magic theories.

The problem (like the model) extends to professional work by social scientists. In fields, or among people, in which there is a strong commitment to being correct, you should expect to find a tendency for social science theories to be magical. As we observed in Chapter Three, good analysis in social science depends on finding pleasure in being wrong.

Example: The Extinction of Subjective Creativity

Many books have been written about creativity. Many attempts have been made to understand how creative people are made. Many complaints have been recorded about the lack of creativity in individuals, organizations, and societies. It is a pervasive and persistent problem. We can illustrate a possible application of our model of adaptation by using it to try to understand why creativity is relatively uncommon among most of us.

> **STOP AND THINK.** Can you see any way in which you could set up a learning model of creativity? *Hint:* What would be the two possible alternative behaviors by an individual?

We begin by reviewing the components of our model. The first is a list of alternative behaviors. We require a way of looking at behavior in terms of alternatives that are relevant to the question of creativity. Perhaps the most obvious one is simply to state two alternatives:

Alternative 1
Act creatively. That is act in a manner that is creative *as far as you can tell*. We can call this behavior *subjectively* creative.

Alternative 2
Act noncreatively.

These form the basis for our model. We will try to understand the process by which an individual might learn to act in a manner that is subjectively creative, or not.

We will assume that each individual has initially some probability of taking a subjectively creative action and that the environment offers rewards that depend in some way on that person's action. We will need to specify the basis on which rewards are made. Perhaps the most obvious way is the most sensible. Let us suppose that the environment rewards behavior depending on whether it is *truly* creative or truly noncreative. That is, the environment does not care that you believe an action is new and creative—it only rewards actions that are objectively new and creative.

We now have an action that is made in terms of *subjective* creativity and a response that is made in terms of *actual* creativity. Since they are not necessarily the same, we will need some way of relating them. Suppose we assume that any act that is actually creative will also be subjectively creative, but that some acts that are subjectively creative are not actually creative. In effect, we assume that the individual sometimes sees noncreative actions as creative; but he never sees creative actions as noncreative. The assumption seems plausible when we remember that any individual is likely to invent things that have been invented before or think thoughts that have been thought before; but he is unlikely to think that new thoughts are actually old ones.

The set of possible events then is defined:

Event 1.   Take subjectively creative action and be rewarded.
Event 2.   Take subjectively creative action and not be rewarded.
Event 3.   Act noncreatively and be rewarded.
Event 4.   Act noncreatively and not be rewarded.

For each of these events we can specify our usual learning equations.

Since we began with the complaints about the absence of creativity in the world, we might ask whether we can specify a set of environmental rules that will tend to eliminate creative behavior.

STOP AND THINK.   **Can you think of an environment that will eliminate creativity? That is, what kind of response behavior, by the world, will eliminate creativity?**

You certainly should have responded with one such world. Suppose that the environment always rewards noncreative behavior and never rewards creative behavior. Such an environment certainly could, and probably does, exist (for example, a highly conservative organization that distrusted anything new and felt comfortable only with previously experienced behavior). In such an environment learning would tend to eliminate subjective creativity. The rate at which subjectively creative behavior is eliminated will depend on the extent to which the behavior is actually creative. Interestingly enough, the *less* the individual is actually creative, the *longer* he will persist in being subjectively creative!

Thus we have at least one type of environment in which, according to our model, individuals would learn to suppress creative behavior: an environment that rewards only noncreative behavior. Are there any other environments that would have the same effect? In particular, is it possible that an environment that rewards *good* ideas could end up suppressing *creative* ones?

STOP AND THINK. We know that "creative" means new. What does "good" mean? What is the relation between creative ideas and good ideas?

A good idea is one that works. It solves a problem or produces what you want. What is the relation between good ideas and subjectively creative ideas? It is certainly possible for a subjectively creative idea to be a bad idea. Consider, for example, the brilliantly creative idea of the child who wants to know what fire smells like and sticks his nose in it. It is also certainly possible for noncreative ideas to be good ones. That is, someone else's subjectively creative idea that turned out to be a good idea can be used by you to solve a similar problem. Much of learning, after all, consists in learning about useful methods and ideas that have helped others with their problems. (The advantages for cultures that have written records is an example.) Thus we have two important parameters of an environment: (1) the probability that a subjectively creative idea will be a good idea; and (2) the probability that a subjectively noncreative idea will be a good idea.

In most domains of action, and for most people most of the time, it seems likely that subjectively creative ideas are likely to be bad ones. Many *apparently* new ideas are old ideas that have been found to have problems and hence have been discarded by the culture; and many really new ideas will turn out to be bad. (This is a self-evident proposition if you have ever watched a child exploring his environment.)

Imagine a child or a young adult learning about the world. He is confronted with a problem: He may either use the standard, noncreative solution that he has used in the past or decide to try a new, subjectively creative solution. He makes a choice, and the world rewards him if it is a good idea and, possibly, punishes him if it is a bad one. The distinction in these last two sentences is important: Our experimental subject is acting in terms of the alternative do *new* action/do *traditional* action while the world is responding in terms of the categories reward *good* actions/ignore or punish *bad* actions. Hence the possible events look like this

Event 1.   Try new behavior, and it works.
Event 2.   Try new behavior and get clobbered.
Event 3.   Try traditional behavior, and it works.
Event 4.   Try traditional behavior and get clobbered.

Now assuming that the world always rewards good ideas and that new (subjectively creative) ideas turn out to be good ones, say 20% of the time, what will the individual learn? That is, assume the world is not stodgy or traditional or conservative; it genuinely likes good ideas and always rewards them. Will the individual learn to be creative or not?

STOP AND THINK about it for a moment. What will happen in such a world?

As you might have observed, the answer depends on the probability that a subjectively noncreative idea is a good one. Figure 6.8 shows the pattern of learning in worlds in which the probability that subjectively noncreative ideas are good ones is 0.1, 0.5, and 0.9. *Q* is the proportion of subjectively noncreative acts that are good. You can see that as long as noncreative ideas have a higher probability of being good (than creative ideas do), the individual will grow up learning to be ordinarily noncreative. If you believe that cultures do "learn" about the world over time and hence that the traditional answers taught at home and in school are relatively likely to be good ones (particularly those that are seen as noncreative by a child), you would have to conclude

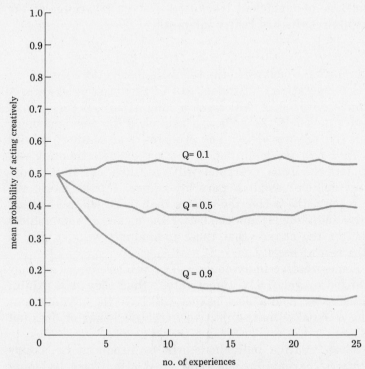

Figure 6.8: The extinction of subjective creativity as a function
of the "quality" of noncreative acts. Simulation of 200 individuals
learning—20% of subjectively creative ideas are good ones. (Initial
probability is 0.5; a is 0.2, and b is 0.2 for all 200.)

that it is quite likely that a society that rewarded good ideas would
tend to extinguish subjective creativity.

STOP AND THINK. This result is sufficiently beautiful
to warrant your attention.

Not all subjective creativity would be extinguished, however.
We would still produce some creative people. Where will you find
them?

STOP AND THINK. Use the model. *Hint:* Since the
model says that learning produces noncreativity, look for

situations of inefficient learning. Give it a try. Some of the possible results are really interesting.

You may have suggested the following derivations:

1. Some creative individuals will be produced by chance. A certain number of people will have a long string of good (*and* creative) ideas even if the odds are against it in any particular person. It is like tossing coins: The probability of coming up with 100 heads in a row is small, but if you try enough times it will eventually happen. Thus everyone will not turn out to be noncreative; we will be saved in part by chance. Furthermore, the larger the society, the better the chance that there will be at least some creative individuals; and the better the means of communication, the better the chance that those individuals will be able to influence the rest of society.

2. Some creative individuals will be produced because they are slow witted or relatively unmotivated; thus they will exhibit slow learning rates. And a slow learner will have the advantage of not learning as quickly that subjectively creative behavior does not pay off.

3. Some creative individuals will be produced by sloppy environments. If parents do not know good ideas from bad ones (perhaps because they have inadequate intellectual or moral training), the relative advantage of noncreativity is muted. Similarly, if the particular domain is one in which the distinction between good and bad is hazy or changing, subjective creativity may be reinforced.

Thus if you want to find subjectively creative people in a typical society, you should look for the inattentive, low-ability child of uneducated parents who is interested in a relatively new field with ill-defined or changing standards.

STOP AND THINK. Before we accept such a prediction, can you think of any complications?

As you may have observed, a theory of subjective creativity may not always be enough. We can increase subjective creativity a good deal without increasing actual creativity or good ideas if we specialize in doing it in the way that is implicit in the preceding prediction. At the same time, however, our model may remind us of some of the complications in intelligence. Educated parents and quick-learning children may, indeed, combine to stunt the development of subjectively creative ideas. Knowledge has some costs as well as benefits.

Some qualifications of the foregoing results are:

1. It is conceivable that a really well-educated parent—maybe one who has read this book—would try to make a local redefinition of the world's response behavior. That is, reward new actions (with lots of praise and attention) regardless of whether or not they are good actions and be relatively indifferent to standard successes. If your modification of the local environment (remember you cannot change the outside world) is sufficiently important to the child and if the child survives (remember, many of his subjectively creative ideas will be nearly fatal), then you can raise creative children.

2. One of the factors that influences motivation, and hence learning rate, is the size and importance of the rewards. If we give especially large rewards to ideas that are both creative and good, then we greatly increase the chances of raising creative individuals. Of course, if these super rewards are mostly associated with adult behavior (children do not have the opportunity or background to make inventions, solve serious organizational problems, or propose legislative solutions) and if the pattern of creative/noncreative response is learned in childhood, then this size-of-reward factor is not likely to make much difference. It does help us to generate an additional prediction, however: Professions that demand a great deal of prior education and that have relatively long apprenticeships will have a smaller proportion of creative individuals in them.

Thus among academic specialties those fields that quickly bring the student to the frontiers of knowledge—for instance, most of the physical sciences, the creative arts, and many of the social sciences—will have a higher proportion of creative people than those fields that demand a long, scholarly background. Or in the business world those companies that give an early chance at significant decision making will have a higher proportion of creative individuals. These will mostly be small companies (or else highly decentralized large companies). This does not mean that those large, centralized companies that value creativity will have no creative individuals: Their very size increases the chances of having some of these people; and they can always recruit top executives from outside, smaller firms. Nor does this mean that those academic specialties or firms will do better. They will do so only if subjective creativity pays off, that is, if subjective creativity is more brilliance than foolishness.

6.5   *SUPERSTITIOUS LEARNING*

We have been discussing situations in which the individual learns to adapt to his environment in order to gain a reward. Subjectively, the individual may reasonably sense that he is manipulating the environment in an instrumental fashion. In this section we will analyze situations in which the environment is indifferent to the individual's behavior; it dispenses rewards or punishments on some basis other than a response to his actions. The individual, however, will not necessarily be able to detect this indifference. Although the environment is not responding to the individual's actions, the individual seems to behave as if he believes the environment is responsive, and he learns in the usual way. We call this phenomenon superstitious learning, and it encompasses some of the most widespread, and most interesting, forms of human behavior.

6.5.1   *BENIGN WORLDS*

We will begin with a simple T-maze example and then go on to the human applications. First we put Alfred the mouse back into the maze again. All the possible events are shown in Table 6.2. Now let us specify a rather special reward situation: Whether he goes right or left Alfred will be rewarded—that is, there is always food on both sides of the T-maze.

> **STOP AND THINK.**   **Given these reward conditions, which of the four events can actually occur?**

Since Alfred is always rewarded, no matter what he does, events E2 and E4 can never occur. It is a benign world. Only events E1 and E3 can occur in this world. What is Alfred likely to learn in such a world? Make a guess about what his behavior is likely to be after, say, 20 trials. Will he always go left, always right, oscillate between them, or what?

STOP AND THINK. **What do you think will happen over time?**

One way to discover the outcome of learning in a benign world is to simulate it. We will now show the outcome of a single simulation.

Initially, Alfred is neutral about which way he will turn; that is, $P_L = P_R = 0.5$; to find out what he actually does on the first trial we use some sort of random number probability generator (as described in Section 6.4). We do so and discover that he goes right on the first trial, and is rewarded; event E3 occurred, and we can calculate his new probability of going right (by assuming $a = 0.3$):

$$P_R(2) = P_R(1) + a[1 - P_R(1)] = 0.5 + 0.3(1 - 0.5)$$
$$= 0.5 + 0.15 = 0.65$$

Now using the new value for P_R we again use the random number probability generator to discover what Alfred does on the next trial. He goes left this time, and we can calculate his new probability of going left on the next trial:

$$P_L(3) = P_L(2) + a[1 - P_L(2)] = 0.35 + 0.3(0.65) = 0.545$$

Notice that whether he goes left or right, the learning rate a is used because he is always rewarded. Using the new value for P_L and the random number probability generator we discover that next time he goes right. We calculate the new value of P_R and continue the simulation. The results of this particular simulation are shown in Table 6.4 and plotted in Figure 6.9. Notice that after some initial oscillation on trials 1 through 4, Alfred settles down to a steady left pattern (with one relapse on trial 8). And notice that the longer the pattern goes on, the greater P_L becomes and hence the less probable a relapse becomes.

Other simulations would yield similar results, some initial oscillation with an eventual steady approach toward one side or the other. Alfred eventually learns to go to one side in order to be rewarded; it becomes more and more unlikely that he will try an alternative behavior. If the mouse were a human, we might expect him to imagine that going left is the best way to succeed, and to believe that his choice reflects a triumph of learning from experi-

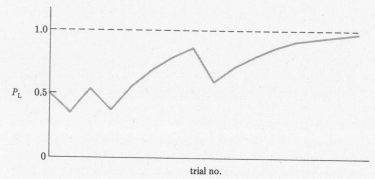

Figure 6.9: Alfred's adaptation in a benign world.

ence. Because we know that going right would do just as well, we call Alfred's model of the world superstition.

Human beings seem to display similar examples of superstitious learning. The following beliefs are illustrations: Never walk underneath a ladder; never open an umbrella inside a house; do not let a black cat cross your path. Some people would defend these, or other superstitions with arguments such as: "I know the belief is true because it works. I have consistently avoided black cats and so I have avoided trouble. That's been my experience." The inference about the world is questionable when the alternative actions have not been explored to see whether they do in fact result

TABLE 6.4   Alfred's Adaptation in a Benign World

TRIAL	WHAT ALFRED DID	NEW VALUE OF P_L
1	Right	0.350
2	Left	0.545
3	Right	0.382
4	Left	0.567
5	Left	0.697
6	Left	0.788
7	Left	0.788
8	Right	0.596
9	Left	0.717
10	Left	0.802
11	Left	0.861
12	Left	0.903
13	Left	0.932
14	Left	0.952
15	Left	0.966

in different outcomes. In fact, it seems possible that many of our beliefs are adhered to in part because we have never had recourse to alternative courses of action.

B. F. Skinner once demonstrated superstitious learning with pigeons. He put a hungry pigeon in a cage and arranged a mechanical device that dropped food pellets into the cage at random intervals, independent of the pigeon's actions. The pigeon would begin moving around the cage. Eventually, a pellet would drop in. Suppose that at the time the pellet dropped, the pigeon was looking over its left shoulder. The pigeon would again resume walking around the cage, but its probability of looking over its left shoulder would be slightly increased. If the next time the pellet dropped when the pigeon was again looking over its left shoulder, this probability would increase still more. Ultimately, the pigeon would "learn" that the way to get food was to look over its left shoulder. Maybe the food did not come immediately, but if the pigeon waited long enough in this position the food would come. This random reinforcement procedure could have caught the pigeon doing any number of strange things and then taught it that this was the proper way to get food. Can you imagine anything sillier than a collection of pigeons in various cages, some standing perpetually on one foot, some with a particular wing extended, some with their heads in the air, and some looking back over their left shoulders, each convinced that it alone knows the best behavior? Can the same situation be said to apply to a group of executives? Or stock market forecasters? Or military theorists? Or educators? Or parents? We will look at some of them in Section 6.5.4.

6.5.2 MALEVOLENT WORLDS

In the previous section we explored the consequences of a basically unresponsive world that gave rewards no matter what the individual did. Again, suppose that the world is unresponsive, but this time we assume that it is unresponsively *non*rewarding. No one ever succeeds, no matter what he does.

> ***STOP AND THINK.*** Under the previous set of assumptions behavior converged, superstitiously, to one strategy or another, even though it was not instrumental to do so. What happens over time when nothing is instrumental?

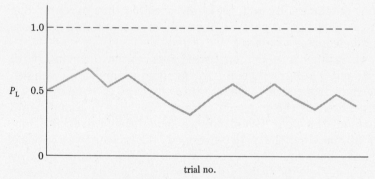

Figure 6.10: Alfred's adaptation in a malevolent world.

We can consider poor Alfred once more. Once again we have the possible events shown in Table 6.2. This time, however, there is never any food in either side of the T-maze. Only events E2 and E4 can occur. That is, Alfred can go left and get nothing, or he can go right and get nothing.

Suppose we simulate the learning in such a world. Table 6.5 shows one such simulation in which we assume $P_L(0) = P_R(0) = 0.5$, and $b = 0.2$. The result is plotted in Figure 6.10.

Other simulations would yield similar results, a persistent oscillation around 0.5. Alfred keeps trying; but every time he goes left, he increases his likelihood of going right; and every time he goes right, he increases his likelihood of going left.

TABLE 6.5   Alfred's Adaptation in a Malevolent World

TRIAL	WHAT ALFRED DID	NEW VALUE OF P_L
1	Right	0.600
2	Right	0.680
3	Left	0.544
4	Right	0.635
5	Left	0.508
6	Left	0.406
7	Left	0.325
8	Right	0.460
9	Right	0.568
10	Left	0.454
11	Right	0.563
12	Left	0.450
13	Left	0.360
14	Right	0.488
15	Left	0.390

It is a cruel world, not unknown to human experience. Consider the behavior of patients seeking a cure for an incurable disease, car owners looking for a reliable mechanic, social scientists looking for a perfect theory, or lovers looking for a perfect mate.

6.5.3 LEARNING LIMITS (OPTIONAL)

We have noted that if two alternatives are always rewarded (the benign world), then individuals will eventually learn either to do one of the alternatives all of the time or to do the other alternative all of the time. Sometimes we may want to know how many people will end up doing one thing all the time and how many will end up doing the other.

STOP. **What do you think? If there are two alternatives and both are always rewarded, how many people will end up doing one of them all of the time and how many will end up doing the other all of the time?**

If you answered that half of the people would end up taking one alternative and half taking the other, you are not correct (except in a special case). The correct answer (which requires some additional mathematics to prove) is that if you expose subjects to a benign world indefinitely, the expected proportion of those who will end up going left all of the time is equal to the proportion of those who go left on the *first* trial. If the initial probability is $\frac{1}{2}$, then one-half of the people will end up always going left. But if the initial probability of going left is $\frac{1}{4}$, then only one-fourth of the people will end up always going left.

Similarly, we have noted that if two alternatives are never rewarded (the malevolent world), an individual will move toward an equal probability of doing each alternative, oscillating around 0.5 with the magnitude of the oscillations depending on the value of *b*. Since each individual approaches 0.5 as a probability, the average probability approaches the same number. The proportion of people going left at the end of a long period of living in a malevolent world will be one-half, regardless of the proportion that goes left on the first trial.

STOP. Be sure you understand the difference between the proportion of people who will choose one alternative rather than the other in the two superstitious situations.

If a population of people with a strong initial likelihood (probability $= 0.9$) of being honest is placed in a world in which *both* honesty and dishonesty are rewarded, the model predicts that some will learn a strong propensity toward honesty and some will learn a strong propensity toward dishonesty, but the proportion of honest behaviors will not change much over time. On the other hand, if the same population of people with a strong initial likelihood of behaving honestly is placed in a world in which *neither* honesty nor dishonesty is rewarded, the model predicts that everyone will learn to oscillate between the two, and the overall proportion of honest behaviors will decline to 0.5.

6.5.4 EXPLORATIONS OF SUPERSTITION

Example: The Case of Hair Color

Some people still have the same hair color they had 10 years ago. Some people have a different color. And other people seem to oscillate. What is it that accounts for these color preferences and changes. Can they be described by some simple adaptation model?

Let us assume that at any given moment people have two alternatives open to them—blonde or brunette. Let P_{BL} be the probability of wearing blonde hair and P_{BR} be the probability of wearing brunette hair. We will assume that the world can respond by either flattering a person or not. Thus there are four possible events: E1 = blonde, flattered; E2 = blonde, not flattered; E3 = brunette, flattered; E4 = brunette, not flattered. Let us assume the $P_{BL}(0) = 0.5$ initially. We shall now try different assumptions about what kinds of behavior are reinforced and see how people adapt to them.

Reinforcement Assumption 1. Blondes have more fun. Assume that blondes are always flattered and brunettes are never flattered. At a given time a person gets up in the morning and picks a hair color, say, blonde. When he (or she) steps out of the house, he will have an enjoyable day and therefore his behavior will be reinforced.

The next day his probability of choosing blonde will increase because that behavior was reinforced the previous day. If instead he had decided to be a brunette, he would not be reinforced. Brunette behavior would have a tendency to decay or be forgotten. Only events E1 and E4 can occur. Under both P_{BL} increases. Over time, under Reinforcement Assumption 1, the world should gradually begin to look all blonde. This is a simple adaptation model; no superstitious learning is involved. People are adapting, rationally, to some social prejudices.

Reinforcement Assumption 2. Pretty people have fun. Here we assume that hair color is irrelevant. Instead we divide the world into pretty people and not-so-pretty people. We assume that pretty people are flattered no matter what their hair color and not-so-pretty people are never flattered no matter what their hair color. Now what happens? If we consider pretty people, only events E1 and E3 can occur. It is a benevolent world for them. Suppose a pretty person gets up and puts on blonde hair. Then when he (or she) goes outside, he will be flattered. Tomorrow his chance of going blonde will increase. Ultimately, he is very likely to end up going blonde all the time. Or suppose that a pretty person awoke the first day and decided to try brunette hair. He would be flattered (thus his behavior would be reinforced), and so the probability of putting on brunette hair the next day would be increased. Ultimately, such reinforcement will most often end up making him go brunette all the time.

In both cases the pretty people act as though the reinforcement occurred because of their hair color. If we assume that the initial blonde probability for all pretty people was 0.5, then over time we should end up with about half the pretty people being determined blondes and about half of them determined brunettes. In every case the individuals will be convinced that their hair color is the proper hair color.

What happens to the not-so-pretty people? For them only events E2 and E4 can occur in a malevolent world. Suppose one of them gets up, tries on blonde hair, goes outside, and is not flattered. Since blonde behavior is not reinforced, it is less probable tomorrow. So the next day he is more likely to try brunette hair. He goes outside and again is not reinforced. Thus his P_{BL} will never deviate very far from 0.5. The same result would occur if he had started with brunette hair on the first day. Thus we conclude that not-so-pretty people will tend to fluctuate between one hair color and the other. On any one day about half of them will have blonde hair, and about half will have brunette. But unlike the pretty people the individual not-so-pretty people will change colors often.

Hair color, of course, is only one of a number of ways in which individuals modify their behavior in response to experience. We also change our clothes, our speech, and our attitudes. One moderately interesting implication of thinking about the case of hair color is the apparent implication that it is the not-so-pretty people who will buy most of the hair coloring and own most of the wigs in the world. Similarly, we would expect (if this model is correct) that it would generally be the people who do not frequently receive social approval who will have large wardrobes of clothes, large repertoires of slang expressions, and flexibility in attitudes. The model may not describe all social situations, but it may interpret some facets of our ordinary experience.

Example: Personality Development

There are many theories of how children (and adults) come to develop characteristic styles of behavior and attitudes. These characteristic styles are often called the personality of an individual in order to suggest that they are relatively persistent and relatively distinctive. Thus we sometimes talk of an authoritarian personality or a selfish personality or an extroverted personality. Theories of personality development generally emphasize some version of the child-is-father-of-the-man hypothesis. That is, they assume that the events of childhood affect the personality of adults. Alternative theories of development, and attempts to verify them, fill the pages of numerous books and articles.

One persistent problem faced by theories of personality development is the variety of personalities that apparently result from very similar childhood environments. Children reared in the same family seem to develop quite different styles of behavior. The same family will include extroverts and introverts, altruists and egoists, risk takers and risk avoiders. The usual explanation of such heterogeneity emphasizes that the same family can (and usually does) provide quite different environments for different children. The oldest child faces a different world from the youngest; boy children face a different world from girl children; pretty children face a different world from not-so-pretty children.

Using our basic model of adaptation in the face of experience, we can provide an alternative interpretation of heterogeneity in personality. In order to do that we need to imagine that a baby learns according to our standard model.

STOP AND THINK. **How would you set up the model? What are the alternatives for the baby? What are the rewards?**

Suppose we imagine that each morning a baby wakes up and does one of three things:

Alternative 1.   He cries.
Alternative 2.   He wets his diapers.
Alternative 3.   He gurgles.

Initially, he has some probability of doing each of these. Let us suppose that the initial probability of each is about $\frac{1}{3}$.

Surrounding the baby is a world of parents. Although parents vary considerably in their behavior, one rather common attribute of parents is that they usually love their children and are concerned about them. This produces a set of responses by parents to the three alternative behaviors:

If the baby cries, a parent goes to the baby, picks him up, and cuddles him.

If the baby wets his diapers, a parent goes to the baby, changes the diapers, picks him up, and cuddles him.

If the baby gurgles, a parent goes to the baby, picks him up, and cuddles him.

No matter what the baby does, his parents pick him up and cuddle him.

STOP AND THINK. **What does the model predict will happen in this situation?**

The baby is in a situation ripe for superstitious learning. According to our model, each baby will learn to do one thing all of the time. Each baby will have the subjective sense of having figured out the world. About ⅓ of the babies will learn to cry all the time; ⅓ will learn to wet diapers all the time; ⅓ will learn to gurgle all of the time.

The model suggests that despite the fact that the environment is identical and despite a learning process that is oriented toward seeking rewards, radically different personalities will be generated. In an enviroment-driven model, we do not need to assume different environments to produce different consistent behaviors. The model also indicates some possible reasons why we find, among adults, some people who cry a lot, some who gurgle a lot, and some who are always wetting their diapers. Perhaps, they all had loving and sympathetic parents.

Example: Successful Executives

Most successful administrators have theories of administration. Some write books about their theories; others confine their expositions to cocktail parties. In either case, one of the most impressive things is the variety of theories: Some propose decentralization, some centralized control; some advocate loose supervision, some tight; some argue for relatively strict insistence on hierarchical channels of communication; others think a more diffuse set of channels works better. Some believe in promotion from within, others from outside; some think planning is the most important activity of an executive; others that it is a waste of time; and some say "it all depends" and that the most important thing is judgment about what it depends on. The list could be made much longer if we wished.

How can it be that successful executives can provide such conflicting theories of their success? Is it possible that our simple model of adaptation might give some clue to what is happening?

> **STOP AND THINK.** Set up the model and see if you can suggest some ideas. What kind of world could produce such diversity?

You might easily have reasoned in the following way: If success as an executive depended primarily on the administrative style (theory?) of the executive, variation in the beliefs of administrators would depend on the fact that they were in different organizations facing different environments. They would learn different things because they were in different worlds. Such a result is certainly consistent with a learning model. Rats that are rewarded on the left learn to go left; rats that are rewarded on the right learn to go right.

But there is another, and perhaps less obvious, way by which the same behavioral result might be produced. Suppose that the success of an executive did not depend much on his behavior. Suppose rather that it depended on the conditions of the market, the chance events of organizational life, and other things outside his control. Then success as an executive would be largely a matter of chance. During certain times, for example, during a boom, almost everyone would be successful. During other times, for example, during a depression, almost no one would be successful. During other times, some people would be successful because they were in the job at the right time; others would be in the job at the wrong time and be unsuccessful.

The successful ones would probably come to believe that their success was related to their style of administration and would develop a theory of administration that would reflect that perception. Since their success was not dependent, in fact, on their behavior, almost any administrative behavior might be associated with success. The sample of successful administrators, according to this interpretation, is simply a sample of superstitious learners living in a benign environment.

Unsuccessful executives rarely publish books about their theories of administration. According to the model, this is also understandable. If they attribute their lack of success to their behavior, they will still be looking for the behavior that works and will persistently cycle through alternative possible administrative styles.

Thus if executive behavior had little to do with executive success, we would produce a group of successful executives who had profound experience suggesting it was important—and a wide variety of administrative prescriptions they are prepared to support on the basis of their experience.

6.6 MUTUAL LEARNING (OPTIONAL)

Thus far we have looked at situations in which an individual is placed in an environment and adapts to it. The environment is assumed to have some *fixed* characteristics by which rewards are determined. For example, one alternative action is always rewarded and the other never is, or one alternative action is rewarded sometimes and the other never is, or either alternative may be rewarded on any particular trial with probabilities fixed in advance, or both alternatives are always rewarded, or neither alternative is ever rewarded.

All of these situations involve an actively learning individual facing an environment that is passive. The scheme for rewards is not affected by the patterns of responses. We can call this class of learning situations, situations of *prospecting*. The rewards are distributed in some way, and the individual tries to find out how to obtain a reward. It is like prospecting for gold.

Not all learning situations are prospecting situations. The world is not always passive. In particular, there are many situations in which the "world" consists of other individuals, who are in turn responding to the environment as they see it. In other words, you constitute other people's environment, and they constitute yours. Hence reward probabilities are not fixed; you and the world are *both* learning to adapt. There is mutual learning. In particular, we can identify two common social situations of *mutual accommodation:*

1. *Mating.* Suppose that the environment rewards only one choice or the other and learns to schedule the reward so that the individual will receive it. It is a common situation. In social life individuals often are more concerned with doing the *same* thing as other people than they are with doing any *specific* thing. For example, male/female relationships are sometimes characterized by mutual adaptation; and in organizations it is often more important that two groups are coordinated in whatever they do than it is that they do any particular thing; and social systems are built on presumptions of extensive mutual adaptation to a common solution.

2. *Hunting.* Suppose that while the individual is trying to learn where the reward will be, the environment is learning to place the reward so that the individual will not receive it. The classic example is the variety of matching games that involve having one person choose an alternative and the other person try to guess what alternative has been chosen. The first individual tries to avoid being correctly anticipated. The situation is common in social life. Competitors try to outguess the competition. Commuters

try to schedule travel when other commuters do not. In some societies, at least, everyone tries to speak only to higher-status individuals than themselves.

There are a number of different ways in which the interdependent learning involved in mating and hunting might be modeled. For example, we could imagine trying to think of how a rational man would act in these two situations. Such considerations have, in fact, led to the development of a whole domain of mathematics and mathematical models called game theory.

Our intention here is different. We want to consider interdependent individuals as adapting their behavior on the basis of experience. We want to extend our simple models of adaptation to the case in which the environment is learning too.

6.6.1   MATING

The natural place to begin a discussion of mating is with mating. Consider the following situation:

> Henry is a 10-year-old boy who walks to school each day. He can walk on 5th Street or 6th Street. The distance is the same. Mildred is a 10-year-old girl who walks to school each day. She can walk on 5th Street or 6th Street. The distance is the same. If Henry and Mildred walk along the same street, they will see each other; if they do not, they will not. Henry likes to see Mildred; Mildred likes to see Henry.

The scenario is familiar to anyone who lives along the way to a school. How do we fit it into a model?

STOP AND THINK. How would you use our learning model to analyze this situation?

We could start by developing a standard learning model for Henry:

1. He has two alternatives: 5th Street or 6th Street.
2. He has some initial probability H_5 of going along 5th Street, and a probability H_6 of going along 6th.
3. On each day there are four events that can occur:

    i. Goes on 5th and sees Mildred.

    ii. Goes on 5th and does not see Mildred.

   iii. Goes on 6th and sees Mildred.

   iv. Goes on 6th and does not see Mildred.

4. For each of the four events, he learns in the usual way:

    i. $H_5(t + 1) = H_5(t) + a[1 - H_5(t)]$

    ii. $H_5(t + 1) = H_5(t) - bH_5(t)$

   iii. $H_6(t + 1) = H_6(t) + a[1 - H_6(t)]$

   iv. $H_6(t + 1) = H_6(t) - bH_6(t)$

Now if Mildred always went on 5th or 6th or if she had some fixed probability of going on 5th, we could use our earlier models. But Milded is also learning; she is trying to adapt too. As a result, our model must include a set of assumptions about Mildred as an adaptive participant:

1. She has two alternatives: 5th Street or 6th Street.

2. She has some initial probability M_5 of going along 5th Street and a probability of M_6 of going along 6th.

3. On each day there are four events that can occur:

    i. Goes on 5th and sees Henry.

    ii. Goes on 5th and does not see Henry.

   iii. Goes on 6th and sees Henry.

   iv. Goes on 6th and does not see Henry.

4. For each of the four events, she learns in the usual way:

    i. $M_5(t + 1) = M_5(t) + c[1 - M_5(t)]$

    ii. $M_5(t + 1) = M_5(t) - dM_5(t)$

   iii. $M_6(t + 1) = M_6(t) + c[1 - M_6(t)]$

   iv. $M_6(t + 1) = M_6(t) - dM_6(t)$

Now we have two individuals, each learning which street to follow in our standard adaptive way. Notice that we have had to introduce two different starting probabilities, $H_5(0)$ and $M_5(0)$. Mildred and Henry do not necessarily have the same initial probability of going down 5th Street. We also have four learning rates (a, b for Henry and c, d for Mildred). Our two individuals may have quite different rates of learning.

STOP AND THINK. Be sure you understand how the model has been developed so far.

Next we need to put our two individuals together so that each becomes the "environment" of the other. And we need to discover what the result of their joint adaptation is.

STOP AND THINK. How would you combine Henry's and Mildred's behaviors? *Hint:* Redefine the events in terms of their *mutual* world.

In the joint world of Henry and Mildred, there are four events that can take place:

E1. Henry and Mildred both go on 5th.
E2. Henry goes on 5th, Mildred on 6th.
E3. Henry goes on 6th, Mildred on 5th.
E4. Henry and Mildred both go on 6th.

We can construct a table that shows for each of these events the changes that take place in Henry's and Mildred's probabilities. In order to do this we need to show first how each of the *joint* world events is related to the list of *individual* events we made for them and then to copy the appropriate learning rule for each individual for each event.

Table 6.6 summarizes the relevant events and the adaptation equations for each event. With this table we can calculate the changes at each time period *if* we know which of the events occurred. For example, consider the case in which initially Henry and Mildred have quite different probabilities: Henry is much more likely to go on 5th $(H_5(0) = 0.9)$, and Mildred is much more likely to go on 6th $(M_5(0) = 0.2)$. Moreover, suppose we know that Henry is a slow learner in the face of reward but a fast learner without reward $(a = 0.1; b = 0.8)$; Mildred is the reverse $(c = 0.7; d = 0.2)$. What are the changes that take place in their probabilities if, on the first day, they should both happen to go on 5th Street?

TABLE 6.6 *Mutual Learning Rules*

JOINT EVENT NO.	HENRY EVENT NO.	MILDRED EVENT NO.	CHANGE IN HENRY	CHANGE IN MILDRED
E1	i	i	$H_5(t+1) = H_5(t) + a[1 - H_5(t)]$	$M_5(t+1) = M_5(t) + c[1 - M_5(t)]$
E2	ii	iv	$H_5(t+1) = H_5(t) - bH_5(t)$	$M_6(t+1) = M_6(t) - dM_6(t)$
E4	iv	ii	$H_6(t+1) = H_6(t) - bH_6(t)$	$M_5(t+1) = M_5(t) - dM_5(t)$
E3	iii	iii	$H_6(t+1) = H_6(t) + a[1 - H_6(t)]$	$M_6(t+1) = M_6(t) + e[1 - M_6(t)]$

STOP AND THINK. **Figure out the answer.**

If both Henry and Mildred go on 5th Street, that is joint event number E1 in our table. Substituting our values in the adaptation rules shown in the table we obtain the following:

Henry

$$H_5(t+1) = H_5(t) + a[1 - H_5(t)]$$
$$= 0.9 + 0.1\ (1 - 0.9)$$
$$= 0.91$$

Mildred

$$M_5(t+1) = M_5(t) + c[1 - M_5(t)]$$
$$= 0.2 + 0.7\ (1 - 0.2)$$
$$= 0.76$$

In a similar fashion we can calculate the changes for the other three possible joint events. These are shown as follows:

JOINT EVENT	IF THIS EVENT HAD OCCURRED, THEN IT IMPLIES	NEW PROBABILITIES OF GOING ON 5TH STREET	
		Henry	*Mildred*
E1	Henry and Mildred both on 5th	0.91	0.76
E2	Henry on 5th; Mildred on 6th	0.18	0.36
E3	Henry on 6th; Mildred on 5th	0.98	0.16
E4	Henry and Mildred both on 6th	0.81	0.06

As you can see, the probabilities of going on 5th Street on the second day depend very much upon what happens on the first day. Is there any way of anticipating what will happen on the average if there are many Henries and many Mildreds and they all go through the same process? That is, can we determine the expected value of $H_5(1)$ and $M_5(1)$?

STOP AND THINK. **What do you need in order to calculate the expected values?**

Since we know the new probabilities that follow from any possible event, we can calculate the *expected* new probability for either individual if we know the chance that each of the four events will occur on the first day. In fact, we know this from the initial probabilities of the two individuals. Since the probability (on the first day) that Henry will go on 5th Street is $H_5(0) = 0.9$ and the probability (on the first day) that Mildred will go on 5th Street is $M_5(0) = 0.2$, then the probability that they both will go on 5th Street is $(0.9)(0.2) = 0.18$. In a similar fashion, we can determine the probability of each of the events occurring on the first day:

Henry and Mildred both on 5th: $(0.9)(0.2) = 0.18$
Henry on 5th; Mildred on 6th: $(0.9)(0.8) = 0.72$
Henry on 6th; Mildred on 5th: $(0.1)(0.2) = 0.02$
Henry and Mildred both on 6th: $(0.1)(0.8) = 0.08$

To obtain the expected value of $H_5(1)$, called $E[H_5(1)]$, we take the value of $H_5(1)$ that will occur *if* a particular joint event occurs and weight it by the probability of the occurrence:

$$E[H_5(1)] = (0.18)(0.91) + (0.72)(0.18) + (0.02)(0.98)$$
$$+ (0.08)(0.81)$$
$$= 0.378$$

Similarly,

$$E[M_5(1)] = (0.18)(0.76) + (0.72)(0.36) + (0.02)(0.16)$$
$$+ (0.08)(0.06)$$
$$= 0.404$$

STOP AND THINK. Be sure you understand the steps we have taken.

Notice that we now have calculated expected values for $H_5(1)$ and $M_5(1)$, but that these values are *actually* true of no one. Henry will have a value for $H_5(1)$ that is either 0.91, 0.18, 0.98, or 0.81 (according to the model). The expected value of 0.378 is what we can expect on the average—but it will never actually occur. Notice also (and for the same reason) that the probability that Henry and Mildred will both go on 5th Street on the second day is *not* $(0.378)(0.404) = 0.153$.

STOP AND THINK. Can you figure out what the correct answer is? *Hint:* Draw a tree—just like a decision tree—of the possible outcomes and their probabilities. *Second hint:* The correct answer is 0.178.

Following all of the possible ways in which Henry and Mildred might change over time is beyond the limits for this book. We can, however, show a simulation of their learning over 15 days by using a random number table to derive the specific events that occur. One such "history" looks like Table 6.7.

TABLE 6.7   *A History of Mating*

| | | MILDRED WENT | NEW PROBABILITIES | |
DAY	HENRY WENT		Henry $H_5(t)$	Mildred $M_5(t)$
1	5th	6th	0.18	0.36
2	6th	6th	0.162	0.108
3	6th	6th	0.146	0.032
4	5th	6th	0.029	0.226
5	6th	5th	0.806	0.181
6	5th	6th	0.161	0.345
7	6th	6th	0.145	0.103
8	6th	6th	0.131	0.031
9	6th	6th	0.118	0.009
10	6th	6th	0.106	0.003
11	5th	6th	0.021	0.202
12	6th	6th	0.019	0.061
13	6th	6th	0.017	0.018
14	6th	6th	0.015	0.005
15	6th	6th	0.013	0.001

The basic result in mating learning is illustrated by the single history. Although there may be some errors at first, the two individuals learn to choose the alternative that is mutually rewarding. In this case, Henry and Mildred learn to go on 6th Street. You should observe, however, that they could very easily have ended up with a joint preference for 5th Street. In fact, if they both had gone on 5th Street on the first day, they might have learned to go that way fairly easily.

Suppose that Henry and Mildred took pleasure in *not* seeing each other. What would happen?

STOP AND THINK. Can you construct the model? (Think about its similarities to the situation we have just analyzed.)

If you correctly specified the model, you should have noted that mutual avoidance is simply another version of mating. The two individuals will learn relatively quickly to choose the mutually rewarding alternative—in the mutual avoidance case Henry learns to go on one street and Mildred on the other. You may think that this is a pathological case of enmity, unworthy of a cooperative society. If you do, you might consider the following simple problem in learning:

> Suppose that individuals learned to choose on which side of the road to drive by experience. We might want to treat a collision as non-rewarding. What would be a reasonable model of the process by which a society of individuals learned where to drive?

Social life is filled with such situations of attractive mutual avoidance.

Can we say anything about properties of our model of mutual adaptation? For example, is there any way of predicting how long it will take for two mating learners to develop a mutually attractive pattern of responses? Is there any way of predicting which responses they will choose?

STOP AND THINK. Can you make any guesses about such questions? Which parameters in the model influence these things?

We saw in our earlier models that the rate of adaptation depends on the learning parameters in the model. The same is also true in this case. In general, the faster the individual adaptations are, the faster the convergence to a mutually attractive pattern is— but not always, however. Suppose, for example, that Henry and Mildred had begun with strong propensities to go on different streets—for instance, $(H_5(0) = 1.0; \ M_5(0) = 0)$—and that they were extremely fast learners—for instance, $a = b = c = d = 1.0)$. What the model predicts is that they would never find each other.

Each would shift to the other street each time and consistently miss the other person. Similarly, two extremely fast learners who want to avoid each other and who start out going the same way would always find themselves running into each other. The particular extreme values are pathological, but the phenomenon is common. Watch two people trying to pass one another in a narrow hall, for example.

The general point is that mutual adaptation between two individuals who initially have quite strong (but different) propensities is usually faster, in the short run, when one learns quickly and the other learns slowly than when they both learn quickly or when they both learn slowly. The results are illustrated in Figure 6.11, in which we show a situation in which 2 quick learners have less success over the first 10 trials than does a pair involving 1 quick and 1 slow learner.

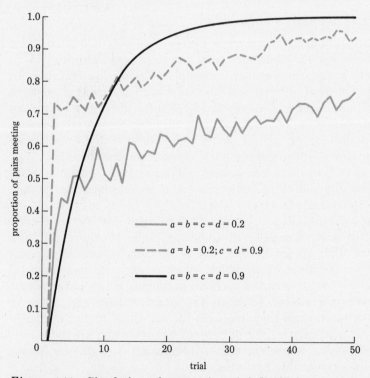

Figure 6.11: Simulation of 200 pairs of individuals in mating learning showing the proportion of pairs successfully meeting. (Initial probability of going "left" equal to 1 for one member of of each pair and 0 for other.)

You should also have noticed another interesting feature of mutual adaptation: Slower learners change less. As two individuals adjust to each other, the one who has higher learning rates changes his behavior more than the one who has lower rates. If we return to our discussion of what is buried in the values of *a* and *b* (see Section 6.3.3), we can recall that:

1. High values for *a* and *b* are associated with situations in which the reward is very important; low values with situations in which the reward is less important.
2. High values are associated with relatively high intelligence; low values with relatively low intelligence.

We can turn these considerations to an examination of some familiar cases of mutual adjustment.

Example: Parents and Children

Parents and children train each other simultaneously. In some cases parents have a clear idea of what they want children to do and do not change their reward schedules during the training. In some cases children have a clear idea of what they want parents to do and do not change *their* reward schedules during training. In other cases, however, both parents and children have a strong commitment to developing a joint pattern of behavior that is mutually rewarding. Initial preferences with respect to exactly what joint behavior is followed are less strong. (Alternatively, extreme stubbornness by the individual can cause the environment to change its reward pattern.)

For example, many parents and children are less concerned with exactly what occupational choice is made by the child than with having that choice be one that is attractive both to parents and child at the time of decision. They engage in some mutual adaptation to try to arrange such an outcome. Many parents and children are less concerned with the exact eating and sleeping habits of children than they are with having these habits mutually acceptable. They learn a joint pattern of behavior and attitudes.

The model suggests some interesting hypotheses about parent-child adaptation:

1. The smarter the parents are, the more "spoiled" the child is. If we associate smartness with relatively high values for the

learning parameters, smart parents will change their positions faster in the direction of the initial position of the child than will less smart parents.

2. The smarter the child, the more "spoiled" the parents. For the same reasons, smart children tend to adapt rapidly to parental initial positions and produce less movement in parents.

3. First-born children will be more spoiled than last-born children. The first child produces a reward situation of considerable importance; by the time of the last born, however, the rewards are of less importance. Thus, according to the model, the learning parameters for the parents should be greater with the first born than with the last born.

The hypotheses may not be true. The last hypothesis certainly contradicts standard folk wisdom and some studies. The model does, however, lend itself to thinking about a familiar situation of social behavior in a new way.

STOP AND THINK. Can you generate any more predictions about mutual adaptation in parents and children?

Example: Seduction

If everyone knew exactly what he wanted all of the time and never changed, seduction would be a ritual activity of some beauty but with little relevance to choice. In fact, however, ambiguity is a feature of ordinary social life; we *learn what we want* through interaction and mutual adaptation. Seduction is such a situation. Many people do not understand seduction because they are inclined to assume either (1) that seduction implies one active and one passive member of a couple or (2) that the process of seduction has only one happy ending. Both assumptions are conspicuously false in many cases of mutual adaptation. The attitudes and behaviors of both members of a couple are changing over time. And most seductive situations end up in mutually attractive relations that do not involve sexual intercourse. As a result, our model of mutual adaptation should have something to say about the way individuals meet and seduce one another.

STOP AND THINK. Use the model to generate some interesting predictions about seduction. *Hint:* What kinds of individuals will be fast or slow adapters; and what kinds of situations might influence adaptation?

6.6.2   HUNTING

Mating is mutual adaptation in which both parties want the same kind of solution—mutual attraction or mutual avoidance. Hunting is a situation of mutual adaptation in which what is rewarding to one person is unrewarding to the other. Consider the following situation:

> Walter is a fashion leader. He likes to be different. If he finds himself wearing something that is the same as what someone else is wearing, he is uncomfortable; if he finds himself wearing something that no one else is wearing, he is happy. John is a fashion follower. He does not like to be different. If he finds himself wearing something that is the same as what someone else is wearing, he is happy; if he finds himself wearing something that no one else is wearing, he is uncomfortable. John and Walter modify their wearing apparel over time in response to their feelings of happiness and discomfort.

STOP AND THINK.   How would you construct a model of this situation? What additional simplifying assumptions might you make? What would be the possible events?

We can suggest some simplifications that make the situation amenable to our models: First, we assume that the society has only two relevant people in it, Walter and John. Second, we assume that there are only two kinds of clothes that can be worn, red and blue. Third, we assume that Walter and John choose the color of their clothes each morning and subsequently spend the day with each other. These assumptions obviously specify a highly unreal situation. We will want to examine later whether the general result would be different in a world in which there were many people and many choices of clothing.

As we did in the case of mating mutual adaptation, we begin by developing a simple learning model for Walter. We assume that

Walter has an initial probability of wearing red $W_R(0)$ or of wearing blue $W_B(0)$ and learning parameters a and b. Similarly, John has an initial probability of wearing red $J_R(0)$ or blue $J_B(0)$ and learning parameters c and d. In each world four events can occur:

Walter Events	John Events
i. Walter red, John red.	i. John red, Walter red.
ii. Walter red, John blue.	ii. John red, Walter blue.
iii. Walter blue, John red.	iii. John blue, Walter red.
iv. Walter blue, John blue.	iv. John blue, Walter blue.

We can now form a model of mutual adaptation under conditions in which what makes one happy makes the other uncomfortable. With each of the four events in the society we associate the appropriate event in the table for each individual and, therefore, the appropriate adaptation equation. (See the table on p. 320.)

Once we have constructed this table, we can compute the changes in Walter and John for each day. For example, let us suppose that Walter and John have the same probability of wearing red on the first day, 0.9. And let us suppose that Walter and John adapt at the same rates $(a = c = 0.3; b = d = 0.5)$. Then we can determine the likelihood of each event on the first day and the changes that will take place, given that a particular event occurs.

		NEW PROBABILITY OF CHOOSING RED	
EVENT	LIKELIHOOD	Walter	John
Both wear red	0.81	0.45	0.93
Both wear blue	0.01	0.95	0.63
Walter red, John blue	0.09	0.93	0.95
Walter blue, John red	0.09	0.63	0.45

The details of what happens in any particular learning experience can be simulated by using a random number table to determine the specific events that will occur. One such experience is indicated in Table 6.8. The result here is quite different from the case of mating adaptation. In mating we see (ordinarily) a convergence toward a commonly attractive solution. In hunting,

JOINT EVENT	WALTER EVENT NO.	JOHN EVENT NO.	ADAPTATION IN WALTER	ADAPTATION IN JOHN
E1. Both wear red	i	i	$W_R(t+1) = W_R(t) - bW_R(t)$	$J_R(t+1) = J_R(t) + c[1 - J_R(t)]$
E2. Both wear blue	iv	iv	$W_B(t+1) = W_B(t) - bW_B(t)$	$J_B(t+1) = J_B(t) + c[1 - J_B(t)]$
E3. Walter red, John blue	ii	iii	$W_R(t+1) = W_R(t) + a[1 - W_R(t)]$	$J_B(t+1) = J_B(t) - dJ_B(t)$
E4. Walter blue, John red	iii	ii	$W_B(t+1) = W_B(t) + a[1 - W_B(t)]$	$J_R(t+1) = J_R(t) - dJ_R(t)$

TABLE 6.8   A History of Hunting

DAY	WALTER WORE	JOHN WORE	NEW PROBABILITIES	
			Walter $W_R(t)$	John $J_R(t)$
1	red	red	0.45	0.93
2	red	red	0.225	0.951
3	blue	red	0.158	0.476
4	blue	blue	0.579	0.333
5	blue	red	0.405	0.166
6	blue	blue	0.703	0.116
7	red	blue	0.792	0.583
8	red	red	0.396	0.708
9	blue	red	0.277	0.354
10	blue	blue	0.639	0.248
11	red	blue	0.747	0.624
12	red	blue	0.823	0.812
13	red	red	0.411	0.868
14	red	red	0.144	0.454
15	blue	red	0.144	0.454

on the other hand, each event tends to reduce the probability of that event occurring again the next time. The system tends to oscillate, making first one individual happy and then the other. In the case of the fashion leader and the fashion follower, what we observe is a strong tendency for the leader to move whenever the follower imitates him, and the follower to move whenever the leader gets away from him. The joint result is one in which the follower tracks the leader.

Although we cannot say precisely what would happen under alternative, more realistic, assumptions without defining them carefully, the tracking/oscillating phenomenon of hunting does not depend critically on the simplifications we have made. With many individuals and many alternative behaviors, the tracking/oscillating phenomenon becomes more complicated; but it still is observable.

Example: Wilderness Lovers

Let us suppose that in the beginning there was a small group of wilderness lovers. They were characterized by the pleasure they took in the natural beauties of the wilderness and by their desire to be alone. After a while, a new group of wilderness lovers came along. They were characterized by the pleasure they received from nature *and* by their desire to be close to other wilderness lovers. Although this second group was initially small relative to the first group, it grew until it was actually larger.

> ***STOP AND THINK.*** **What would you expect to happen in the wilderness over time?** *Hint:* **Think about three phases: first, only type 1 people around; second, mostly type 1 people around but some of type 2 also; and third, substantial numbers of both types. How would they distribute themselves, spatially, during each of these phases?**

You might have noticed that the situation in the beginning was one of mating. The original wilderness lovers were jointly pleased at being away from each other. You would expect them carefully (and cheerfully) to avoid each other's company while enjoying the scenery. Through mutual adaptation, they would converge on a solution in which each individual found a place to himself. When the second group first started to appear, you would observe a shift (partly) to a situation of hunting. The old-timers want to be alone; the newcomers want to be with people; but the old-timers represent most of the people with whom one could be sociable. You would expect a period of oscillation, with old-timers settling down in serene privacy only to be discovered by friendly newcomers who then were hurt when the old-timers chose to be left alone. Finally, however, enough newcomers appear so that they can find one another (an easier task because it is mating search). People who want to be with other people occupy one part of the wilderness, ordinarily the most easily accessible part. People who do not want to be with other people have wandered off farther into the wilds where they only have to avoid other people who want to avoid them. So long as there is enough wilderness, it works reasonably well.

Example: Business Versus the Internal Revenue Service

Most corporations are run by managers rather than by the people who actually own the corporation. The gross income that a company receives from its sales can be used for many purposes: expenses, research, shareholder dividends, hiring new employees and erecting buildings to make the company grow bigger, and so on.

Obviously, there are some choices to be made here. Suppose that managers are primarily interested in high salaries, executive perquisites (such as fancy offices, expense accounts), and company growth. We leave aside the fascinating question of manager-shareholder conflicts and examine another one instead.

The Internal Revenue Service (IRS) is also interested in corporate gross income. But the IRS is interested in having as much of that income as possible be called profits, because profits are subject to taxes; expenses are not. It may seem like a word game as to whether a dollar of company expenditure is called profits or expenses, but the financial stakes are enormous. It is a classic hunting situation.

The following are examples of how the game has thus far been played:

1. Managers decide that managers should be given the free use of company cars for their own personal transportation. This reduces company profits and increases (effective) management salaries, with nice tax consequences for both. The IRS rules that free automobile service is part of management income and hence is taxable (that is, managers have to pay higher taxes). Managers then define an "automobile road-test simulation program," which asks high-ranking managers to drive company-owned vehicles, at company expense, in order to determine "how well these vehicles hold up under real driving conditions." Thus the free cars become a developmental expense and are no longer taxable. The next round of oscillation has not yet occurred.

2. Managers decide that the company ought to own a yacht that will be available for their personal use. The IRS decides that this is part of management's taxable income. Management redefines the yacht as a necessary business expense for entertaining customers. The IRS redefines, very strictly, what a business purpose might be. Management redefines the yacht as part of a pilot research venture in oceanography and hence a legitimate research expense—and so on and on.

These are real examples. You might want to think about the kinds of oscillations that can occur and who will usually be on the "winning" side, given that business can make quick decisions (that is, have high learning rates), while the IRS often requires new legislation by Congress (that is, slow learning rates).

References

Robert R. Bush and Frederick Mosteller, *Stochastic Models for Learning* (New York: Wiley, 1955).

William Kruskal, ed., *Mathematical Sciences and Social Sciences* (Englewood Cliffs, N.J.: Prentice-Hall, 1970), Ch. 1.

R. Duncan Luce, ed., *Developments in Mathematical Psychology* (New York: Free Press, 1960), Pt. II.

Notes

[1] There are other models of the learning process. Some of these are more complex versions of the one we will discuss; others are quite different.

[2] Note that it would be impossible to do such a thing for real subjects. We cannot observe a single subject's probability on a single trial. We *can*, however, observe the *behavior* of many subjects and use that to *estimate* the underlying probability; and we can compare the model's predictions about changes in the behavior with our observations.

[3] See M. F. Norman, *Markov Processes and Learning Models* (New York: Academic), 1972.

[4] Albert Bandura, *Principles of Behavior Modification* (New York: Holt, Rinehart, and Winston, 1969), provides further information if you want to pursue this topic.

Problems 6.3

1. You are trying to train your pet hamster to go to the right in a T-maze. You have decided you will reward it only if it goes to the right. From your long evenings of hamster watching, you know that its current tendency to go right is 0.4, that its learning rate, a, when it is rewarded is 0.5, and that its learning rate for unrewarded behavior, b, is 0.2.

   (a) The following tree shows all possible occurrences during the first two training trials.
   What are the values of a, b, c, d, e, f, g, h, i, and j?

   (b) What is the *expected* probability of the hamster's going right on the second trial?

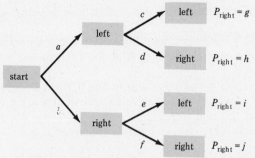

2. Herman notices that his dog Zot is visibly afraid of him 95 out of every 100 times when he approaches the dog. The local dog psychiatrist suggests that this might be due to Herman's custom of whacking Zot with his hand. The psychiatrist indicates that an alternative would be to hold a biscuit out for Zot every hour. If Zot comes closer, he gets the biscuit; if he shies away or shows fright, he does not. Assume that for dogs of Zot's pedigree $a = 0.1$ and $b = 0.9$.

(a) What is the expected probability that Zot will shy away from Herman after two trials of the new treatment? Draw a learning tree.

(b) Suppose that after many hours of training, Zot has a probability of 0.95 of being friendly. Herman, however, loses his temper and strikes the dog. What is the probability Zot will come closer on the next trial?

(c) How would your answers differ if $a = 0.9$ and $b = 0.1$?

3. Hollywood Productions, Inc. (H.P.), has always made two kinds of movies: family movies (full of grinning children) and animal movies (full of grinning animals). H.P. used to make the decisions about what kind of movies to produce each time, but recently the company has decided to turn the problem over to a mechanical mouse who presses one button for family movies or another for animal movies. The mouse has made three decisions so far: a family movie (which flopped); another family movie (which also flopped); and an animal movie (which was a big box-office hit).

You have some spare cash and have been given the opportunity to invest in an H.P. film, either the fourth or fifth production (the offer is good for two weeks only; you cannot wait until the returns are in from the fourth movie to decide about the fifth). Your conviction is that the world has changed and no longer likes family movies. You hope that the mouse has kept abreast of these changes.

After a little undercover work you ascertain that the mouse was programmed with a standard adaptation equation; initially, he had a 4-to-1 preference (that is $p = 0.8$) for family movies; and that his a is 0.3 and his b is 0.4.

(a) What is the probability of the mouse's fourth choice being an animal movie?

(b) And, on the basis of your convictions about the world's preferences, what is the expected probability that the fifth movie will be a moneymaker?

(c) Comment on the advisability of investing in the fifth as opposed to the fourth movie. Consider expected value and what your convictions are worth in the real world.

(d) Would your answers to (a), (b), and (c) be diffierent if $a = 0.1$ and $b = 0.4$? How?

4. Imagine a typical worker at the Widget Engineering Company. W.E.C. builds widgets used by the central bureaucracy in Wonderland. In Wonderland there are two political parties, the Hearts and the Diamonds. Our typical worker has an initial bias toward supporting Diamonds (that is, his probability of voting Hearts is initially only 0.4), a learning rate of 0.6 from rewarded behavior, and a learning rate of 0.4 from unrewarded behavior.

W.E.C's president is a Heart party stalwart. Consequently, she expects all of her employees to make contributions to the Heart party campaign fund. Each year she gives pay raises to all employees who make contributions during the year; no pay raises are given to those who do not make contributions.

Assuming our typical worker learns in the usual way:

(a) What is the fewest number of years in which our typical voter could become a staunch Heart supporter (that is, have a probability on contributing greater than 0.9)? How would he have to behave each year in order to reach that point in that short a time? Why? Plot the yearly probabilities associated with such a path.

(b) What is the greatest number of years it could take him? How would he have to behave each year in order to have it take that long? Why? Plot the yearly probabilities associated with such a path.

(c) On the average how many years will it take the typical worker to become a staunch Heart supporter?

5. You have a test cage with two doors, left and right. When a rat is placed in this cage, it will eventually choose to go through one or the other. On your instruction your assistant can arrange to place a reward of food behind either (or both) doors. If a rat chooses a door with a reward, it will be able to eat the food.

You have 10 holding cages, each containing a great many rats. Each cage contains a particular breed of rat. Different breeds may (or may not) behave differently. For example, some breeds of rats have a preference for the left; others have a preference for the right; others seem to have no preference. A rat's choices can sometimes be modified by a system of rewards. Some breeds of rats adjust their behavior rapidly when they receive a reward; others adjust more slowly; others not at all.

You have a theory. It is the model presented in this chapter.

For each of the following problems, you have a research budget that will allow you to place a rat into the maze 1000 times. That is, you may place 1 rat in the maze 1000 times; 1000 rats in the maze 1 time each; 10 rats 100 times each; 1 rat 900 times and 100 other rats 1 time each; or any other combination that involves no more than 1000 trials.

To specify an experiment you must identify a procedure so that your assistant will know for each of 1000 trials:

 i. What rats to use.
 ii. What choices to reward.

An *efficient* experiment is one that provides the greatest amount of information in the number of trials available.

(a) Specify an efficient experiment to tell us whether there are differences between cage 1 rats and cage 2 rats in their preferences for left and right.

(b) Specify an efficient experiment to tell us whether there are differences between cage 3 rats and cage 4 rats in the rates at which they adjust their behavior in response to receiving a reward.

(c) A political scientist has hypothesized that rats in cage 5 are more easily trained to go left than they are to go right. Specify an efficient experiment to test this hypothesis against the alternative that there is no difference.

(d) An economist has hypothesized that rats in cage 7 are more likely than those in cage 8 to exhibit negative recency, that is, a tendency to believe that if a reward has been behind one door recently, it is likely to be behind the other now. Specify an efficient experiment to test his hypothesis against the alternative that there is no such effect.

(e) A business administrator has hypothesized that rats in cage 6 act so as to maximize expected value (that is, they assume the reward scheme will not change and select the door that will maximize their expected value). Specify an efficient experiment to test this hypothesis against the alternative that they learn.

(f) An educator has hypothesized that the differences among breeds of rats are the result of socialization rather than genetics. Specify an efficient experiment to test his hypothesis against the alternative that the differences are genetic.

Problems 6.4

1. Consider the standard T-maze learning model presented in this chapter. Assume that $a = 0.5$ and $b = 0.2$. Using any standard random number table, simulate the learning behavior of two rats through 10 trials for each of the following situations. Assume that the initial value for the probability of a left response is 0.5. For each case and each rat show (for each trial) the trial number, whether the rat actually went right or left, whether the rat was rewarded, and the probability of a left response after adaptation.

    (a) Suppose the reward is always on the left.

    (b) Suppose there is always a reward on either the left side or the right side but never on both; the probability of the reward being on the left side is 0.7.

    (c) Suppose the reward is placed on the left side with probability 0.7 and on the right side with probability 0.3; but the two probabilities are independent (the reward may be available on either side, both sides, or neither side on any one trial).

2. (*Note:* This problem cannot be done feasibly without the use of a computer and computer program for simulating the behavior of rats in a T-maze.) Using the standard learning model presented in this chapter, comment on each of the following questions:

    (a) The number of trials required to learn in a T-maze depends on the values of a and b. Which of the two learning parameters affects the number of trials more?

    (b) Suppose that there are 20 training periods available to you. During the first N of those periods, you must always reward on the left; during the last $20 - N$ of those periods, you must always reward on the right. How sensitive is the expected value of the probability of going left on trial 21 to the value of N ?

    (c) Suppose that there is no difference in the probability of a reward on the two sides. That is, probability of reward on left = probability of reward on right $= W$. How is the variance of the probability of going left on trial 21 affected by the value of W ?

    (d) Suppose that the probability of reward on the left side is L and that there is always a reward on one side or the other but not both. After 10 trials what proportion of the subjects will have a probability of going left that is less than 0.5? Show how this proportion depends on the value of *L*.

3. Tennis is a game played by two people who hit a ball back and forth according to certain rules. Points are scored by one player when his opponent fails to hit the ball back. The two players face each other as indicated in the diagram below. A ball hit to Player A will land either to his left (Area 1) or to his right (Area 2).

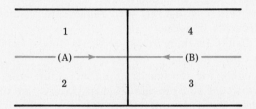

He then can hit the ball either to the left of Player B (Area 3) or to the right of Player B (Area 4). This continues until one player or the other fails to return the ball. As a general rule, right-handed players are better able to retrieve balls that are hit to their right sides (Areas 2 and 4) than balls that are hit to their left sides. In other words, a right-handed player is both less likely to miss a shot on his right and better able to hit a more forceful return.

(a) Outline a learning model of how players learn where to hit their return shots.

(b) If all players were right-handed, what would you expect to have happen? Show how you derive your expectation from your model.

(c) If most players were right-handed but some were left-handed, would you rather be a right-handed player or a left-handed one? Would you expect right-handed players to be over- or under-represented (relative to the total population) among professional tennis players? Show how you derive your answers.

(d) To what extent do your answers depend on the quality of the competition that a young tennis player faces when he is learning the game? What does your model predict will happen if a player is consistently much better than his competition? What will he learn? What will he learn if his competition is consistently much better than he is?

(e) If people learn to like what they are good at, would you expect left-handed people to enjoy competition more or less than right-handed people with respect to physically interactive sports (tennis, boxing, polo, football, basketball, wrestling, baseball pitching/batting, and so on)? Explain.

4. Consider the way in which teachers learn from their experiences in teaching.

(a) Outline a model of how teachers learn to teach on the basis of their experiences with students.

(b) Use the model to discuss each of the following:

    i. Most teachers talk too much.

    ii. Experienced teachers give fewer examinations than do inexperienced teachers.

    iii. Most teachers like good students (namely, students who receive high grades) better than poor students.

    iv. Experienced teachers tend to direct their remarks to the most accomplished students in a class.

    v. Most teachers dislike teaching; most students dislike being taught.

(c) If you were responsible for teacher training at a university, what kind of advice would you provide teacher trainees on the basis of your model? What potential pathologies of learning would you note? How would you modify the usual training experiences? What else would you do?

5. Human beings can be seen as learning from experience how to allocate their time among the various things they might be doing.

(a) Develop a model for adaptive learning of personal time allocation.

(b) Use the model to make some predictions about the ways in which business executives will allocate their time.

(c) Use the model to make some predictions about the ways in which community leaders will allocate their time.

(d) Use the model to make some predictions about the ways in which college students will allocate their time.

(e) Comment on any social complications you see in the implications of your model for these various groups. Under what circumstances will the allocation of time be individually or socially perverse?

6. One of the problems in considering parent-child relationships is the fact that almost everything written about the subject is written by someone who either is a parent, or wishes he were, or wants to sell books to people who are. As a result, we normally consider only the socialization of children by parents. The reciprocal relation—the training of parents by their children—is at least as important and interesting.

(a) Specify a model of learning that might be used to consider the rearing of parents by children.

(b) According to your analysis, which of the following will be more easily trained:

    i. Mothers or fathers?

    ii. One-child parents or multichild parents?

    iii. College-educated parents or noncollege-educated parents?

(c) Under what circumstances (if any) would your model predict intergenerational (or cultural) consistency in parent behavior?

(d) A major fad during the 1960s was concern about the mutual alienation of the older generation (parents) and the younger generation (children). Since the concept of generation itself is relational, the generation gap necessarily is associated, at least in part, with the pattern of relations between children and parents.

    i. To what extent and in what ways did the problem stem from inadequacies in the parent-rearing behavior of American children?

    ii. How could parent rearing be modified to alleviate the problem?

    iii. What side effects would you expect?

(e) One of the problems for parents as they grow up is the problem of adjusting to the independence of their children.

    i. What are the different ways in which children prepare parents for this difficult time?

    ii. What are the consequences of the differences?

    iii. Outline a sensible parent-rearing strategy to facilitate parental adjustment to the problem and show how the strategy is consistent with your model of parent learning.

Problems 6.5

1. Suppose that you have a large number of business managers, each learning how to treat employees. Imagine that each manager has a choice between two general strategies:

Strategy I. Be tough. Fire employees who are not performing adequately; make it clear that any kind of sloppiness will not be tolerated.

Strategy II. Be sympathetic. Work with unsatisfactory employees to develop their skills and motivation; make it clear that you accept them as people.

A person who first starts working as a manager has a probability of 0.7 of using Strategy II, a 0.3 probability of using Strategy I. Assume that managers learn from their experience in the standard way assumed by the stochastic learning model.

(a) For each of the following situations draw plots of the proportion of managers who will use Strategy I over time:

    i. If the managers work in a firm in which profits are very good regardless of the behavior of managers.

    ii. If the managers work in a firm in which profits depend on the actions of managers and Strategy I is certain to lead to profits and Strategy III is certain not to do so.

    iii. If the managers work in a firm in which profits are very bad regardless of the behavior of managers.

(b) In the case of the managers what interpretation can you give to differences in the values of the parameters *a* and *b* in the model? What managers would have high values of the parameters? Which low?

2. Suppose people have two choices each day—to lie or to be honest. Suppose the world may reward honesty or it may not—people do not know which. Assume that our standard adaptation model accurately describes the way people's truth-telling propensities change over time, with $a = b = 0.2$, and with everyone having an initial tendency to lie of 0.5.

(a) If lying always results in doing poorly in worldly affairs and being honest always results in doing well, what will eventually happen? Draw a tree; calculate and plot exactly the proportion of people who will lie on the first 3 days (with the y axis measuring proportion of people lying for each day along the x axis), and plot roughly that proportion for the first 20 days.

(b) Suppose some people are intelligent, and intelligent people always do well, no matter what. Plot (roughly) the proportion of *intelligent* people who will tell the truth on the 1st through 20th days. Explain. How might the learning curve for an *individual* intellectual differ from that for the intelligentsia as a whole?

(c) Suppose some people are dumb, and dumb people always do poorly. Plot (roughly) the proportion of *dumb* people who will tell the truth on the 1st through 20th days. Explain. How would an individual's 20-day curve differ?

(d) Suppose the world is like (b) and (c). Will anybody believe that "honesty is the best policy"? Who?

3. Suppose that we are interested in understanding the adaptation of female human beings in a simple two-alternative world. In this world the only two behavioral alternatives we will consider are *passive* behavior and *assertive* behavior. Passive behavior consists in allowing others to take the lead, in conciliatory responses to argument, and in generally shy styles of relating to other people. Assertive behavior consists in leading, in argumentative responses to argument, and in generally outspoken styles of relating to other people. At any point

in time, we will imagine the female as having a probability (p) of using passive behavior and a probability $(q = 1 - p)$ of using assertive behavior.

Let us assume that whenever a female behaves in one way or the other, she is either rewarded by others around her or she is not. As a result of this reward, or lack of it, the female changes her probability of passive behavior.

Consider two models of this adaptation:

Model I. Anytime a specific kind of behavior is followed by reward, the probability of that behavior is increased by an amount proportional to the difference between the old probability and 1. Thus if passive behavior is rewarded:

$$p_t = p_{t-1} + a(1 - p_{t-1})$$

And if assertive behavior is rewarded:

$$q_t = q_{t-1} + a(1 - q_{t-1})$$

On the other hand, if behavior is not rewarded, the probabilities remain unchanged. Thus if passive behavior is used but not rewarded:

$$p_t = p_{t-1}$$

Similarly, if assertive behavior is used but not rewarded:

$$q_t = q_{t-1}$$

Model II. So long as behavior is rewarded, the result is the same as in Model I. However, when behavior is not rewarded, the probability of doing that behavior *decreases* by an amount proportional to the present probability. Thus if passive behavior is used but not rewarded:

$$p_t = p_{t-1} - bp_{t-1}$$

And if assertive behavior is used but not rewarded:

$$q_t = q_{t-1} - bq_{t-1}$$

Answer the following questions, assuming in each case that the probability of passive behavior is initially one-half for everyone and that a and b are positive fractions.

(a) Suppose passive females are the norm in the sense that passivity is always rewarded and assertiveness never is. What would happen to passivity among women over time according to Model I? According to Model II?

(b) Suppose pretty females are always rewarded regardless of behavioral style and not-so-pretty females are never rewarded. What kind of behavior would you expect according to Model I? According to Model II?

(c) If you strongly suspected that neither Model I or Model II was correct but were unsure which, what kind of observations would you plan to test the models?

(d) To what extent are such models consistent with your observations of contemporary female behavior? What inconsistencies do you see? How would you modify the model?

(e) Adapt your model to an analysis of male behavior and make some predictions about the conditions under which you would find passive and assertive aggressive males.

4. Assume the world is divided into two kinds of people: Those who see themselves as "winners," who work hard and emit confident behavior and those who see themselves as "losers," who work very little and project the very image of failure. Assume that at any particular time an individual has a probability (P_t) of emitting winner behavior (also of working hard) stemming from his self-image. Reward (such as good grades, compliments) increases self-confidence and thus the probability of emitting winner behavior. Nonreward (such as bad grades or indifference) decreases the probability of emitting winner behavior (conversely, it increases the probability of emitting loser behavior). Assume that all students have the same innate abilities but that differential effort produces differential performance; and, finally, that all students have the same a and b.

(a) At Silverado Tech, the teachers follow a strict policy of giving good grades only for good work. Sally Sad starts at Tech with an 80% conviction that she is a loser; Winnie Winner starts at Tech with an 80% conviction that she is a winner.

  i. State a mathematical model of the adaptation process.
  ii. Graph P_t, as their schooling goes on, for each girl.

(b) At Permissive University the teachers are specially selected to give students love regardless of the quality of their work. Assuming Winnie and Sally start there, with the same convictions, redo i and ii.

(c) For (a) and (b) graph (total of 4 graphs) the hours of homework done per week for each girl at each school as their schooling goes on.

(d) Sally has become disgusted with herself for being a loser, and she has decided to try to become a winner. Use the adaptation model to predict what might happen if she undertook each of the following alternative plans of action designed to produce a "new and better Sally." (Assume that she is at Silverado Tech.) *Show how you get your results.*

    i. Take the six hardest courses in school next quarter in order to catch up.

    ii. Continue taking her normal course load.

    iii. Do i plus give up smoking, resolve to be nicer to her roommate, lose weight, and read at least one good book per week.

(e) In many years of advising students, it has been noted that students trying to improve themselves most frequently choose alternatives i or iii in (d). Draw a moral from this.

5. Consider American presidential elections. Suppose that there are only two parties (Republican and Democratic) and that each voter can be described at any point in time as having a probability p, of voting Republican, and $1 - p$ of voting Democratic. Each voter modifies his own probability on the basis of experience. However, voters make the modifications in two different ways:

Type A Voters

These consider general prosperity as a reward. The presence of general prosperity one year after an election for president *reinforces whatever voting behavior he exhibited* at the election. Absence of prosperity one year after the election leads to a reduction in the probability of repeating the same vote.

Type B Voters

These also consider general prosperity to be a reward. However, they consider that the outcome of the election *reinforces the chance of voting for the party that is in office.* Absence of prosperity one year after the election leads to a reduction in the probability of voting for the party that is in office. Answer the following questions using the standard learning model and assuming that $p_0 = 0.7$, $a = 0.3$, and $b = 0.2$ for both types of voters. (*Note:* As long as the number of voters is as large as it is in the United States, the following statement is correct: If all members of a large group of voters have the same independent probability, p, of voting Republican, then the chance is nil that the Republican proportion of the vote within that group will vary by any appreciable amount from p.)

(a) For each of the following situations explain and plot the Republican proportion of the vote in each of three successive presidential elections. Do this for each type of voter separately, assuming in each case that that type of voter is the only type in the country.

    i. If prosperity only occurs when the Democrats are in office.
   ii. If prosperity is guaranteed regardless of who holds office.
  iii. If prosperity never occurs.

(b) Suppose that 70% of the voters were Type A and 30% were Type B. Explain and plot the Republican proportion of the vote in each of three successive elections under the three conditions indicated in (a).

(c) Suppose American business cycle history consisted in relatively long periods of prosperity divided by relatively short periods of depression. According to the model used previously, what would American political cycle theory look like? To what extent would it depend on the relative numbers of Type A and Type B voters?

(d) American national party politics has exhibited the following broad characteristics over the past 100 years:

    i. Two parties fairly equal to one another in voting strength.
   ii. Long periods of dominance (in terms of occupancy of the presidency and control of the Congress) by one party or the other.
  iii. A tendency for parties (in power) to lose voters when there is a relatively strong shift downward in economic conditions.

Comment on the extent to which such attributes are consistent with the kind of adaptation model you have developed. What implications do you draw?

(e) Suppose that learning occurred not in response to general levels of prosperity but in terms of individual incomes. What differences would it make to your answer to (c)?

(f) What income redistribution strategies would your model in (e) suggest for political parties during good times? During bad times? To what extent does your answer depend on whether the party is in or out of power?

Problems 6.6

1. Suppose we have two independent and simultaneous binary choices. In the first choice the alternatives are A1 and A2. In the second choice the alternatives are B1 and B2.

$p_t =$ the probability, at time t, of a choice of A1.

$1 - p_t =$ the probability, at time t, of a choice of A2.

$r_t =$ the probability, at time t, of a choice of B1.

$1 - r_t =$ the probability, at time t, of a choice of B2.

In addition, assume the following adaptation rules:

If *A1 and B1* are chosen at time t, then:

$$p_{t+1} = p_t + a(1 - p_t)$$
$$r_{t+1} = r_t + c(1 - r_t)$$

If *A1 and B2* are chosen at time t, then:

$$p_{t+1} = p_t - bp_t$$
$$r_{t+1} = r_t + d(1 - r_t)$$

If *A2 and B1* are chosen at time t, then:

$$p_{t+1} = p_t + b(1 - p_t)$$
$$r_{t+1} = r_t - dr_t$$

If *A2 and B2* are chosen at time t, then:

$$p_{t+1} = p_t - ap_t$$
$$r_{t+1} = r_t - cr_t$$

Finally, suppose that the following values hold:

$$p_0 = 1.0$$
$$r_0 = 0$$
$$a = 0.2$$
$$b = 0.4$$
$$c = 0.3$$
$$d = 0.5$$

(a) Compute and plot the relative frequencies of events (A1, B1), (A1, B2), (A2, B1), and (A2, B2) from time t_0 to t_3.
(b) Compute and plot the expected values for p_t and r_t for $t = 0$, 1, 2, 3, 4.
(c) Comment on the general properties of the model.
(d) Identify two different situations in social science for which the model might be used. Indicate clearly how you would associate the model to the situations. Comment briefly on the implications of the model for understanding such situations.

2. Consider the following game, which is played by two people. Each player has in front of him a deck of cards. Each player selects a card from the deck and gives it to the experimenter. He may give any card, but he may not expose the card to the other player. If both players choose the same color (black or red) card, each scores a point. Otherwise, they score nothing. This procedure is repeated 20 times.

   (a) Outline an adaptation model to predict what will happen.

   (b) Run the experiment. Record the results. Compare the results with the predictions of the model.

   (c) Now change the game so that one person receives a point if they have different colors and the other person receives a point if they have the same. Adapt your model to predict what will happen.

   (d) Play this second game. Record the results. Compare the results with the predictions of the model.

   (e) Comment on any implications you see from either the model or your results for the understanding of interpersonal learning processes.

3. Consider a two-person conversation as a learning process. Suppose there are two kinds of responses that a person can make to another person's conversational statements: (1) supportive, agreeing, encouraging comments; (2) rejecting, disagreeing, discouraging comments. Suppose further that the first kind of response is reinforcing of conversational utterances, and the second is not.

   (a) Develop a model of two-person conversational learning and use it to make specific empirical predictions about the following:

      i. The length of conversations. When and with whom will you tend to have long conversations? Short ones?

      ii. The content of conversations. How will what you talk about differ as a function of the kind of group and kind of society involved?

      iii. The distribution of conversational time among the participants. Who will talk a lot? Who will talk little?

   (b) Extend your model to deal with three-person conversations. Then discuss what differences you would expect between two-person and three-person conversations with respect to their length, their content, and the distribution of conversational time in them.

4. American football is a game played between two teams. At any point in time one team is on *offense*. At that time, the other team is on *defense*. The team that is on offense can choose between only two alternative offensive maneuvers—pass or run. The team on defense similarly can choose between two alternative defensive postures—pass defense or run defense. The combination of offensive maneuver and

defensive posture leads to an outcome. The following listing summarizes these combinations:

    i. Team 1 pass—Team 2 pass defense.
   ii. Team 1 pass—Team 2 run defense.
  iii. Team 1 run—Team 2 pass defense.
  iv. Team 1 run—Team 2 run defense.
   v. Team 2 pass—Team 1 pass defense.
  vi. Team 2 pass—Team 1 run defense.
 vii. Team 2 run—Team 1 pass defense.
viii. Team 2 run—Team 1 run defense.

With each combination we can associate a probability—the probability that Team 1 will be pleased with the outcome of the combination. If Team 1 is not pleased with the outcome, then Team 2 will be. Thus every game is described by the following:

a_1, a_2, b_1, b_2—the learning rates of Team 1 and Team 2.
p_1, p_2—the initial propensity to use pass on offense.
s_1, s_2—the initial propensity to use pass defense.
r_1, r_2, r_3, r_4, r_5, r_6, r_7, r_8—the probability that Team 1 will be pleased with the outcome of combinations 1 through 8 respectively.

(a) Outline a model of mutual adaptation by which the offenses and defenses of each team might learn.

(b) Use your model to make some predictions about football for each of the following situations (defined in terms of the values for r_1, r_2, ..., r_8):

Situation 1: Equal, Perfect Teams
$r_1 = r_4 = r_6 = r_7 = 0;$ $r_2 = r_3 = r_5 = r_8 = 1.$

Situation 2: Equal, Imperfect Teams
$r_1 = r_4 = r_6 = r_7 = 0.2;$ $r_2 = r_3 = r_5 = r_8 = 0.8.$

Situation 3: Equal Teams, Unequal Game
$r_1 = r_2 = r_7 = r_8 = 0.8;$ $r_3 = r_4 = r_5 = r_6 = 0.2.$

Situation 4: Unequal Teams
$r_1 = r_4 = r_6 = r_7 = 0.5;$ $r_2 = r_3 = r_5 = r_8 = 0.9.$

(c) Can you extend the general ideas of the model to say something about the habits of football teams over the course of a year in the real situation? What specific predictions would you make about teams in the National Football League?

5. Outline a theory of how husbands and wives (or, if you prefer, lovers) train each other. Use your theory to derive some delicate and intricate implications for everyday life. Use your observations to report whether your predictions appear to make sense.

chapter seven

diffusion

7.1 INTRODUCTION

We are familiar with the general phenomena associated with the spread of contagious diseases. Measles, chicken pox, cholera, and a host of other familiar diseases diffuse through a population in predictable and interesting ways. In this section we examine the diffusion of other kinds of "diseases." We will be concerned with a group of models that have been devised to explain situations of the following types:

1. Suppose a major disaster (for example, a flood, an earthquake, an assassination) occurs somewhere in the United States. This information is rapidly translated into radio and television bulletins, telephone calls, and conversations among residents of the country. Initially, only a few people know of the disaster.
2. In a high school teachers observe one day that one of the students is wearing shoes that do not match. A few days later several students are doing so. Before long, many students are wearing unmatched shoes.
3. At one time, the word "hopefully" was an adverb. It was used in sentences such as this: "He waited hopefully for his father's return." A few people occasionally used it (incorrectly) as a dangling interjection: "Hopefully, father will return." After a while almost everyone was using "hopefully" in this way, even some English teachers.
4. The Colleges of Agriculture and the Agricultural Experiment Stations in the United States have a long tradition of doing research to develop better farming methods (for example, new fertilizers, new crops, new farming techniques). Each of the new developments has gone through a similar process: At first, only a few farmers try it; then sometimes quickly, sometimes slowly, other farmers finally adopt the innovations.
5. Drug companies do research to develop new drugs for use in medical treatment. When a drug is introduced, reports about it are published in medical journals, information is sent by the drug company to doctors, and drug salesmen call on doctors with samples and specifications. Initially only a handful of doctors use the drug. As time passes, more and more do so.

All of these situations involve the diffusion of something—the spread of some "disease." The something might be information, an innovation, or almost anything in fact: an emotion as it spreads in a crowd (or in a couple); an ideology as it spreads in a sub-culture; a child-rearing practice as it spreads over generations; a belief as it spreads among acquaintances.

The typical cases involve a simple pattern over time. Initially, the information (or fad or behavior or belief) is known to (or distributed among or used by) a small number of people. As time goes on, the item seems to diffuse among a greater and greater number of people. Sometimes this diffusion is rapid at first; some-times it starts slowly and then speeds up later. In the end, a large number of people are involved with the item, and it is no longer "new" to many people.

Such a pattern is, of course, the pattern of a "successful disease." Not all news, fads, behaviors, or beliefs travel so success-fully. Sometimes an item fails to spread much at all. Some news never goes anywhere; some would-be fads are never accepted; some new products never find a market; and some ideas do not catch on.

Our objective in this section is to examine some models for thinking about this kind of phenomenon. We want to be able to talk about how and why a particular item spreads through a par-ticular society. How fast does it spread? Where does it spread? What are the factors that determine the rate and pattern of dif-fusion? How can we make the item diffuse faster or slower?

7.2   A SET OF BASIC ASSUMPTIONS

In order to examine social diffusion, we will need a set of basic ideas about how things spread within a society. Consider the following simple situation.

A large manufacturing company is about to have a new manager appointed. Early one morning a senior executive, Herb Carter, is told (in confidence) that he will be the new manager. We wish to study how this information diffuses through the com-pany.

What sort of assumptions do we need in order to develop a model of diffusion for the information about the new boss?

STOP AND THINK. What does it take for this news to spread? What kind of additional information do you need in order to trace the course of this rumor?

To follow, or predict, the spread of the rumor about the new boss we will obviously need some knowledge about those who know the information initially, because at least one of these people will have to act as a source, an agent of contagion. We will also need some knowledge of communication patterns in the company, who talks to whom. In this case the information that Carter will be the new boss can only spread if someone who knows the information has a communication contact with someone who does not. Since we will want to apply our basic ideas to the whole range of things that spread—information, fads, emotions, beliefs, sentiments, and so on—we will need a descriptive term for the thing being spread; we will call it the *object of diffusion.* The object of diffusion in the case of the new manager is information. The object of diffusion in the case of market acceptance is the product. The object of diffusion in the case of the spread of political allegiance is party affiliation. In each case, the object of diffusion is the idea, the behavior, the attitude, or the information that is diffusing.

Diffusion in a society presumes that individuals are connected to one another. In particular, they must be connected in some way that allows transmission of the information, idea, emotion, feeling, or style.

Assumption 1. In order for diffusion to take place between individuals they must be connected by some kind of relevant communication link.

STOP AND THINK. What might be meant by a "relevant communication link?" Can you specify the relevant communication link for the spread of a rumor, a fad or an emotion?

When we talk about the spread of rumors or news, we will naturally think of communication links as being friendship networks or the contact patterns of ordinary life or the more institutionalized contacts provided by mass media—the whole variety of ways by which people speak to one another. When we speak of the diffusion of fads or styles or emotions, the contact patterns of sight become more important. Who can see whom?

These exposure patterns among people in a society may vary substantially. They are influenced by technology. Telephones, television, mass-circulation national magazines, and movies have all produced systematic changes in contact patterns. In a society without one or more of these, information travels more slowly and less generally.

The study of exposure to mass media is an important area of applied social science. Politicians use it to determine how they should present their campaigns. Manufacturers use it to discover what advertising media would be particularly useful for their product. Scientists use it to assess where they should publish the results of their research. Any of us who are interested in the spread of an idea, product, mannerism, or piece of information are interested in the pattern of attention to mass media.

Exposure patterns are also influenced by a variety of social factors: Age, sex, status, language, and social norms affect who is exposed to whom, not only through the media but also face-to-face. Consider, for example, the direct exposure pattern of a typical college student. Most of his contacts are within his own age group, his own sex group, his own economic and racial group. His pattern is not unusually narrow but, on the contrary, is probably relatively broad compared to members of the society who are not in school. The pattern of contacts through which diffusion occurs is a *social* pattern.

One convenient way of representing the contact pattern within a society is an exposure pattern. Suppose we had a society consisting of three boys (Abe, Bob, and Carl) and three girls (Donna, Elaine, and Felicia). Then we can describe the pattern of exposure in a matrix, as follows:

	ABE	*BOB*	*CARL*	*DONNA*	*ELAINE*	*FELICIA*
Abe	1	1	1	0	0	0
Bob	1	1	1	0	0	0
Carl	1	1	1	0	0	0
Donna	1	0	0	1	1	1
Elaine	1	0	0	1	1	1
Felicia	1	0	0	1	1	1

In this matrix each name appears as both a row and a column. If 1 appears in the matrix, it means that the person whose name is attached to the row is exposed to (that is, can, see, hear, or otherwise receive information from) the person whose name heads the column. For example, in the first row, the 1 under Carl means that Abe is exposed to Carl.

STOP AND THINK. **The matrix has a particular social pattern in it. Can you recognize the pattern? What kind of society is this?**

The hypothetical society shown in this matrix is obviously one in which most exposures are between people of the same sex. However, everyone is exposed to Abe. Abe is apparently a conspicuous member of the society. Abe himself is not exposed to everyone, but everyone else is exposed to him.

STOP AND THINK. **How can this be? Why is exposure not symmetrical? How can Donna be exposed to Abe while Abe is not exposed to Donna?**

Everyone is aware of what Abe does, but he in turn does not pay attention to all of them. Such a situation is, in fact, quite common. Consider the President of the United States. Many people are exposed to him not only through television or newspapers but also directly in public places. At the same time, the President is aware of only a small proportion of all of those people. Many kinds of exposure are symmetrical—if I am exposed to you, you are exposed to me. But many other kinds are not.

Exposure networks are one of a class of similar matrices that are used to represent features of social structure. When these matrices are intended to describe friendship relations (that is, who chooses whom), they are usually called sociometric matrices. When they are used to describe communication links (that is, who talks to whom), they are usually called communication nets.

For many purposes, however, we may want a somewhat different matrix. In our exposure network, the entries are either 1 or 0—people either are exposed to someone or they are not. Suppose that although Elaine *might* be exposed to Bob, it is not *certain* that she will be. How can we represent such a situation?

STOP AND THINK. How would you describe a society in which exposure is possible but not certain?

What we do, of course, is to say that there is a certain *probability* that Elaine will be exposed to Bob during some interval of time. This probability may be 0 (it probably is very close to 0 for any two people chosen at random in the United States for any period as short as say a week or so). The probability may be 1 or very close to it. For people who are exposed to one another fairly regularly, the probability is somewhat more than 0 and somewhat less than 1. Moreover, it varies depending on the time of the day, the day of the week, and the matters at hand (that is, there is some news that might cause you to seek out a particular person in order to communicate the news to him). We could incorporate this probability knowledge into the exposure array by writing probabilities instead of 1 or 0.

In order for an object of diffusion to spread, an individual who does not have the object must have contact with an individual who does have it. Contact alone, however, is not enough. If I know that Carter is going to become boss and you do not, simple exposure between us will not necessarily lead to your learning the information. In addition, there must be some kind of transmission of the object.

Assumption 2. In order for diffusion to take place between any two individuals, the object of diffusion must be transmitted by the person who already has it.

How do you transmit a piece of information? You tell it, because if you have exposure without verbal communication, the information will not spread. How do you transmit a style fad? You wear it, because on the days you are not wearing the style, exposure to you will not lead to spread of the fad. How do you transmit an emotion? You exhibit it, because an unexhibited emotion does not spread easily.

Given that there is exposure between two people, there is some chance that the object of diffusion will be transmitted. We can represent that chance as a probability in a transmission matrix if we wish. Such a matrix would look similar to the contact matrix, but the entries now become the chance *if Donna is exposed to Abe* that Abe will transmit a particular object.

> **STOP AND THINK.** What factors will influence the chance that transmission will occur? For example, what might cause you to repeat a piece of information or not?

News is transmitted if the sender thinks it is important or interesting. Innovations are more likely to be transmitted if they are viewed as important. Ideologies are transmitted if they are important.[1] Emotions are exposed if they are felt to be important. News about Carter's appointment is more likely to spread from people who are actively concerned about the decision.

Some objects of diffusion are easier to transmit than others. For example, a piece of information has to be repeated at each new contact, and at each new contact a "decision" to communicate it further must be made. A beard, on the other hand, pretty much communicates itself in any face-to-face contact. We would expect the objects requiring positive action every time would be transmitted somewhat less frequently than objects that communicate themselves. This is one of the prime reasons why manufacturers like to produce products that are self-advertising through their distinctiveness. Simple ideas are more easily transmitted than complex ones.

Some objects of diffusion are more satisfying to transmit than others. A piece of information that contributes to the self-esteem of the communicator is more likely to be transmitted than one that does not. For a dramatic demonstration of this, listen to children talking about their grades in school, the last baseball game in which they played, or their sexual adventures; listen to businessmen talking about their day in the office, scientists about their research, your parents describing you to others, or yourself talking about your children. In our example, we would predict that Carter would have some difficulty keeping the secret.

Given that there is contact between someone who has the object of diffusion and someone who does not and given that the person having the object of diffusion undertakes to transmit it, there still will not be diffusion unless the transmission is accepted. (A disease must be transmitted from the sick person to the well one.) It is possible that the information about Carter might not be heard or believed.

Assumption 3.   In order for diffusion to take place between any two individuals, the transmission of an object of diffusion must be accepted by the person who does not already have it.

To accept a piece of information is to recognize and believe it. To accept an idea is to perceive and adopt it. To accept a fashion is to see and wear it. To accept a saying is to hear and repeat it. To accept an innovation is to know and use it. Not all transmissions will be accepted.

> *STOP AND THINK.*   **What are the factors that affect the chance that a transmission will be accepted? For example, what determines the acceptability of a piece of information?**

The acceptance of a transmission depends in part on the sender. In particular, the higher the status of the sender (in the sphere represented by the object), the greater the likelihood of acceptance. Status may come from expertise. Information on automobiles is more likely to be accepted if it comes from an experienced mechanic than if it comes from an experienced painter. Status may come from general social prestige. Information on the ills of society is more likely to be accepted if it comes from a professor of chemistry than if it comes from a high school teacher of chemistry. Status may come from popularity ("If you read it in *Reader's Digest,* it must be right") or from inference ("Never believe a beardless rabbi").

The sender's trustworthiness influences acceptance. As is well known in the practice of law, messages from husbands about wives are not to be automatically accepted—regardless of the status and general probity of the husband. Advertisers distinguish "unsolicited" praise from simple advertising copy, presumably because they have discovered that their readers do. We all make estimates of the credibility of a source.

Clearly, these attributes of the sender do not exist in isolation of the person exposed to him. In many ways we are thinking of properties of the sender *in relation to* the recipient. Trust and status are relational, and they can be modified by experience in the relation. A person gains status and trustworthiness through interaction. As a result, characteristics of the recipient also affect acceptance. What is his own expertise and status in this area? How will his own self-esteem be affected by accepting or not accepting the transmission?

At the same time, these attributes of the recipient relate to some characteristics of the object of diffusion. How "contagious" is it? A transmission will be particularly acceptable if it is consistent with, and flatters, the existing beliefs, behaviors, customs of the recipient. Indeed one of the most common procedures for discovering latent attitudes is to observe the relative acceptance of alternative messages. What you repeat of a story tells something about you as well as about the story.

Finally, we need to make two more assumptions explicit to tidy up the loose ends of the model. According to the first of these, at any point in time an individual either has the information or he does not. This enables us to describe a society as a collection of people divided into two groups: one group that has the information and one group that does not have it.

STOP AND THINK. Although this seems to be an obvious assumption, it is not the only possible one. Can you think of an alternative assumption about how people possess the object of diffusion? What consequences does the alternative have? *Hint:* probability.

As you may recall in the chapter on adaptation, an individual had a *probability* of doing something, not a *certainty*. Here we are proceeding in a quite different way: We say that the individual either has the object of diffusion or does not. After we have completed the development of the basic models of diffusion, you may want to return to this assumption and examine the implications of modifying the all-or-nothing approach to allow for the gradual shift of a person from knowing nothing to knowing everything.

Assumption 4. At any point in time any individual in the society either has the object of diffusion or he does not.

Given this assumption we have a natural way of describing the state of any society at a point in time. We can do so with a single number—the *proportion* of the total population that has the object of diffusion at that time. For example, we can describe the company that is appointing a new manager in terms of the proportion of the total employees who know that Carter will be the new manager; or we can talk about the proportion of the student body who are wearing unmatched shoes.

For most purposes we are interested in looking at how this proportion increases over time. Obviously, it does not necessarily increase at all, and it may, in fact, decrease. Information may be forgotten or replaced by more valid information. Fads may become passé even to former enthusiasts. Beliefs may be adopted, then changed. Emotions do not continue indefinitely. Nevertheless, it may be useful to limit our model to situations in which the proportion of people having the object of diffusion increases over time. When we are interested in the relatively early stages of diffusion, this may not be too severe a restriction. Initially, we will assume that when something has diffused to an individual in society, it stays diffused to that individual.

Assumption 5. Once any given individual in a society has the object of diffusion, he continues to have it indefinitely.

This assumption assures us that the proportion of individuals who have an object will not decrease over time. If there is any diffusion at all, it will increase.

The diffusion models we will discuss build upon these basic assumptions to produce concrete predictions of the spread of almost anything. They represent the elementary framework of a theory of social diffusion.

1. *Contact.* In order for diffusion to take place between any two individuals they must be connected by some kind of relevant exposure link.
2. *Transmission.* In order for diffusion to take place between any two individuals the object of diffusion must be transmitted in some form by the person who already has it.
3. *Acceptance.* In order for diffusion to take place between any two individuals the transmission of an object of diffusion must be accepted by the person who does not already have it.
4. *You Have It or You Do Not.* At any point in time any individual in the society either has the object of diffusion or he does not.
5. *You Never Lose It.* Once any given individual in a society has an object of diffusion, he continues to have it indefinitely.

7.3   INTERGENERATIONAL DIFFUSION

The basic ideas of diffusion just outlined are usually applied to the spread of things over a relatively brief time period. Such a perspective is not necessary, however. For example, we can consider the diffusion of behavior or attitudes across generations.[2] Children catch the behavior and attitudes of their parents. They, in turn, spread the objects of diffusion to their own children. Such a perspective can be applied to such things as the intergenerational spread of child-rearing behavior, occupational preferences and styles, political attitudes, and language.

STOP AND THINK. Can you think of anything else that might be viewed as spreading through intergenerational transfer?

When we study intergenerational transfer, we ask the same questions that we ask in any diffusion process: What are the characteristics of contact, transmission, and contagion? How frequently do parents and children interact? How conspicuous is the object of diffusion? How likely is it that the child will adopt it? We can, in fact, discuss much of the literature on child socialization in exactly these terms.

Our primary interest, however, is *not* what happens in a single generation. We want to use some assumptions about the process of transmission in a single generation in order to show what happens over several generations.

For example, many people have suggested that the political-economic-social events of young adulthood combine with childhood training to produce the political attitudes parents transmit to their children. If this is true, we should be able to predict how the events of the present decade will spread over the next few generations.

STOP. What would such a prediction require? What kind of assumptions would you make?

Example: The Spread of Divorce

We can illustrate a simple model of integenerational diffusion by considering the spread of divorce from generation to generation. That is, we will assume that if a couple has a divorce, their children will be more likely to seek a divorce. Divorce spreads like a disease. (If you prefer to think of nondivorce as a more patho-logical state, you can develop the model in terms of nondivorce spreading like a disease.)

The basic ideas of our model are that parents are married at one point and either stay married to each other or secure a divorce, that each child can be described as either having divorced parents or not, that children marry, and that those children who have divorced parents are more likely to end up divorced than those who do not. We want to know what will happen to divorce as time passes and generations come and go.

In order to do this, we will need some simplyfying assumptions. We can start by noting that divorce is something that happens to couples. In any generation there are four kinds of couples (in terms of the parents of the couple) :

Type I
The parents of *both* the husband and the wife were divorced.

Type II
The parents of *the husband* but not the wife were divorced.

Type III
The parents of *the wife* but not the husband were divorced.

Type IV
The parents of *neither* the husband nor the wife were divorced.

Our interest in the contagion of divorce leads us to assume that the divorce rate will be higher in Type I marriages than in Type IV and that Types II and III will have an intermediate rate. In effect, we assume that all parents and children have about the same contact, that divorce attitudes are spread as a result of that contact, and that parents who have themselves been divorced communicate a more positive attitude toward divorce than those who have not been divorced.

STOP. **Think about each of the assumptions. Make a list of any interesting alternative assumptions you might want to consider.**

Although we could make more complicated assumptions, suppose that we start with the simple idea that *any* Type I couple will certainly end up divorced; that *no* Type IV couple will ever divorce; and that exactly 40% of Type II and Type III couples will divorce. In this way we can explore how divorce spreads in a highly specific, numerical example. As we have discovered earlier, we will subsequently want to relax the numerical specificity.

Now we need to develop our model so we can talk about changes in divorce rate from one generation to another. In order to do that we will need some assumptions. In particular, we will need some way of determining—in each generation—the proportion of marriages that fall into each category, or type.

> *STOP.* What kinds of assumptions do we need? What are the simplest assumptions we can make?

In order to talk about the changes in the distribution of couples into types of marriages we need two different kinds of assumptions:

1. A birth-rate/marriage-rate assumption. That is, we need to know the average number of children (of each sex who subsequently marry within this generation) produced by each type of marriage each generation.
2. A marriage-pattern assumption. That is, we need to know the rate at which a child of one type of marriage marries a child of any other type.

We will make some very simple assumptions initially. We will assume that all children marry and that they marry within their own generation; that the average number of boy children produced by each type of marriage is equal to the average number of girl children; that each of the four types of couples has, on the average, the same number of children; that marriage pairings are random; and, finally, that the rate of intermarriage between a boy from a Type I couple and a girl from a Type III couple is proportional to the number of such boys and girls in the population.

> *STOP.* Be sure you understand what each assumption is and why it (or some other) is necessary.

With these assumptions we can now proceed to examine the spread of divorce through generations. We will need one final piece of information, the current (initial) rate of divorce. Let us suppose that rate is 0.2. We assume that 20% of couples in Generation 1 will obtain a divorce, and we will attempt to discover what the rate will be in later generations.

Our first job is to determine the distribution of couples according to types in Generation 2. What proportion of the second generation will have Type I, II, III, and IV marriages? From our assumptions we know that the proportion of boys who have divorced parents is 0.2. This is also the proportion of girls who have divorced parents. If marriage takes place randomly, what proportion of the marriages will (on the average) end up as Types I, II, III, and IV?

STOP. **See if you can determine the Generation 2 distribution of marriages according to types.**

You should have observed that 20% of the boys come from divorced parents. Of this 20%, 20% will marry girls from divorced parents, and 80% will marry girls from nondivorced parents. Thus 4% of all the couples will be Type I, and 16% will be Type II. You should also have observed that 80% of the boys come from nondivorced parents. Of this 80%, 20% will marry girls from divorced parents, and 80% will marry girls from nondivorced parents. Thus 16% of all couples will be Type III, and 64% will be Type IV. Table 7.1 summarizes these results.

From our previous assumptions we know what the divorce rate is for each type of couple. Using these assumptions we discover that the overall divorce rate in Generation 2 is 0.168.

TABLE 7.1   *Results in Generation 2*

MARRIAGE TYPES	DIVORCE RATE	PROPORTION OF COUPLES	DIVORCES
I	1.0	0.04	0.04
II	0.4	0.16	0.064
III	0.4	0.16	0.064
IV	0.0	0.64	0.0
Total	—	1.00	0.168

STOP.　Be sure you understand how the number 0.168 was obtained.

We can now continue the analysis for additional generations. In Generation 3 we know that 16.8% rather than 20% of the children will come from divorced couples. Otherwise, the analysis repeats itself. If we continue for five generations, we obtain the results indicated in Table 7.2.

STOP.　Before you continue, be sure you understand exactly how the entries in Table 7.2 were determined.

The result is a record of divorce rate over time. As you can see, our assumptions lead to a steady decline in divorce over the five generations, and thus nondivorce spreads. This result, however, depends on the specific assumptions we have made. In particular, it depends on two assumptons that might seem too specific: (1) the assumption that the initial divorce rate is 0.20; (2) the assumption that the divorce rate among couples having "mixed" parents is 0.40. We do not know what the result would be with different rates. Suppose that we now examine how the assumptions might be made more general.

STOP AND THINK.　How would you do that? How would you build a model that did not contain specific numerical values?

You should, by now, be familiar with the standard theoretical trick of substituting arbitrary letter values for numerical values when you are not sure of the numerical values or want to extend the generality of results.

The remainder of this section is optional. If you can delight in, or even tolerate, some simple algebra, please continue reading. Or you may postpone this discussion for a while and skip to Section 7.4.

Let us define terms:

TABLE 7.2   *Results Through Generation 5*

MAR-RIAGE TYPES	DIVORCE RATE	GENERATION 1	GENERATION 2		GENERATION 3		GENERATION 4		GENERATION 5	
		Proportion Divorce	*Proportion*	*Divorce*	*Proportion*	*Divorce*	*Proportion*	*Divorce*	*Proportion*	*Divorce*
I	1.0	—	0.04	0.04	0.0282	0.0282	0.0196	0.0196	0.0135	0.0135
II	0.4	—	0.16	0.064	0.1398	0.0559	0.1204	0.1204	0.1025	0.0410
III	0.4	—	0.16	0.064	0.1398	0.0559	0.1204	0.1204	0.1025	0.0410
IV	0.0	—	0.64	0.0	0.6922	0.0	0.7396	0.0	0.7815	0.0
Overall Divorce Rate		0.20	0.168		0.140		0.116		0.096	

TABLE 7.3 *Generalization of the Results Through Generation 5*

MARRIAGE TYPES	DIVORCE RATE	GENERATION 1		GENERATION 2		GENERATION 3	
		Proportion	Divorce	Proportion	Divorce	Proportion	Divorce
I	1	—	—	D_1^2	D_1^2	D_2^2	D_2^2
II	a	—	—	$D_1(1-D_2)$	$aD_1(1-D_1)$	$D_2(1-D_2)$	$aD_2(1-D_2)$
III	a	—	—	$D_1(1-D_1)$	$aD_1(1-D_1)$	$D_2(1-D_2)$	$aD_2(1-D_2)$
IV	0	—	—	$(1-D_1)^2$	0	$(1-D_2)^2$	0
Overall Divorce rate			D_1		$D_2 = D_1^2 + 2aD_1(1-D_1)$		$D_2 = D_2^2 + 2aD_2(1-D_2)$

MARRIAGE TYPES	DIVORCE RATE	GENERATION 4		GENERATION 5	
		Proportion	Divorce	Proportion	Divorce
I	1	D_3^2	D_3^2	D_4^2	D_4^2
II	a	$D_3(1-D_3)$	$aD_3(1-D_3)$	$D_4(1-D_4)$	$aD_4(1-D_4)$
III	a	$D_3(1-D_3)$	$aD_3(1-D_3)$	$D_4(1-D_4)$	$aD_4(1-D_4)$
IV	0	$(1-D_3)^2$	0.0	$(-D_4)^2$	0.0
Overall Divorce rate			$D_4 = D_3^2 + 2aD_3(1-D_3)$		$D_5 = D_4^2 + 2aD_4(1-D_4)$

$D_i =$ the overall divorce rate in generation i.
$a =$ the divorce rate for couples with mixed parents.

Now we can prepare Table 7.3.

> **STOP.** **Review each step shown in the table to be sure that it is clear to you.**

You will notice that the divorce rate in each generation can be written in terms of the divorce rate in the immediately preceding generation. Therefore,

$$D_{t+1} = D_t{}^2 + 2aD_t(1 - D_t)$$

and this is true for any generation.

We can manipulate the simple diffusion expression to find out how the value of a affects the outcome.

> **STOP.** **Spend some time doing it. See if you can summarize how a affects the diffusion of divorce.**

One simple way of examining the effect of a is to ask when the divorce rate will stay constant from one generation to the next. Thus we want to know what else is true when

$$D_{t+1} = D_t$$

To develop the point we use some elementary algebra.

$D_{t+1} = D_t$ (This must be true to produce
 steady-state equilibrium.)[3]
$D_t{}^2 + 2aD_t(1 - D_t) = D_t$ (This equation substitutes D_t for
$ D_{t+1}$ in our basic equation.)
$D_t{}^2 + 2aD_t - 2aD_t{}^2 - D_t = 0$
$D_t{}^2(1 - 2a) - D_t(1 - 2a) = 0$
$(1 - 2a)D_t(D_t - 1) = 0$

Thus we can see that the conditions are met if any one of the following is true:

$$D_t = 0$$
$$\text{or } D_t = 1$$
$$\text{or } a = \tfrac{1}{2}$$

If a (the divorce rate for couples with mixed parents) equals $\tfrac{1}{2}$, the divorce rate will never change from one generation to another (if the model is correct). Also, if the divorce rate reaches either 1.0 or 0, there is no further change. By using the same analysis with the inequality

$$D_{t+1} > D_t$$

we discover that if a is less than 0.5, the divorce rate will decline steadily toward zero; if a is greater than 0.5, the rate will increase steadily toward 1.0.

STOP. **Review the explanation. Be sure you understand exactly what has been proved.**

The model of divorce diffusion that we have developed is a simple and unrealistic one. Our next step is to take such a model structure and gradually make it a more realistic representation with more interesting implications. You can undertake the first steps in such a program in the problems for this section.

Notice that so far we have simply taken a familiar phenomenon and explored what we might learn by treating it as an example of a diffusion process. This led us to make some assumptions about contact, transmission, and contagion, and to try to develop their implications. Divorce is not usually looked at in this way, and intergenerational changes are not usually viewed as diffusion processes, which is why the approach has a certain amount of beauty.

7.4 SOME MODELS

The assumptions for a model of diffusion that we have outlined in Section 7.2 suggest a series of analogies. For example, the study of the diffusion of substances under various conditions of pressure, temperature, and physical restriction is an important part of chemistry. Perhaps the most obvious analogy, however, is to the study of epidemics—the diffusion of diseases. It should not be surprising, therefore, to discover a close relation between the ways in which epidemiologists look at diseases and the ways social scientists look at the diffusion of information, ideas, or sentiments. Many of the same basic models are used by both.

When we study diseases or social diffusion or both, we ask two primary questions:

1. What is the rate of diffusion? How fast does the object spread through a population?
2. What is the pattern of diffusion? Who has the object first? Who is relatively slow? What is the sequence of individual movement from not having the object to having it?

Although it is possible to make models that predict both the pattern and the rate of diffusion, the most common models for understanding diffusion do not, in fact, say anything directly about the pattern of diffusion. Rather, they are models of the rate. They can be elaborated, however, to give more attention to pattern by introducing some ideas about the social structure within which diffusion occurs. We will return to such considerations later.

7.4.1 THE IDEA OF RATE OF CHANGE

Though rate is a familiar concept, it warrants some extra attention. We use the concept of rate every day, as in reference to speed (rate of change of distance, measured in, say, kilometers per hour), interest rates (charges per year), wage rates (payments per hour), weight loss (kilos per week), and so on.

When we talk about rates, we are usually interested in some figure that portrays the average rate over some time period. What is our average speed in driving from New York to Chicago? What is the average annual interest rate on a short-term automobile loan? What was our average rate of growth over the past three years?

Imagine that George has just been given a new sports car by his rich aunt. He starts driving toward the city (50 kilometers away), and arrives after 30 minutes of driving. Since he covers 50 kilometers in 30 minutes, his average rate is $50/30 = 1\frac{2}{3}$ kilometers per minute.

It is unlikely that he was always traveling at the same 1⅔ kilometers per minute, during every minute of the journey. There are many problems in which it is useful to know something about the variation in this rate, faster or slower. We need more information to compute rate during the different portions of his journey.

Can we describe George's travels and compute changes in his rate? He covered the first 10 kilometers in 10 minutes; thus his rate was 10 kilometers/10 minutes, or 1 kilometer per minute. He then speeded up, and his rate was 30 kilometers/10 minutes, or 3 kilometers per minute. During the final part of his journey his rate was 10 kilometers/10 minutes, or 1 kilometer per minute again. This is a *rate of change* of distance. George's total distance traveled has changed after each 10-minute period. The *slope* of the graph in Figure 7.1 shows his rate of change of distance: steep slopes represent fast rates of change; gentle slopes represent slow rates of change.

Figure 7.2 is a more detailed representation of Figure 7.1. Notice that between minute 8 and minute 9 the car moved forward by exactly 1 kilometer. Thus its rate of change was 1 kilometer per minute. Between minute 11 and minute 12 the car moved forward by exactly 3 kilometers; hence a rate of change of 3 kilometers per minute.

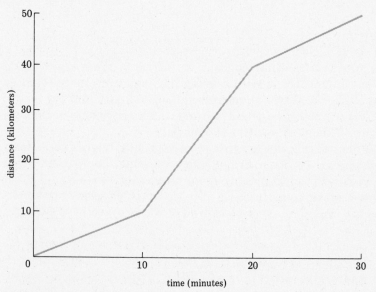

Figure 7.1: George's rate of travel.

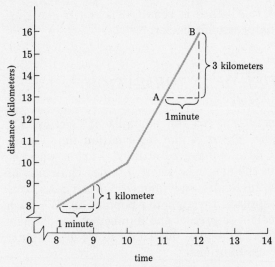

Figure 7.2: George's rate of travel (detail).

STOP AND THINK. **Suppose the slope were perfectly horizontal. What would that mean; what would George's rate of change be?**

A horizontal slope means that time goes on (increases), but distance does not change; that is, the rate is 0 kilometers per hour, and George is stopped.[4]

You have undoubtedly noticed that we compute the rate by dividing 2 *differences*, the difference in distances divided by the difference in times; for example, the difference in distance between A and B is 3 kilometers, and the difference in time between A and B is 1 minute. All of our rate formulas will involve such differences (for instance, the difference in the number of people who have heard a rumor between Monday and Wednesday). It is convenient to have an abbreviation for difference, and so we use the Greek letter delta, or Δ, as our abbreviation. Thus the formula for speed that we have been using becomes Δ distance/Δ time. Δ distance is the *increment* in distance traveled—so another way of thinking about the rate is as the increment in distance divided by the increment in time. This average rate of change can be measured over very long periods (a year or more) or very short periods (a second or less). All that is required is that some time has passed. The denominator cannot be zero.[5]

7.4.2 A MODEL OF INFORMATION EXPLOSION

Suppose we begin by returning to the example of Section 7.2. There we talked about the spread of the information that Carter would be appointed the new manager. Initially, Carter was the only individual present in the firm who knew it. (The chairman of the board is vacationing in Brazil and phoned Carter.) As time passes, the information spreads through the population. We wish to study the rate of diffusion, to predict the number of people who will have the information as time goes on. To do so we might start by making a few specific assumptions.

Assumption 1
During each hour, every person who has the information tells it to three persons who do not have it.

Assumption 2
Each person who receives the information believes it.

These assumptions are simple specifications for the exposure, transmission, and acceptance assumptions in Section 7.2. We are assuming that each hour every person who has the object of diffusion (the information) contacts three persons who do not, that he transmits the information to them, and that they accept it.

How many people would know the information at the end of the second hour (assuming that only Carter knew the information at the start of the first hour)?

> **STOP AND THINK.** Be sure that you follow through the assumptions carefully. How many people (the *total* number) will know about it by the end of the second hour? *Hint:* Perform two steps. How many will know by the end of the first hour? Then figure what happens during the second hour.

In order to develop the implications of this model, you might have prepared a table similar to Table 7.4. Under our assumptions

TABLE 7.4   Spread of a Rumor

HOUR	EXPOSURE-TRANSMISSION	ACCEPTANCE
	Each hour each person who has the information tells it to three persons who do not have it	*Each person who receives the information believes it*
1	Carter tells it to A. Carter tells it to B. Carter tells it to C.	A believes it. B believes it. C believes it.
	During hour 1, 3 *new* persons learn the information; at the end of hour 1, the *total* number of persons knowing the information is 4.	
2	Carter tells it to D, E, F. A tells it to G, H, I. B tells it to J, K, L. C tells it to M, N, O.	They believe it. They believe it. They believe it. They believe it.
	During hour 2, 12 *new* persons learn the information; at the end of hour 2, the *total* number of persons knowing the information is 16.	

16 people will know the information by the end of the second hour.

The process, of course, does not end after two hours. How many people will have the information after five hours?

STOP AND PREPARE THE TABLE.   **It is easy to do and is good practice.**

Once we have worked through a few time periods with our detailed table connecting the assumptions explicitly with what happens in each time period, we can shift to a somewhat more numerical version, as in Table 7.5. Now suppose that we wished to draw a graph of this process over time. We might begin by providing some symbolic notation for the variables. Suppose we denote the hour by t (for time) and the number of people having the information at the start of the hour n (for number). Then what would you call the number of people learning the information during the hour?

TABLE 7.5   *Spread of a Rumor*

HOUR	NO. OF PEOPLE HAVING THE INFORMATION AT THE START OF THE HOUR	NO. OF NEW PEOPLE LEARNING THE INFOR- MATION DUR- ING THE HOUR	TOTAL NO. OF PEOPLE HAV- ING THE IN- FORMATION AT THE END OF THE HOUR
1	1	3	4
2	4	12	16
3	16	48	64
4	64	192	256
5	256	768	1024

STOP AND THINK. What is the symbol you would use to represent the change, or increment, in the number of people who know the information? If you are not sure, reread the end of Section 7.2.1.

The number of people learning the information during the hour is the change, or increment, in the number of people (that is, Δn) having the information during a one-hour change in time. It is the rate of change in number, and we would denote it by $\Delta n/\Delta t$. Thus our table becomes a table of t, n, and $\Delta n/\Delta t$ (or Table 7.6).

Now let us graph n as a function of t; that is, let us show the total number of people who know the information each hour. The result is shown in Figure 7.3. Notice that the total number seems to be growing faster and faster. The slope of the lines connecting the time points is getting steeper and steeper. That is, the rate of change of informed people is increasing. We can

TABLE 7.6   *Spread of a Rumor*

t	n	$\Delta n/\Delta t$
1	1	3
2	4	12
3	16	48
4	64	192
5	256	768
6	1024	3072
7	4096	12,288

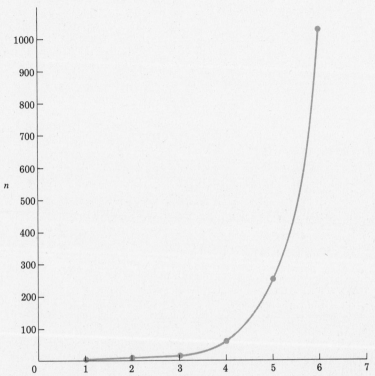

Figure 7.3: The number (n) of people who know at the beginning of each hour.

illustrate this by plotting $\Delta n / \Delta t$ as a function of t, as in Figure 7.4. Figure 7.3 shows that the *number of persons* knowing the information increases over time. Figure 7.4 shows that the *changes in that number* also increase over time. Why does the rate of growth get faster and faster? Because there are more and more informed people available to spread it: The people who are told become "converts," and themselves become active in spreading the rumor. It snowballs.

The diffusion process we have described by our assumptions belongs to a broad class of phenomena called "birth process" models. The name comes from the fact that such a model is a first approximation to what happens in rabbit reproduction. Suppose we put a pair of healthy rabbits in a very large valley full of grass and devoid of predators. Soon there would be a litter of baby rabbits. These would in turn grow up and produce more rabbits. Meanwhile,

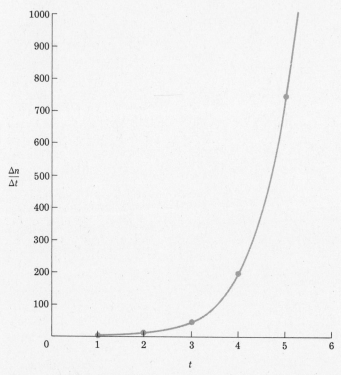

Figure 7.4: The change in number (Δn/Δt) of knowers during the hour.

the first pair would have another litter. The more rabbits there are, the greater the number of baby rabbits, and thus (in another generation) there will be even more rabbits, and so on. Each contact between male and female rabbits produces a litter of rabbits.

The diffusion of the rumor about the new boss and the reproduction of rabbits are basically similar processes: In one case we have rabbits begetting rabbits; in the other we have rumors begetting rumors. We say the diffusion is like a birth process. These birth process models apply to a wide variety of phenomena, not just to rabbits and rumors. It will be useful then to formulate the model in more general terms. We try a simple algebraic model first.

What is the relation between $\Delta n/\Delta t$ and n? The relation is shown numerically in Table 7.5, and graphically in Figure 7.4. The rate of change of n is always equal to $3 \times n$.[6] That is,

$$\frac{\Delta n}{\Delta t} = 3n$$

This is an exact algebraic description of the birth process model, for the case of spreading information about the new manager. The algebraic description of other birth process models should be similar.

STOP AND THINK. Does this particular equation apply to the case of rabbit reproduction exactly as written? What would you have to change to make it describe the rabbits?

Remember that the number 3 in the equation is the product of our assumptions about exposure transmission and acceptance for the case of the new boss. It is unlikely that these same specific assumptions will apply in the rabbit case; thus the number 3 will be changed to some other number. If we use the letter a to represent the net effect of the assumptions, or conditions, in any given situation, we can rewrite the equation in a general form to cover all cases that involve the birth process model:[7]

$$\frac{\Delta n}{\Delta t} = an$$

Although a will be some constant for any given situation, it will obviously differ among various situations. It summarizes, in a single number, the specific forms of our exposure, transmission, and acceptance assumptions. Changes in the assumptions cause changes in a. In the rumor case, for example, if we assume that everyone talks to five people per contact period, then a would increase. Or suppose that only half the rumors spread are believed; then a would decrease. Any of the factors discussed in Section 7.2 as affecting exposure, transmission, or acceptance will influence the value of a. We will treat this topic in more detail in Section 7.5.

Obviously, changing the value of a will change the speed at which the process grows. Figure 7.5 shows the graph of n as a function of a for various values of a. Examination of Figure 7.5 shows that although rates of diffusion differ substantially (depending on the value of a), the basic shape of the diffusion curves is the same. All birth process models tend to grow explo-

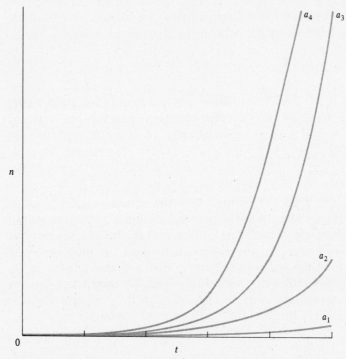

Figure 7.5: Growth curves for different values of a: *a₄ is largest value.*

sively; that is, they grow faster and faster and faster as time goes on.

STOP AND THINK. What are some possible problems in applying this model to an actual situation? Think about the implications of explosive growth.

The model pictures information (or whatever the object of diffusion may be) as spreading without limit. For example, our simple model of what happens with the story about the new boss in a business firm indicates that by the end of 20 hours the information would be known by 274,877,906,944 people! The model works reasonably well over a wide range of situations when we are observing the diffusion process near its beginnings (when it is still far from its ultimate theoretical limits) or else when we are observing some process having a relatively small a (whose ultimate limit is distant in time). We will need to consider some alternative models for other situations, however.

7.4.3   A BIRTH PROCESS WITH LIMITS

The birth process model in the previous section grows explosively and hence ultimately becomes ridiculous for any limited situation. For example, it makes no sense to calculate that, say, 12,288 new people will learn the rumor during the next hour when only 1000 people are employed by the company. We will need a different kind of diffusion model to use in a case in which growth is limited. To formulate such a model we first discuss the kind of growth properties we think would be realistic for limited environments.

Look at Figure 7.3 again. Suppose we draw a horizontal line across the graph at the $n = 1000$ level. This line represents the possible limits of growth for the rumor, assuming that the firm has 1000 employees. We know that the portion of the growth curve above the $n = 1000$ level cannot exist, but what about the portion of the curve below this limit?

> ***STOP AND THINK.***   **Does the shape of the growth curve below the $n = 1000$ line seem reasonable to you? That is, will diffusion of the rumor go faster and faster, then suddenly stop?**

To answer this question it would be useful to think about the process by which the rumor is spread: Someone who knows the news has contact with someone who does not and tells it to him. Toward the end of the process, when almost everyone has the news, it will be very difficult to make contact with someone who does not know it. Most of the people contacted will already have been exposed to the news and cannot be converted. Suppose that everyone has an average of three contacts with other people at which the information is transmitted. In the beginning the process will be relatively efficient because there is a high probability of talking with someone who does not have the news. Hence the growth rate of the rumor is rapid. Toward the end of the process, however, most contacts will be unfruitful because there is a low probability of talking with someone who does not already have the news. Hence the growth rate of the rumor is very slow because most of the three random contacts that each one has will be with people who already know the rumor.

The analogy with disease contagion is helpful. Suppose you are the first person in your neighborhood to have Danish flu. Initially, it will spread to everyone whom you contact and, in turn, to everyone whom they contact, thus causing a rapid rate of contagion. The contagion process slows down though as everyone in the neighborhood is exposed to the disease and becomes immune to it. The *total number of people* who have had the disease continues to increase day by day until everyone has had it. The growth rate, the *number of new cases* produced each day, increases at first but then must decrease as the process nears its limit. Going back to our imaginary version of Figure 7.3 with the horizontal limit line at $n = 1000$, we know that the curve must flatten out and become less steep as it approaches the limit line.

It would be useful to have an algebraic formulation of this new model that implies rapid initial growth followed by decreasing growth near the limit. One possible formulation is as follows:

$N =$ the growth limit (for instance, 1000 in the preceding case).
$n =$ the number of people who have the information at the start of the hour.
$t\ =$ the number of the time period.

$$\frac{\Delta n}{\Delta t} = an(N - n)$$

The *constant, a,* summarizes the diffusion properties of the situation: the facts about exposure, transmission, and acceptance. N is a *constant* that expresses the growth limit of the process. n is a *variable;* it grows, rapidly at first, then slows down. The first term in the right-hand side of the equation, *an,* is identical to the original birth process model. We know that the *an* term will grow explosively. The second term $(N - n)$ will be large initially because n will be small. As n gets bigger, the term $(N - n)$ gets smaller; when everyone knows the rumor (that is, when $N = n$), the term will equal zero. Our growth equation is the product of these two terms: the *an* term, which gets bigger and bigger, and the $(N - n)$ term, which gets smaller and smaller.

It might also be helpful to express the equation in words: Since N is the total number of people in the population and n is the number who already know the rumor, then $(N - n)$ is the number of people who do *not* know the rumor. Thus the formula could be expressed as a times the number who know it times the number who do not. It is the contact of "actuals" (those who already have the rumor or the disease) with "potentials" (those who do not yet have the rumor or the disease) that produces the growth process. Initially, the number of potentials is high so that the actuals can be very effective. Eventually, the number of potentials becomes so small that most contacts produce no spread of the rumor.

Table 7.7 shows a numerical example of this growth process. We assume a total population of 50 people; that a is 0.01 for this group; and that only 1 person knows the rumor initially at time 1. You can see that the rumor takes a while to pick up speed; at the beginning of the fifth period only 4.8 people know the news. But it then spreads quite rapidly; it starts slowing down after the midpoint (25 people); and it eventually becomes very slow again.

TABLE 7.7 Spread of a Rumor in a Limited Population

t	n	$\Delta n/\Delta t$	$an(N - n)$	
1	1	0.49	$0.01(1)(50 - 1)$	$= 0.49$
2	1.49	0.72	$0.01(1.49)(50 - 1.49)$	$= 0.72$
3	2.21	1.06	$0.01(2.21)(50 - 2.21)$	$= 1.06$
4	3.27	1.53	$0.01(3.27)(50 - 3.27)$	$= 1.53$
5	4.80	2.17	$0.01(4.80)(50 - 4.80)$	$= 2.17$
6	6.97	3.00	$0.01(6.97)(50 - 6.97)$	$= 3.00$
7	9.97	3.99	$0.01(9.97)(50 - 9.97)$	$= 3.99$
8	13.96	5.03	$0.01(13.96)(50 - 13.96)$	$= 5.03$
9	18.99	5.89	$0.01(18.99)(50 - 18.99)$	$= 5.89$
10	24.87	6.25	$0.01(24.87)(50 - 24.87)$	$= 6.25$
11	31.12	5.88	$0.01(31.12)(50 - 31.12)$	$= 5.88$
12	37.00	4.81	$0.01(37.00)(50 - 37.00)$	$= 4.81$
13	41.81	3.38	$0.01(41.81)(50 - 41.81)$	$= 3.38$
14	45.19	2.17	$0.01(45.19)(50 - 45.19)$	$= 2.17$
15	47.36	1.25	$0.01(47.36)(50 - 47.36)$	$= 1.25$
16	48.61	0.68	$0.01(48.61)(50 - 48.61)$	$= 0.68$
17	49.29	0.35	$0.01(49.29)(50 - 49.29)$	$= 0.35$
18	49.64	0.18	$0.01(49.64)(50 - 49.64)$	$= 0.18$
19	49.82	0.01	$0.01(49.82)(50 - 49.82)$	$= 0.01$

***STOP AND THINK.*   How can 4.8 people know the news?**

According to our model, an individual either has the news, or he does not. It is not possible for one person to have $\frac{8}{10}$ of the news. Nor is it understandable to speak of $\frac{8}{10}$ of a person. The model is an approximation. We could "correct" it by requiring that we round the number off to the next higher integer; but we will leave it as a reminder that the model—like all models—is not a complete picture of the world.

Figure 7.6 shows a graph of n versus t. You can see that initially n grows faster and faster, and the lower half of the graph is similar to the shape of the explosive growth curves. Growth is fastest—that is, the slope is steepest—at the point when half the population knows the rumor. From that point on growth begins to slow down, the curve gradually flattens and becomes horizontal.

It is also interesting to look at the change in the growth rate as the rumor spreads. Figure 7.7 shows a graph of $\Delta n / \Delta t$

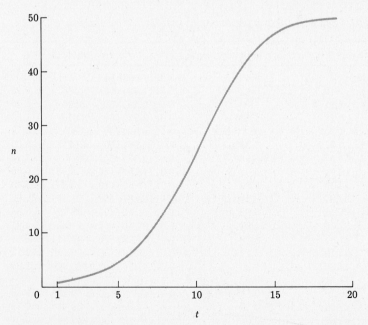

Figure 7.6: Graph of n *as a function of* t *when* $\Delta n / \Delta t = an(N - n)$; $a = 0.01$; $N = 50$; $n_1 = 1$.

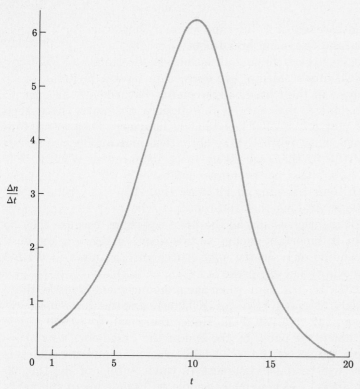

Figure 7.7: Graph of $\Delta n/\Delta t$ *as a function of* t *when* $\Delta n/\Delta t = an(N - n)$; $a = 0.01$; $N = 50$; $n_1 = 1$.

versus *t*. You can see that the growth rate becomes faster and faster until the halfway point, then levels off and reverses.

A close look at the equation suggests, of course, that if we want to be sure that $n + \Delta n$ is never greater than N , we must restrict the value of a to be no greater than $1/N$. The restriction is not overly burdensome; so we continue the Δ notation a bit longer. Since we exclude the possibility that the number of people having the news will decline with time (see Assumption 5), we also require that a be nonnegative.

7.4.4   A BROADCAST PROCESS

The preceding two models both assume that the object of diffusion propagates through *contact* between those who have the object and those who do not. There are some situations in which the object of diffusion spreads in a different manner, however, for example, newspapers and television broadcasts.

Consider the following situation: Radio station WBBB, the local classical music station, has decided to have a birthday party for Beethoven in their studio this coming Saturday. It is open to all their listeners, and they will announce the party once each hour from now on. WBBB has 100,000 listeners. They are a fun-loving bunch, busy with diverse activities, and during any given hour only 10% of them are likely to be listening to WBBB. It is a random 10%; that is, everyone listens only 10% of the time, rather than some listening much more than 10% and some listening much less. Assume that those people who hear the announcement do not themselves spread the news (perhaps because they do not consider it important enough to talk about or they are too busy to gossip, and so on). So the only source for the news is WBBB itself. How will the news spread?

During the first hour when the announcement is made, there will be 10,000 listeners (10% of 100,000), and the announcement will come as news to all of them. Hence there will be 10,000 people who know about the party by the end of the first hour. What happens during the second hour? Again, when the announcement is made, there will be 10,000 listeners (a random 10% of the 100,000 possible listeners). So how many people will know about the party at the end of the second hour?

STOP AND THINK. **Bob and Carol think that the correct answer is 20,000; Ted and Alice think that the correct answer is 19,000. What do you think?**

Remember that the 10% who listen are randomly distributed among the total audience. At the end of the first hour there were 10,000 who knew about the party and 90,000 who did not. During the next hour 10% of this total tunes in: Thus the 10,000 second-hour listeners will consist of 9000 new listeners and 1000 who already know the news. So WBBB can only convert 9000 people during the second hour, and the total number who know about the party will be 19,000. During the third hour, the 10,000 listeners will consist of 8100 new people and 1900 who already know about the party.

This broadcast phenomenon has a simple algebraic description:

$$\frac{\Delta n}{\Delta t} = a(N - n)$$

As in the previous models, a summarizes the net effect of the contact-transmission-acceptance process. The term $(N - n)$ is simply the number of people who do not yet know the news. Thus the model says that each broadcast converts a constant fraction of the remaining uninformed people. In Table 7.8 we show the calculations for the WBBB example.

As in our previous example, we need to limit the possible values of a. Since we want $n + \Delta n$ to be no greater than N, we require that a be no greater than 1. And since we want diffusion to occur, we require a to be nonnegative.

Figure 7.8 shows a graph of n versus t. You can see that the information spreads very rapidly at first, and then slower and slower as it becomes increasingly harder to find people who do not already know the news.[8]

In Figure 7.9 we plot the growth rate versus time. It starts high and gradually decreases over time.[9]

Table 7.9 summarizes the main characteristics of the diffusion models we have explored so far.

TABLE 7.8   Diffusion via Broadcast Model

t	n	$\Delta n/\Delta t$	$an(N - n)$	
1	0	10,000	$0.1(100,000 - 0)$	$= 10,000$
2	10,000	9000	$0.1(100,000 - 10,000)$ =	9000
3	19,000	8100	$0.1(100,000 - 19,000)$ =	8100
4	27,100	7290	$0.1(100,000 - 27,100)$ =	7290
5	34,390	6561	$0.1(100,000 - 34,390)$ =	6561
6	40,951	5905	$0.1(100,000 - 40,951)$ =	5905
7	46,856	5314	$0.1(100,000 - 46,856)$ =	5314
8	52,160	4784	$0.1(100,000 - 52,160)$ =	4784
9	56,944	4306	$0.1(100,000 - 56,944)$ =	4306
10	61,250	3875	$0.1(100,000 - 61,250)$ =	3875
11	65,125	3488	$0.1(100,000 - 65,125)$ =	3488
12	68,613	3139	$0.1(100,000 - 68,613)$ =	3139
13	71,752	2825	$0.1(100,000 - 71,752)$ =	2825
14	74,577	2542	$0.1(100,000 - 74,752)$ =	2542

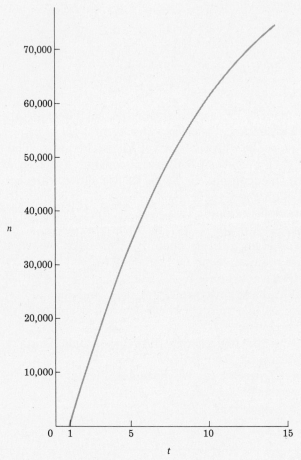

Figure 7.8: Graph of n as a function of t when
$\Delta n/\Delta t = a(N - n)$; $a = 0.1$; $N = 100,000$; $n_1 = 0$.

7.5 EXPLORATIONS OF SOCIAL DISEASES

We now have a collection of models for a variety of possible diffusion situations. The models are relatively easy to use, but it must
have occurred to you that they can only be used if you are given
some value for the diffusion constant a. How do you know what
a is in a given situation? It is easy to discuss the factors that
influence a in terms of the exposure-transmission-acceptance
process.

TABLE 7.9   Summary of Diffusion Model Characteristics

	BIRTH PROCESS	BIRTH PROCESS WITH LIMITS	BROADCAST PROCESS
GROWTH EQUATION	$\dfrac{\Delta n}{\Delta t} = an$	$\dfrac{\Delta n}{\Delta t} = an(N-n)$	$\dfrac{\Delta n}{\Delta t} = a(N-n)$
GROWTH CURVE			
SOURCE OF GROWTH	contagion from those who already have the object	contagion from those who already have the object	constant source of some kind, not from other people
ASSUMED POPULATION	unlimited size	limited size	limited size

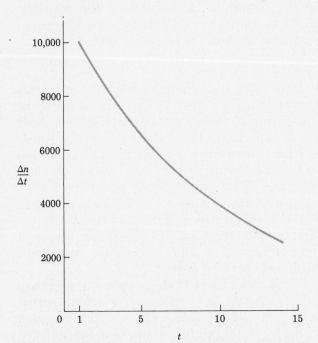

Figure 7.9: Graph of $\Delta n/\Delta t$ as a function of t when $\Delta n/\Delta t = a(N-n)$; a = 0.1; N = 100,000; $n_1 = 0$.

Exposure. Other things being equal, more frequent contacts mean a greater *a*. A rumor will spread faster among residents of a dormitory then among the students who live at home and commute to school; a cold or flu will spread faster in the winter when people are more concentrated indoors with poor air circulation than in the summer; and news of world events will spread faster through a literate population than through an illiterate population.

Transmission. Other things being equal, ease of transmission will affect *a*. Simple, uncomplicated rumors will spread faster than ambiguous, complex ones. Thus there is a kind of natural selection process operating when disasters or other notable events occur. Simple-minded explanations and descriptions are going to spread faster than more complex, balanced ones. (In situations having riot potential this is an especially significant conclusion. By the time the more correct version of an event has had time to diffuse, it may be too late.) Also, other things being equal, the more important an item is, the faster it will diffuse: someone is more likely to repeat information that he considers important or that he thinks his listener will consider important. A story about the president of a university is likely to diffuse faster, and to a broader population, than a story about a professor (assuming that the type of story is similar).

Acceptance. Other things being equal, a high probability of acceptance means a high value for *a*. A story is more likely to be accepted when it comes from a credible source. Information about an innovation in cars is more likely to be accepted when it comes from an engineering journal than when it comes from an advertisement. Advertisers make use of this principle by having an automobile commercial narrated by an "engineer" or by having a drug commercial narrated by a "doctor." Also, other things being equal, the more important and useful an item is to the listener, the faster it will diffuse. A better mousetrap will diffuse faster among a population with rodent problems; an improved shaving cream will diffuse relatively slowly in a bearded society.

In terms of disease, an illness that spreads via sneezing, in which case the affected person is contagious for a long period of time, will spread much faster than a disease that spreads through personal contact. (In this kind of disease the affected person is usually only contagious at the very peak of the illness, when he is likely to be home in bed.)

We can illustrate some of the behavioral factors summarized in the value of a by looking at the diffusion of inventions. Almost all of the technological processes used to produce our economic goods today are radically different from the processes that were used a hundred years ago. Hybrid corn is grown instead of native corn. Furniture is made with power-driven tools instead of handsaws. Light is produced by electric bulbs instead of kerosene lanterns. What accounts for these changes? Certainly, the genius of numerous inventors accounts for a large part of the answer, but only part. Though there have been millions of patents issued, very few of the patented devices have ever received wide usage. Why did some inventions diffuse while others did not? What determines the rate at which an invention diffuses?

Such questions are important to more than our own history. They bear on current world problems as well: Why are some nations rich and others poor? At least some social scientists believe the answer is simple: "Western society uses modern technology, whereas the underdeveloped nations do not. If the latter would only adopt modern methods of farming and manufacturing, they would become rich, too. But instead they insist on clinging to traditional ways of doing things."

Even if such an explanation were a good one, it should be pointed out that the problem is not simply an instance of "bold, progressive Westerners seizing each new opportunity and adopting it instantly" versus "tradition-bound societies." Diffusion has been a slow process in Western society, too. Hybrid corn was demonstrated all over the American farm belt by thousands of government agricultural specialists, and it was conclusively shown that its corn yields were much higher than those of conventional seed. Yet even well-educated American farmers did not adopt it immediately. In fact, it took 18 years before hybrid corn was being used by 80% of American corn farmers. Although the spread of information (contact and transmission) was quite rapid, the rate of adoption (contagion) was much slower. What factors influence the contagion of an innovation?

Example: Economic Development

The government of Mexico was concerned about the problem of improving agricultural output to increase the welfare of its people. It asked a team of agricultural experts from the Rockefeller Foundation to make a study of Mexican agriculture and then suggest ways in which the farmers might improve their productivity. The Rockefeller team started work in the early 1940s and was spectacularly successful. This example is adapted from their experience.

The team initially formulated two plans for increasing corn yields. Assume that you have the task of choosing between them. Plan 1 involves irrigation: A large increase in corn output per acre can be obtained if modern irrigation techniques are used; implementation of this plan involves the construction of a network of water-storage reservoirs and irrigation canals by the farmers. This would require that all of the farmers agree to work together and donate their labor to the project during the slack season. *All* will have to work together during the building, but all will share in the benefits once it is completed.

Plan 2 involves the introduction of improved corn seed. This improved seed yields higher output per acre, even with the existing irrigation techniques, and costs no more than the conventional seed. You plan to make the seed available to any *individual* farmer who wishes to give it a try.

STOP AND THINK. Put yourself in the position of the Rockefeller team. You are an adviser, not a dictator. You can make suggestions and try to persuade the farmers, but you cannot simply issue orders. You are faced with the problem of diffusing an innovation. Which of the two innovations would you try to diffuse?

At first glance it seems as if the irrigation project is better since it makes a quick improvement in the output of an entire area, whereas the improved seed plan only increases the output of those farmers who are willing to try it. But if you think that there might be difficulty in persuading a significant number of farmers to try the new seed, think of the difficulty of persuading *all* of the farmers to work together on an irrigation scheme. It is obviously easier to persuade a few farmers than it is to persuade all of the farmers. You do not have to solve the problem all at once. The point about diffusion is that if an idea is a good one and if you can get it started among some farmers, it will spread through contact without any further persuasive effort from you. Improved seed can be adopted incrementally; irrigation is virtually an all-or-nothing proposition.[10]

Once the Rockefeller group had decided to concentrate on seed improvement, it still had two choices to make. Again, put yourself in its place and decide which choice you would make. Plan 2A involves synthetic seed, and Plan 2B involves hybrid seed. Synthetic seed which is essentially just an improved version of the seed that the farmers are already using, improves yields by about 25%, but it can still be used exactly the same way as traditional seed. Hybrid seed increases corn yield by 50%, but it requires that the farmer change his techniques at the same time: Since the hybrid is sterile, he must buy new seed every year (instead of his customary practice of simply putting aside some of the corn harvest to be used for next year's seed). Hybrid corn also needs to be planted and cared for in new ways.

STOP AND THINK. Which of these innovations would you try to introduce and why?

The hybrid corn gives the most spectacular results, but it is the most complex innovation. In effect, it is not one innovation but many. The synthetic corn is only a single innovation. It is very similar to what the farmers are already using in every respect but one (improved yield). Hence, the Rockefeller group decided to concentrate on diffusing the synthetic corn first because it was the most familiar innovation and the least complicated. We will discuss the results of this strategy in a moment.

7.5.1 DIFFUSION AS INDIVIDUAL CHOICE AND ADAPTATION

From our discussion of the diffusion of an agricultural innovation we derived the general principle that innovations that can be adopted incrementally diffuse more readily than those that must be adopted on an all-or-none basis; and that innovations that are uncomplicated and similar to existing practices diffuse more readily than those that are complicated or quite different from existing practices. Our focus has been on understanding the overall spread of an innovation without asking why an individual farmer tries a new method of farming—or why a manufacturer tries a new process— or why a consumer tries a new product.

You might have noticed that we could have looked at the diffusion process in terms of any of our previous models: as an individual making a *choice* to try something new; as an individual *exchanging* something old for something new; as an individual *learning* to try new things. Any of these models might cast additional light on the diffusion process.

We can look at innovative behavior, for example, as though it were the result of a rational choice. The choice model outlined in Chapter Four involved maximization of expected value. In those terms a possible explanation of why some farmers do not innovate could be: Considering the two alternatives, innovate or not-innovate, the expected value of not innovating is higher; therefore, the farmer does not try the innovation.[11]

> *STOP AND THINK.* **Using the explanation as a starting point, think of some way to make the farmers accept the innovation.** *Hint:* **How could you increase its expected value? Remember, expected value equals probability times payoff.**

The explanation offered is potentially circular (see note 11), but it does focus our attention on the expected value of the innovation. Presumably, there is no question in the farmers' minds about the *value* of an innovation that increases yield per acre. So the low expected value must be due to the farmers' skepticism about the chances that the innovation will work. That is, the farmers apparently have a low subjective *probability* that what you are telling them is correct. They do not believe the claim you make about increased corn output with the new seed. (In terms of the earlier example, you could say that the irrigation innovation requires you to obtain the trust of all the farmers, whereas the improved seed innovation only requires that you obtain the trust of a few.)

As you contemplate the problem of changing the farmers' beliefs about the likelihood of a successful innovation, you may want to use the models in Chapter Six to understand how farmers could come to believe that the innovation will be successful. Before the farmers will believe in (assign a high probability of success to) your future innovations, they will have to experience rewards as a result of believing in your past innovations. Thus you begin with the synthetic corn. Some farmers will be willing to try it, and their success will prompt other farmers to adopt it. As the innovation diffuses, your credibility rises. You might then try introducing hybrid corn. This is a more complex innovation, requiring other contingent innovations along with it, but a few farmers will be willing to try it because of your increased credibility, and eventually this innovation will diffuse as well. Finally, you will be in a position where enough farmers trust you to enable you to suggest the cooperative irrigation project.[12]

All of the foregoing considerations are useful in assessing relative rates of transmission. They will not give an actual numerical prediction for a. An epidemiologist deals with the situation by generalizing from past diseases: He can study statistics on prior outbreaks of flu, determine the value of a that describes these prior events, and then use it to make predictions about current diseases. He might modify the prior estimate of a to take into account increased geographic mobility (more air travel now), the season of the year, the infectious period of the disease, and so on. But in practice he could make relatively good predictions. An advertising agency might make predictions about the spread of a new product by studying the spread of similar products in the past. They would presumably try to find products with similar characteristics that were introduced into similar situations in the past.

Therefore, for many diffusion phenomena it is possible to estimate rate of diffusion by evaluating similar past events. And knowledge of the relevant factors underlying a (which is, after all, only a summary of many diverse facts) sometimes enables useful predictions.

7.6 DIFFUSION IN A SOCIAL STRUCTURE

The basic models of diffusion that we have discussed in Section 7.4 share a common assumption: They assume that the collection of individuals involved in the diffusion process is homogeneous and that the connections among the individuals can be ignored. For many purposes the assumptions work, and the models seem to fit the phenomena. Sometimes, however, we will want to modify the models to reflect the fact that individuals are organized into a social structure that affects the diffusion of things.

7.6.1 THE ELEMENTS OF SOCIAL STRUCTURE

By social structure we do not mean anything as general as a complete sociology or geography of modern society. Rather, we think of three attributes of social organization. The first attribute is the *interconnectedness* of individuals or groups. Social and technological rules define the extent to which different individuals in the society see, talk, or write to one another. The inventions of the telephone, radio, printing press (and literacy), and television have changed the interconnectedness of society. The changes have increased some connections among individuals while they have reduced others. It has been argued, for example, that television has had the consequence (through diffusion) of reducing the heterogeneity of American society. In effect, the argument is that the connection between a few style leaders (as reflected in the television networks) and individuals has been strengthened while the connections within smaller groups (region, family) have been weakened.

The second attribute is closely related. It is the *distances* among individuals or groups. Distance here refers partly to physical distance, but it also includes social distance. It reflects the variety of factors of social life that make people behave as if they were physically distant (or close). Social class is the classic example of a factor in social distance. From the point of view of diffusion, two individuals of different social classes may be quite distant, even when they are standing in the same train station. In an urban society it is often true that two neighbors are more "distant" from one another than either is from work associates.[13]

The third attribute of social structure is the social *regulation* of behavior. From a social point of view some objects of diffusion are not feasible for some individuals or groups. The economic and political system limits contagion. Some diffusion, for example, requires money; the spread of yacht owning, for instance, is constrained by the social distribution of wealth. Some diffusion is regulated by law; the tendency for crimes of violence to spread is inhibited by laws against them. In addition, there is a complex maze of social rules about behavior. These norms affect the rate and pattern of diffusion. If anyone doubts the power of such regulations, he should consider the errors that would be made by a simple diffusion model in studying the spread of a new swimsuit style in a population that included both men and women.

STOP AND THINK. Identify some other features of social interconnectedness, distance, and regulation as they affect diffusion. What are some of the major forms of social organization?

Social interconnectedness, distance, and regulation are all related to the ways in which society organizes individuals into subgroups. These include primary groups like the family, the work group, or the neighbor group. Different societies organize these groups in different ways. In fact, the study of the social structure of kinship is one of the major domains of modern research in anthropology. We would expect diffusion to be different in two societies that, although otherwise similar, had a different way of organizing extended family relations.

Social subgroups also include various relatively formal associations, such as churches, unions, clubs, and professional associations. Modern Western society tends to be an organized society. It has organizations with newsletters and staffs and meetings. Some people are tied in extensively to the network; some are not. As a result, we typically come to recognize the phenomenon of "the establishment" in science; it consists of those people who are tied into the network of science associations, committees, panels, and meetings. There is an establishment in radical causes too, and in city affairs, high society, and education. The establishment structure influences the process of diffusion.

Social subgroups include a variety of social classes, ethnic groups, age groups, sex groups, and national/regional groups. By belonging to such groups individuals are linked to each other in ways that affect the spread of things. People in different groups talk to each other at different rates, at different times, about different things, in different ways, and with different consequences.

STOP AND THINK. How would you go about making changes in the simple models of diffusion to accommodate the problems of social structure?

Our approach is conservative. We will try to suggest some modest changes in the models that will capture some parts of social structure sometimes. They are not profound changes, and they all involve one simple strategy: We assume that society is segmented into subgroups and that diffusion within and among subgroups follows our basic diffusion model.

7.6.2   *RELEVANT GROUP MODEL*

Perhaps the most common procedure for accommodating elements of social structure is to note that social structure divides society into two groups—those people who are relevant to an object of diffusion and those who are not. If we want to consider the diffusion of new fertilizers, we limit our attention to farmers. If we want to consider the diffusion of footballs, we limit our attention to football players. If we want to consider the diffusion of $500,000 yachts, we limit our attention to rich people. If we want to consider the diffusion of a new engineering computer, we limit our attention to engineering organizations.

All of these segmentations are social segmentations. They reflect various social restrictions on diffusion—money, professional training, occupation, sex socialization. The success or failure of our models when we apply them to the relevant group will depend on (1) the extent to which the boundaries between the relevant group and the rest of society are permeable and (2) the extent to which there is additional social structure *within* the relevant group. If it is possible to identify one group that is homogeneously relevant and another group (including everyone else) that is homogeneously irrelevant, the relevant group model is a good way of accommodating social structure.

STOP AND THINK.   **Can you think of some situations in which such a strategy might work?**

You might have thought of the following kinds of examples:

1. *Potential Group of Customers.*   A manufacturer of baby diapers wishes to establish a diffusion model to examine the spread of information about a new product. He defines a relevant group as all parents of diaper-wearing children and proposes to ignore other people.
2. *Organizational Participants.*   A student of organizations wishes

to apply a diffusion model to the contagion of participation in a profit-sharing program. He defines a relevant group as the group of all employees in the firm.

3. *Caste Society.* An analyst of folk humor wishes to test a diffusion model for the spread of a particularly unattractive joke told by men about women. He defines the relevant group as the group of all men.

The assumption in each case is that the situation effectively eliminates the possibility of diffusion to other parts of the society. The assumption is reasonable in each case, but it could be wrong. Parents might be the wrong group in the diaper case because there is social structure within the relevant group; mothers are different from fathers. Employees might be the wrong group in the organizational case because the boundaries may be permeable; many employees have families, and families sometimes talk. Men might be the wrong group in the folk humor case; it is possible that some man might tell the joke to some woman and that the spread among women might then be relatively rapid.

7.6.3 SEPARATE GROUP MODEL

A second procedure (closely related to the first) is to notice that the parameters underlying the diffusion process might vary in different groups. Each group is viewed as separate, with no diffusion from one group to another. The process affects each group, but differently. We still assume that the segmentation is effective, but we allow more than one group to be relevant. For example, it is possible that an advertising campaign might spread a new product simultaneously through two unconnected groups—but at different rates.

To illustrate such a model suppose that diffusion takes place by some combination of rumor transmission and broadcast transmission. Many situations involve both dissemination from some central source and transmission from one individual to another. Most information that is spread by radio, television, or newspapers is subsequently spread through rumor. This is true of advertising, news, learned opinions. Professional innovations spread through the professional journals and through contact among professionals. Dress fashions spread through broadcast from magazines and by observation of others.

In order to reflect the combination we can produce a combined expression for the rate of change in the possession of the item being diffused. We do this with two individual equations:

Rumor Transmission $\quad \dfrac{\Delta n}{\Delta t} = a_1 n (N - n)$

Broadcast Transmission $\dfrac{\Delta n}{\Delta t} = a_2 (N - n)$

If both processes are occurring at once, we might speculate that[14]

$$\frac{\Delta n}{\Delta t} = a_1 n (N - n) + a_2 (N - n)$$

Now how can we reflect the fact that the rate of diffusion is different in different groups?

STOP AND THINK. **How would you do it?**

Suppose that we had two groups of doctors.[15] One group consists of doctors who are socially isolated from their colleagues, who have relatively few contacts with other doctors, and who rarely talk about professional matters with them. The other group has relatively frequent contact and relatively frequent talks. If we wanted to apply the foregoing diffusion model to these two groups as they adopt a new drug, what would we do?

STOP AND THINK. **You should be able to see a concrete way to adapt the model to reflect the difference.**

Coleman, Katz, and Menzel reasoned that for the doctors who were socially isolated, the value of a_1 would be quite small and might be approximated by assuming a value of zero. Both groups would learn from reading journals about the new drug, but only the socially integrated doctors would learn from each other.

The sociologists obtained the cooperation of local drug stores and made an examination of their prescription records for the 15 months following the release of a new drug, which had been introduced a few years before. From these historical records they noted the first month when the new drug was prescribed by each of the doctors in the community. From this information it was easy to make graphs of the proportion of doctors who were using the drug at the end of each month after its initial introduction. In addition, each doctor was asked to name the other doctors with whom he talked most frequently for advice or discussion, as well as the doctors whom he met most frequently in social-friendship contacts. It is easy to construct social structures from such information. For each of the three social structures (advice, discussion, friendship) the researchers counted the number of times a given doctor was named by his colleagues. Presumably, those doctors who are named most often by other doctors are more integrated into the social structure. The researchers then divided the doctors into two groups, those with a high degree of integration into the structure and those with a low degree of integration. The group having a high degree of integration was comprised of those doctors who were named by three or more other doctors. Separate diffusion curves were then plotted for the two groups. With respect to the friendship network, the data showed that approximately equal proportions of the integrated and nonintegrated doctors were using the drug after the first 2 months. But the integrated doctors reached the 80% adoption point after 7 months, whereas the nonintegrated doctors did not reach this point until 15 months after introduction. That is, the two groups started out about the same, but the *rate* of growth among the integrated doctors was much more rapid. The obvious explanation is that the integrated doctors are part of a much tighter contact network, and the news spread among them like a rumor process. It snowballed, with each converted doctor in the network acting to convert others in turn. Those doctors who were not well integrated with their local medical community learned of the drug more slowly through some kind of broadcast process. Both groups of doctors were equally exposed to the constant source of journals and drug salesmen, but the integrated doctors had the additional factor of rumor diffusion as well—so the overall, total diffusion rate was much higher for them. Similar results were obtained for the advice and discussion networks.

By adopting similar procedures, we can adapt the simple combination model of diffusion to separate groups simultaneously spreading something. We simply establish the groups and vary the group values for a_1 and a_2.

STOP AND THINK.   Can you think of situations in which this strategy might be appropriate?

You might have considered situations such as the following:

1. The diffusion of information about a local scandal through the ranks of the military base. We might speculate that there would be one process among the "insiders" (for example, among the officers if the scandal involved an officer) and another process among the "outsiders."
2. The diffusion of commitment to the ideology of the women's liberation movement. We might speculate that there would be one process among men and another process among women.
3. The diffusion of a tax-avoidance procedure. We might speculate that there would be one process among those taxpayers who use tax consultants and another process among those taxpayers who use the I.R.S. booklets.

7.6.4   SEMIPERMEABLE GROUPS (OPTIONAL)

A final procedure is to assume that the groups involved are neither completely separated nor completely mixed. Rather, there is some diffusion within the groups and some diffusion across the groups; but the rates of diffusion across group boundaries are different from the rates within groups.

For example, suppose that you were interested in the diffusion of a language fad in a high school.[16] You might observe the following general features of diffusion in a high school:

1. Upper classmen (seniors and juniors) rarely copy the language fads of lower classmen (sophomores and freshmen).
2. Lower classmen often copy the language fads of upper classmen.
3. Upper classmen talk mostly to other upper classmen.
4. Lower classmen talk mostly to other lower classmen.
5. Upper classmen listen to TV programs (the main source of new language fads) less than do lower classmen.

The problem is to translate these general observations into a model that might capture key aspects of the diffusion of language fads in high schools.

STOP AND THINK. **Think about how you would set up the model to deal with semipermeable groups.**

The first thing is to notice that we have two populations just as we did in the previous case. As a result, we might start with the same general kind of equation:

$$\frac{\Delta n}{\Delta t} = a_1 n (N - n) + a_2 (N - n) \text{ (for upper classmen)}$$

$$\frac{\Delta m}{\Delta t} = a_3 m (M - m) + a_4 (M - m) \text{ (for lower classmen)}$$

Notice that we have done two important things. First, we have recognized that our two groups have different sizes and different numbers who already have the language fad. This is reflected by talking about n and N in the case of upper classmen and m and M in the case of lower classmen. Second, we have recognized that the rates of talking and listening may be different among upper classmen than among lower classmen.

If we stop here, however, we would have the model for our separate group case described in the previous section. We need to change the model to allow for the fact that the two groups are not completely separate.

STOP AND THINK. **How would you do it? What additional term would you add to each equation?**

We need to add a term that reflects the rate of cross-group contagion. If there are n upper classmen who have the fad already and $M - m$ lower classmen who do not, then the contagion *from* upper to lower classmen should be proportional to $n(M - m)$. Similarly, since there are m lower classmen who have the fad and $(N - n)$ upper classmen who do not, the contagion *to* upper from lower classmen should be proportional to $m(N - n)$.

STOP AND LOOK IT OVER. **Is it clear why we assume this?**

Thus we end up with a two-equation model:

$$\frac{\Delta n}{\Delta t} = a_1 n (N - n) + a_2 (N - n) + a_3 m (N - n)$$

$$\frac{\Delta m}{\Delta t} = a_4 m (M - m) + a_5 (M - m) + a_6 n (M - m)$$

STOP AND THINK. Go over the equations carefully to be sure that you understand each term and what it means.

Within this model we can also say some things about the relative values of the constants, a_1, a_2, a_3, a_4, a_5, and a_6. Since upper classmen rarely copy lower classmen and lower classmen often copy upper classmen (and assuming that there are equal numbers of upper and lower classmen and that the rate of talking within class is the same in the two groups), a_3 will be less than a_6. We also know that a_1 will be greater than a_3 (assuming that upper classmen copy the fads of other upper classmen more often than rarely). But we have more difficulty knowing the relative values of a_4 and a_6. Finally, we know that a_5 is greater than a_2 (assuming that the contagion rate from each exposure to TV is the same for both lower and upper classmen).

STOP AND THINK. Review the statements and accompanying assumptions. Is it clear why they follow from the general features listed earlier?

With such a specification of the model, we could now derive some implications of the spread of a language fad through a high school that was divided into two semipermeable groups, a group of upper classmen and a group of lower classmen. Notice that as soon as we know the values for a_1, a_2, a_3, a_4, a_5, a_6, for the size of the two groups N and M, and the initial number of persons who use the fad in both groups, we can compute the number of individuals who will have the fad at each point in time. Normally, we would plot those numbers as a time path in a graph on which each point shows the number of persons in one group who have the fad

n along the horizontal axis and the number of persons in the other group who have the fad m along the vertical axis.

In our present example, let us suppose the values are as follows:

$a_1 = 0.02$
$a_2 = 0.01$
$a_3 = 0.01$
$a_4 = 0.02$
$a_5 = 0.02$
$a_6 = 0.03$
$N = 20$
$M = 30$

Now we can plot the path of diffusion from a starting point, where $n = m = 0$, to a final point, where $n = N$ and $m = M$. The path is displayed in Figure 7.10. The path of the system through

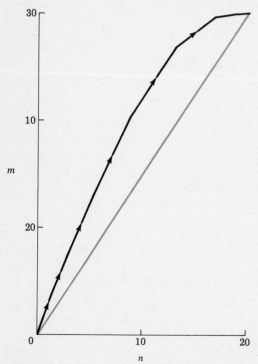

Figure 7.10: Example of the time path of diffusion through a two-strata social structure.

time is shown by the line connecting the several time points. You should notice that the fad grows slowly at first, then rapidly, then slowly again (as it approaches saturation). Also notice that it spreads more rapidly among the lower classmen until the end; and throughout the process a higher proportion of lower classmen have the fad than do upper classmen.

Circumstances involving semipermeable groups are common. They include:

1. Diffusion through groups of professionals (for instance, ministers, teachers, architects) and their clients (for instance, prisoners, parents, home builders).
2. Diffusion through organizational strata.
3. Diffusion in an industry.
4. Diffusion through different language groups.

In each case we would need to assume different rates of contact, transmission, and acceptance between groups than within groups.

The *within*-group rate of contagion is not necessarily higher than the *between*-group rate.

STOP AND THINK. **Can you think of an example of the opposite situation?**

The classic example is the diffusion of sexual technique through a population of males and females. Techniques diffuse through broadcast (from books, television, and movies) and through sexual experience. Since most female sexual experience is with males and most male sexual experience is with females, the rate of contagion of technique is faster between sex groups than within them.

STOP AND THINK. **Can you figure out what the time path (see Figure 7.10) will look like when between-group contagion is faster than within-group contagion?**

Example: Interracial Hostility

To explore a case of between-group contagion we can consider the problem of interracial hostility. Suppose we examine the spread of hostility toward members of the other racial group in a population consisting of N blacks and M whites.

STOP AND THINK. **Take some time to lay out the basic model you would use.**

We can start by making our standard assumptions: A black is either hostile toward whites or nonhostile; once he becomes hostile, he stays hostile. Similarly, a white is either hostile or nonhostile toward blacks; once he becomes hostile, he stays hostile. These assumptions permit us to use our basic models. In addition, we will need some assumptions about how hostility spreads. Though we could imagine a number of alternative ideas, we will focus on one: Hostility develops as a response to the expression of hostility. A black becomes hostile toward whites as a result of seeing hostility against himself; a white becomes hostile toward blacks as a result of seeing hostility against himself.

In model terms we let M be the total number of blacks and m be the number of blacks who are hostile toward whites. Let N be the total number of whites and n be the number of whites who are hostile toward blacks. Then:

$$\frac{\Delta m}{\Delta t} = a_1 n (M - m)$$

$$\frac{\Delta n}{\Delta t} = a_2 m (N - n)$$

Now suppose that we have a society of 10 blacks and 40 whites and that the value of a_1 is the same as the value of a_2:

$$a_1 = a_2 = 0.02$$

Finally, suppose that initially there is 1 hostile black and 1 hostile white. What happens to hostility over time?

STOP AND THINK. **Can you figure it out?**

Figure 7.11 shows the result. After 5 time periods there are 3.3 hostile blacks and 7.0 hostile whites. After 10 periods there are

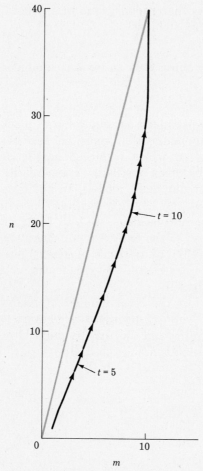

Figure 7.11: The diffusion of racial hostility.

8.4 hostile blacks and 21.3 hostile whites. Notice that in the early time periods the *number* of hostile whites increases more rapidly than the number of hostile blacks, but the *proportion* of hostile blacks increases more rapidly than the proportion of hostile whites.

STOP AND THINK. What produces this effect? Is it significant in the real world?

If we were interested in reducing interracial hostility and we believed the model, what could we do? The behavior of the model depends on the values of a_1 and a_2. Figure 7.12 shows what happens over 10 time periods and three sets of values for a_1 and a_2.

But what are a_1 and a_2? If we review our earlier discussions, we can determine that a_1 is a measure of three things:

1. The opportunities hostile whites have to show hostility toward blacks (contact).
2. The extent to which those opportunities are used to express hostility (transmission).
3. The extent to which the expression of white hostility toward a black produces a feeling of hostility in the black (acceptance).

Similarly, a_2 is a measure of three things:

4. The opportunities hostile blacks have to show hostility toward whites (contact).
5. The extent to which those opportunities are used to express hostility (transmission).
6. The extent to which the expression of black hostility toward a white produces a feeling of hostility in the white (acceptance).

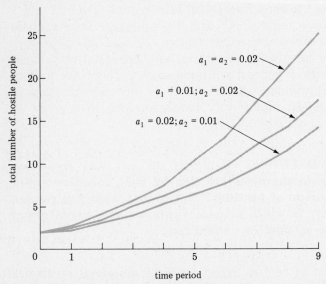

Figure 7.12: The effect of changes in a_1 and a_2 on the total number of hostile people over ten time periods.

The model indicates that we can reduce the rate of increase in hostility by reducing a_1 or a_2 or both. In effect, this means changing one of the six factors. How might a society accomplish this?

STOP. Make a list of some possible social policies that would affect the spread of hostility.

According to our model, any of the following social procedures will stop the spread of interracial hostility:

Apartheid
Eliminate contact between the two races.

Civil Rights Laws
Prohibit (successfully) the overt expression of hostility by both races.

Love
Persuade both races that the proper response to hostile acts is patience and love rather than hostility.

Apartheid reduces factors 1 and 4 to zero and thereby reduces a_1 and a_2 to zero. Successful laws reduce factors 2 and 5 to zero and thereby reduce a_1 and a_2 to zero. Love reduces factors 3 and 6 to zero and thereby reduces a_1 and a_2 to zero.

One of the complications with all of these social procedures is that they require a general willingness throughout the society to act. We might wonder whether there is any possible way in which one race might *unilaterally* reduce or stop the spread of hostility.

STOP AND THINK. Can you see any way by which (according to the model) action by only one race would stop the spread of hostility? Notice that what you require is some way in which actions within a single racial group make both a_1 and a_2 equal zero.

There seem to be two broad types of unilateral strategies possible according to the model. One is unilateral withdrawal; that is, in principle, at least, one group can unilaterally decide not to have anything to do with the other. By eliminating contact a single group can prevent the spread of hostility.[17] This strategy has been captured in folk wisdom by the expression: "Good fences make good neighbors." (Like most folk wisdom, it does say something true.)

The second unilateral strategy is passivity. If blacks do not express their hostility toward whites overtly and if at the same time they do not respond to hostile acts with hostile feelings, the diffusion process stops. Similarly, if whites do not express their hostility toward blacks overtly and if they do not respond to hostile acts with hostile feelings, the process stops.

There are two classic forms of unilateral passivity. The first is racial subjugation. If the minority race is enslaved, it normally is expected never to act in a hostile manner toward the dominant group and never to react to overt hostility on the part of the masters. The second is pacifism. The pacifist creed requires that a person (and thus a racial group of persons) abstain from expressing hostility or responding to overt hostility with hostile feelings.[18]

Either subjugation or pacifism will work (according to the model) to eliminate the spread of hostility, provided interracial communication is good. If the communication is good, then the refusal to express hostility will be perceived. If the communication is not good, it is quite possible that *intendedly nonhostile* behavior will be perceived as hostile. Under such circumstances the other race would become increasingly hostile over time. For example, paranoia is a standard limitation on the effectiveness of unilateral passivity as a device for restricting the spread of hostility.

Our model also allows us to say something about the relative advantage of applying various strategies in one race rather than the other. Figure 7.12 indicates that if we want to retard the spread of hostility, we can do so by reducing either a_1 or a_2. However, reductions in a_2 are more effective in the early time periods than are comparable reductions in a_1. This suggests that a strategy of inhibiting overt hostile feelings by whites as a result of hostile actions by blacks will be more effective than the converse strategy. If you must choose, it is better to teach tolerance to the majority group and behavioral discipline to the minority group than the other way around. If you note that discipline in the expression of hostility often is derived from fear and that tolerance in responding to hostility often is derived from security, you may want to derive the prediction that interracial hostility will spread relatively slowly in a situation of strong, stable racial colonialism.[19]

STOP AND THINK. If the conclusion is wrong, there must be something wrong with either the model or the procedures for derivation. What is wrong?

It may have occurred to you that we are not simply talking about blacks and whites. We are also, in effect, talking about blacks and chicanos, labor and management, Democrats and Republicans, men and women, psychoanalysts and patients, old and young, Hertz and Avis, China and Russia. And we have in our wanderings discovered the main theoretical base for pacifism, segregation, and colonialism as responses to conflict. If our model is right, you should be able to stimulate or inhibit the spread of hostility in the groups in which you live.

STOP AND THINK. Is the model right? What are some potential problems? What are some alternative models? How would you choose among them?

One possible alternative model that might have occurred to you is a model for diffusion of competing feelings. Suppose, for example, that an individual can either be hostile toward members of another race or friendly. And suppose that both hostility and friendliness spread through the expression of them so that the number of hostile people can increase, decrease, or stay steady with time. You might wonder what would happen if we assumed:

$$\frac{\Delta m}{\Delta t} = a_1 n (M - m) - a_2 m (N - n)$$

$$\frac{\Delta n}{\Delta t} = a_3 m (N - n) - a_4 n (M - m)$$

It is a good thought and a possible reason for questioning the earlier model, but unfortunately we cannot pursue it further here. In the classic tradition of models, it is left to the reader as an exercise!

References

Norman T. J. Bailey, *The Mathematical Theory of Epidemics* (London: Griffin, 1957).

James S. Coleman, *Introduction to Mathematical Sociology* (New York: Free Press, 1964).

Georg Karlsson, *Social Mechanisms* (New York: Free Press, 1958).

Notes

[1] We exclude here the interesting cases in which the situation calls for secrecy of important objects of diffusion, for example, with national or industrial secrets. In such cases the situation is obviously more complicated; but as both nations and industrial firms have discovered, keeping an important secret is not something that most people find routinely easy.

[2] Genetics can be viewed as the study of diffusion across generations of those attributes that are genetically controlled. One of the classic complications in studying human behavior is the extent to which biological diffusion (genetics) and social diffusion (child rearing, socialization, and migration) interact.

[3] Notice that if we can find some situations in which $D_{t+1} = D_t$, we will have found a situation in which the divorce rate will not ever change. This is a stable equilibrium value for this model. Any particular model may have one, more than one, or no such equilibria.

[4] In Figure 7.2 the straight line between point A and point B indicates, by its slope, the *average* rate of change during that time period, 3 kilometers per minute. It is unlikely that he was always going *exactly* 3 kilometers per minute during that period and if we had more detailed information on George's ride, we would undoubtedly discover that sometimes he was going slower (say, 2.8 kilometers per hour) and sometimes faster. With this more detailed information we could make a more accurate graph and discover that the line connecting points A and B would be wiggly or curved instead of straight.

[5] It may have occurred to you (or you may have recalled from your study of calculus) that it would be useful to be able to talk about the rate of change at a point, or instant, in time. A procedure does exist for this procedure, and its conventional symbol is dx/dt. This symbol is not a fraction but means simply the rate of change of x at time t.

The usual mathematical development of the models of diffusion about which we will talk often uses the dx/dt formulation rather than the $\Delta x/\Delta t$ formulation. But this detailed mathematics is not necessary to our discussion. We will be talking about changes in the *rate of change* as time passes. We mention the dx/dt notation to alert you to the importance of continuous equations concerning the rate of change (differential equations) to the more advanced study of diffusion and to the more advanced study of many areas of social science.

[6] You may also have noticed that the first seven numbers in Table 7.3 can each be formed by multiplying the previous number by 4. That is, our

table of n is a table of the powers of 4. When $t = 2$, $n = 4^1$; when $t = 3$, $n = 4^2$; and so on. Thus you could write the function $n_t = 4^{t-1}$.

[7]Or alternatively, the continuous approximation to that equation:

$$\frac{dn}{dt} = an$$

[8] The curve in Figure 7.8 should remind you of the learning curves discussed in the adaptation chapter. The curves are similar because of the similar underlying models: In one case we assume that the subject always learns a constant fraction of the amount left to learn; in the other case we assume that a broadcast always converts a constant fraction of the people left to convert.

[9] You do not have to worry about the possibility that everyone who knows the information will show up at the party. Those who know about the party will not necessarily attend: They are too busy, they do not have transportation, they prefer Prokofieff, and so on. It is similar to any advertising situation: After four commercials in a half hour, all the listeners may know that a new miracle soap contains vitamin B_{12}, but most of them simply will not care about it. You might want to define the acceptance part of the process as meaning that the person not only knows about something but will also act on the knowledge. The same set of models will still fit, but obviously the value for a in the models will be lower. We discuss some of these issues at greater length in the next section.

[10] This same principle is also applied to each separate agricultural unit. It is possible to have incremental adoption within a single farm. That is, a farmer can try some of the new seed while still keeping the majority of his land planted with the old seed. Thus the farmer minimizes the risk associated with trying the innovation; if it does not work, he is not completely wiped out. Unfortunately, incremental adoption is not always possible; many innovations can only be adopted as a whole; for example, sanitation; there would be little improvement in health from cleaning dishes only occasionally or from washing only one of your hands.

[11] At this point you are wary enough to realize that this explanation has some serious potential problems. If it is only used as an explanation, after the behavior has occurred, it can *always* "explain" what happened. For example, if the farmer has adopted the innovation, then the explanation could be changed to this: Since the expected value of the innovative alternative is higher, the farmer decided to innovate. Used at this level of analysis, after the fact, the explanation is only bad history. To break out of this potential circularity you must develop the process of drawing out further implications and predictions, which you will have a chance to do shortly.

[12] The T-maze has two alternatives for the farmer. Alternative 1 is to trust your statements; Alternative 2 is not to trust them. Whenever a farmer tries something you said would work and it does work, he becomes more likely to follow Alternative 1. You can expect that the values of a, b, and the initial probability of trusting you will vary considerably among farmers (which explains who will become the early adopters of your synthetic seed). This is essentially the procedure followed by the Rockefeller team in Mexico, and it worked—food production was increased enormously. A research group from Cornell University achieved similar results in Peru.

[13] You should note that social distance and social interconnectedness are not necessarily reflexive. That is, Mary may be able to communicate with John without John being able to communicate with Mary; a person of high status may be of considerable importance to a person of low status without

the converse being true. The distance from *a* to *b* may be different from the distance from *b* to *a*.

[14] Notice that the restrictions on a_1 and a_2 are becoming more complicated. We will continue the $\Delta n/\Delta t$ notation in the remainder of this section without formally specifying the restrictions. In fact, you might well want to move to a differential equation model and speak of dn/dt. The general discussion would be the same.

[15] This example is taken from an actual study by Coleman, Katz, and Menzel. For a discussion of it, see James S. Coleman, *Introduction to Mathematical Sociology* (New York: Free Press, 1964).

[16] This example is taken from some actual research by Coleman. The details have been modified. For the original, see James S. Coleman, *ibid.*

[17] Note, however, that many individuals would question the model at this point. It is possible that hostility might spread within a group by word of mouth.

[18] The behavioral similarity between pacifism and subjugation produces considerable difficulty in persuading many individuals to give a pacifist response. As a result, it normally is a viable strategy only for those who have no serious doubts about their personal status either because of profound moral beliefs or because of secure social position.

[19] For an alternative theory see Frantz Fanon, *The Wretched of the Earth* (New York: Grove Press, 1965).

Problems 7.2

1. Assume that on Monday morning one person in the city of Las Pulgas has a specific piece of information. What is the expected total number of people who will have the information on Friday evening under the following assumptions:

   (a) The population of Las Pulgas is 10 million. Each day, each person who has the information tells it to 3 other people chosen at random in the city. Each person who hears the information learns it immediately, and no one ever forgets it.

   (b) The situation is the same as in (a) except that a person does not learn the information until he has heard it twice.

   (c) The situation is the same as in (a) except that the population of Las Pulgas consists of only 5 people.

2. The final examination in Humanities 1 has been canceled. The decision to cancel the examination was made at 11:00 P.M. on Sunday. News of the cancellation first reached the residence halls at the college at 1:30 P.M., when the instructor called a student friend to tell him. This friend lives with five roommates. The six roommates each lunch together every day, in pairs, and exchange news. They pair off at random. Suppose that the news about the examination is not particularly important to them; anyone who hears the news for the

first time one day will mention it at lunch the next day but will thereafter not view it as current and will not pass it on. Outside of the lunch conversations, news about the examination is not transmitted.

(a) What is the earliest evening by which all six roommates could know the news?

(b) How many of the roommates will have heard the news by Monday evening? Tuesday? Wednesday? Thursday? Friday? Saturday?

(c) How likely is it that at least one of the six roommates will never hear the news?

(d) What would be the effect on the rate of diffusion if:

  i. Twice as many people received the information initially.
  ii. Each person talked to twice as many people each day (that is, if there were two "lunches" a day).
  iii. Each person talked twice as long about the news (that is, repeated it two lunches in a row before treating it as no longer current).

(e) Specify one important modification you think would make the model more realistic as a description of the diffusion of information in a college and show how your modification would change the predictions.

3. Callipygia is a small community in eastern California. Recently, the government has been thinking about trying to introduce fertility pills in Callipygia to increase the productivity of Callipygian couples. A recent month-long study in the community has produced the data indicated in Tables 1 and 2. In Table 1 we show the number of days during the study month that each pair of couples talked to one another. (Thus the circled number indicates that Couple 4 talked to Couple 2 on 4 of the 30 days during the month.) In Table 2 we show the likelihood that one couple will imitate the behavior of another couple *if they communicate*. (Thus the circled number indicates that Couple 2 will imitate the behavior of Couple 3 about 40% of the times that they communicate.)

TABLE 1

COUPLE NO.	1	2	3	4	5
1	—	2	7	1	8
2	2	—	10	4	12
3	7	9	—	6	15
4	1	(4)	6	—	10
5	8	12	15	10	—

TABLE 2

COUPLE NO.	1	2	3	4	5
1	—	0.1	0.1	0	0.1
2	0.3	—	0.2	0.3	0.1
3	0.6	(0.4)	—	0.4	0.6
4	0.1	0.3	0.2	—	0.4
5	0.2	0.1	0.1	0.3	—

(a) How common is this pattern? Explain.

(b) If you had data in the form of Tables 1 and 2 for a society, how would you determine who the key individuals were (in other words, which individuals would you try to have adopt the pills first in order to maximize the rate of diffusion)? Illustrate by using the data in the tables.

4. Take the map of a community you know well. Locate a major intersection. Assume that 50 people collapse and die from smog at that intersection between 4:50 P.M. and 5:00 P.M. on Monday.

   (a) Predict the diffusion of information about the disaster by showing the densities of knowledge (that is, the proportion of people in a given area who have the information) in various parts of the city at 5:30 P.M., 6:00 P.M., and 6:30 P.M. Explain your predictions by identifying the assumptions you are making about the way in which such information would spread.

   (b) Using the same assumptions, indicate how your answer would be different if the disaster occurred on Sunday instead of Monday.

5. Consider an extended family group consisting of your parents, children, siblings, and spouses as well as all of their parents, children, siblings, and spouses.

   (a) List all of the people involved and locate them in some simple kind of family tree.

   (b) Construct a description of the contact, transmission, and acceptance patterns within this extended family group.

   (c) Take some kind of news that might spread through the extended family (for example, news about your choice of occupation, life style, or love life) and suggest some implications of your answer to (b) for making predictions about the spread of the news.

Problems 7.3

1. The model presented in this section is simple. One obvious way we can make it more complex is to relax the strong assumptions that couples in which both individuals have divorced parents will divorce and *no* couples in which neither individual has divorced parents will divorce. Suppose, instead, that each child in a generation has a "divorce proneness" that depends on whether his parents were ever divorced. Call q the proneness for children of divorced parents and r the proneness for children of nondivorced parents. We will assume q and r are between 0 and ½. Further suppose that the divorce rate within a couple type is the sum of the divorce proneness of each (thus $2q$ for Type I, $q + r$ for Type II or Type III, and $2r$ for Type IV). What happens now? Plot the values of q and r that lead to stability at several different divorce rates.

2. Show what would happen in the model given in this section if we assume that divorced couples have (on the average) fewer children than nondivorced couples.

3. Modify the model to show what would happen if children from divorced parents are more likely to marry each other than you would expect by chance, as are children from nondivorced parents.

4. If these models were correct and we wished to inhibit divorce in a society, what social actions might we take? Show what differences they would make.

5. Take some other area of intergenerational diffusion and show how you would construct a simple model of the phenomenon. Use the model to derive some interesting implications. (*Examples*: intergenerational diffusion of religious preference, taste in food, political loyalty.)

Problems 7.4

1. For each of the following situations indicate what model of diffusion you would use and why:

   (a) The spread of laughter through a movie audience.
   (b) The adoption of pass-fail grading by American universities.
   (c) The spread of the news that the stock market has gone up substantially.
   (d) The spread of dissatisfaction with an American President.
   (e) The spread of a report that the Queen of England is contemplating a divorce.
   (f) The use of a particular automatic weapon by terrorist groups.
   (g) The use of a particular youth expression by middle-aged women.
   (h) The use of a new dress fad in a high school.
   (i) The adoption of a new illegal drug substitute for heroin.
   (j) The adoption of a new fertilizer by farmers in the United States.

2. The Acme Soap Company recently introduced a new soap into two test communities. In each community they used a steady radio campaign to advertise the product. The two charts that follow show the results over the first 10 weeks of the campaign. Each chart shows the number of people in the community who have used the product by the end of the indicated week.

   What differences would you suspect might exist between the two communities? Why?

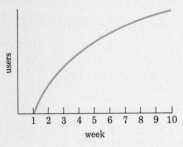

Test Community A

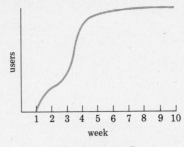

Test Community B

3. You are the manager of a market research consulting firm. In each of the following cases you have been asked to advise a company on its market tactics. In each case indicate what advice you would give and why.

   (a) Wunderbar Electronics has developed a new three-dimensional color television set. The designers report that they have two alternative designs for the antenna. Design 1 is indistinguishable from the standard outdoor television antenna except for a small (1 inch high) box attached to the base. Design 2 looks radically different from the standard antenna. Under what conditions should the company use Design 1? Design 2?

   (b) Smithers Wickets has a superior new wicket. It wishes to advertise and sell this wicket over the next two years and plans to spend $10 million on the advertising. The company is considering two alternative plans. Plan 1 calls for spending 75% of the advertising budget during the first four months. Plan 2 calls for the budget to be spread evenly over the two years. Under what conditions should the company follow Plan 1? Plan 2?

   (c) Suppose the new wicket in (b) was actually inferior to existing wickets. Which plan would be better if the company wants to maximize sales?

   (d) Conglomerate Pills, Incorporated, has invented a drug that cures symptoms (for instance, friendliness, a sense of well-being, absence of worries about the future) exhibited by natives of the island of Euphoria (population 100,000). In order to sell the pill, Conglomerate must convince the Euphorians that they have a disease. Two tactics have been proposed. Tactic 1 involves hiring 100 residents to spread the rumor that tomorrow will come. Tactic 2 involves advertising the same message on television once a day. The company knows that people never discuss TV commercials with each other but always pass on anything that someone else tells them. Under what conditions should the company follow Tactic 1 (assuming both tactics are equally costly)? Tactic 2?

4. The following three schemes have been proposed for turning a nation (population 1 million) of illiterates into a nation of readers:

Scheme 1

One teacher teaches one person to read. This takes a year. During each subsequent year, each person (including the teacher) who knows how to read seeks out an illiterate and teaches him to read.

Scheme 2

One teacher teaches one person to read. This takes a year. During each subsequent year, the teacher teaches one new person to read. Each person who learns to read is obligated to spend the immediately following year teaching one additional person to read, and then he stops teaching.

Scheme 3

One teacher broadcasts reading lessons over the national radio. Learning to read over the radio takes one year. Every home in the nation has a radio, but only 10% of the homes (a random 10% of all of the homes) listen to a complete set of the year's reading lessons each year.

(a) How many readers (not counting the teacher) will there be in the society after four years under each scheme?

(b) What is the equation for $\Delta n/\Delta t$ for each scheme?

(c) What is the numerical value of the constant in each of the equations in (b)?

(d) Suppose that Scheme 1 were modified so that citizens in the nation were paired off randomly each year and only when the pair included one reader and one nonreader did a reader teach a nonreader to read. Only one pairing occurs per year. What would be the equation for $\Delta n/\Delta t$? Why?

(e) How would you modify the basic model in Scheme 1 if the rules in the society were that men were forbidden to teach and therefore no man ever teaches anyone else?

5. The Quick Buck Smoking Company is planning to introduce two new products:

Product A

A new filter cigarette using Bulgarian tobacco.

Product B

A new cigarette with marijuana-like effects.

The Federal Trade Commission has obtained a court order prohibiting any advertising of the second product pending further testing. However, the company is planning immediately to have an active advertising campaign (in newspapers) for the first product and to give away 1000 packages of *each* product to 2000 random customers during the next month.

(a) What will be the rate of new adoptions for the two products during the first few months? What is the model? How is the rate derived from the model?

(b) Who will be the early adopters of the new filter cigarettes? Who will be the early adopters of the new marijuana-like cigarettes? Why?

(c) The company is particularly interested in the Alaskan market. Would it make any difference whether the products were first introduced into Alaska in winter or summer? Why?

6. The Icelandic Record Company has decided that, starting next year, it will no longer send free records to American radio stations. KROK, a monthly disk jockeys' magazine, writes an editorial complaining about the decision. Those disk jockeys who read the editorial feel moved to comment on it once every day over the radio. Assume that listeners do not care enough about the news to repeat it; that disk jockeys compete so strongly that they never speak to each other; that each station has a separate audience of 100,000 listeners; that a for rumor models is $1.0/N$; that a for broadcast models is 0.1; and that only the 1000 morning shift disk jockeys *ever* read KROK (they only look at it once, as soon as it comes out, then throw it away).

(a) How many total listeners will know about Icelandic's decision three afternoons after KROK comes out (if the magazine is on the newsstands around 3 P.M.)?

(b) Explain verbally or using calculations show how your answer would be changed if some disk jockeys read KROK as late as three or four days after it is placed on the stands.

(c) Suppose that once a year the disk jockeys suspend hostilities and have a one-day convention in New York. KROK comes out the afternoon before the convention; during the convention the morning-shift disk jockeys do not read or broadcast but manage to exchange gossip once. How many listeners will hear about Icelandic's decision the day after the disk jockeys have returned home?

7. You are introducing a new food product to the college market. In particular, the product looks like one that will have a special appeal for the students at Outland University. (OU students are notoriously neurotic eaters, and your product is filling, sensuous, and nonfattening.) Unfortunately, you have found that the students at Outland are lonely, shy people. They are willing to listen to anyone, but they never have the courage to talk to one another. You decide to import some gregarious transfer students from the University of Virginia to spread the word about your product.

(a) Specify a diffusion model for the spread of information among students at Outland and indicate what each part of the model represents.

(b) Assign some specific values to the constants and variables in your model and calculate how many Outland University students will know about your product after two days.

8. Your research division has just made a startling breakthrough in automobile gasoline consumption, and you wish to market this product as Super Blintz. The problem is to explain the advantages of Super Blintz to the public so that they will buy the product. You are considering four alternative strategies:

Strategy 1
Import a specially trained group of personable drinkers who will fan out among the local bars and casually pass on a story about how wonderful Super Blintz is (assume that bar patrons only talk to other bar patrons and only while in the bar).

Strategy 2
Make hourly announcements over the local classical music station. You know that their listeners are isolated types who never talk to anyone else.

Strategy 3
Make hourly announcements over the local rock station. You know that their listeners are gregarious types who gossip a lot.

Strategy 4
Spend your whole budget as a "consulting fee" for the editor of *Truth Digest* magazine in order to induce him to write a story about the marvels of Super Blintz in the next issue. The magazine will run the story only once, and *Truth Digest* readers are moderate gossips.

(a) Draw a diagram (perhaps with circles and arrows) showing how you would expect information to diffuse from each of these alternative strategies, and show the rate of spread (perhaps with a graph).

(b) For each of the strategies, make up an algebraic diffusion model.

Problems 7.5

1. For each of the following situations indicate what factors would influence the value of the constants in the models (see Problem 1 in the preceding section) and discuss the differences you would expect between occasions when the diffusion would be rapid and occasions when it would be slow:

(a) The spread of laughter through a movie audience.
(b) The adoption of pass-fail grading by American universities.
(c) The spread of the news that the stock market has gone up substantially.

(d) The spread of dissatisfaction with an American President.

(e) The spread of a report that the Queen of England is contemplating a divorce.

(f) The use of a particular automatic weapon by terrorist groups.

(g) The use of a particular youth expression by middle-aged women.

(h) The use of a new dress fad in a high school.

(i) The adoption of a new illegal drug substitute for heroin.

(j) The adoption of a new fertilizer by farmers in the United States.

2. Suppose a society consists of two kinds of people: supporters of the regime and opponents. Good news about the society travels by word of mouth. Specify a diffusion model for the spread of good news and suggest some implications. Then compare the implications with the results of a model for bad news (which also travels by word of mouth). Be sure to make your assumptions clear.

3. Comment on the following statement. Indicate why it might be true and the circumstances under which it would not be true:

> The breakdown of the extended family, the increased residential mobility of Americans, and the advent of the automobile culture all combine to increase substantially the impact of mass media on political attitudes in the United States.

4. Herman Smith is an infantry squad leader. Next week his squad is scheduled to go into action for the first time. He has sent his men into the city for a last weekend of cultural activities while he considers the following problem:

> His troops are inexperienced. Since he is scared witless, he supposes they probably are too. For the good of the whole group it is important to avoid a panic reaction to the first sight of blood.

What steps can Smith take (or might he have taken with more time) to minimize the risk of contagious panic? Show how your answer follows from an analysis of the spread of panic.

5. Some parents are quite concerned about the apparent tendency for attending college to be associated with changes in the behavior, dress, and attitudes of their children.

(a) Specify a diffusion model for the spread of ideas in a college and discuss what factors in the model might make college students particularly susceptible to diffusion.

(b) Using your model, make some suggestions for a strategy to be adopted by a parent who wanted to control a child's development without appearing to do so.

(c) How would your model explain the shifts in college sentiments over the past 20 years? What would it predict for the next few years?

6. From time to time students of education proposed some new procedure for education (for instance, ability grouping, union school districts, team teaching, new mathematics, free schools). These procedures spread through the world of education over time.

   (a) Outline a diffusion model of the process by which new educational ideas spread through the educational establishment. Make your assumptions explicit.

   (b) According to your model, what would be the pattern of adoption of new ideas in education? What schools would adopt first? Last? What kinds of ideas would spread rapidly? What kinds of ideas would never spread? Be sure your answers are tied clearly to your model.

   (c) On the whole, would you expect educational institutions to be relatively slow in adopting new ideas or relatively fast? Explain your answer by showing what factors in your model affect the rate of adoption.

   (d) Suppose you were a consultant to a school district that was concerned about too rapid change. What concrete suggestions can you make (from your model) with respect to how the district might protect itself from the diffusion of new ideas?

Problems 7.6

1. Suppose you are a manufacturer of ready-to-wear clothing for men and women. You have a new kind of jacket that you expect to become fashionable, primarily through people noticing other people wearing it.

   (a) Suppose you assume that the use of the new jacket among men spreads only by exposure to other men wearing it, and among women only by exposure to other women wearing it. Specify a model of diffusion to describe such a situation.

   (b) Assign some reasonable values to the constants in the model in (a) and plot the spread of the use of the jacket in the society over time.

   (c) Suppose you assume that although most of the diffusion occurs by exposure to other people of the same sex, there is a smaller tendency for men to copy women and for women to copy men. Specify a model for such a situation.

   (d) Assign some reasonable values to the constants in the model in (c), plot the spread of the use of the jacket in the society over time, and compare the results with those obtained in (b).

   (e) Suppose you assume that although most of the diffusion occurs by exposure to other people of the same sex, there is a small tendency for men to copy women. However, there is also a small tendency for women to *stop wearing* jackets that they see are worn by men. Specify a model for such a situation.

(f) Assign some reasonable values to the constants in the model in (e), plot the spread of the use of the jacket in the society over time, and compare the results with those obtained in (b) and (d).

(g) Assuming that three magazines have equal total numbers of readers, under what circumstances would a ready-to-wear manufacturer of unisex clothing prefer to advertise primarily in magazines read mostly by women? In magazines read mostly by men? In magazines with equal numbers of male and female readers?

2. A number of studies of the introduction of innovation (particularly, but not exclusively, agricultural innovation) have shown the existence of so-called opinion leaders. Opinion leaders are people who seem to adopt an innovation relatively early after learning about it through some reading or special contact with experts. The innovations seem to be adopted first by these leaders and then to spread through the population.

(a) Specify a reasonable model of this process for a population of N people, of whom M are opinion leaders.

(b) Identify the major things in your model that determine the rate of diffusion of an innovation.

(c) What real world interpretation can you make about the model factors determining rate of diffusion?

(d) Some people have suggested that so-called opinion leaders may be mythical; that obviously someone will adopt a new product before others and to call this someone an opinion leader is quite misleading. Does your model suggest any way of examining the validity of such a criticism by looking at the cumulative number of innovation users over time?

3. Most societies wish to protect themselves from socially disruptive ideas. Many social reformers and revolutionaries wish to encourage socially disruptive ideas. Both social defenders and social reformers are particularly interested in the problems of corrupting (or preventing the corruption of) college students.

(a) Why (or why not) would it be reasonable to believe that college students are particularly vulnerable to corruption? Show how your answer follows from a model of diffusion.

(b) Why (or why not) would it be reasonable to believe that college students are particularly useful people to corrupt? Show how your answer follows from a model of diffusion.

(c) You have been hired as a consultant for the Movement. It is considering three basic strategies with respect to college students:

Strategy 1
Isolate students from contact with establishment people and ideas.

Strategy 2
Expose students deliberately to establishment thoughts and people but do it in small, well-spaced doses.

Strategy 3
Expose students deliberately to establishment thoughts and people in large doses.

The Movement wants to adopt the strategy most likely to produce adults having socially disruptive thoughts. Prepare a recommendation outlining a model and showing the circumstances under which each alternative would be best.

4. Read carefully the material on interracial hostility in Section 7.6.

   (a) Use the model to derive additional predictions; discuss the predictions; develop a critique of the assumptions; show how alternative assumptions would produce different results.
   (b) Develop the model suggested in the last paragraph of the chapter. Derive some implications and discuss them.

5. Missionary movements (religious, social, or political) are confronted with a dual problem. On the one hand, they need to keep their old believers loyal. On the other hand, they need to recruit new believers. In solving the second problem they sometimes have to run the risk of failing to solve the first—and vice versa. Missionary work can involve contact, and it is always possible that the missionary will be converted to nonbelief before he converts the nonbeliever to belief.

   (a) Develop a model for two-way diffusion of beliefs.
   (b) Use your model to indicate under what circumstances a missionary movement would want to do any of the following:

       i. Insist that missionaries live together.
      ii. Require missionaries to wear distinctive clothes.
     iii. Make missionary work a short-term commitment.
      iv. Encourage missionaries to leave the movement and live among the people as ordinary citizens.
       v. Specialize in radio-television appeals rather than direct contact.

   (c) Would your model predict any change in the tactics of missionary movements as the number of adherents to the cause changes (up or down)? Can you use the model to develop the first part of a natural history of missionary movements?

6. For each of the following, discuss three things:
   i. What special problems are there in applying a diffusion model to the situation?
   ii. What kinds of predictions can you make from such a model?
   iii. How would you use the model to make recommendations for dealing with the problem, and what recommendations would you make?

   (a) The problem of crime in the city.
   (b) The problem of low morale in an organization.
   (c) The problem of the Americanization of Europe.
   (d) The problem of drug abuse.
   (e) The problem of social violence.
   (f) The problem of intergenerational alienation.

index